Blueprint

Blueprint

Gautam Bhatia

MAPIN PUBLISHING

First published in India in 2018 by
Mapin Publishing Pvt. Ltd
706 Kaivanna, Panchvati, Ellisbridge
Ahmedabad 380006 INDIA
T: +91 79 40 228 228 • F: +91 79 40 228 201
E: mapin@mapinpub.com • www.mapinpub.com

International Distribution
Worldwide (except North America and South Asia)
Prestel Publishing Ltd.
14-17 Wells Street
London W1T 3PD
T: +44 (0)20 7323 5004 • F: +44 (0)20 7323 0271
E: sales@prestel-uk.co.uk

North America
Antique Collectors' Club
T: +1 800 252 5231 • F: +1 413 529 0862
E: sales@antiquecc.com • www.accdistribution.com/us

South Asia
Mapin Publishing Pvt. Ltd

ISBN: 978-93-85360-33-6

Copyediting: Vineetha Mokkil / Mapin Editorial
Proofreading: Mapin Editorial
Design: Sarayu Narasimhan / Mapin Design Studio
Printed at Manipal Technologies Limited, Manipal

Contents

Foreword

Blueprint is an artist's testimony about his work, nothing more and nothing less. For that reason alone, it is an unusually welcome event in Indian architectural discourse.

I have long believed that Bhatia's is among the most original imaginations at work in contemporary Indian architecture. Yet, Bhatia is probably better known for his architectural writing—whether taking down bourgeois fakery, or illuminating the felt poetry of spatial experience—than for his architectural practice. This book is therefore important as the first consolidated presentation of his creative practice—not just the body of his work—as an architect. It is also important for the way in which Bhatia presents the ideas behind his work, as well as moments from the process and experience of making it. For once, it is the ideas (and their unexpectedly persuasive idiosyncrasies) and the experience of translating them into design and built form that predominate in a book on architecture. But even rarer and truly original is the indirect illumination of the creative self that is the ghost in the book's machine: steering as much as steered by the tumult of artistic and everyday practice, endlessly plagued by self-doubt and yet always straining for latent worlds of value that lie just out of reach. Like any good testimony, it presents rather than argues, and thus invites quarrel deeper than debate.

The personal is Bhatia's register, in architecture and its telling. A thoughtful and well-read architect whose first degree was in the fine arts, Bhatia draws, sculpts, writes and designs from the gut. His creative practice hinges on emotional response: his own, to spaces and places produced by others whether named artists or authorless histories; and that he anticipates, manipulates and hopes for in the inhabitants he imagines into his buildings. The bile he hurls at the city, as well as the wonder for architecture he reports, issue from the same unfashionable source: deepest feeling. Surprise, engineered through distortions that yield unexpected caricature, or poetry, is the fulcrum that balances swinging contraries in word, image and building.

What is the value of such a personal testimony in our times? *Blueprint* attempts a personal account of the creative process that is free of the noxious fumes of self-congratulation. At the same time, the substance of this testimony offers a fascinating glimpse into the challenge of being an artist today, especially in the unpromising role of a service provider.

Bhatia takes architecture—and indeed, the city—personally. Unlikely as it may seem at first glance, it is difficult to disentangle the city from his architecture. Going by so much of his writing, he will probably never make peace with the Indian city. We thus have the wild, vulgar, violent urbanism of Bhatia's New Delhi to be grateful to for the ruses of escape into nature, solitude and conviviality that his architecture plots in the hills, forests, and plains of other places. Baiting or surrendering to nature—undulating scrub land by the lake, or forest in the hills—or the ever-fresh pursuit of the ideal of retreat—underground, or in an upper floor study—are among the themes he brings alive differently in different settings.

Bhatia's method is to seek contradiction, even stage it where it does not emerge naturally out of the predicament of design, as a point of departure and as an axis around which a design or its meaning may spiral out. Doubtless, for him, contradictions have the potential to open a crack in entrenched structures of habit and convention which produce and sustain the soul degrading reality around.

Of course, since the architect usually builds for others, in a context that is socially produced, there is no shortage of contradictions. Among other things, Bhatia's testimony illuminates a common but rarely articulated question: how can one respond to imperatives that might contradict the very foundation of one's approach to life and work? Subversion is one answer as at Bhatia's remarkable design for a drama school on an urban plot. Behind the straight-faced façade, its roof subsides into an amphitheatre that becomes the institutional commons edgily bringing together spaces of everyday life and creative activity against neat bureaucratic classifications of time, space and human action.

Engaging contradictions is risky business, of course. Bhatia's unbuilt design for a skyscraper and an entry for a library competition in Varna, Bulgaria, are fascinating in this regard. We wonder: how will he retain the disaggregation, intricacy and the love of internal contradiction visible in his smaller works, in addressing these monstrous projects? The journey through the critical idiosyncracy of his design reasoning in each project reveals the value of Bhatia's architecture and telling, as an opening gambit in a conversation. Yes, the skyscraper and the big urban building are increasingly a given for the architect, and yes, perhaps, there is a need to rethink it from scratch but no, turning it into an integrated vertical township does not make me feel warm. But, yes, the broken-up pile, textured rough to help weave an unlikely social fabric, is an apt response. At Varna, yes, the reader 'detached' from the library building, is a beguiling image; but does yet another city need a glazed, convex, architectural totalization on its streets?

The conversationality of Bhatia's practice may perhaps be traced to his simultaneous affiliation with contrary spirits, say, collage and classicism. Everything is, deeply, what it seems to be and its opposite. An almost classical penchant for (Kahnian) repetition is interrupted or deflected by a change in alignment, or an unexpected, inescapable, and potentially incongruous element in his architecture. The otherworldly harmony of his collaborative miniatures in traditional style, heaves with invisible antibodies ready for combat with the disgusting profanity of flesh depicted with care. And, as testimony, *Blueprint* is equal parts commentary.

Indirectness, allusion, the love of secrets. This book disavows systematic, transparent and comprehensive argument or documentation. Buildings are not presented in full as plans, sections or photographs. Drawings fade into blue vapour. Building plans and photos are accompanied by surreal and sometimes dire visualisations of related themes, sometimes ballooning into the ridiculously insightful. Anything but the direct declaration of the detached or overobsessed observer. Circumlocution over the axial approach. Reverb as itself melodic progression. And the exaggeration of the ridiculous inherent to all human practice, especially architecture, to keep us anchored to the common ground of everyday bodily existence. The obliquely delivered message can be frustrating to the receiver; yet sometimes it is the only way of communicating the artist's struggle with the incommunicability of what is really worth sharing.

What is really worth sharing, then?

Blueprint, for me, is allusive autobiography. Its contents—intimations of what Bhatia has created over more than three decades in word, image or building—are like mirrors, variously angled, redirecting our gaze endlessly till we stop looking for a definite object. It is the dizziness of criss-crossing our own paths in following Bhatia's narrative journeys, instead, that may be the point.

Creative practice can be dizzying, when it is schizoid. Being shown this schizoidness (as in the double role Bhatia gratuitously, but effectively, slips into at the end of "Palace") is a valuable gift at a time when the quick smart pose is regularly proffered in place of a carefully considered position. *Blueprint* invites us into the internal-external confusion and contradictions that the thoughtful artist must grapple with in holding on to the integrity of his vision and therefore, of the self. Bhatia must write, paint, and sculpt alongside his practice not because he is trained as a visual artist first, but perhaps because he must keep shifting between media of differing privacy and indirectness, to find modes and trajectories of formulation with which to negotiate the constant translation between private and public imperatives of architecture. Architecture, for Bhatia, lies in the sometimes disorienting to and fro between intention and its enactment that marks the process of conception and its always ongoing realisation as place.

To persevere critically in creative practice is to consolidate hope. If there is value in the boundary walls that secure Bhatia's socio-economic privilege, it lies in the fact that they sustain that practice and that hope, however unreasonable it may appear. Too much of his writing, for me, has been fueled by a blinding rage. But we see here, most clearly, that it is in architecture that Bhatia gambles on hope.

Himanshu Burte
November 1, 2017

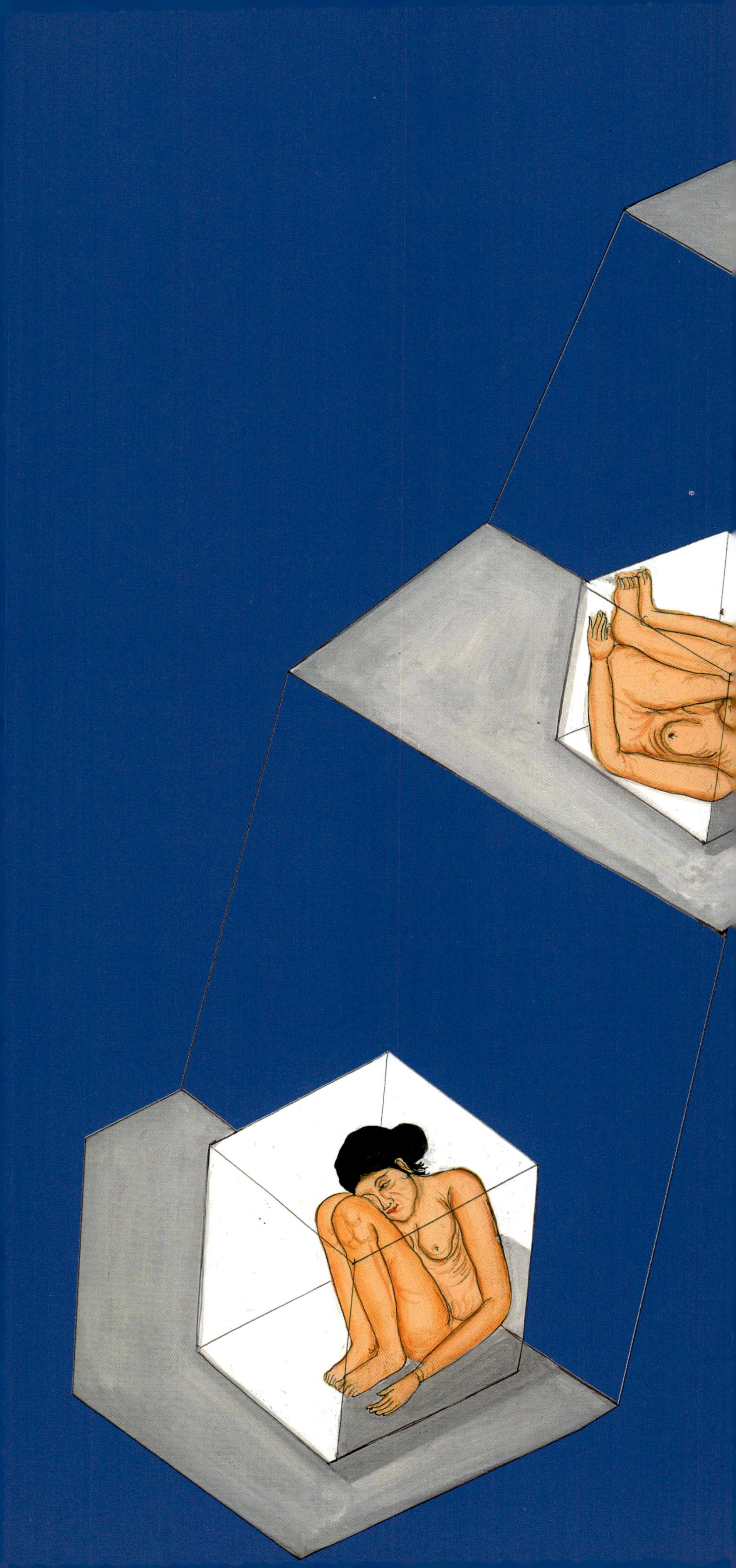

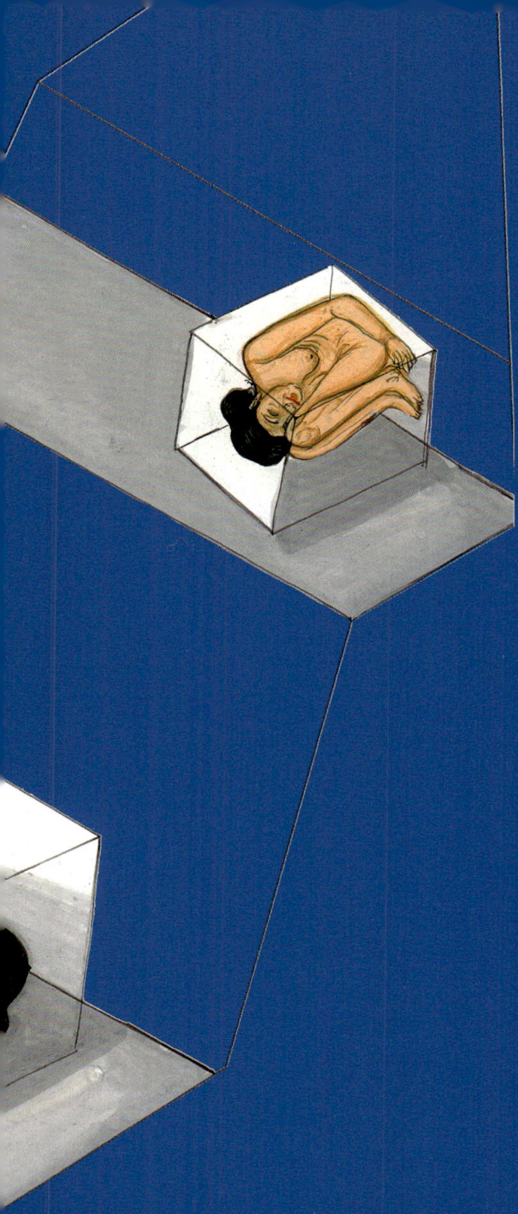

Building

How do you view the cumulative work of your life—the record of which is far more complex than what a studied view can provide? All lives have their own history, geology and archaeology, and any written record can only be a self-conscious, visible and conspicuous scaffold on which a selective history is constructed. This is not a planned architecture book, the kind with wide-angled double spreads of photographs and plans that make architecture a seductive picture. No, in India, such a perfect picture is elusive and often a complete lie. The real record of Indian architecture is the gut-wrenching reality of rooms filled with too many people—people whose habits don't lend themselves to photography, and for whom architecture stands for nothing more than a place to settle in for the night.

Anthropology gives an altogether different reason for architecture. In fact, in the course of building, for better or worse, so many peripheral activities take place. I always feel the need to account for the many decisions I had to take in order to arrive at the construction that stares me in the face. The seeming arbitrariness of most of those decisions makes me want to apply some design logic to the social and cultural incoherence. Writing is a way of understanding your intentions: why you did, what and when. Unlike medicine or accounting that are processes towards specific ends, getting well, fudging books, architecture is just a process towards yet another process, a social structure of life that is never ending, but is itself used to construct a physical structure, that too, is often unending.

Architecture draws inspiration from ordinary life, and gives it back with equal maladjustment. I find that the only reason for writing a book on architecture is to record a static design idea that turns into a dynamic process. Others may see it as self-indulgence, but for me, a profession that doesn't go by the book deserves a book that traces ideas and the upheaval they cause in the process of construction.

This is a book of uncertain ideas and mixed sources. It emerged untested, as a collaborative of personal applications that straddle art, architecture, sketch and writing. Much of its content has been derived from my own professional practice, the written diaries, and the speculative sketches and artworks that support particular architectural projects and conceptions. In the search for a method to building, I have been a reluctant problem solver. It is in the nature of any work in India, a country that has an unwieldy, shifting population and few material resources, that everything is seen as a problem. Yet for me, that narrow path of conventional practice remained elusive. I was never at the receiving end of large commissions or a participant in urban resettlement programmes. Instead, the institutional and private work that came my way contained precise and limited building programmes. In it, beyond the resolution of stated requirements, I found possibilities of raising a variety of architectural questions related to modernity, to the architect's treatment of history and archaeology, to forgotten and misplaced attitudes to design. All this, beyond conventions of style and theory, the lies and evasions which have become a false measure of architecture.

The continual presence of people, techniques and places imposes arguments whose validity is constantly tested on the architectural idea. Such contamination is not always a magnification of the initial thought, but it does perform the useful task of giving it due respectability, or denying it a place on the trophy shelf. Most of the time the architect himself takes the added precaution of isolating the work behind high walls and hence invokes professional privilege. Such a luxury is not accorded to buildings that involve themselves in the structure of urban life. For me, working on architecture commissions was the most legitimate way to trespass into the private terrain of family life, institutional set-up, domesticity, and even into the business structures of politics and administration. To use architecture as an instrument of sociology was the greatest gift of the profession. Within the practice, architecture had become not just a mode of personal expression and a method of experiencing building as a momentary spectacle, but a sustained thrill over time. At every stage of building the profession would assert its own design morality and impose a conscience on people who were too used to their own private ways: regionalism, vernacular traditions, globalization, green architecture. To be true to a collective destiny, you were expected to build within the chosen framework of the moment.

Architecture's place was in an automated brain-wash that cleansed private sins as it emerged, glistening and packaged, on the other side. I chose instead to adopt a private method to this, the most public of professions, and even allow explorations in art and drawing to encroach on building. The foundation of architecture was the loose chain of ideas expressed in charcoal or pencil, ink or bronze. They came from the exponentially invasive, unregulated way of Indian life that was the background in which I lived; India loomed as large as an untameable beast, baring its fangs with regularity, leaving me reeling, and sometimes wounded in retreat. Everything outside the boundary wall of my house was an exaggeration, a place filled with daily upheavals—migrations, *puja* rooms on the road, pavements for defecation or selling orchids, incomplete buildings, piles of refuse, human debris and construction matter; I witnessed it all every day. Its influence on my architecture was but natural.

I suppose in every society, the middle class bears the burden of dysfunction. People are forced to belong out of human needs and inadequacies. And people of my background, privileged and pretentious, aloof, and always judgmental, are easily unhinged in an untamed country. The practice of architecture then was less a picture of how people lived but how they *could* live. Architecture was a corrective measure, a hope... The idea of a return to a future reality is not a new one, nor does it purport to invent a different way of living. It does however recall the direct and narrow path to a material and textural reality and a spontaneous experience of building mass, light and surface. To see the structure for what it is, where it exists, and under what conditions it is experienced. Devoid of sentimentality and association, the perception seeks to re-establish the link between intent, visibility and reality, that is to say, the association between the architecture, the people for whom it was built, and eventually the settled condition it created.

Beyond the house, beyond the street, the physical world was a collection of houses and highways and trees and people. Each, among them, a library of individual ideas and meanings. Were they meaningful as they were, or because they had something to say collectively? Ultimately when an entire social or natural heritage is examined, their value lies in contemplation without myth or memory. Merely a direct material comprehension of the object, its substance and structure, an appreciation of its origins, its process of construction or fabrication has no meaning. It is true that I was living and practising in a period when architecture was perpetually escaping the familiar comfort of physical sites by denying their existence, or escaping behind high walls. It was also moving rapidly into other allied or unrelated arts—theatre, scenography, history, nostalgia, and even futurism. The architect's use of archaeological references, ironic colonial representations, or symbolic twists and allusions to different periods had made building into a caricature of style, and every new design was a testament to the architect's discomfort and unease with the old definitions.

One of the serious flaws of the profession is the absence of choice in the life of an architect. Private individuals or institutions issue the demands that provoke architectural thinking. The architect is always trying hard to stay away from the receiving end of instructions to retain a level of independence outside of the client's instructions. The incoherence and randomness of the process is inevitable when the message is garbled by arbitrary and personal wishes, backed by an uncertain culture and a history prone to misinterpretation, including constantly changing demands and parameters that have no established reason. Unlike the novel, honed by precise editorial marksmanship, or a painting provoked by personal expression, architecture struggles to retain its integrity and cohesion.

Sadly, architecture's only expression of value remains in the first draft, for the idea is soon taken over by a team, mutilated by client confrontations, or reduced to a whimpering mass by the architect's own censorship, or modified during construction by the builder. There, in the uncertain armature of mismatched forces, the architecture idea is rapidly altered to suit commonly held perceptions. The unlearning of the conventions of design, building techniques and practice then becomes the misinformed palette of private expression. In the final analysis, the structure is an unrecognizable mutation that awaits demolition by the critic and the wrecking ball.

As a result an architect's working life is filled with residual thought that is peripherally connected with his/her current preoccupations. It is in the nature of architecture that every attempt to make a building requires a cultural, social and artistic examination of the people, places, technologies and materials that make the eventual construction possible. Such digressions often do not get recorded in a book on architecture. But these are the critical scaffolds to the eventual goal, and their record illuminates the process of visual and verbal thought. Beyond the record of a process, every building asks the fundamental question: how do we begin to question the way we live? Not just a matter of realignment, but the very motivation to create architecture must emerge from primary cultural and social roots and find a form through idea, innovation and technology.

The illusory nature of architecture as a problem waiting to be solved rankles mainly because it sees life as a dreary drudgery, often limiting all possibility to the standard conventions of space: room 10x10, built of mud or cement or steel or glass—an image of confinement that has held architecture to ransom for a century, and refuses to be replaced. The idea is to question basic forms of space; the home, the apartment, the office, the hotel. Such agglomerations have come about through a multiplication of the basic unit: the room, the bath. In them is expressed the innate nature of privacy itself: the living room, the office space, work and recreation; actions of daily life that must necessarily take place behind walls and closed doors. The building begins by first describing individual privacy as its smallest unit. It grows then, frame by frame, into something else, bigger, more complex; its understanding of the forces that shape it are always a discovery, an inevitable testing ground that questions its origin, its links to other buildings and the landscape, its value as a work of architecture.

The Western tradition has continued to stress the value of such originality. Before any practical work was undertaken, architects were encouraged to make the historic pilgrimage to Rome, to sketch, draw and interpret. Architecture was the testing ground to see what had been done, what could be done. Andrea Palladio, one of the more influential Renaissance architects, methodically reconstructed many of the ruined structures, providing at times an imaginative interpretation from a mere fragment, so much so that even his own constructed work began to draw inspiration from the reconstructions. Though not all great architects produced interesting drawings, and conversely not all great drawings produced interesting architecture, Piranesi was one architect to whom the phrase, "the greatest architect who never built anything", could easily apply. His reconstructions of Roman ruins inspired architects through the Renaissance upto the Beaux Arts, opening up new ways of seeing old things, of attaching imaginative stories to discarded foundations, and breathing life into distant and remote forms. Yet part of the problem lay with his excessively fertile architectural imagination and in drawing buildings too great to be ever physically realized, he produced a range of fantasy projects—plans and perspectives of structures of such exaggerated scale and dimension that could only remain a two-dimensional tribute to his own genius.

Drawings in European private collections, drawings of nuclear reactors in dense city neighbourhoods, apartment blocks built on toxic waste sites, suicide bridges on the Hudson River, fast food restaurants in the shape of a burger, the Ugly Duckling Beauty Parlour, Bouelle's drawings for a penis-shaped brothel, the SITE architects' version of the garden city as a skyscraper, architecture could be a dark, often private, joke, tucked away between the sheets of a drawer full of serious drawings. For visionary architects (as conventionally understood), are the products of less traditional societies. In their own ways 20th-century America, Renaissance Italy and Roman Rome were open and permissive to a point that encouraged thinking beyond their cultural borders. The creation of problems was in themselves beyond the scope of their time and place. Sixteenth-century Italy had no explicit need for a flying machine, yet Leonardo da Vinci's drawings for his model came from his own mental mappings. Similarly a glass dome over New York City was one of architect Buckminster Fuller's many far-fetched ideas, a suggestion of the ecological problems he foresaw. Both were ahead of their time. Having achieved some notoriety in official circles for their inventiveness, and a social label that varied from genius to crank, both enjoyed a certain immunity from the conventions of the time. They were allowed to be themselves.

In India this is often not possible. Architecture, like other professions, falls squarely in the realm of the objective activity directed towards a specific goal, discouraging, so to speak, the tangential view. There are no patrons, only clients. And theirs is not an exploration of architectural ideas, merely an expression of details for eventual construction. So in seeking to express ideas, the architectural task becomes harder, if not downright impossible. Architectural practice today produces professionals, not artists. The insistence on professional discipline is unfortunate only to the extent that it destroys a way of thinking, and the possibilities of arriving at wildly incongruent conceptions that may or may not be part of the solution sought.

The artist's studio has for long been the threshold of innovation and ideation, where too often the impracticality of continual trial and error is not constrained by time frames, work schedules, etc. A person who thinks of a project only between nine and five is not unlike a warehouse packer who punches in and out of his workplace. Do the eccentric and the fantastic then fall outside the imagination of architecture in India? From looking at buildings around us, so it would seem. The profession of architecture today is formed from restraint and repose, not exhilaration, conflict or expectation. All of these are the wrong instincts for a supposedly creative endeavour.

An interpretation of design and style keeps the architect firmly situated in the realm of the problem stated, and problem solved. Like medicine or law, its reach is neither reflective nor self-searching. Other than servicing the client, it serves no purpose at all. What then is the purpose of a profession that doesn't serve the interest of the architect? The confusion stems from the fact that architecture begins as a service profession that strays distressingly into the realm of manufacturing. The uncertainty of its aims and processes leaves the architect on an unsure footing, something that requires as much engagement with a client as with the messy entanglement of the production of building. The eventual result is nowhere as interesting as the process that gets you there. This is not the norm for architecture.

Why then does architecture warrant a book? To my mind, there are three conditions that qualify buildings as architecture, and consequently require a record. First, self-belief. The single most important idea, which cannot be learned or acquired, but is an unconscious attitude. This is like an involuntary organ that comes into play at the time of architectural conception. You instinctively know about the "rightness" of your idea. The strength may not be the idea itself, but your belief in its applicability for the situation you will address. This places great value on architecture as inheritance, the architect's absorption of the building experience into subconscious thought. What you make is not just part of you, but has been part of your history, your background. That is the critical difference between architecture and other construction arts like engineering or interiors.

The origin of self-belief is then your own history, the way you have lived, your understanding of the life of buildings and the way it manifests in you. It appears as a subconscious value in your constructions. Second, conceptual clarity. This is an essential vision that immediately dispels the myth of other possibilities. The strength of the idea drives the design into the narrow path of construction. There is no exploration of the concept, the idea occurs fully-formed and whole.

Once you know for certain what is to be made, the "how" of its making is an open question. Conflicting, violating, testing tendencies arise much later, when there are questions of materials and techniques. The practice of architecture is like a confessional. Every time you build, you go beyond the conventions of the profession and seek a sort of imaginative reconciliation for yourself, another step in the step towards greater clarity, an added reason for how architecture informs your life. That's why building is a sort of liberation, triggered by a remote sense of integrity, even some inner state of happiness, both of which come as much with practice as with ageing. Architecture then goes beyond a simple wishlist of completed buildings and becomes a state of wellbeing.

Third is the question of place. The cultural measure of architecture can only be gauged against the background of the people around and the place it is set in. All other things like climatic, local materials, history and techniques of construction are a given. They are like the gloves and tools a surgeon needs for an operation. They are never the justification for architecture. To this I add the fourth, and most critical, architecture imperative: distillation, for lack of a better word, it signifies not so much simplicity as simplification. Like music, the tonal quality of the complete building—its structure and details—as a receptacle for ordinary life, and free of the anxiety of design interrogation. Architecture as a private background to life, your own life.

In artistic terms, it records the quiet maturity of Cezanne who in his later years painted the same mountain innumerable times; the work of film-makers like Bergman whose camera stood still in Nordic landscapes, or Satyajit Ray whose frames were similarly slow to define his subjects, and instead lingered on mundane details, the transit of life. Architecture is similarly absorbed by indolent realities; a picture that evolves slowly over time and leaves an impression of serenity, rather than the striking or the spectacular; a growth then into a maturity that sees all architecture as a continuous process over time. The building tests the concern for meaningful presence, like the slow fading monumentality of places that are expected to erode, rather than die a sudden death. So slowly, that even when they disappear from sight or experience, they remain ignited and purposeful in memory.

Of course, the working time frame of a building is itself immense. It emerges beyond a precise distillation and conception over the years through a wavering of calcified and prejudiced thought, finally into the sticks and stones of a building site. Except to its architect, its journey is of no consequence or interest to anyone. I've tried to replenish architecture's season of deprivation by drawing unlikely relationships and links. The focus of this book is a set of ideas that are rooted in architecture, and have an expression in varying artistic mediums. Notions of luxury, death, recreation and natural living have sociological meaning, but they also have a reflective resonance in the buildings they generate.

In the course of writing, I also realized the importance of drawing and writing over actual photographs. An image—a painting or sketch—resonates with imaginary possibilities, which are only a display of reality in a photograph. A photographic repeat of what the eye witnesses on the building site onto a page is both a significant loss to the senses and a mere convenient ploy. The picture exclaims the point already made in words. The tangential approach of using mixed media to take a generic bash at the subject is a form of delayed gratification wherein the reader is left to imagine his/her own reality in the space. A lack of imagination in architecture can only be compensated by a willful integration of the reader's imagination with the ideas of buildings. So this is a picture book about the process of architecture. In exploring building ideals however, it is not exclusive and analytical, but derivative and wholly inclusive.

Where thoughts have a visual dimension in art or in tangentially related ideas, they are presented in a loop that includes building, sculpture, painting and drawing. Obviously you make drawings because you want to build. But art is just a wider frame of reference for architecture; its tools can be used to discover architectural ideas, not necessarily build them. Central to sketching, photography, writing and sculpture is the common idea of elaboration, to set out a frame for myself. Bits of writings, pencil drawings, or moulded mud or wax, become a sort of residue of visible matter around me. Like the necessary bits of evidence in a legal battle, they help me build my case in a court where I am the accused, the plaintiff, the jury and judge. It is a sort of personal resonance that a process in on towards some unknown end. This isn't creative writing or art as formal creation, just a set of physical images described for myself. They become irrelevant once the process is over.

By keeping the writing to a minimum, I have tried to present my own personal connection between related ideas in a wholly visual form. I found no literary precedence for such a presentation. At the same time, it was important to present the work and sequence with graphic coherence, where the viewer could easily gauge the connection between the various media presented. Standard layouts were abandoned for a nonlinear format that allows viewing and reading simultaneously, a process that may be frustrating at first, but is true to the disparate content. The book uses architectural drawings rather liberally. Such a layout is not meant to merely depict the standard technical dimensions of a building, but also to state the importance of drawing in conveying something of the atmosphere of the proposed structure.

It also shares some of the thinking that went into its resolution; ideas that often cannot be communicated by photographs alone. Doubtless, the reliability of the varied sequences will be viewed with suspicion, and many in my own fraternity will question the method of elucidation. When the material falls under architecture, artistic and literary mass, the question invariably arises whether one is an architect, artist, or writer and critic. When the goal of the book is self-examination, it becomes impossible to exclude any of the variables that went into examining an idea, without self-consciousness or pretence. Many sketches were quickly, even badly, drawn to delineate an idea. Sculpture and painting were done at times merely as restless references to thought that had no easy translation into art. Collectively, the mediums I hope, convey an idea.

Certainly, much of what I do—what most architects do—is dictatorial. Dictatorial tendencies grow in advancing age. More and more, the practice becomes less of a studio and more of a family-run business. With the patriarch sternly watching, outsiders are not expected to make decisions but merely to follow orders. They are not even in the know because decisions are made without justifications, excessive testing, or visible logic. Their reasoning remains embedded in my own mind and do not need airing. The process of design needs to be more clearly defined than the product pictured as perfect architecture, and the stifled individual spirit that has produced such incoherence in the streetscape. It requires the most vociferous condemnation. Architecture's ambitions are so grandiose that the resulting buildings can only be partial and incomplete successes.

In a descriptive profession that straddles art, ecology landscape engineering, sociology, history and anthropology, the canvas needs set a limit to its expression and exploitation. The buildings in the book are therefore minor studies for a single subject that falls under the broader heading of architecture. Incomplete in many respects, some unbuilt, each focuses on precise matter, enlarged to engage with particularities of site, materials and people. Appendages to a larger idea, they are meant not so much as to draw attention to themselves, but incite thoughts on a web of relationships. The challenge architecture faces, particularly in India, is not a design ideal, but a confrontation with multiple realities, and consequently options. To adopt the hand-me-downs of other cultures, or to use architecture as an evolutionary step that traces insights into materials, resources, labour, ecology, relationship with land, ideas of consumption, emissions, the processes are relevant only to the way we chose to live.

In the long term, the attempt is to analyze architectural ideas, not for their own sake. As mentioned earlier, I use my own buildings only to examine methods by which places can lend meaning to people's lives. Though this may seem too grand an ambition in itself, I hope the exercise will raise questions on why architecture should be relevant to all. By describing the intention rather than the result, the plans and pictures used here only offer clarity on the idea. Many projects lose that clarity in construction. Even if my buildings do not warrant a presentation, I hope the way of thinking about them does. I wrote this book in part to escape redundancy, to remain relevant to the profession. The book is not a denunciation, but a confessional, and an all-out expression of gratitude for a profession that has given much beyond its limited scope. Inspite of its absence of literary or artistic merit, I hope it remains an informed reference to a practice.

Introduction

Increasing populations, growing urban centres, chronic unemployment, a marginalized economy and changing political situations have, during the last 60 years, set the tone for the built landscape of India. Rapid urbanization has necessitated large designed and planned zones within the uncontrolled sprawl of the old city. In tune with 20th-century statistics, the government had taken on the responsibility for providing markets, housing, schools, universities, offices and other infrastructure. Yet, now into the 21st-century, the growing pressure on urban land has led to congested city centres, and to enterprises with a new scale of public space and architecture.

The unimaginably wide disparities in living situations, the stranglehold of building laws, crowding and overpopulation, have all forced unimaginative make-shift solutions to the design of places for living, working, play and entertainment, and to the space of the city itself. Do the results then, the collective effort of what has appeared on the ground, convey anything of people's needs and aspirations? Do the places we make reflect something about the sort of places we would like to live in? Had different ideas and attitudes been expressed in building, planning, urbanism and design, would we be living another life? Is it still possible to find something of the innocence and optimism with which this country began at the time of independence?

The perception of the city as a bounded place historically started as an establishment of the inside and outside, a perceived division that could be made by a simple line, or some impregnable high walls with gates. Its essential character lay in separating space that was organized and settled from the disorder and transience of the surroundings. City walls were meant to be permanent, and an exit from any of their gates was a trespass into an arena of uncertainty. You were leaving an organism whose landscape was objectified and settled over time—a terrain that was shaped by human activity and ancestral memory and a multitude of historical and personal associations. In returning through the gates, the resident was keenly aware of these links, knowing fully well the shared history he was about to enter, and indeed the importance of his own citizenship.

A city like Samarkand additionally bore the burdens of religion, culture and commerce in ways that made it a crucial centre along the old trade routes. The integration of markets and Islamic centres for scholarship, all within the proximity of Registan Square (the focal centre of mosque and mausoleum) and the cultural confluence

■ WC City, pencil on paper, 2014

made the city plan a willful reminder of places wherein like walled geometry becomes the definitive reading of the city. Attempts at reviving the old quarters of medieval towns have been many, and have largely been weighed by concerns about integrating contemporary commerce and culture into the ancient city fabric. A new attempt sought to weave a street culture that linked Registan Square to the rest of the city, in ways that fragmented and stretched the orthogonal geometry of the urban site. But if the medieval city had changed, so too had its citizens.

The closure of city walls traditionally was meant to contain an altogether different life, and it held within its masonry compaction the growth of a significant and ordered community under powerful governance; the hierarchical arrangement of palace, city square and public building—the ground sequence of monuments, visible in Jaipur and Chandigarh, and in the new cities of Amravati and Naya Raipur. If the picture looked divisive and bleak right from the beginning, if the political ideology that generated it was archaic and isolating, it wasn't difficult to see how deadening and forlorn its monuments would be. In the convulsing remains of its future ruins, the real inhabitants spread like a worn carpet, a heterogeneous city of private people and places, no longer made to order, but built quickly in small parcels—urban violations and transformations in private hands. No one in the tenement was part of the sight line and axial arrangements of the old monumental order. No one could care less.

Where then is the city that is still the container of private rights, responsibilities and citizenship? The modern citizen has lost something of the timebound links to places and now operates in free time. The change is visible everywhere. Syrian refugees live in Berlin; they mix there with earlier settlers from Turkey and Ghana. They buy Italian pasta from a restaurant owned by an Afghan. Meanwhile, the native German resident commutes to Amsterdam to work on a project in Dubai... Given the racial and economic polarities, the old perception of a citizen as a permanent resident confined to a fixed geographic location has mutated into a collage of shifting sites and explorations.

People live somewhere, work elsewhere, recreate in yet another, carrying their own inner cities of memories with them wherever

- **ABOVE** Migration 1, bronze, 2012
- **BELOW** Migration 1, bronze, 2012

they go. They populate the unfamiliar with the familiar, setting up a transit camp in places made for movement and impermanence like the potted plants and family photos in gilded frames that make a private setting of an anonymous open plan office work-table. In European and American cities, the debate between "the melting pot" and "multiculturalism" creates an unnecessary rift where conventions of citizenship are still practised. New people are not only required to pledge allegiance to the flag and learn the national anthem, but they must have a strict grounding in local history.

The Indian necessity of publically proclaiming the country's greatness through vocal renditions of "Bharat Mata ki Jai" is a similarly archaic belief, where the majority tries to shout orders to the minority inside the ghetto. Maybe there still exist places where people are born, live and die within the small radius of a medieval town, but in the transitory, fragmented nature of modern city life and global citizenship, such calls are awkward attempts to relocate a presumed past in a desperate nostalgia, and a future that is the figment of a hyperactive political imagination.

So is the paltry offering of the city analogous to the meagre offering that the resident offers the city itself? Conceived as a primitive urge, the new resident merely uses city space as an opportunity to quench his growing appetite, where public engagement is only related to the city as economic entity: to eat well, raise a family, fatten your purse and children is the singular purpose even if you live in a sewer pipe. The instinct of the jungle and the city is the same; the only difference lies in the quality of public regulation, and the agreement

TOP Migration 2, bronze, 2013
ABOVE City Chessboard, pen & ink, 2010

to follow it. In urban terms, they govern land and building, the quality of food, nutrition and hygiene, the immediacy of communication, the security of banking and finance, and the extent of political control. Their power is meant to be used for a collective enhancement of life, the continued evolution of public good. At least this is true on paper. But is it?

Turkey's adoption of European Union regulations for its urban infrastructure saw a dramatic improvement in living conditions: safer neighbourhoods, cleaner air and a more abundant and equitable distribution of energy and utilities. It was from this sudden commonality of experience that the city benefitted. But elsewhere, two separate cities had come into existence, appalled at each other's split and dissonance. One saw place as a distinct world of private objects divided by boundaries in which lives were insular and static. The other was steeped in a dynamic process that ensured that living, working, consuming and dying followed an unprogrammed routine that required no fixed address, no specified time or place, no personal or material attachment; nothing that would jeopardize the process itself. In its public life consequently, the city was a diffuse and unmappable entity, with no focus, outer wall, internal structure, or landmark. That the two worlds existed side by side was itself a pleasant shock, a leap of good faith. It demonstrated that human will was capable of multiple urban realities.

■ **LEFT** Queue 1, bronze, 2011
■ **RIGHT** Queue 1, bronze, 2011

When the common ground, where both ideals could exist intermeshed and dependent, is eventually destroyed, there will be little choice but to divide and then fight for the spoils... The European vision of an ideal society may be altogether different, but if the urban disturbances and distensions that routinely disrupt the life of Indian towns are to act as instruments of change, then a realignment of civic patterns needs to be seen from a new perspective. Also, if the constant search to correct the wrongs of the Indian city sets only painless statistical targets, the lackluster thinking is emboldened by those who hold seemingly unrealistic and "utopian" views. In both cases, implementation is either cursory or impossible.

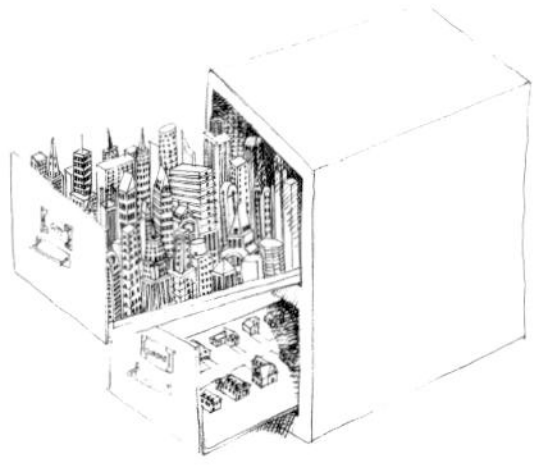

The paranoia of failure, stuck in unrealized plans that derail preceding ones, form an endless stumbling block to the culture of ideas. Bureaucratic planning has guaranteed the public's continued submission to a preordained order. People lived the way they did, because they had no choice. The state's institutionalization may have given a formal shape to public architecture, the secretariat at the head of King's Way in Delhi, or Le Corbusier's government buildings in Chandigarh, but the advocacy of formal structures to urban privacy has always been tainted with mistrust and failure. By imposing a cosmology, geographical axes and terrain to position public monuments and assert bureaucratic authority, civic plans deplored the pattern of traditional settlements.

Private homes and housing were the leftover space from formal bureaucratic order, the tyrannical defense of a displacement that came from a lack of finite position; in its absence, the public was left rudderless, free to move into institutional space—roads, parking lots, flyovers, bridges and railway tracks. At its lyrical best people will move, bag and baggage, and set up private homes in commercial arcades or within monumental settings like parliament buildings and public plazas—places that feel need a human presence. In Louis Kahn's Dhaka and Corbusier's Chandigarh, the width of the open plain separates a notoriously invasive humanity from the grand architectural vision. When the floodgates open, it would be impossible to reconcile the crowds and their new relationship with the monuments. This will fill the sublime emptiness with an exercise of human rights that will once and for all dignify isolated public space with private occupation. Then, all notions of autonomy, self-governance and public rights would require a rethink.

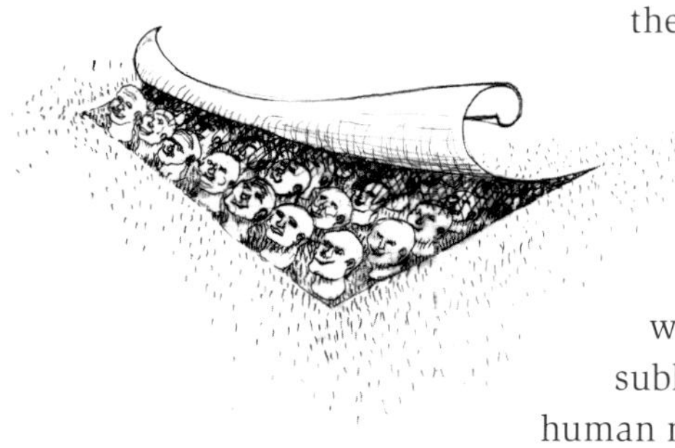

■ **ABOVE** Cabinet City, pencil on paper, 2014
■ **BELOW** Labour 1, pencil on paper, 2014

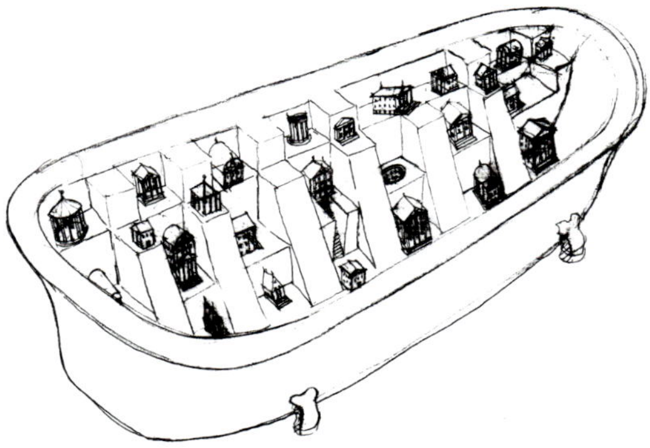

The reversal of the planning process seeks to guard against the view of public space as a self-conscious, isolating entity, as opposed to one with unselfconscious activity. The utopian tendency to define divisions through a reading of space as an element of the sublime, opposes the reality of the new ideal of the 21st-century city, which enhances people's participation, and is based on the tacit belief that the unpredictability of innumerable human actions create their own dynamic of public space. Architects, when they choose to become planners, as Le Corbusier in Chandigarh, Louis Kahn at Dhaka, and Edward Stone in Islamabad, are unable to abandon the specific tonality of precise architectural dimensions for the more fluid strains of civic design. In developing places like India, Pakistan or Bangladesh, with no civic models to absorb migrations, the city becomes a notorious testing ground of urban ideas. And architecture's willful confinement is unsuited to the incomprehensible assemblies of new citizens.

Without knowledge of traditional assemblies and social norms, the tendency of architects to isolate functions, as opposed to supporting diverse and mixed uses, only results in outlandish over-simplifications. The results are forms that become in the long term vast chasms of emptiness, assiduously maintained on the basis of the belief of their art. Without the introduction of metropolitan life into the bland space between public structures, traditional forces will continually erode urban centres; local tendencies of life slip into crevices and undesigned pockets, and spoil individual and heroic decisions of the architect.

Does the civic work of individual architects border on totalitarian extremes then? Is Le Corbusier's planned and unforgiving isolation of the government citadel in Chandigarh acceptable as a work of civic art, but Mussolini's design for New Rome fascist and unacceptable? Is the Imperial City in China, with its formal layout, seen as a form of civic perfection, and Hausmann's rigid restructuring of Paris a sham? Such ideals are less a reflection of architectural sensibilities than a recognition of the

■ Gated Community, pencil on paper, 2015

prevailing social and political regimes of the time; regimes that use architecture merely for public legitimacy. Moreover, where is the need for public space when all human needs are met in the private sphere—the right to own land, build as you wish, to own a car and drive it wherever and whenever you want, eat the food of your choice, own a gun, commute to any place for work, communicate your opinions on a range of electronic devices and across mediums to people entirely disconnected from your life? To give birth, and die as you wish. What other freedoms or choices remain?

Every aspect of public life was available in private space. In the 21st-century, civic architecture has been thoroughly discredited as an archaic practice, a leftover of 20th-century idealism that once saw the city as a great work of man. Its mistaken belief that the confining envelope of unencumbered public space would eventually produce, for all those under its shadow, a great society. The mass of people that readily occupied public space, without regret or apology, were all too aware of the complexities of habit and routine and the truly experimental nature of the life they had chosen for themselves. Their investment came not from a belief in pictorial civic space, but from a crucial mix of sweat and toil, and the blind spot of hope and personal imagination. Somewhere in their sightline lay the hope for a better life, but the city had no part to play in it. Instead it proclaimed its own private ideals.

If city planning models in the '60s were devoid of human scale, and were wholly based on statistical demand, urbanism came in the '80s as a much-needed corrective. Perhaps it was the obvious outcome of a modernist ideal that had begun so savagely: vast repeating blocks of housing, isolated and alone, built on the strategy of ever increasing accommodation. In the wake of the collective failure of that vision, the discrediting of the planning model was inevitable. Urbanism's promise to return the city to a connective fabric of walkways and small streets was a facile localization of efforts that had exaggerated the urban condition into an apocalyptic image, gone completely out of control. Underlying the suspicion of all that was new and big and misunderstood was the belief that architects read every change as a crisis from which they were somehow being excluded.

Even if the problem lay in the ingrained utopian idea that every act of architecture was meant to be an act of upliftment of the human

■ **LEFT** Pipe Dreams, pencil on paper, 2011
■ **RIGHT** Tree Houses, pen & ink, 2010

condition, the reality was different. School-learnt tricks only offered the profession as a seduction, a carefully manicured compound that excluded and divided and left you the proud owner of a gigantic object that could be placed in a book for safekeeping. The profession's alternating surges between high-end design and people-centric sociology left the architect's conscience adrift and confused. In the midst of modernism's fatalistic changes, and the urge to satisfy the increasing numbers, the profession had shamelessly marginalized itself.

The architect's feeble attempts to restore the city and diligently map its space was like assembling pieces of a jigsaw puzzle that could never realistically be completed. The futility of his interventions where statistics were always overwhelming could only leave the city as a permanent construction site. Efforts either dissolved under the absolute form of draconian planning, or were privatized, to remain outside the framework of the plan itself. Either way, the architect's proposal was inconsequential in a place that had exploded into a demonic parasite, eating up its own boundaries. The potential for an urban life without architecture could only be generated by a resolution of migratory forces operating in the city and encoding something of their own culture, on their own terms.

The central idea of the city as a contained, self-governing entity changed; and in its transformed state, so did its engagement with citizens. Unlike its medieval conception as a place bounded by walls and gates, the new city is without physical boundaries; it stretches beyond visibility, as well as physical comprehension, housing people, places, incidents and ideals that often never intersect. Its dimensions consequently, can only be vague—measured in mounting kilometres, on GPS maps, and as expanding statistics—number of homes, number of homeless, division into districts, etc. Within its vast agglomeration however lay smaller cities, places with personal boundaries prolonged and experienced over time, places that form a limited private engagement for each of its residents.

While the larger city is in the constant flux of migration, construction and demolition, along with other less easily measurable incidents—crime, marriage, rape, accident, political

■ **ABOVE** Gated Home 1, pen & ink, 2013
■ **BELOW** Gated Home 2, pen & ink, 2013

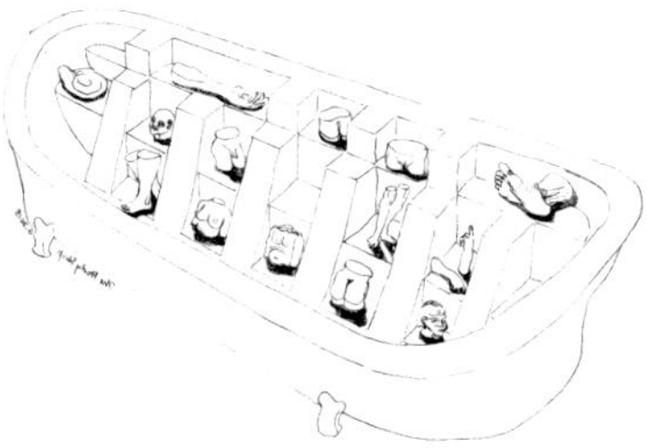

protest, religious festival—the personal city remains unchanging; its sites are traversed daily and still engage the senses in much like a traditional city, in a real, physical way—in walks, in drives to the workplace or market, in recreation and sport, in domestic activity, teaching and school...If the architect had once been the professional who dealt with the description of the city, its silence and emptiness, the relinquishment of that duty was an unstated attack on urbanity itself. Not merely abandoning the child on an unknown doorstep, but giving up parenthood altogether.

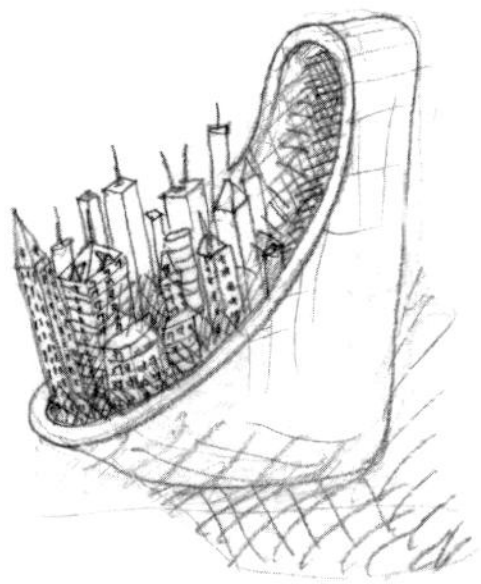

The objectification of architecture's individuality into privately designed products retained not even cursory references to where buildings were placed, against which wall, in which city. The city of divide and rule was intentionally constructed as a place for the homeless, to the precise dimensions of fitted bodies; unlike the real cities of history, the former place of citizenship and privacy, the new residents had begun to feel at home in uninhabitable space, even calling it home without ever feeling the real ache of homesickness. The privatization of the city then became the most logical form of urban control.

To be able to run a large office complex, a housing estate, or a shopping mall required the administration of a municipality. A daily staff of officers and bureaucrats, machinery for upkeep and maintenance, controls for entrance and exit, offices for records, safety and security were all required. The efforts at urbanism were then contained within the boundary wall; while the outer dimensions and events were beyond reckoning, distorted into unrecognizable entities. The architect and urbanist rediscovered the virtues of their applications—the shaded streets, squares and neighbourhoods of shops and playgrounds; a pedestrian city, made slower, accessible, within dimensions that could be understood, all inside a private boundary wall.

This was hardly a suitable alternative, but in the surrounding gloom of infrastructure, once under the control of the pencil of the architect, every situation was consumed by impossible dimensions. Dimensions that no longer fit the drafting table. Satellite townships, industrial

- **ABOVE** Body Shop, pencil on paper, 2014
- **CENTRE** Urinal, Suburb, pencil on paper, 2014
- **BELOW** Ghetto, pencil on paper, 2014

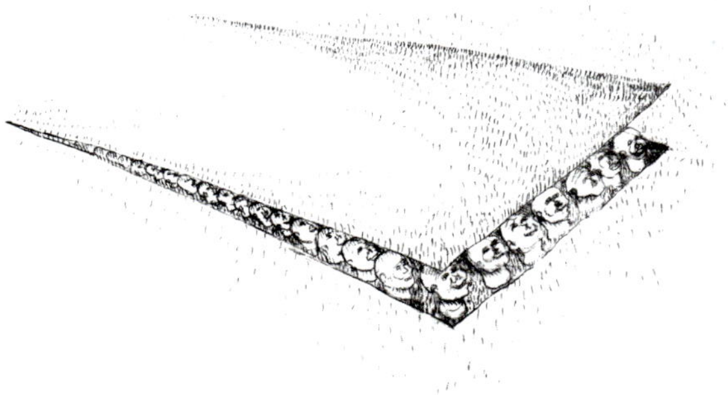

cities, transport hubs, expressways, skyscrapers, model housing, eco-cities, even the terminology was baffling in the movement and settlement of impossibly large populations. The architect's unwillingness, and incapacity, to deal with these new alignments pushed him quickly into redundancy.

When the form of the new city was no longer just physical, it needed the nurturing of a new philosophy of living. Not just something that emerged from the magnified dimensions of the infrastructure, but had a basis in human relationship with its size. Only then would the incomprehension and awe help to dismantle the narcissism of architecture's minor design and artistic claims, and help to direct the profession towards reinventing itself. It was hard to understand why the city had given in to such violent self-abuse and annihilation, surrendered completely to permissive private moments and veered away from hope, reform, or will to collective action. If it continued to function as a social device with an indeterminate formlessness, its technical containment in place would always be embroiled in chaos.

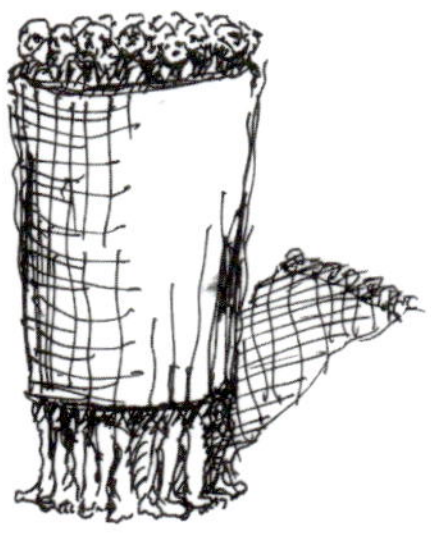

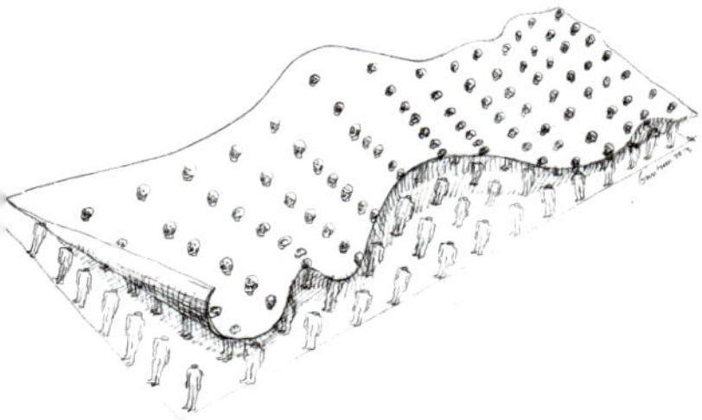

People could manoeuvre into its crevices, even live a life of desire; but the physical structure and order was held in contempt, as if the expression of the collective was an agonizing antithesis of the city's private lives; a falsification, a fabrication of implied order that served no purpose at all. Perhaps the question was no longer whether one cancelled out the other, or whether the two could possibly co-exist. Given the grainy, parasitic growth of urban centres, it was inevitable that any future form of urbanism could not rely on the permanence of architecture, and the fixed

- **ABOVE** Labour 2, pencil on paper, 2012
- **CENTRE, LEFT** Crowd, pen & ink, 2011
- **CENTRE, RIGHT** Crowd, bronze, 2011
- **BELOW** Labour 2, pencil on paper, 2012

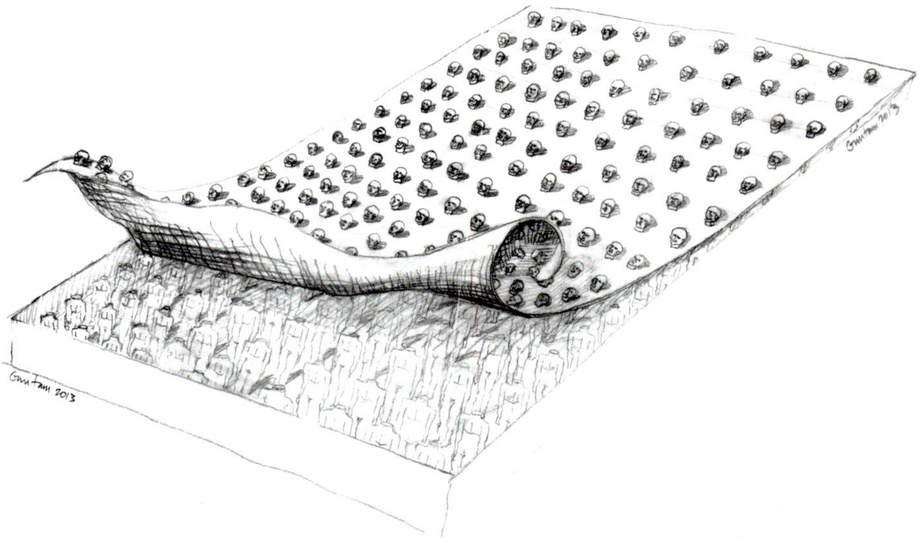

position of objects and cores—even that settled view of the world with home as a fixed and finite place.

The house was once a physical entity built on its own ground; it approached the city from a private vantage of ownership and identity. A personal refuge, an escape from the indignities of civic strife; it later assumed a more tenuous position as air-space. The future city may see its physical obliteration altogether. The view of architecture as settlement may be altogether archaic and will, in the migratory struggle, create shifting alternatives to place. Just as office space was replaced by a connective tissue of interactive information conveniently exchanged between workers, the home's transience too was assured.

The potential to purchase or construct your privacy when required was an enactment of civic life claimed by the city of constant movement. The pen drive and hard disc could promote the new form of housing; a storehouse of memories that was always available when private familiarity and comfort was required. The animation of the old house and family life was at hand as simulated possibility. Was this to be viewed as a failure of the traditional position? Redundancy was the position of the architect himself, who used objects as a defining outline of the city.

- **ABOVE** Labour 3, pencil on paper, 2012
- **BELOW, LEFT** Dhaka Ruins, pen & ink, 2012
- **BELOW, CENTRE** Dhaka Ruins, watercolour, 2011
- **BELOW, RIGHT** Chandigarh Ruins, watercolour, 2011

No longer was such an approach required or desired. It was instead easy to fill the city with numbers, and believe that a statistical order could satisfy the demands of urban life. The numbers too were divided among themselves: guests one day, hosts the next. They only sought privileges they had designed for themselves, playing roles that made the city a place to constantly act, and never just be; resident, commuter, worker, shopper, consumer, always an addict. The city of the future was a visibly unstable configuration, but its values were grounded in a shifting stage set of people, food and employment. Home was a job, a quenching of thirst, a place to lie down.

A movement between these variables no longer made it possible to capture it in diagrams or statistics—the two traditional benchmarks of planning and architecture. In the future, the public fields of bureaucratic intervention will be enablers of migratory tasks, accommodating potential, discovering hybrids and making physical possibilities happen on ground space. The city's potential for human action and spectacle would confer new definitions on civic life, and the resulting architectural brief would doubtless be informed by fluid transformations, rather than setting physical limits and boundaries. The order of architectural activity will always remain in flux, and live in the hope of new diversification.

It will be impossible to use architecture's conventional characteristics to suggest changes in the public realm. The promise of a future formlessness not only denies the architect a livelihood but sets up an autonomous framework without architecture and even without a stated physical requirement. If the case for redundancy looms large, so does the promise of brighter alternatives. When so much of the profession regressed into facile statements of design, architecture had itself sunk to civic irrelevance. At the very outset, architectural culture had learnt to applaud the mediocre, and create a cult that resonated only among the elite. Architecture's inclusion in the new world of visible design was fuelling its quick demise. Just the way art has lost its relevance by becoming entirely political, architecture lost its way by being wholly apolitical and merely fumbling in private shadows.

While art's inclination resides in a normal purpose that validates its position as a beacon in society, architecture concerns itself with providing solutions to political concerns or atleast extend the realm of social responsibility. Without its presence in uncomfortable issues of settlement and migration, public space, urban culture, etc it is condemned to the peripheries of design, an immodest position somewhere in between low art and complete decline. Perhaps in through alternative thinking, public participation, broadcasting and television and restrictive zoning, construction will tangentially gain relevance and retain something of its claim to improving lives.

The civilizing influence of building, seen in symbolic representations of government—justice, legislature, parliamentary assembly, and the democratic ideals of Greece and Chandigarh—will be trampled in the stampede and replaced by forces of a mass struggle. Not the physical revolution of the 19th-century, but a social cohesion formed out of private needs. For all its grandiose past and all the historic remnants encased in its aging monuments, the new

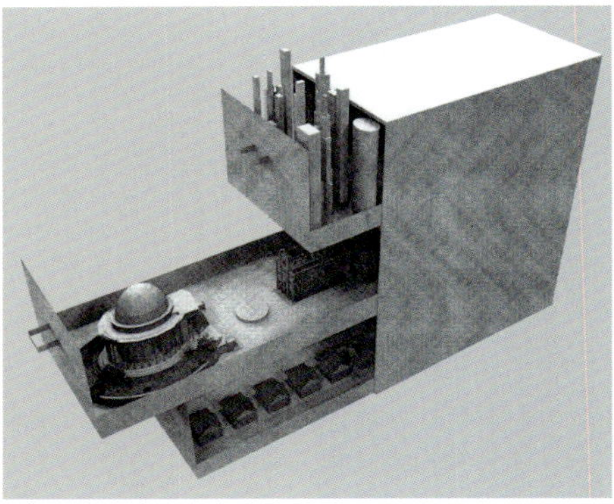

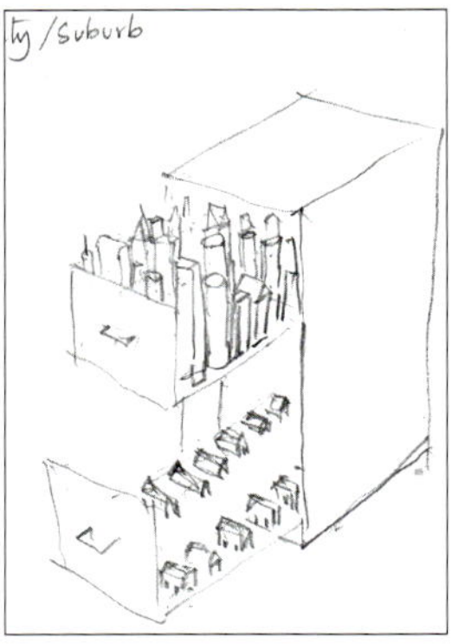

city is a reminder of struggles yet to come. The constantly changing signatures of its streets and neighborhoods, and its new arrivals, are bound to become a daily erasure of memory, and the framing of new forms of urbanism's participatory democracy, which is formed out of private norms of survival.

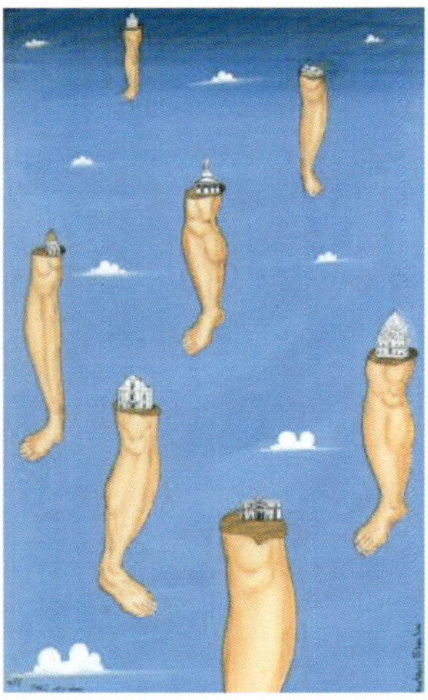

Among the newly landed masses, architecture will itself struggle to suggest new forms of physical cohesion. In the expectations of political upheaval, migratory flows, and social demands for civic space lies the hope that changing urbanity would itself lead to a radical shift in architecture. The city's formlessness will then be its most positive attribute. In a culture of expediency and spectacle, architecture will have none of the responsibilities of its glory days, as a master builder, the architect and planner will become just another citizen on the run.

The city's inexorable decline as a magnificent, dynamic entity was a cause to grieve. The architect had not only misunderstood its situation in timeless time, but willfully and with utter disdain,

- **ABOVE, LEFT** City–Country–Suburb, simulation, 2014
- **ABOVE, RIGHT** City–Country–Suburb, pencil on paper, 2014
- **BELOW** Footings, watercolour, 2011

defeated the remarkable evolutionary arrangements of its many parts that had given it long-term meaning. The city existed in an elastic timelessness; its eternal presence, a conclusion that never resisted the ceaseless migration of people and buildings. People and buildings were in fact finite and linked to each other in measurable ways—building against building, the marginal and tentative growth of families and their evolving homes, the changing densities of streets and neighbourhoods, the ceaseless rise and demolition of downtown areas, the proliferation of commerce and slums.

In every architectural act was a measure of temporary upheaval, permanent only for the generation that occupied it. The ideological process was compressed in a miniscule and personal timeframe, enlisted by private land and building ownership; the city merely surrendered to its whims, constant erosions, additions and adaptations. The endless additions and subtractions made architecture a record of perennial interruption—concrete silhouettes and profiles rising, decaying, eroding, renovating, demolishing and re-erecting. Architecture's influence on the texture of the city was miniscule, and often overrated. It was much like a cupboard whose shape is unaffected by the items stored in it. The subjective imposition of small ideas, inebriated by design, technology or new social trends, could hardly impose on the seemingly objective, political and economic struggle of the city.

The endless autonomy of private expression in homes, offices and businesses was a feeble characteristic of people wishing to exercise visual physical control over their lives and to offer a picture of resistance to collective regulations and codes. Only the temporal, changing framework of architecture remained its innately humane characteristic. Material aged, altered and decayed like human skin and left you pained by its passing, delighted by its renewal. In the experience of daily encounters, architecture conveyed its fragility and informed the resident with its subliminal, and most crucial, psychic sense.

The temporal, generational nature of such private protest however made it impossible to alter the memorial space of the city. Architecture could then only remain a partial symbol of a temporary condition. Its minor influence tried to rescue culture from oblivion; but it could never be in competition with the city, a ceaseless force of memory and archaeology. The collusion between architecture and the city therefore never endorsed the fractured conditions of one on the perceived order of the other. The city could never control the ensuing disorder of architecture; conversely architecture's chaos was self-contained and insular, unable to make a dent on the great civic pile. Where architecture had begun to move away from its material massing into self-indulgent prophecies of disorder, its own structure and existence was suspect—the elaboration of its subversive solutions to self-made cause and effect.

In its most fastidious falsification, architecture offered itself as disguise, a willful representation of itself as another; the enveloping skin showed one thing, the inside another. An exterior of grand aspirations, concealing the innards of biological frailties. The architect was a cloak fitter, tailoring the perfect suit on an empty garbage landfill. The inherent complication of the simplistic envelope was a professional necessity and it gave the working life self-obsessed meaning. In a peculiar position between self-conscious will and public embarrassment, the architect stated his position, first by articulating the design ideology on the facade, and then, in a moment of flourish, taking an important, visible risk with it, for the sake of other professionals who may notice his work.

The courtesies of reticence and restraint could no longer be practised when the building's role was reduced to message; the distortion of the familiar, the only language of communication. The end result was the hope of a mystical aura that demonstrated both a resolution of architectural history and the process of building production and emerging trends. "Watch this space", without it, the building fell flat. The old understanding of architecture as a place settled in time and place had altogether disappeared. There, the inclusion of all—people, building, ground and landscape—in the frame had grown together to give coherence to the composition. The reading of age and decay as positive attributes of surfaces gifted architecture with the patina of time, legend, even myth.

This drew a blank on exactness of history, construction and technology, eroding the precision under which a building had originated. The aging quality of much of its architecture was itself relegated to the ruin—buildings in stone, wood and brick receded restfully into Arcadian landscapes, throwbacks to a time that recorded seasonal and site variations on their surfaces. Their place in the setting was informed not by their value as individual, identifiable objects, but as markers permanently embalmed in the ground and foliage, for posterity, forever. However, the transformation to a new perception grew in a flash. The unchanging visibility of the new building was a continuous record of its

■ **PAGES 38-49** Model Buildings, pen & ink, 2010

inception throughout its short life. Every structure looked as if it were built yesterday; its synthetic materiality an asset that never grew old, never showed its age like television programmes that aired their seasons for the short duration of a specified time, buildings grew and died with omnipresent quickness.

With everyone asserting a private identity, the value of design dimmed. With every object seeking its moment of fame, its short life under the sun, its planned noticeability went unnoticed. Buildings did not even last long enough to cast a shadow; only their birth and demise was recorded, their time on earth was simply a distraction without experience, visible for that instant as a jolt of shock and awe. Unable to resolve into the surrounding mass, the architectural landscape was a blinding impression that stayed in the mind as a trifling residue—weightless and without content. In the long term, it affected the people who moved in and around the characterless, featureless terrain, their indifference and dislocation an unrecognized threat to themselves.

In the larger picture of a world with too many visible and planned differences, everything and everyone was the same, a tireless stream of images sparked with nervous delight, but afloat like sewage; a surface stream in an even current. But architecture's measures were isolated and restricted to the professional sphere. In the conventional view its reading had been intrinsically tied to geometry. It was also considered a display of the forces of gravity. The heaviness and lightness of structure, its shift of weight from top to bottom, its contact with the earth, was more a lesson in physics, far removed from the weightlessness of the new architecture.

My admiration of traditional architecture stemmed from its stark and honest statements of structure, the transfer of loads that shaped its piers and gave windows their size, the way gravity defined weight and agility, the way columns were shaped by scientific entasis, the presence of domes and vaults that let you know, in no uncertain terms, the upper limits of construction. The physics of form was then a given, and the architect was left with few choices and fewer causes for making erratic and whimsical decisions. However, its most critical resolve, to create intimacy in the exterior, and to deliberately slow or enclose exterior space, was in defining moments so essential to enact civic life.

In forts, city walls, plazas, courtyards and streets, architecture learnt how best to define the city. Its most pervasive

FOLLOWING PAGES Wallpaper Architecture, watercolour, 2010

शंकर लाल भोपा

influence lay in the meeting ground of privacy and community. Older cities were forever in debt to their architecture. Without it, they were nothing, nothing but industrial wasteland. In the shadows, the shade of arcades, the soft focus of public grasslands, water channels and stone streets, the design of public life had the same texture as the private, as if you had merely walked out of your own living room into another that included some strangers. Strangers not for long. Urban territories were additional attractions that flowed in indivisible, connected space; they took you by the hand and led you deeper into familiarity.

This was something that the 21st-century had lost forever. From the Hindu temple to Le Corbusier, the definition had varied only in degree. But in the 21st-century much of that singular god-given truth stood altered, paralyzed. Architecture's object-making destroyed the logic of the city. Buildings sprung up in China that displayed structures that were more hand-weave than orthogonal geometry, as if the architect had deliberately chosen to be obtuse and indeterminate. The Corbusier logic of the plan being the generator would no longer hold if applied to the Bird's Nest Stadium. Try doing this and you will end up with a dull halo of a building. Its outer face provides no front and back elevation, no sense of up or down—part of the logic of buildings whose structure is generated through a complex computer programme. By itself such architecture clarifies a vision that is altogether revolutionary and has evolved out of wholly new considerations.

First and foremost, it requires no visual reading. You do not stand before it to make a physical study of its envelope, the resultant logic of orientation or connection to surrounding buildings or the neighbourhood, in order to arrive at the core of its design. No. An instantaneous revelation is formed in experience, and through a hazy recollection of form, as if in the mind's eye, everything—shape, material, structure, time and space—affords a multivalent perception. The ambiguous definition of its physics contributes to the eventual experience. And no single reading of it from any one vantage point is true to the total experience.

Architecture is nothing or everything, all at once. You consume it without nuanced expectation, or it spits you out like dirt. After all the noble clarity of modernism, after all the need to express intent and display the structure and mechanics of building, and reveal the process of construction was a thing of the past. Architecture's complicity with structural engineering and building mechanics produced the Pompidou Centre. The exposure of its many parts was to an extent the concluding statement of Le Corbusier's "machine of living in". Prefabricated parts, standardized elements, lighting, cooling, heating, water drainage, circulation were all reduced to systems operating the building, but ensured that the efficiency of consumption was beyond the pale of human error or control.

When building had embraced the logic of construction, it had sailed beyond preference and personal choice. Renzo Piano's exposed pipes and steel trusses at the Pompidou Centre were the last defining triumph of the archaic idea. The building finally lay buried with all the French honours in a neighbourhood of stone facades, a reminder now of its place in history. Architecture's anonymity had begun to grow with the partition-free office space. The industrial shed was a landmark structure that gave commercial building the unrelieved span, and a continuous set of mechanical services and utilities that could be tapped at will. It was a new type of magnificence, not by detail or design, but by choice—the free-wheeling envelope that could adjust to any and all individual needs.

Technology's takeover was full and certain. It grew from the belief that the value of scientific advance could best be demonstrated in architecture and engineering, not in the laboratory. Buildings and bridges were big, physical things and required no proof of their existence. When spans could get longer and structural conditions optimized, the private, diminutive quarters of traditional building could be relegated to the dung heap. The anonymity of the endless space, air-conditioned and conceived in modular increments without a pre-programmed diagram of activity, was a new utopian order.

People and their private spaces could be made as a minor afterthought, with little or no affect on the structure itself. In fact, people were involved in only arranging the partitions inside the envelope at will—an act that let the architecture remain untouched. Consequently, architecture as a statement in the city had lost its urban value. The sheer gigantic scale of a building that operated on the scale of a ship did not allow it to connect with other ships in the city. The connective tissue of material, scale, texture and height were obliterated once and for all. The sights and sounds of the neighbourhood convulsed into a factory yard, and space, vacant—both inside and out—was unlike anything experienced in day-to-day life.

I had always presumed architecture to be a part of a closed system, a story that had a beginning, middle and an end. In every project the process proceeded to ensure closure of the kind that built walls, created boundaries, and could be stated in square feet. The universal statement of building and its intention was an essential condition, and geometry's most primary forms gave a recognizable definition to architecture. No cultural or social differences were brought into play to understand height and size, front and back, door and window, ground and road. The visual relationship of building to building established a continuity with the street and became an essential measure of urban design.

The strategy of commonality—a consensus on materials and heights drove the eye along a neutral track, and happily removed architecture from the visual sense as mere background to life. This is where globalism had a pervasive impact. Often misunderstood as a homogenizing influence on architecture, it betrayed a negative connotation, especially so in a profession that was judged solely on its appearance. Such judgements made quick and often erroneous mockeries of local situations. Yet, architecture's adaptive qualities remained unrecognized, and its major attributes were brushed under the carpet, mostly by professionals who saw globalism as a form of cultural invasion. Accusations came primarily from sources that were in themselves too weak to fend off the onslaught.

In places like India, China and parts of West Africa, globalism was a marauding threat, a looming gray fog that filled the emptiness of cultural space with its own facsimiles. Without a precise definition of architecture or settlement, it was mistakenly viewed as a borrowing, an imposition. In the culturally cohesive societies of Western Europe and Japan, there were no visible blemishes of globalism. Nothing was to be seen that said that new buildings were inconsistent with the evolutionary nature of their own local traditions. Global architecture merely infused local building traditions with ideas on materials, technologies and space without altering the cultural and social fabric of urban design. Even the multiple projections and material inconsistencies of the new Whitney Museum in Chelsea do not seem to be out of place within the severe rectilinear structure of New York City.

The idea that the building's shape is no longer a significant measure of architecture is perhaps then only a 21st-century sentiment. Diller-Scofido-Renfro had deliberately turned space into an undefined mass of vapour in their Blur Building project—a formless structure without space requirement or function. Was that then the new architecture—

the faceless building that had travelled the distance from the self-conscious Renaissance of proportion and subtle element variation to a formlessness that was now complete? This was the architecture of fog and smudge, something that could not be placed on a drawing board or captured in photographs.

As its creator, Charles Renfro remarked that its public dimension encompassed only a universal measure of things; the state of the digital world, of altered states, love, the self and the universe. What more was there to say? When material and elemental relationships were no longer valid measures of architecture, the only choice was to build distension, decay and disintegration into the premise of future practices. It was easy to build large structures, but harder to hide their physical presence in a liquid pixilation that was as much eye-wash as mechanical deception. Working with sculptor Isamu Noguchi, Kahn had earlier chosen to practise a deviation from the physical order of building into a celestial and transcendental direction, as a way to link the visible to something greater. It was not enough that the Salk Laboratories were just good laboratories, fine workspaces in which scientists and researchers worked in magnanimous surroundings.

No, the conscious focus of science in the lab was rewarded with a stark metaphysical condition in the landscape—a thin strip of water that connected land, ocean and sky in an artistic vision so fundamental that it set you adrift somewhere between the built world and emptiness. If Noguchi's sculptural idea complimented Kahn's architecture it was only because both had learnt to test the physical world as much through construction as through its absence. Noguchi physically chiselled away at matter; Kahn's solids were formed out of voids. The two worked in geometry so primary—cubes, cylinders, cones—that the form was an unquestionable given, and entirely irrelevant.

Architecture or sculpture was not a choice to be made, it was something beyond description. Its physical invisibility was its greatest asset, a step in the right metaphysical direction. In the Roosevelt Memorial in New York, Kahn's room—a reminder of Franklin Roosevelt's Four Truths of freedom—had a missing fourth wall that opened completely into the East River. Its incompleteness was an imagined enclosure, where the water and the distant ocean were also inducted into the architecture. If in the search for formal integrity, architecture had to paradoxically disintegrate, the message was interpreted in wildly disparate ways.

When I saw Frank Gehry's Bilbao Museum, it informed me in no uncertain terms about the destructive attributes of the new architecture. It was not so much about the shock of its silvery

presence in a place with such a magnificent history, but about the continual prismatic distension of its many planes. Architecture made it abundantly clear that the whole was no longer the sum of its parts, but the atomization of the parts itself. I imagine Gehry had chosen its display deliberately to antagonize the traditions of the surrounding city.

The building defied all conventions of architectural design: there was no front or back, no elevations, no prescribed entrance, no serving bay, no distinction between wall and floor, floor and cladding. No difference between window and wall, transparent and opaque, no visible division into floors, no prescribed height, or building crown. Yet the constructed pathway through the galleries was an ambulatory of such delight and surprise that the building lost nothing of its power to condense and illuminate the artistic experience. The galleries were absorptions of such enormous variables of light and space that the art could only partake of its glorious iridescence.

I stood by the waterfront in the evening light and watched as the architecture's vivid sheen turned into a burnished brown. The building never lost its sculpted shapelessness even at night. More guarded in his break with tradition, Jean Nouvel's work takes only the external presence of building as an opportunity for serious play. Even when the internal layout follows the rigid pattern of required space, the window and wall confound the viewer with synaptic variations, so deliberately subtle that the building is seen as a visual trick. At his new apartment block in Chelsea, window frames pivot and slant in minor angular variations, setting up the glint and sparkle of a fresh-cut diamond (an idea he first developed at the Arab World Institute), a camera aperture opening and closing in accordance with the light outside.

The clarity of such private perceptions has suddenly altered into a multi-polar view to a geometry that stretches in elastic ways, and conforms to no literal rectilinear dimension. Herzog and de Meuron's Olympic Stadium in Beijing confronts the viewer with a structure and shape that emerges from the strains and stresses of an elaborate basket weave, an inventiveness that relies on computer-generated structural programmes; the plasticity of form is both a devise to invent and camouflage.

Diller + Scofidio's work on the High Line, so intensely physical in its demand for human weight and continual sensory reaction, happily obliterates the old relationship with geometry and materials. The trusting, amalgamating, truly inclusive nature of its design intoxicates and wills the walker into modes of serious divergence. You are drawn all along conceptually down the straight and narrow path; yet a sensory gravitational pull is exerting its own force from the sides: a bench built into a side extension, a sudden bowing out reshapes the relationships of walk to plantation for views down the street, past rectangular window frames of traffic. Everywhere, new moments of rest find a treasury of expression among the long movement.

The ambiguity of the transformation itself invites participation. You sit on a bench that is in fact a sidewalk, the interweaving fingers of the sidewalk are encouraged to grow weeds, every tertiary activity unfolds from the primary act of walking, every additional design is merely an impulsive resolution of the concrete pathway into something else. The highlight of the journey is the journey itself. No start, no finish. Just a literal, physical slicing of the walkway where it ends. You can join the experience anywhere. Part of the problem in reading such architecture lies in the nature of representation itself.

Much of the work—the Blur Building or even the High Line—does not conform to conventional drawing. When buildings have no start, no end, obey no geometry or orthogonal axes or linear limits, they defeat the line representation of rendering. No plan, section or elevation allows you to construct the structure in the third dimension. Spray paint, charcoal or the ink smudge come close to the statement, but the computer mesh frame begins to capture something of its illusive angularity, the complexities, concave and convex. A slow and seemingly self-conscious process of destruction has taken architecture from an object that is carefully constructed, piece by piece in space, occupying ground and air rights to complete oblivion, and a deliberate denial of its physicality.

In the early '80s, Sculpture in the Environment (SITE), began by destroying the very buildings they first carefully constructed, a dual process that constructed and de-constructed. The denial of architecture was perceived in its decay, and designed in the building itself. In the Best product showrooms, walls developed cracks, whole brick parapets crashed in confounding piles, foliage ripped apart facades—the seemingly

■ **FOLLOWING PAGES** Warehouse Architecture, pen & ink, 2011

innocuous archaeological process of decay that stretches across centuries was compressed into a foreshortened present, leaving the visitor suspended in a time-warp transformation.

The architect's critical grasp of the present, past and future expressed in a single moment was the primary call for the architect. For the most part, the current work only reinforces this quest for geometric redundancy and an expression that overcomes the right of the building for a patient expression of its materiality. In my own reading of these recent projects, I was also seeing an awkward distention to the idea of institutional private space; a lack of dimensional clarity that ordinarily gave precise definition to institutional design. The nature of reading and study had changed in a library; office privacy was denuded into an open plan; the museum and gallery no longer initiated a private conversation between viewer and object.

Obviously, technology's interception and interference had left a disturbing footprint in a long-held, intimate relationship. In the presence of autonomous space, the library reading room, the airport terminal and business office could all be fitted into the androgynous template. The closed, dark, secretive and shadowed spatial combinations that endowed space with multiple meanings had been abandoned as naive, claustrophobic and presumably archaic. I was always looking to engage with the mysterious unknown of space, in places that surprised you.

Unfortunately there was a growing tendency among architects to politicise the very physical actions of architecture. Space was a democratic medium if it allowed multiple uses. At the Seattle Public Library, the reading hall is also reception, meeting room, playground, plaza and civic space; everything a citizen wants it to be; the newspaper office open plan makes no distinction between reporter, administrator and editor, or encourages private enclosures for thinking and writing. The insularity of closed chambers, small rooms and divided halls is anti-democratic. So individual identities are blurred; private actions are assembled like furniture in public vastness.

In Rem Koolhaas's Seattle Public Library, the open field of incessant motion and public exchange is justified as a street plaza made indoors. Is this really the nature of a public library? Or is it closer to a public playground? How does the magnified openness of such a raucous interior gain validity without contrasting privacy?

When architecture becomes a mere instrument of design rather than social structure and cohesion, it loses its value, and becomes a mere object, visibly gratifying, but nothing more. Much of the new architecture then works as a perfunctory instrument of territoriality. Animals too have learnt to define and demarcate their space, but they rarely possess the power to invoke a message of constructive engagement. What then is the difference spatially between the Seattle Public Library and a sheep barn outside Seattle? Other than momentary sparks of intellectual gratification, how do the recent works of Diller-Scofido-Renfro enlarge the architectural experience in space and time?

I had begun to see in the architecture around that the profession had become a genuinely useless activity, a rare form of high art that embodied the three ignoble truths of contemporary urban culture: architecture as fashion icon and trendsetter, architecture as heroic structure, and architecture as intellectual statement. One of those rare professions that needed no depth of inquiry, no investigation or philosophical thought to convey ideas. Instead, photos were enough to tell its story. Architecture's most pervasive fear, the fear of banality became paradoxically an escape into greater banality. When renowned structures made statements about skin and shadow, transparency and opacity, materiality and temporality, they were merely expressing a designer's concerns with design.

Obviously then, one of the more serious changes that has occurred in recent architecture is the architect's perception of design itself. If the earlier approach conceived buildings as complete entities within which a specified program of space occurred, the new way dissects and fragments buildings into residual parts and then gives identity to each in some distinctive material expression. It recognizes patterns of diversity within the building mass, rather than consigning everything to a common framework. Much of it is a cause for sensory appreciation—a delight and instant gratification. Its most visible form, I found in the work of Jean Nouvel. Where classical approaches accepted sunlight as an orderly magnificence on floor and walls, and described the changing glow as an eternal phenomenon, Nouvel split light's radiance into manmade fragments—dealing with it not as perfect density and colloidal mass, but a fluid imperfection, to be sieved, grated and manipulated to private order—almost like ingredients of a cooking show. Much of the new work is consequently patterned to an exuberance of serial pleasure and private technical wish fulfillment. Architecture becomes a statement in product design and 3D graphics, at times even alleviating cognitive dysfunction with decorative flamboyance and distraction. The disturbing aspect of such sensory manipulation is the ultimate dissolution of building clarity. Such private attitudes to design follow in the wake of a crucial absence.

A critical aspect of architecture lies in a realm outside of itself—a decisive link to a social or political history. Soon after Indian independence, architects gratefully received the story line of freedom and partition; practices aligned their narrative to the new political thinking. In the 1980s global—and Indian—concerns narrowed to regional issues, and to stories of private and local identities. When public perceptions are expressed in architecture its private and insular tendencies can be effectively curbed, and a more cohesive picture emerges.

Sadly the reality of the 21st century is that a generation of architecture has no story to tell. Climate change is neither narrative nor a creative of collective consciousness; it is merely political expediency that has a technical resolution. The ambivalence of architecture and its easy fallback on design is a convenience that is eccentricity, flash and delirium. Not a peculiar condition of time and place, but a product. In that distant time, when architecture grew into its own engagement with silence, it remained outside the shackles of design; but in a new world it has fallen prey to the noise. And the social reality of the rich world is too exclusive to offer anything but programmed requirements of architecture packed into private ideas.

Rarely did the building or its architect talk about human beings and habitation, culture, the nature of occupancy or social norm, or even the old dictum that architecture is background to life. I wondered why people asked so little of their buildings. With such low expectations, how did architecture continue to even survive as a profession? If there was a restatement of the relationship between the building and the user, it was a parallel repeated in art and literature where the narrative reached no conclusion, and most times, resolved the story line in a subversion of space and time, and a complete absence of cultural situations. Without culture as a hinge, architecture loses its essential of the “eternal” where its archaeology becomes a link to the surrounding buildings and landscape.

No such conditions are imposed on architecture anymore. The anonymous and the universal were now one and the same thing. The generalities of architecture: the importance of site, landscape, techniques, building and labour practices, consciousness of climate, etc., have too often been cited as the morals of any building story. The purpose of citing specific examples from a private practice are now like a sampling from a cook’s set of tested recipes. Still, in my opinion, what matters is the specifics of a particular location, the details and difficulties that are personally experienced, made and unmade in a precise time and place, the intention and the result. Only the evocation of that experience can describe and resolve diversity. More than ever a case needs to be made now for architectural complexity, away from the serious delusions and entrapments of the visible object into the telling of a deeper and more profound tale that is more engrossing, and within which the inhabitant becomes an active protagonist, a participant not just lost in the storyline, but for whom the story is written. Without it, architecture has no place in history.

The idea is to go beyond the visible appeal of the building (something that architects have shamelessly exploited), and to see how places can be assessed critically and form a psychic basis that influences our lives. I approach architecture then from a perspective of experience. Beyond its professed inclinations to aesthetics, order and legibility, the overwhelming purpose is a record of its various readings; what architecture makes in the space of a room, its perceptions of history, its relation to the land, its participation with the landscape, its record of height and size and its confinement to the underground. Though every building expresses moments from all these, it also controls the central premise of its existence where one idea overrides the rest, and becomes the defining moment of the architecture.

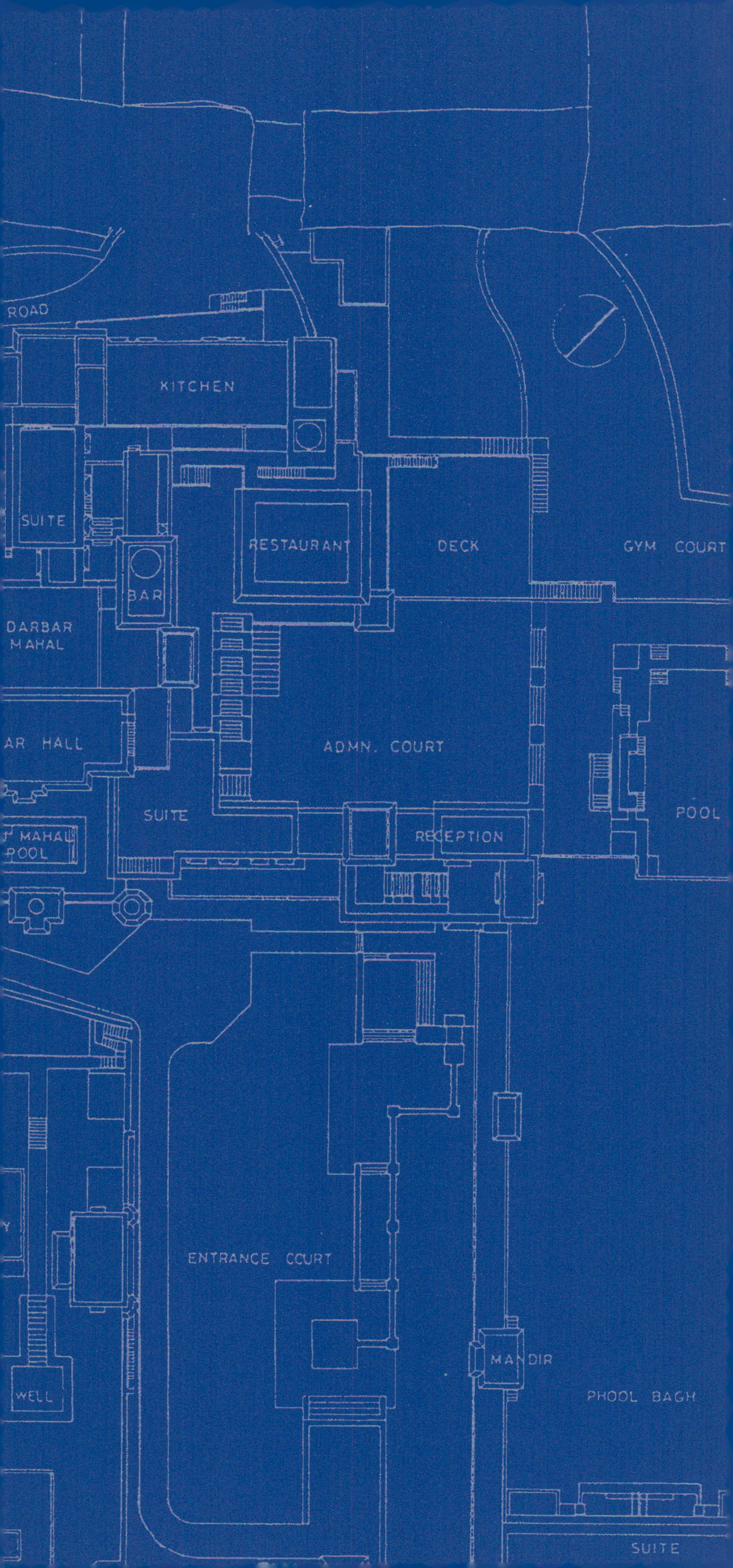
ROAD
KITCHEN
SUITE
RESTAURANT
DECK
GYM COURT
BAR
DARBAR
MAHAL
AR HALL
ADMN. COURT
POOL
SUITE
MAHAL
POOL
RECEPTION
ENTRANCE COURT
MANDIR
PHOOL BAGH
WELL
SUITE

Palace

In a remote village far from the great civic amenities of London, unconnected to universities or institutional bureaucracy, there exists an archive of rare 18th-century manuscripts related to the English landscape heritage. Funded originally by private initiative, a Baron with a love for the countryside, the collection is now in public hands, endorsed and maintained by local funds, and accessible to anyone with an interest in the subject. For over two centuries, the scholastic upgrading of this growing and ingenious collective has quietly turned the private obsession of an 18th-century crank into a public archive of serious academic value. It exists without fanfare, lovingly maintained, but utterly disconnected from the mainstream media or the government.

It is merely part of a daily municipal directive of local civic responsibility that also oversees street cleaning, sidewalks, and the maintenance of public order. Some years ago, the archive was willed a hefty sum by a wealthy local resident who saw value in its

■ Sponsoring Jantar Mantar, pencil on paper, 2001

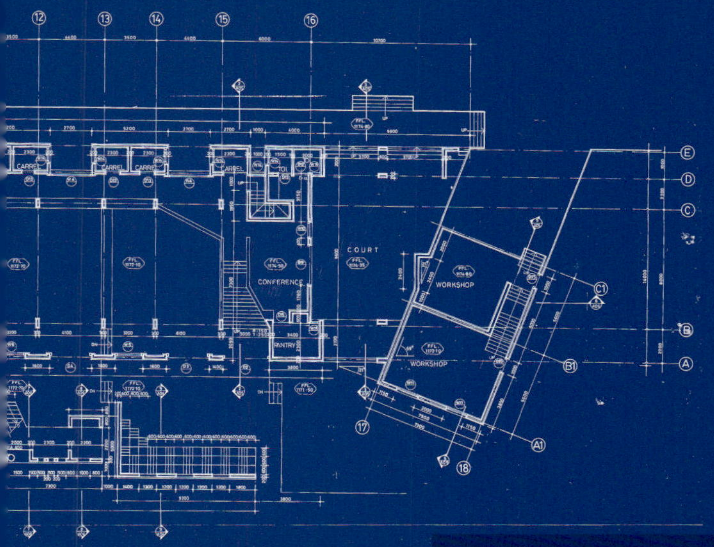

State Museum (unbuilt), Sikkim, 1991

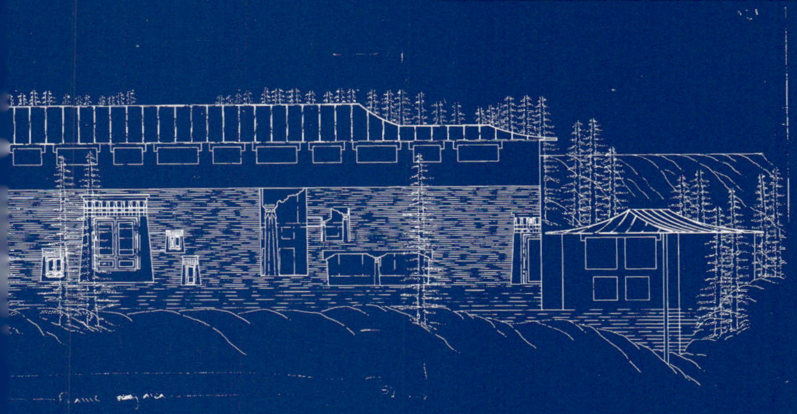

perpetuation. At the time, the documentation was assiduously upgraded and computerized; the building added a small wing to it named in memory of the donor. The old Gothic bulk of a structure was given a wash and a skylight was added to the main archival hall. However, most of the money was directed towards better storage and display facilities and making access easier for scholars. A place of characteristically English understatement, it is hard to believe it exists in the middle of nowhere.

Yet, there are similar facilities for marine research along the coast, private institutes for astronomy and medicine, a gallery of skulls collected during the war, an archive of world crime and criminals—some useful, some fanciful and whimsical—but all preserving cultural and antiquarian memories without judgement. Repositories of such richness speak of cultural integrity that far surpass efforts by older civilizations unable to integrate the old and the new. The particular lesson of English institutional history, apart from its enormous range and variety, is the value it places on ensuring the growth of intellectual

■ **FOLLOWING PAGES** Discovering Archeology, watercolour, 2012

Devigarh Palace Hotel, Udaipur, Rajasthan, 2000

collections and ensuring them public support and longevity. Many resources remain happily obscure in the English countryside, located in small villages and towns, making them truly a part of the peoples' heritage.

Compare this to routines in an Indian town. City life is firstly an outcome of physical distress: the painful stratification of its residents, the disparity of slum and baroque mansion, the overrun streets, broken roads and encroached sidewalks, open defecation, the absence of utilities. Certainly all these contribute to the Indian city's unmade and incomplete character. But these are the mere fallout of civic inadequacies that are being constantly fixed by urban budgets and municipal manifestoes. The real stench of despair rises from the stifling lack of civic activity—the city is a place bereft and deprived of participatory life. All primary civic sensation is formed out of acquisition of land and

- **ABOVE** Shah Jahan inspects the Taj, watercolour, 2015
- **BELOW** Shah Jahan's Ambassador at the Carwash, watercolour, 2008

home; civic activity is contained within the superfluous borders of shopping and eating.

In the struggle to make Indian cities liveable, there is perpetual talk of public space. The belief that somehow public space will save the city from street crime, rape, and inequities, and bring the citizens together, is an odd myth. What use is public space without public culture? A purposeless citizenry will do little but use that public space for its own private purposes—selling, hawking, encroachment, privatization and more crime. Without ascribing descriptive value and purpose to a particular amenity, public space is meaningless. The reconstruction of Dresden's public space after WWII was a civic imperative for a city that had lost so much of its cultural heritage in the rubble. The importance of baroque churches, theatres and museums of course cannot be disputed, but their real value lay in returning the city to an active cultural life. The restoration of specific activities that enhanced social conditions far outweighed the symbolic standing of buildings.

Devigarh Palace Hotel, Udaipur, Rajasthan, 2000

Today, the city's historic centre is a hub so intimately connected to the life of Dresden, its resurrection was a matter of urban urgency. The idea of long-term settlement then implies a city with a varied history, where historical remains are not merely consigned to a dead archaeological heap, but participate in daily reality. In India, the value of much of archaeological history is suspect. Sporadic walled compounds of *madrassas* and tombs that appear in erratic corners of Indian towns remain fleeting reminders of some past glory and nothing else. Other than odd moments of pride, their participation in civic life is hollow and disjointed. Is it any wonder then that they need to be physically protected from vandalism by their own citizens?

In my neighbourhood in Delhi, a sultanate *madrassa* had stood for many years in splendid isolation. But when the area began to grow from single to

■ **LEFT** Aurangzeb stops at McDonald's before a beheading, watercolour, 2007
■ **RIGHT** Wrecking ball rock-cut temples, watercolour, 2007

three-storied homes, the ancient structure was unfortunately dwarfed by houses that were becoming multiple dwellings; soon the structure became an insignificant reminder of its own history. A few years later, builders branched on to apartments and built high walls along its southern face, threatening the building. Since then, some of the *madrassa*'s domes have collapsed, and at night, the old structure is used by a floating population of migrant labourers as a shelter. A sign at the entrance remains the only reminder that the building was once a place of eminence. Was its protection a civic responsibility?

For too long I had envisioned history and its relics as a fixed and unquestionable form of goodness from which to measure the present. Archaeological remains were like cemeteries where aspects of real value lay buried under the tombstones and only a minor sign showed up on the surface. I never feared the

■ **ABOVE** Chandigarh Ruins, watercolour, 2011
■ **BELOW** Dhaka Ruins, watercolour, 2011

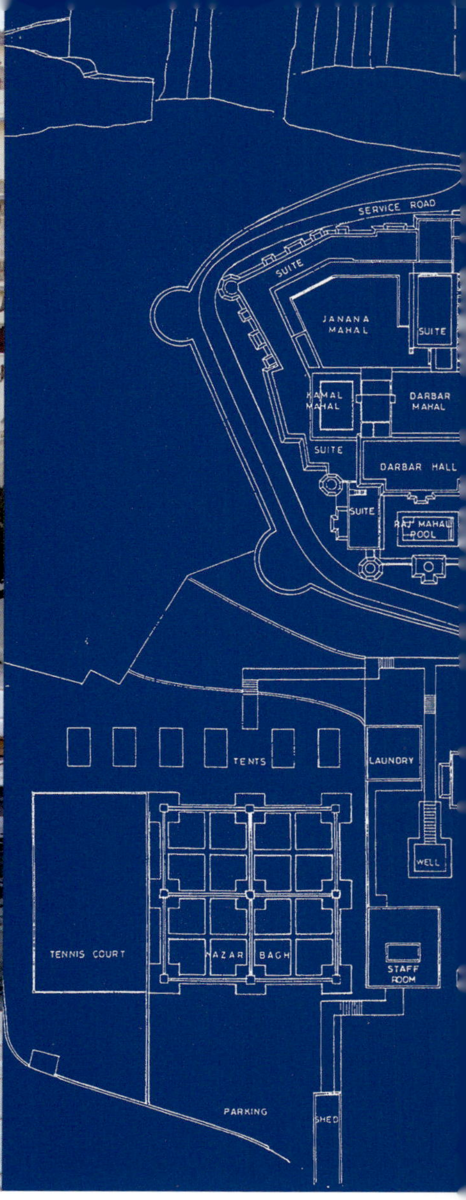

destruction of the *madrassa*. Even after the domes were willfully destroyed, I often went there to bask in their silence, to remind myself of the actual life that throbbed in the foundations. In the semi-darkness, the light that entered the broken roof magnified the flapping of bats' wings, and hastened new plant growth in the interior. The archaeology of the place could not be ransacked, only its building artifacts could.

How then does archaeology contribute to a city's urbanity? In a proposal for a museum in Gangtok, it seemed important to give an indication of the larger historic setting of Sikkim of which it was a part. In between the traditional and the contemporary, the thin line between continuity and the expression of change, a vocabulary of exposed concrete block was developed along with a painterly expression applied to individual elements. In contrast, the important enclosing forms of the building were designed to reflect prevailing techniques. It was a position of compromise that used adaptation ahistorically in the hope

■ New York Ruins, watercolour, 2011

Devigarh Palace Hotel, Udaipur, Rajasthan, 2000

that the final expression would be unique in itself. Part history, part contemporary entity. But it was an uncertain pictorial approach to salvage.

In an urban study done several decades ago, Leon Krier, a Luxembourg architect, had foreseen this state of the Indian city and suggested the possibility of providing temporary quarters to its migrant poor. Through elaborate drawings, he found living space on the great open plazas of Le Corbusier's government buildings in Chandigarh, along the open flanks of Fatehpur Sikri in Agra, in old forts and tombs, and in other large-scale monuments. Employing the historic space of Indian landmarks, he found ways to accommodate some of the millions who trespass into urban areas daily. Unlike bureaucrats and historians Krier did not see antiquity and the modern city as incompatible.

Both belonged to the citizens, and if imaginatively harnessed, he felt, their spaces could be used equitably and efficiently. Yet, in the present state of urban indifference, history and the

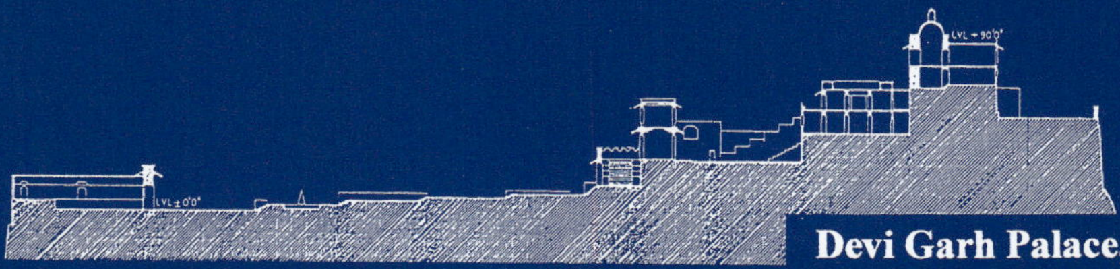

Devi Garh Palace, Udaipu

modern city exist as natural enemies, needing each other, but carefully demarcating their boundaries. The fear that if you allow people to use their monuments in unconventional ways, they will then destroy these places, still persists. As a result archaeological ruins are enclosed behind high walls, or controlled by draconian legislation.

Obviously when local residents around the citadel at Fatehpur Sikri and the palace at Jodhpur began to remove stones from the building's outer walls for their own use, government action was swift, and indeed essential. But in less drastic situations, would a less rigid reverence for history make for a better city if the use of its monuments was made more flexible? Most Indian cities have already witnessed the actions of heaving populations that squat on uncomplaining, unprotected monuments. Mosques, *madrassas* and tombs in Delhi, Georgian neighbourhoods in Mumbai, Nawabi buildings in Lucknow, colonial structures in provincial towns, the old architecture is besieged by the growing squalor of the city's unrepentant growth.

Devigarh Palace Hotel, Udaipur, Rajasthan, 2000

Three, four and five storeys of ramshackle plaster walls in a relentless cordon of blight surround the ancient facade till little remains. Where visual plunder has happened, can physical plunder be far behind? The old structure occupies an awkward place in its changing surroundings. The fight to save it will always be a losing battle. The coexistence of monuments and malls can hardly be a matter of pride these days, especially when physical activity spills so frequently and easily onto historic ground. In the civic strata of such diverse and conflicting social and economic values, how then do you balance the city's needs with the requirements of urban history and scholarship?

Should the rising tide of migrants not be allowed to make their homes in unused space? Should the architect work with private intentions alone or be informed by ancient forms? The argument has too often led the professional down an inconclusive path where the expression of cultural and economic realities far outweighs

■ Excavated Dynasties, watercolour, 2009

Devigarh Palace Hotel, Udaipur, Rajasthan, 2000

other options. Unless the extremes of conservative preservation and the uncontrolled way in which Indian cities are settled find some form of physical reconciliation, the monument will remain a zone of conflict.

Many years ago when working in Philadelphia, I was chosen to be part of a small team of architects entrusted to examine the upgrading of a derelict section of the city along the river. An area prone to crime, the edge of the water was occupied by abandoned warehouses. After numerous trips to examine the structures, I came to believe that the place had no future other than demolition and replacement by sturdier warehouses. So it came as a surprise when Clark, the leader of the team, suggested that we salvage the wooden ruins and convert them into houses. Not just any housing but upscale homes for executives working in downtown Philadelphia. So outrageous was the suggestion, it fell into place immediately!

To fit an idea into a building so completely the opposite of its original intent would obviously be the only possible resolution. In the grey winter light of a Philadelphia evening, the broken structures,

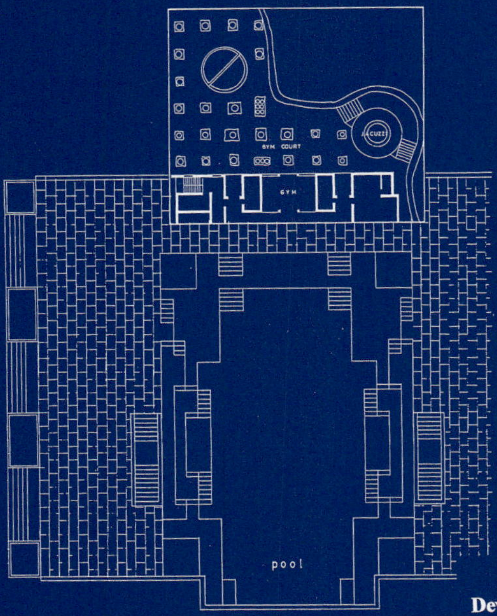

POOL

Devi Garh Palace, Udaipur

splattered with graffiti on the outside, and filled with broken syringes belonging to local drug addicts, the setting looked like a war zone. For its uplift and resurrection, the idea that the same structure, the same neighbourhood, would become the home of the city's business community was fitting, or rather wholly retrofitting.

Too often retrofitting is an unplanned exercise, the outcome of a sudden opportunity. Battleships have been converted into floating luxury hotels, buses, restaurants, shipping containers and houses. Such a design engagement may seem frivolous compared to the elaborate insertion of new functions into historic buildings. They do however serve the more pressing need to recycle. In the vast spread of Indian heritage, the 4000 monuments under the Archaeological Survey of India form a select minority. For the most part, an examination of archaeological remains suggests two conditions: either a conservative preservation that saves the structure in its historically authentic state, or abandoning it to complete dereliction.

RESTAURANT

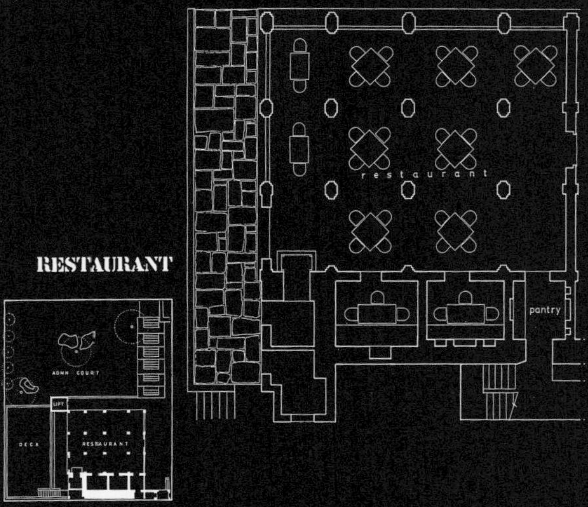

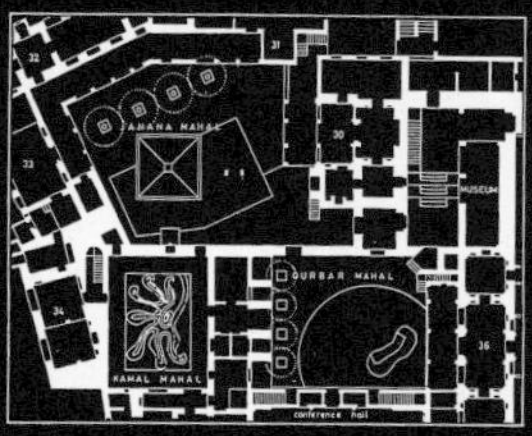

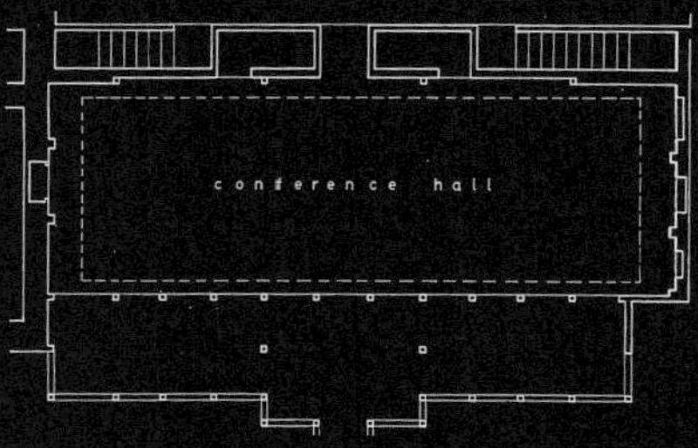

CONFERENCE

Devi Garh Palace, Udaipur

Structures like Humayun's Tomb or the Gateway of India, always in the public eye, will be saved and restored. But what of the numerous churches of Kumaon, the hundreds of abandoned wood and stone structures in the Nainital and Almora districts? Or for that matter the wooden temples of Himachal? The great masonry mountains that make up the forts of Rajasthan, colonial post offices, forest rest houses and PWD bungalows, wooden stations on mountain train routes, *havelis* and hunting lodges that are no longer in use, all require a serious rethink of their place in history.

Do all palaces in Rajasthan need to become heritage hotels or museums? Isn't it possible to maintain our historical buildings without succumbing to the lure of international tourism? Such selective preservation of a few distorts history and creates a mismatch between reality and the eternal promise of the historic ruin. How does the inhabitant of the tarpaulin tenement gain from his proximity to the elaborate stone *madrassa*, the Housing Board Colony in Lucknow from the Imambara?

A closer association between the needs of the city and the potential of heritage buildings could make for more vibrant surroundings.

Devigarh Palace Hotel, Udaipur, Rajasthan, 2000

The association between village and palace was one that I observed closely while renovating the derelict ruin of Devigarh. Whenever I went there, the dry, dust-filled air was a typical Rajasthani greeting. Something or someone on the ground was always stirring up the dirt: cows, shepherds, children, goats, impromptu cricket. In the evening light, the sun dipping onto the shallow hills of the Aravalis, viewed high up from the ramparts of Devigarh, the village and its fields appeared to be caught in a perpetual haze. I learnt to accept it as a condition of the desert. The mossy green surroundings of the palace and the yellow walls of the low-lying village and its stepped well; this mixed characteristic of poverty and royalty was a hard one to imagine.

The reluctance partly stemmed from the sheer neglect of rural life itself. How was it even possible to link the magnificent scale and abundance of palace life with the scarce, weak-boned lives of the people who lived in its shadow? The proximity of both extremes was a visual disturbance that resolutely disassociated one from the other, and it left me searching for a more egalitarian association. But there was none. The village was the servants' quarter of the palace itself; the royal employers were a necessary

evil in a land blighted and lacking resources. It was evident that a resolution of their differences was not possible, not in the heyday of 17th-century royal life, and not now. People's survival was always going to be linked to some form of servitude to the palace. If a building worked to maintain the royal lifestyle, its new incarnation was to be a replication of the luxury of the past.

The foremost test of the villagers' allegiance was in the restoration of the structure itself, and in the revival of the belief that any association with the palace was for their own good. I wondered if there existed a precise benchmark that would reconcile the available relic of history with its transformation into a new future. Did the surviving archaeology give indications of salvage? Or was a more definitive operation possible when planning the future of a heritage building? Were we truly stumped in assuming that the only future was a thoughtless recreation of the past? If that were so wasn't such a restorative future a lie in architecture's evolution?

It was easy to access the flexibility of an 18th-century fort, which wasn't built on a fixed programme of requirements. The insertion of a hotel did not necessarily require any destruction, only because the superfluous excess of the palace lent itself admirably to new and unpredictable insertions. The structure's easy changes were the outcome of its generous outlines and the capacity to accommodate even opposing interpretations.

Devigarh Palace Hotel, Udaipur, Rajasthan, 2000

The standard that history was a good thing and needed perpetuation blurred any reasonable rethink and forced the architect to commit to blind faith. The careful replication of cornices, the restoration of marble columns, and the process of bringing to the fore the physical visage of things as they existed 400 years ago, invigorated the masons and stone-cutters. The exactness of that picture could not be made possible, for in the intervening years, several additions and alterations had taken place. These changes had taken an important piece of Rajput architecture and given it both Mughal and colonial flourishes.

As history played out in the state and around the site, it had its expected impact on the building. The growth of imperial arches and an altogether English pavilion at the top of the building obviously came out of the Raja's acquiescence to his English masters and their influence, giving the building an appropriate transition from traditional to colonial design. The structure's hybrid architecture was a positive attribute of a building that had not only aged, but had in its three-hundred-year-old history happily displayed all its additions and incarnations, warts and wrinkles. Peepal trees had rooted in its crevices, and stone roofs had cracked and shifted into precarious positions.

The lime wash given to its columns, walls and cornices had accumulated into layers of paint that hid the intricate stone

Devigarh Palace Hotel, Udaipur, Rajasthan, 2000

carvings from view. The building was a smudged facsimile of its former self; but there were enough members of the old guard of great grand children of the original masons and stone carvers around who knew the secret behind the veil of plaster. The idea that a revival was going to be initiated stirred many of them into remembering stories about the last Maharajah and eventually led to a resuscitation of the palace itself. It took a team of 60 people two years to restore the palace structure, and to bring its hidden wealth back on to the surface.

Invariably architecture weighs its self-worth against the impermanence of other human endeavours. Its historic preciousness lay obviously in its age, in outlasting its own residents, the ravages of time and climate that erode people as well as the vegetation and the physical support of other implements. While things decayed and died in and around buildings, the death of architecture in historic terms lay in its passage from construction to archaeology to geology, and was celebrated as transformation. When old buildings sank into ground as rubble, it was a form of extinction. And this was often equated with other catastrophes—the death of a species or race. When architecture transgresses the scope of the imagination, then its loss is truly felt. The destruction is not just physical, but also the loss of common ground and the erosion of a public belief.

Devoid of bats and broken masonry, it became possible to traverse the building for the first time. I had stood many times in front of it to observe the facade—a seven-storeyed structure that arose obliquely (sloped walls, windowless for four floors) upto the delicate traceries of

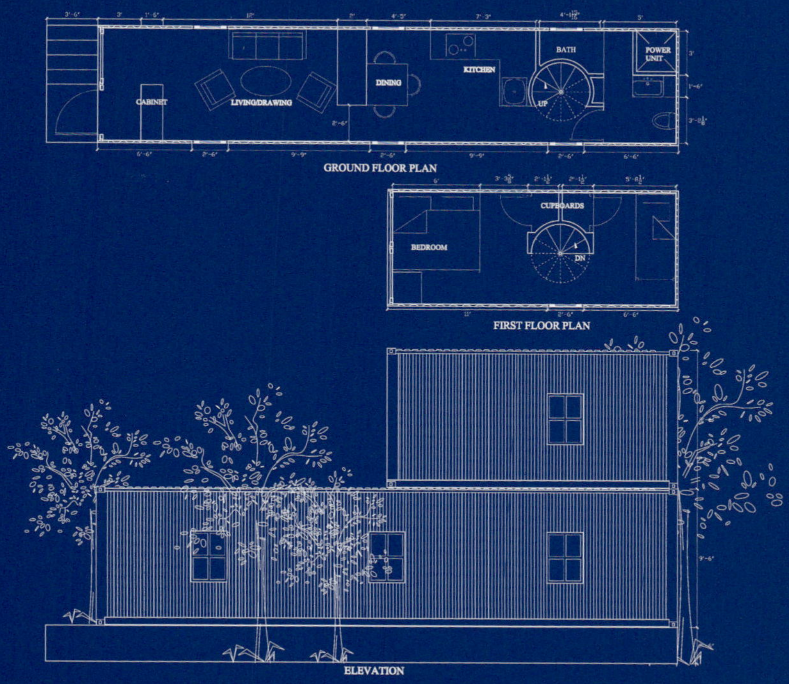

Container House, Kotabagh, Uttarakhand, 2010

palace design. The solidity of these lower floors merely masked the series of rocky outcrops on which the building grew—a clever ploy to give added monumentality to the architecture. The steps within the structure reveal a series of courtyards at different levels, the Lotus Court, the Durbar Court, the Zenana Court, each intimately bordered by rooms.

Above, within the renovated rooms and raised high above the ground, the mossy green of the Aravalis was revealed, at distances that didn't disturb the privacy of the interior—for instance, in a jacuzzi or a tub bath, the royal life, was once again duplicated, and connected to the distant landscape. On the day before the palace opened to tourists, I stood at the topmost parapet, pretending momentarily to be the old owner and the new user of the palace all at once: an 18th-century monarch and a retired eye surgeon from Ohio, in temporary possession of a restored, simulated life. And I thought about how inaccurate our simulation really was, a mere replication in visual terms and nothing else.

As an American surgeon, I wanted to lie on my Rajasthani bed under a two ton air-conditioner, but as the Raja, I needed an open, well-ventilated room with a *pankhawallah*. I would need to sit on my haunches to relieve myself down a hole open to a peripheral collection, ambulatory below, for the scavenger. I gazed out at the unchanged ridge of mountains beyond and felt remote and entirely disconnected from it all.

Socialite Rita Bansal
who has a live in boy friend
Sabir, a stock market analyst
and a part-time astrologer,
denied her affair with Rajaya
Sabha MP Sushil Ahmed, stating
irreconcilable differences in choice
of bed linen, even though she is currently
carrying social activist Rocky Madan's
child, himself 19 years old. At Don Balram
Ansal's funeral—whose blood-soaked body
wrapped in Tricolour, lay in state in the Defence
Colony Nallah and was discovered accidentally
by the Vice President who had come to defecate
nearby—Rita denied it again, stating categorically
that it wasn't Sushil Ahmed in her bed but just a
hot water bottle that belonged to land grabber and
bureaucrat Raman Anand, formerly extortionist and finance
secretary for the Bihar Chief Minister. When Raman was
contacted by two reporters at his secluded Baroque beach
villa in Delhi's posh Tirlokpuri Extention Part II, a harassed
Dimpy Ahuja answered the phone (No 011-2351-0162) and
denied all charges, including those that had not been levied
against her. She said she had only met Babbu, alias Jonathan
at a polo match hosted by the then Maharajah of Khadipur, his
Royal Highness Ching-Do-Ling of Shanghai Proper Part II, and
was nothing between them but for the two children, Aman 5,
an exclusive orphanage

Terminal in New York [illegible] — a 7-year old Buick, and a 3-year old custody of the two kids — a 7-year old Buick, and a 3-year old Toyota pick-up truck — was to be jointly shared. The Greyhound bus had gone on to marry a German shepherd that had been chasing it for some years. Sadly, some years later, Dimpy died in an accident when a pedestrian rammed into her SUV, while she was on the way to her new apartment in the Andamans, being decorated by the interior design firm of Waha, Naha, and McDonaldo, Attorneys at Law. Explaining the concept to Dimpy, as she lay critically wounded in the ICU of Delhi Piggery and Meat Company Limited, Cyrus Waha said that "I'd like to do the Living and Dining areas in Early Tudor," because it was an old favourite of his uncle, Sherlok Holmes, and he owned a copy of a book by Arthur Conan Doyle which he had used to prop up the bed, when his daughter Ramola, now 62, had been conceived. The servants quarter would be 'ideal in a Rajasthani Baroque, because most servants came from Bihar and preferred to live a relatively frugal lifestyle. Sensing a note of discord, two reporter had gone on to question Cyrus, a bystander, if he was not the illegitimate son of his own father Nochir, now 83, and a respected tribal chief in Nigeria with his own very successful company, Rent-a Cannibal, now listed in the New York Stock Exchange

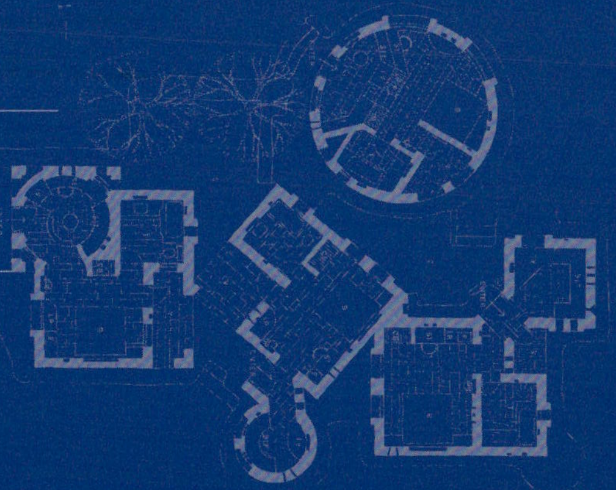

Commerce

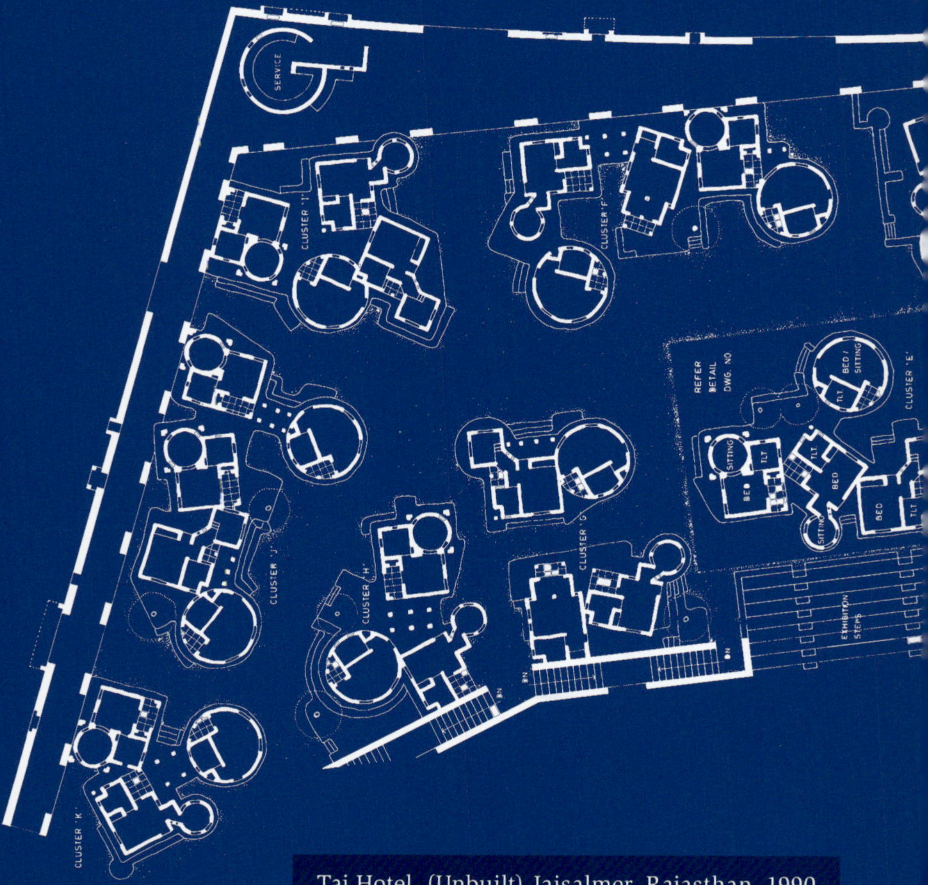

Taj Hotel, (Unbuilt) Jaisalmer, Rajasthan, 1990

It is hard to believe that within barely half a century, technology could so radically change the face of commerce. What had begun as a small store at the end of the street grew into an arcade of shops that slowly acquired a structure and identity of their own; the market's eventual growth into a commercial facility for the city led to the birth of a shopping centre, a focal point that drew in the residents of the neighbourhood. The mall is a relatively new phenomenon whose integration of shop, restaurant, hotel, movie theatre and parking lot, all under one roof, owes its conception neither to architecture nor the sociology of commerce.

The escalator and air conditioning are the two technological advances that were wholly responsible for the mall. The uniqueness of the structure lay in its size and physical spread. New Jersey malls, the Dubai Mall, the Mall of the Emirates, the building was an additive conglomeration in all of them, with an up and a down, but limitless in the horizontal direction. Within

■ Body Shop, watercolour, 2009

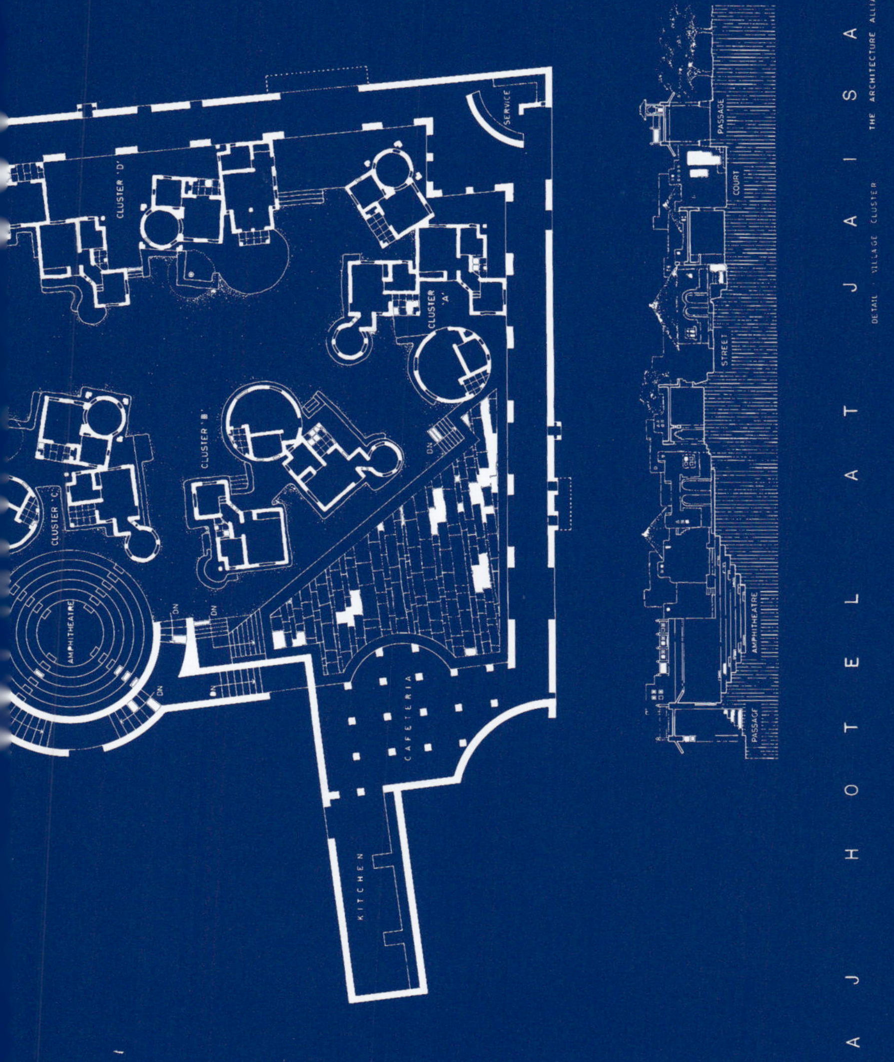

its continually extending profile, it defied the urge to intimacy and the compaction of closed space. Its vastness was always meant for the collective throng, not the isolated individual. Only interior design rendered the space with momentary sobriety and pause—a break-up into multiple enclosures in which individuals were removed from the mall's disconnected isolation. The contradictory inclusion of multiple space, however, defied the original intent where the mall was conceived as integrated infrastructure rather than architectural space.

The mall and its related parts that had functioned for so long as independent buildings could afford to unite only under the cohesive umbrella of infrastructure and technology. The control of climatic conditions within a glass envelope of such immensity saw the rise of a monumental scale that encompassed shopping, sports stadiums, airports and rail terminals. Within this space, the collision of diverse functions kept the visitors in hermetic comfort and spatial enthrall. Space moved up and down, stretched across internal sidewalks and bridges; floor

upon floor, its verticality stretched to atrium heights that connected burrows of basement parking to sunlit glass roofs. Within the envelope the dimensions were always changing because every action was related to movement.

The entanglement with space had a kind of order of disorientation made all the more diffuse and erratic by the nature of commerce itself. The visibility of the diverse attractions filled the atmosphere in random sequences and made people rush up and down, sideways or straight like atoms in a heated cylinder. The escalator as an architectural feature fed into the fantasy of commerce, making floor to floor connections, its simultaneous horizontal and vertical movement unifying the multiple dimensions of mall space. It wasn't possible to move up or down without moving frontally. The body's ascent was a cascade into space that itself had no fixed route. You abandoned yourself as much to the

■ **ABOVE** Upmarket Restaurant, watercolour, 2009
■ **BELOW** Organ Sale, watercolour, 2009

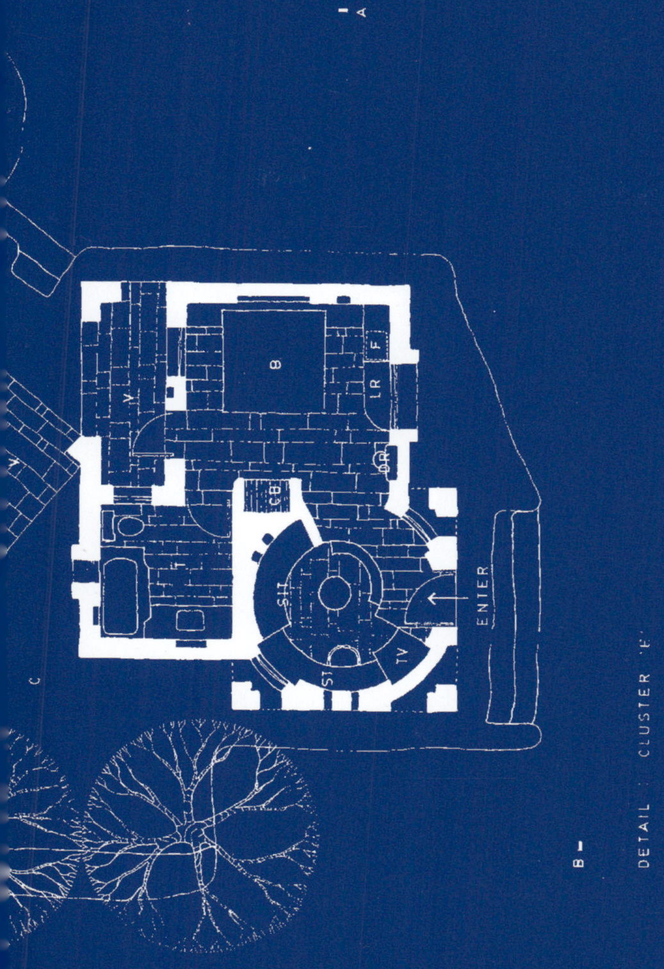

Taj Hotel, (Unbuilt) Jaisalmer, Rajasthan, 1990

flash and sign of commerce as to the random shuffle of space.

The same was true in other forms of commerce. In hotel projects, the self-consciousness of place draws an imitative blank on architecture surfaces. So inebriated was hotel architecture with the pretence of local classicism that its innate characteristics were dulled into a prosaic sameness as if the act of arrival and departure were the only indications of identity. Thus the importance of numerical identification, the proximity to the elevator on arrival, the help desk on departure. The building's originality was never questioned because it was never seen. Unlike other buildings that instinctively gain characteristics that help to engage with it and identify it, the hotel is so often served by new

■ **ABOVE** Connaught Place Ruins, watercolour, 2004
■ **BELOW** Brand Building, watercolour, 2009

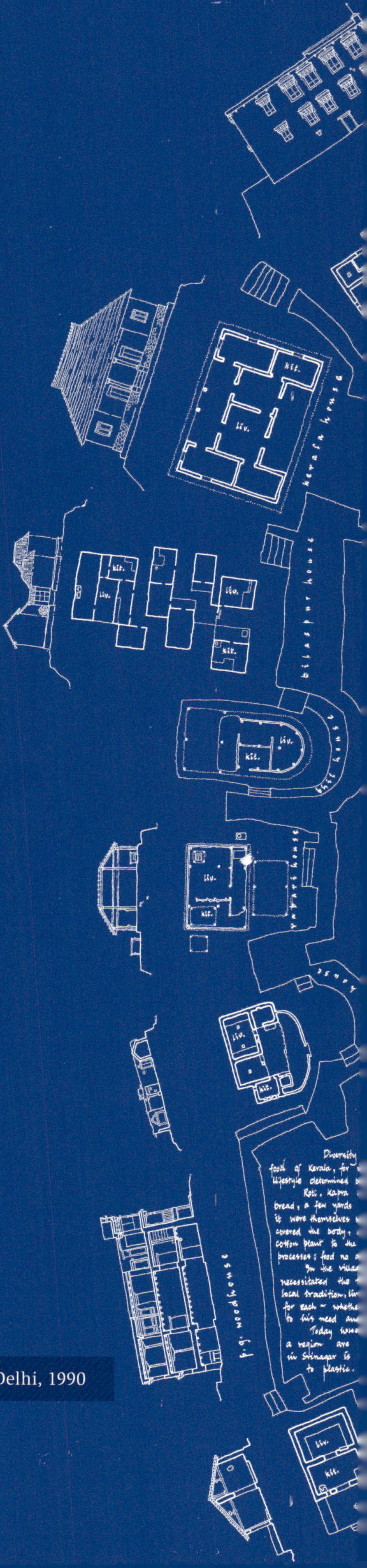

Living India, Proposal for ITDC, Delhi, 1990

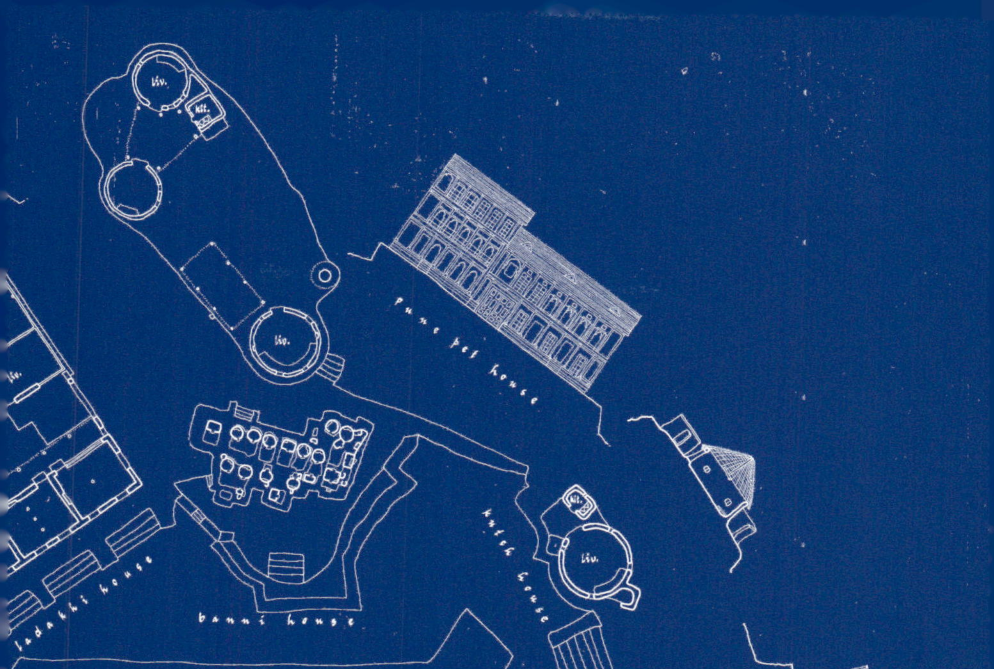

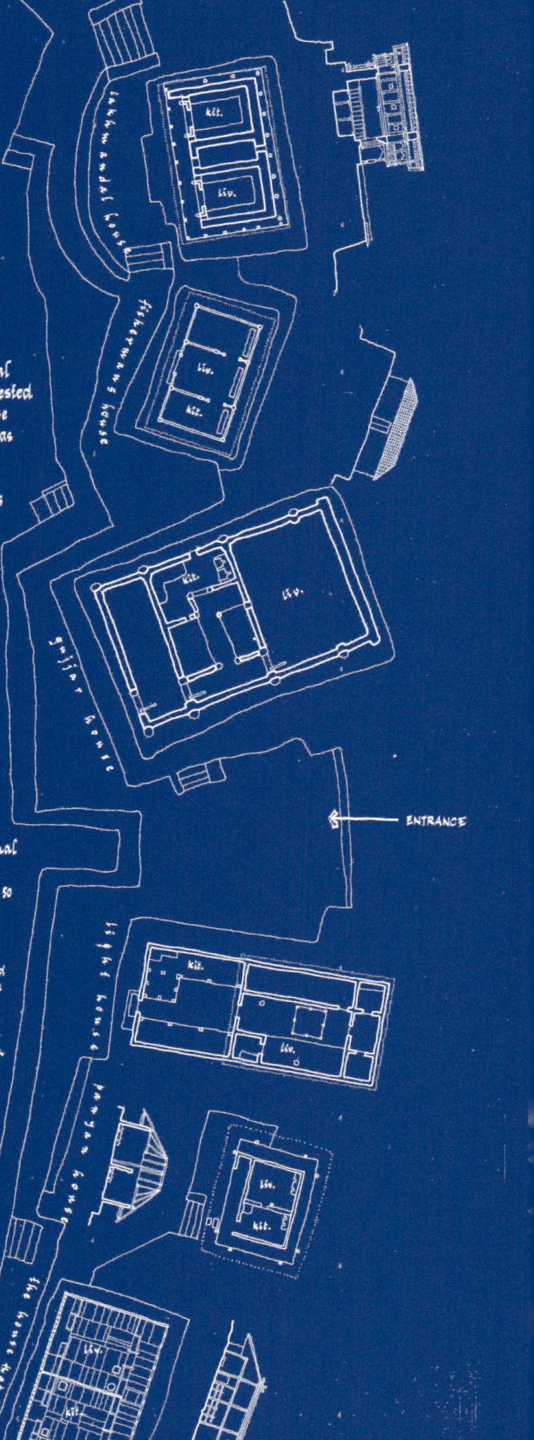

Living India

construction, craft, cuisine and costume
arts and eats
eat your art out (eats meets west)
roti, kapra aur makan.

ose of living India is to establish a center for traditional
hitecture, craft, cuisine and costume, and to record time-tested
of traditional construction techniques by providing at close
view of regional house types. The attempt would be to create as
ally as possible an India we are fast losing by assembling the
ould function both as a restaurant as well as a museum of
ure, each building and its related cuisine will represent its
with an open air amphitheatre for cultural programs, dances,
s – with a small museum and cultural center affiliated to
emic institution and serving primarily to document catalogue
use aspects of traditional Indian culture – folk music of each
a kind of ethnic dinner theatre – a weekly culture program –
environment and preservation – planned as a village street
nsistent with contemporary village life, a banyan tree, an open
an annual arts / crafts / food fair.

nate purpose of the project with its documentation center and
is to develop complete habitats in keeping with local custom
ition, and to set up a museum of architecture / shelter a model
ith house types from all parts of India: a Gujarati pol house –
od, a Punjabi mud house – dhaba, a Ladakhi house – kashmere food,
use – goan food, a kerala house – south indian food, a bania gothic
naggi noodles / fast food.

n will simulate within the given constraints of the site, the actual
ent of each region, from local plant life, trees, vegetation, to the
re, craft and the life patterns of its inhabitants. Each house will so
a museum of craft for the state.

effective selling point for India. At one time, the architecture, craft, costume and
ly different from the architecture, craft, costumes and food of Kashmir. People lived a
ition, climate and topography.
ies this simple phrase summing up life's necessities meant only a round wheat
rdinary mud dwelling. Survival was not difficult because the essential ingredients for
and affordable. Home grown wheat was baked and eaten for food; home spun cloth
es provided the necessary shelter. The transformation of the wheat to the roti, the
to a house was direct, simple, easily understood. Cloth required no chemical
atives; construction, no college degrees, no education.
not an artist. The simple mundane needs of housing, cooking and clothing
ally available material into objects of utility. Out of this understanding of
climate, and after generations of trial and error a particular form emerged
shelter. The craftsman recognized these limitations and designed according

changed. And the differences that characterised a particular state or
deed become one – if not politically, at least culturally. A modern house
in Trivandrum, as is the dress and food. Local craft has given way

museums are repositories of high culture and art with collections
ifacts from glorious civilizations, from forgotten kingdoms and ancient
pires. Through carefully labelled archaeological evidence they trace
in vivid detail the rise of political dynasties the peaks in its painting,
music, sculpture, or the monumental expressions of its architecture.
Yet for the millions of ordinary lives that have created in their own
mall ways a living folk culture historical continuity means little,
and museums have little time or energy for their art. In our own
times, when culture has itself become a fashionable commodity
to be marketed abroad or to be discussed on urban cocktail
circuits, the art of the common man is of little value to
the common man.

By itself the idea of a folk museum is not new. Several
arts and crafts museums already exist in the larger cities.
The establishment of yet another cultural repository would be of

PROMOTED BY : THE LIVING INDIA FOUNDATION
&
THE ARCHITECTURE ALLIANCE
FOR ITDC HOTELS

Taj Hotel, (Unbuilt) Jaisalmer, Rajasthan, 1990

eyes; its perennial newness stands as a reminder of the original, and leaves the visitor with a residue that is both a perfect picture, and a calcified image. Only the plan serves to distance the picture from the experience.

For the most part, the commercialization of history has lead most entrepreneurs down a narrow, messy path that is both eclectic and wrong. History's worth as a business proposition is an archaeologist's nightmare for it packages and twists facts into a marketable commodity. Living India grew from sites and domestic histories that were dead. Their revival into a garden congregation was hardly due to a genuine concern for their future. But individual houses were seen as relics, assembled as in a museum for a set fee. This was a tourism master plan that fit them into an integrated partnership for an occasion. Nowhere else would you find a Chettinad house next to a Kashmiri home, a mud house from the Banni region of Kutch up against a Gujarati haveli. The artificial congregation was the new background from which commerce infiltrated culture and made it saleable. But unlike the assured containment of shop and hotel, the mall was an anomaly; it constructed a multitude of visual directions and left you in charge of your destiny. It differed from the precision of movement in rail terminals or airports where action preceded intention. You moved in at one end of the terminal space and out of the other end, onto a train or a bus.

The mall, however, was conceived in endlessness, an amorphous mass of semi-integrated social functions that thrived in a bubble. Without the two traditional signals of architecture, the entrance

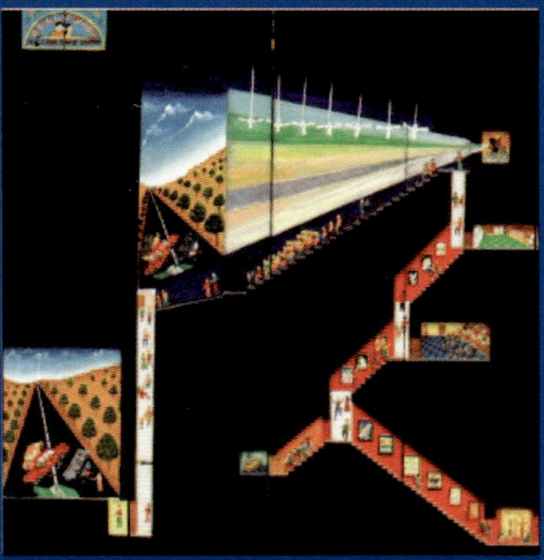

PVR Cinema, watercolour, 2004

and the exit, the front and the back, the structure could only be navigated by GPS, or by elaborate directories at interior street junctions. Its disorientation encouraged a self-induced aimlessness. Families with softy ice-creams strolling by on Sunday afternoons...The mall is and will be for a long time, the commercial ambition for any architect and builder. Its promise of bright lights, air conditioning, atrium space, automatic movement via escalators and glass lifts is an architectural experience that dismisses the provincial misery of the ordinary market place: heat, flies, congestion, and the absence of window shopping. Dubai's decision to make the mall a centrepiece of its social, cultural, artistic and commercial life was of course fuelled by the desperate need to escape the desert heat. And what better way than to do it than to keep it all under a single roof?

So the malls arrived. Mile upon mile of concrete roofscape filled with every form of public and private facility sprung up. The Mall of the Emirates, three million square feet of retail. The Dubai Mall at 4.5 million square feet. These commercial palaces glittered with gold souks, jewelry stores, aquariums, ski slopes, skating rinks, movie theatres and restaurants. The Mercedes taxi glided down a dark ramp and deposited me at the hissing automatic doors of the mall.

From the *sh* ... of the taxi to the *hmm*... of the mall, from air conditioning to air conditioning, it was a movement from one darkness to the next. Spread out and sprawling, the difficulties of orienting oneself in so demanding an obstacle course requires

continual direction. At every junction, information counters give answers in recognized languages: English, French, Spanish, German and Arabic. At the largest single aquarium in the world, the glass-encased seascape rises three storeys; sharks and octopi look out from their cases at Gucci and Louis Vuitton and Chanel. Given the monumental scale of consumer proximity, they must wonder how the ocean floor has suddenly acquired this high-end commercial edge. So you eat, you drink, you gawk, you file past empty gold stores, 50-60 of them located in a darkened cavern of flickering starry lights like something out of the Arabian Nights; you walk another mile; under the canopy of a European street café you sip a latte and nibble on a blueberry muffin.

You piss in a sanitized rest room diligently manned by an Indian, Pakistani, or Sri Lankan, in a black uniform dispensing towels, wiping sinks, a simpering slave stuck in the service recess of an interior wonderland. You walk for several hours oblivious to the sun's movements in the sky. The lights are always changing in the mall, giving you the illusion of daylight, evening, even night. Electric reflections in tinkling waterfalls and shiny floors of granite and glass.The sheer size dwarfs the minor intentions of the day time visitor.

■ Connaught Place Ruins, pen & ink, 1990

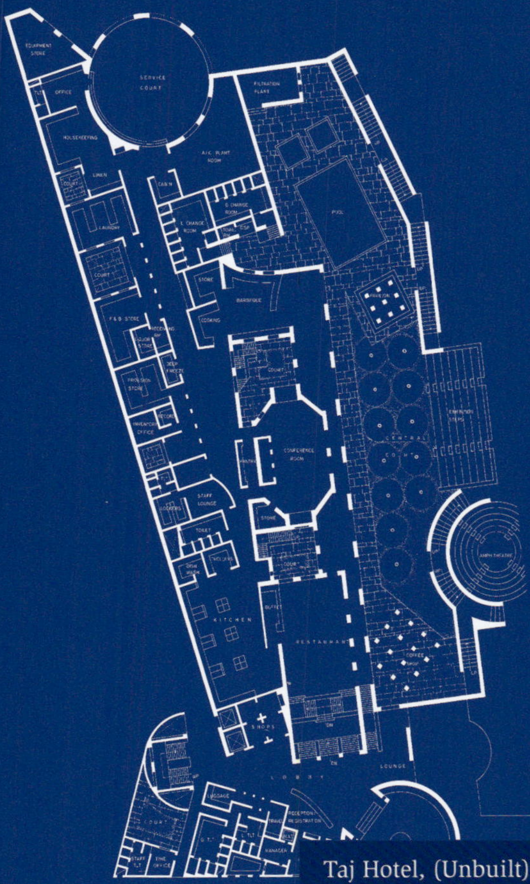

Taj Hotel, (Unbuilt) Jaisalmer, Rajasthan, 1990

A city inserted into the air conditioning system—such a possibility had never existed earlier, and it called for an altogether different organization. The smaller measures of geometry that traditionally defined the minimum yardage of space required for a human task had mutated into a monster of unbelievable girth; atleast at ground level, it denied the existence of any dimension. Only somewhere from the air, as in the Great Wall of China, could the balloon spread of a mall town be seen breathing under the glass. It was a monster at rest, blowing out hot air from its steel nostrils, able to expand its wings across blacktop parking lots, protecting its innards with fire fighting gear and air filters. After centuries of history of construction, the mall had reversed the old myth that people needed buildings; it had cast itself into the city as a mass of material—pipes, steel, glass that changed urban scales and perceptions forever. People drove along its glassy endlessness, thinking they were better than animals. And every day, at the appointed time, its mouths open and people flock in, providing food and fodder for its gargantuan guts. It works as an antidote to Corbusier's machine for living in.

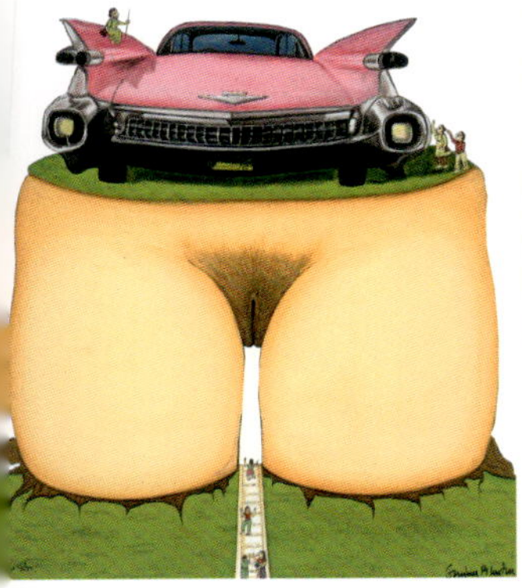

■ Rear Elevation, watercolour, 2009

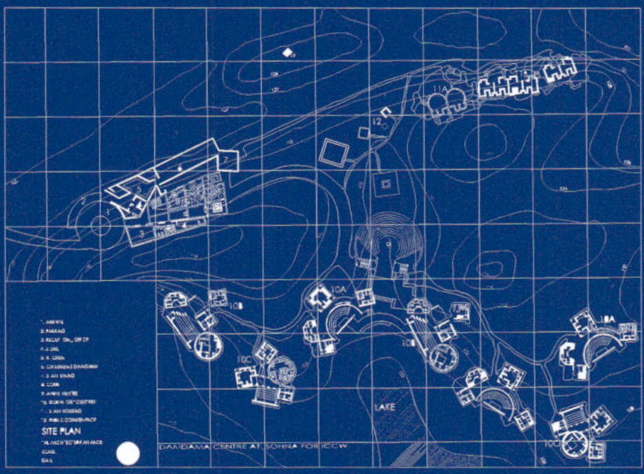

Retreat

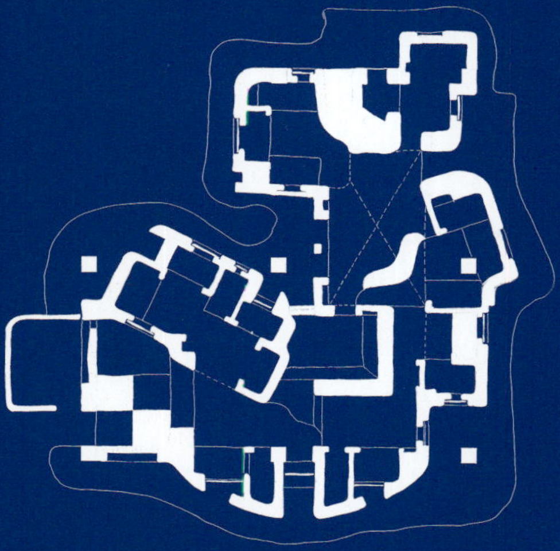

Where nature has played a pivotal role in the dispersal and placement of architecture, the building has been created in an open, outward orientation. But the absence of a natural landscape has often led architects to creating nature for their own purposes—a desperate idea, where the replenishment of green is instantaneous and totally artificial. Some places however are so green, and the growth so organic and rooted, that they bring into question the nature of construction itself. If building is to occur, where should it happen, and what form should it take, if any at all?

Containing the destructive nature of construction on ecologically sensitive sites makes the reading of nature a critical part of any architectural exercise. At the very outset is the question of entitlement. Does building, in fact any form of construction, deserve a place in the natural setting? If the answer is that

■ Landscape 1, watercolour, 2011

Children's Retreat (Competition entry) Sohna, Delhi, 1989

architecture is a denudation of nature, then should any building spring up at all? The argument that nature's constantly changing growth can never be really measured confers a more democratic settlement of a site, where the natural and man-made reconcile over time and resolve like a ruin into a composite state. The endlessness of nature is too elusive to be comfortably drawn into the ambit of architecture.

I had to establish my own working limit on the landscape, and what was accessible and visible from the site itself. For a project for a children's retreat, I was filled with an architect's fears related to expressions in nature. It was not just paranoia about where to draw the line on a site that was an undulating, unkempt treasure of rock, hillock, water and scrub, but also about what shape that line may take. The fear too that an architect's organic intentions may clearly differ from nature's organic core. Working in the rarefied atmosphere where earth and water were in muddled collusion, the place offered no clues as to how outside influences may alter them.

It was on this issue that the understanding of expression was the most difficult. In a place that had no man-made definition, no edges or boundaries, nothing of human presence, the idea of control became all the more delicate and ephemeral. I was neither geographer nor ecologist. I was unable to examine the place as a natural system or an organic container. In my mind, the architectural approach was a calculated misdemeanor using which I could exercise physical control of the place temporarily without affecting the larger environment.

Architecture was a minor desecration that lasted a few decades before nature returned the place back to itself, for itself. The eventual resolution was thus a deliberate fragmentation of functions into minuscule parts, each expressed in primary geometry. A circle, a cube, a rectangle, a half-circle were free-floating molecules in a viscous

■ Landscape 2, watercolour, 2011

Children's Retreat (Competition entry) Sohna, Delhi, 1989

plasma, moving at will, jointed and disjointed, fusing with each other, but herded in a composition that itself remained fluid. Buildings were transitory things that grew into formations, and were caught and anchored at the lake edge like tumbleweed. The accidental nature of each formation was a carefully worked ploy that resolved the shifting mass into a community of buildings grouped around their own amphitheatre.

Much of the actual architectural design was an exercise in connection and overlap. Sometimes the circle fused with the square, sometimes it stayed apart; but such actions allowed links between structures to exist through absence. Together the minute archipelago confronted its own relationships within

■ Landscape 3, watercolour, 2011

Children's Retreat, Sohna, Delhi, 1992

itself and to the surroundings, and found its anchors on the lake edge. But the setting raised other questions. Is nature made more abundant in the presence of architecture? Does architecture gain in a confrontation with a natural setting or does building always decrease the value of nature? Architecture's confinement is too often placid and straight-jacketed in a conforming geometry. While the geometry invents a rigid ordering, making the distribution of functions into an easy formula, its control over the plan becomes totalitarian. It is as if in the ensuing occupation of the building, the residents are condemned to a preordained plan dictated by the grid.

We think that the repetition of the orthogonal, the alliance to symmetry and axial divisions, all form necessary tools for containment and orientation. But too often the converse is true, and the site, its terrain, slopes and features, dictates the geometry, design and placement. Yet by their very nature as independent entities on a site, architecture becomes a motivation to connect and assemble them in a way that modifies their nature into a more complex entity. In rougher terrain, the exercise resorts to both a linking of

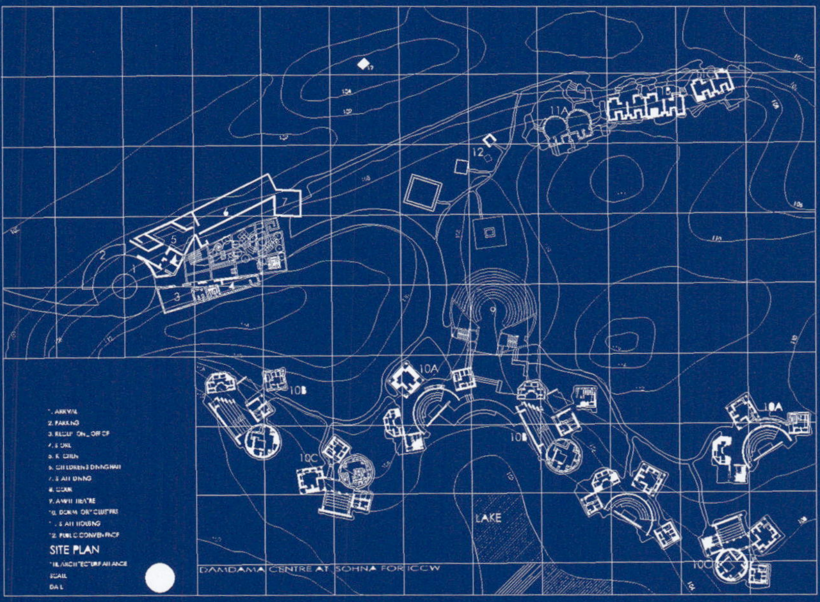

buildings to each other and a reconciliation of buildings with the land. The dormitories of the retreat started as free-floating cellular structures. Once they combined with the amphitheatres they became autonomous objects, structured in the desired architectonic combination. The fluid sparseness of their existence then called for a more robust attachment to the site and its lake.

By repositioning each grouping in a manner that gave resonance to the lake, architecture was used to redefine the water's edge, and give habitable three-dimensional meaning to it. By extending its influence beyond the building, the landscape gained from an unusual act of urbanism, enacted in the open wilderness. The final residue of the place is always difficult to grasp because it exists in multiple images that contract and enlarge as you walk through it. The limits of the architectural frame focus the eye on precise intentions, anchoring the sight on components that are geometric and formal. Yet their presence is meant equally to offer a distillation of the place in which they are located. It is

also meant to encourage the eye to move away and select a variety of surrounding clues that fuse the whole composition in the mind's eye.

The final scene hopes to make no distinction between what has been built now, and what has existed forever. Too often it becomes a perennial wish to help dispel architecture's newness in the hope of establishing a "fleeting eternity". At the retreat, the nature of construction was itself plastic and spatial. Not laid out in a reclusive geometry, but like its residents, free to roam among the boulders. The impregnable nature of walls, built in brick and random rubble masonry, outwardly provided the picture of a dense stronghold, even a fortress; its monolithic quality may be forbidding but in design, it refused any centralized control—a focal point that stated a singular intention. Instead the variables of protection and openness were drawn immutably into the plan.

Enclosed in a deliberate and secure form, but freed across the lake in a diaphanous extension, part open, part closed, contracting and stretching at will, ensuring that the wide expanse of lake was

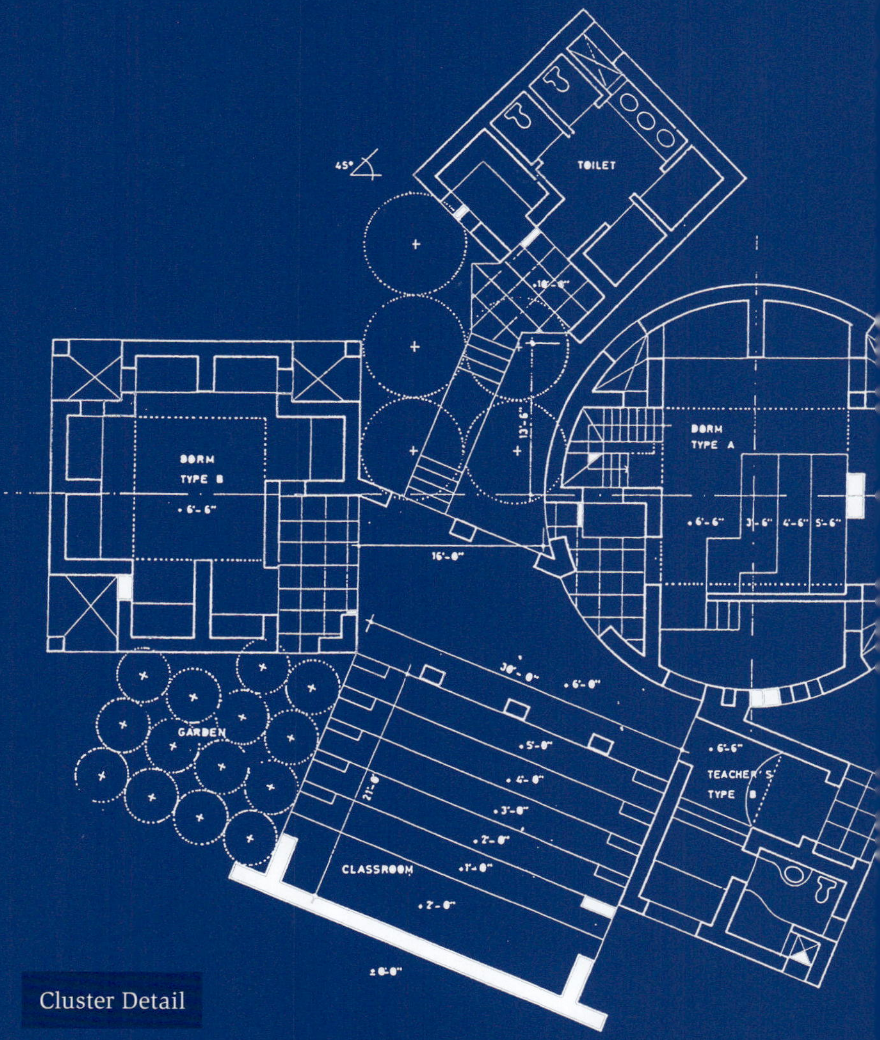

Cluster Detail

within its grasp, as was the protective cocoon of the building whenever nature loomed as a threat. The willingness to be both at once engages the resident in the same instant with the site and the building. It was there that I began to read the edge of the lake as crucial to the design. What made the building clusters conscious of that threshold was the shifting water level itself; consequently the relationship between architecture and the lake was always changing.

During the monsoons, the water invaded the building, leaving a part of each amphitheatre submerged; later in the year, the waterline receded to the entrance of each cluster; in summers, at its lowest, a wide swath of earth separated the building from the lake. The narrowing, expanding, overlapping threshold was the defining moment between building and site, nature and architecture. There is a tendency then to make a place between the known and the unknown, to slide a function to the edge of some hopeful darkness. The move to the unfamiliar is the constant search to deliver a tension to space that is too often

just a package of requirements; to sit at the edge of a valley, to build only partially on stable land or in a raging river was part of the urge to rescue architecture from familiar territory and deposit it on a precipice.

Fallingwater, or the Viaduct at Maillot, may be equated with technological conquest, but at the heart of the exercise lay the human urge to seek deviation from the scourge of static space. The changing strata of water were the only feature that gave seasonal, territorial resonance to architecture. Without it, the buildings could have been located anywhere. It had taken a long testing period

Verandah, Children's Retreat

to find the right location for the various clusters. At first, they were independent buildings overlooking the lake, once even as structures that straddled the water in the lake. But the clarity of the final decision lay in the shifting lake edge itself—the narrowing and enlarging threshold that kept you guessing about the terrain, the weather, the surrounding hills and rocks.

Each time I visited the place in a different season, the building's connection with the water left me wondering whether it was the water that was shifting or the architecture. I was never sure...

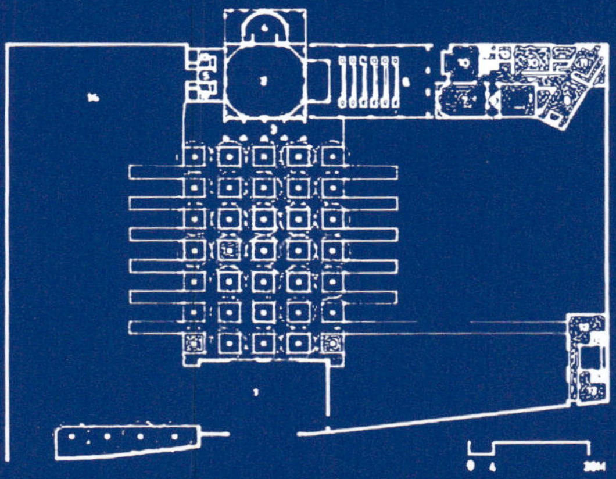

Church

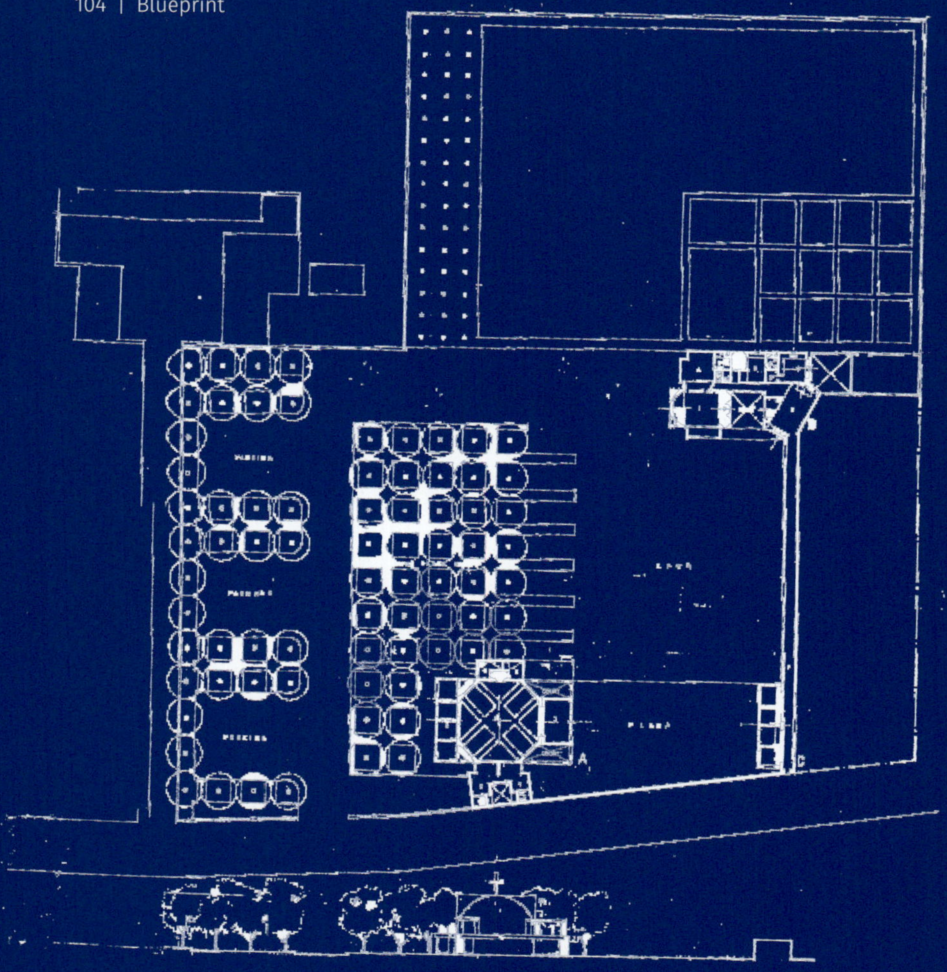

For one of our earliest projects, I was approached by Father Narayan of the Catholic diocese for designing a low-cost church in Panipat, Haryana. "We want a simple structure," he told me quietly. Father Narayan was himself a reserved man from a provincial Kerala town. His words were always accompanied by a generous smile and his permanent expression was that of benign conviction. His manner reflected, I felt, the kind of building he desired: simple, symbolic, low-key, and attractive in its Christian austerity.

The St. Mary's complex, when realized, was set at a distance from the country road and comprised a church, a priest's residence and a caretaker's house. The emptiness and flatness of rural Haryana was all around. The church stood among endless wheat fields relieved only by a few lines of eucalyptus. This lent the extraordinary quality of contrast to the building's compact solidity. Its sudden and unreal presence would, I hoped, appear from the approach off the country

■ Perfect Race, watercolour, 2011

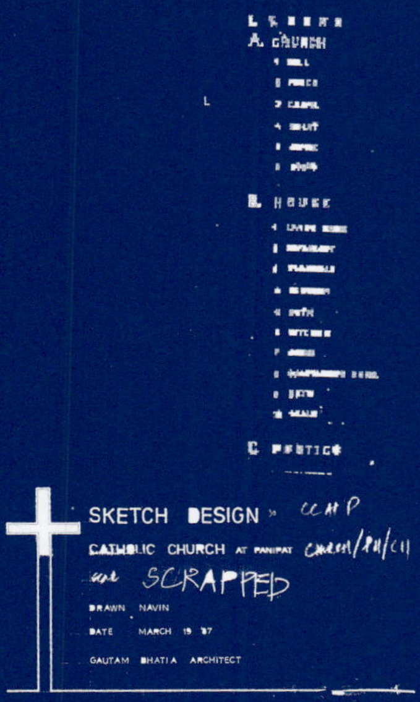

Proposal for Catholic Church, Panipat, Haryana, 1988

road as a kind of ravaged medieval construction, a building that had always stood there, but for some reason had gone unnoticed. The church was the focus of this allegedly ruined Christian compound on a two-acre plot surrounded by a high wall. The priest's residence was an extension of the church as priest's residences had always been; and the caretaker's house, as always, was an organic growth at the corner of the boundary wall.

The formality and significance of the church was expressed in the formation of a tower and a dome, both symbolically acting as the architectural links to a "Christian memory" and thus drawing in the local congregation across. Exposed brickwork was the only material used for all the buildings as well as the enclosing boundary. Brick cruciform *jalis*, repeated along the parapets throughout the complex, served as religious symbols. Such symbols became increasingly important in view of the

■ Family Beheading, watercolour, 2011

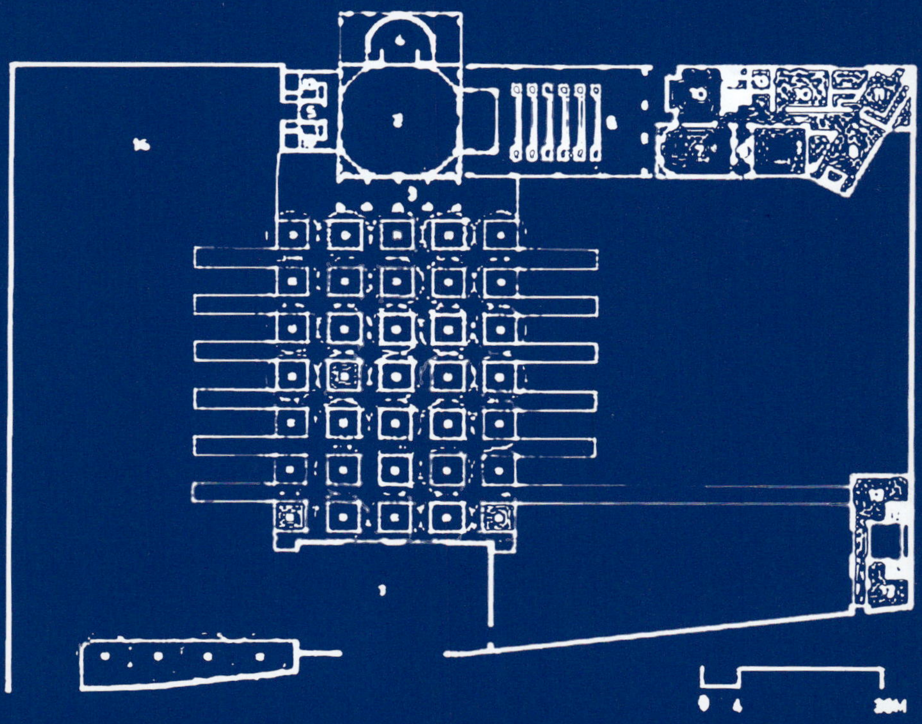

Proposal for Catholic Church, Panipat, Haryana, 1988

building's isolated presence in a rural landscape. Yet the open, rural site of the church, its relation to the fields and the distant horizon, suggested that the buildings, in material and form, displayed a kind of elemental ruggedness.

The forms used were therefore geometric and primary, framing the landscape and casting deep shadows. At the same time, the experience of the building at close range, I thought, had to have a certain delicacy, even appearing to dissolve into its natural surroundings. Elements such as the screen wall, the court, the arcade and the *jalis* became crucial to the composition because they were neither building nor landscape in their partial enclosure; but forms that mediated the transitions between inside and outside, land and sky. They were also both building and landscape. And in the absence of any background or urban setting they helped to reconcile the two extremes.

The body of the church was designed as a square, the corners chamfered into triangular wells from which diffused light entered the interior. The main axis which members of the congregation were to follow began from an entrance porch and ended in a semicircular chapel, indirectly lit from the

■ Inconvenient God, watercolour, 2013

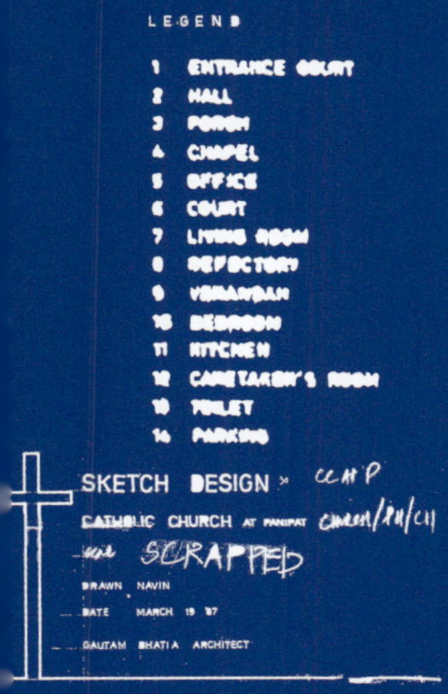

sides; ancillary services and stage areas were grouped along the secondary cross axis. In the combined schemes of the church and the priest's residence was a suggestion of architectural communication between the two buildings. The church opened onto a high, corbelled arcade, the house onto its private court. But a curved brick screen became the means to link the two and terminated the movement in the stair tower.

A comprehensive landscape plan was submitted and it was meant to unify the buildings and create a formal sequence through the gate. Close coordination between architecture and landscape became essential to make a series of separations between the discordant outside, and to set the mood for quiet and prayer on the inside. Passing through a grove of trees you proceeded into the arcade and the church hall along the axial pathways that culminated in the chapel. The idea was to use the landscape to suggest the solemnity of the procession into the church's interior.

In the open, bare fields surrounding the site the columnar placement of shade produced an architecture made from an organic element and treated as shaded

■ Convenient God, watercolour, 2013

enclosure. The trees planted in repeating dimensions extended the church arcade seamlessly into the outdoors. The structured fusion was less a method to use the landscape in an architectural way and more of a device to enlarge the shade of the church without drawing attention to the design. In the scheme, the building was far less important as a symbol promoting a particular faith than as a means of providing a religious setting conducive to meditation and prayer. While construction was going on, Father Narayan saw the *shikhar* of a Hindu temple rising across the street. To me it appeared to be a nondescript brick spire of no design significance, an ineffectual backdrop of an ordinary roadway.

But Father Narayan regarded its rising silhouette in the manner of an Olympic sprinter who notices that his lead in the race was fast diminishing. He was disturbed by it. The plans for the rising church were put on hold till a high bell tower and steeple could be incorporated into the structure. Prayer and meditation can go hang when religions start vying for architectural air space: then, a symbolic assertion becomes critical. I could not understand why the sight of a temple or a mosque or a gurudwara could turn even the most benign of religious people into rabid fanatics.

The *shikhar*, the church steeple, the dome and the minaret were once raised above the jumble of the ordinary city street, above the

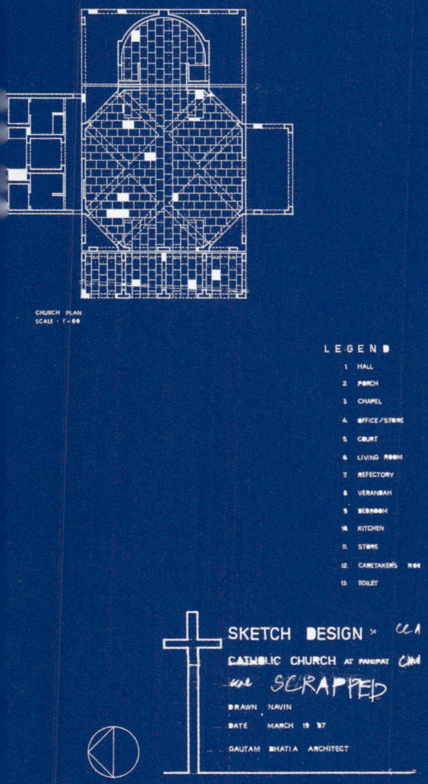

Catholic Church, Panipat, Haryana

anonymity of uncharismatic skylines to signify the existence of special places, a kind of public call of citizens to prayer. These were merely appendages to the buildings; as architectural indicators of intention, they served no real spatial function. Religious architecture, unlike others, was painstakingly built, and ensured that something remarkable on the nondescript skyline would act as a reminder to the faithful. At the time, the architectural symbolism was not planned as a competition between faiths, but merely in order to issue a resonant building outline to the devout.

Father Narayan's increasing fanaticism on account of the Hindu *shikhar* across the road was a reminder of a national malady—

■ **LEFT** Christian Family Photograph, watercolour, 2012
■ **CENTRE** Muslim Family Photograph, watercolour, 2012
■ **RIGHT** Hindu Family Photograph, watercolour, 2012

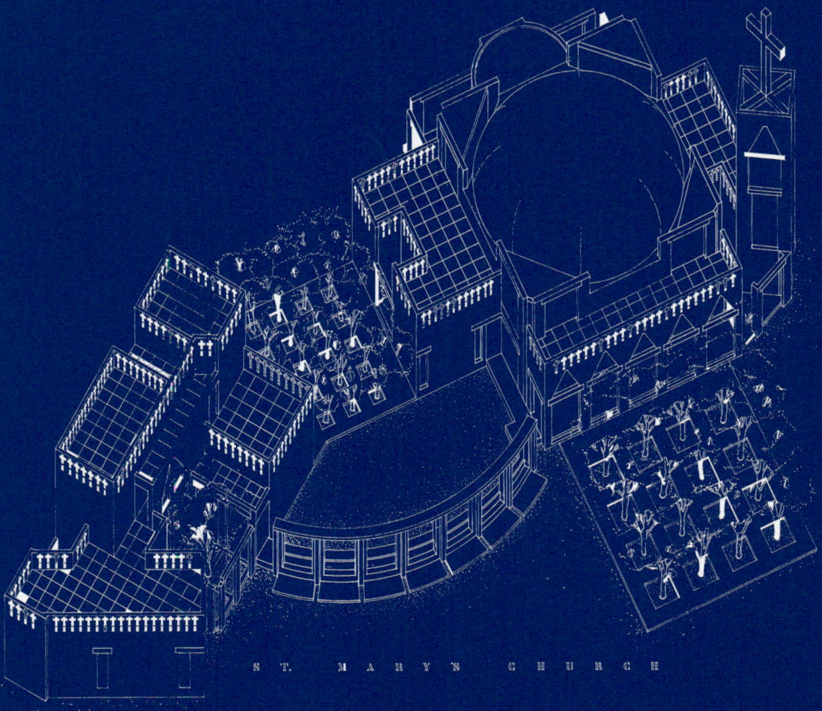

a seemingly sudden and fervent religious upsurge in the country. Each religious group was channelling a seperate identity. There was a show of strength to be made and religious architecture and its mild protagonist, Father Narayan, were merely caught in the middle of this strife. In the six months prior to completion, the numerous changes made on the site rendered the idea of integrating architecture with the landscape totally meaningless. Father Narayan's rapidly rising religious fervour had begun to affect his position as an architect's client; he was becoming its more insightful practitioner.

Throughout our earlier discussion he had remained an innocent bystander, nodding approval at the plans and smiling benevolently at the bills we submitted. Suddenly he became an over-active participant in the process of design. The blueprints had been unintelligible to him but the rising brickwork had a physical presence to which he could react. And react he did with a range of disjointed nuances—images of Catholic splendour—drawn from a career consisting postings across the country, and a fleeting memory of

- **ABOVE** Khajuraho Cola, watercolour, 2001
- **BELOW** Ruins of Church-Temple-Mosque, pencil on paper, 2001

Catholic Church, Panipat, Haryana

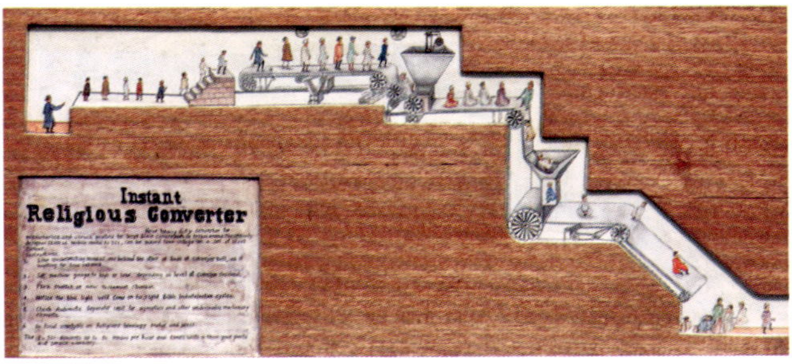

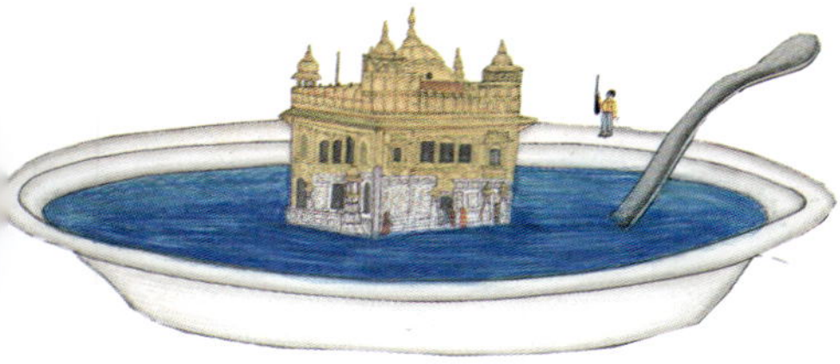

photographs and excerpts from religious books and ecclesiastical journals. He showed us pictures of stained glass clerestory windows, drawings of difficult Gothic traceries. He brought us calendars, pulled out picture postcards from his cupboard. Austerity no longer had the desired association with architecture. The final building was the outcome of unfortunate compromises, a mishmash of uncertain fancies, testifying ultimately to an idea that was only partially realized.

- **ABOVE** Instant Religious Converter, watercolour, 2001
- **CENTRE** Temple Soup, watercolour, 2001
- **BELOW** Temple Soup, pen & ink, 2012

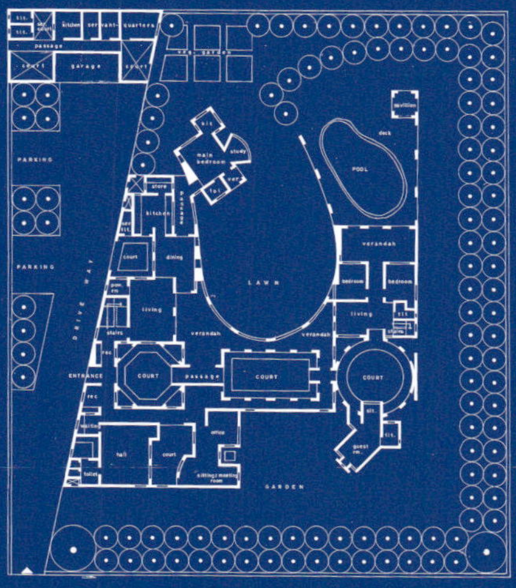

City House

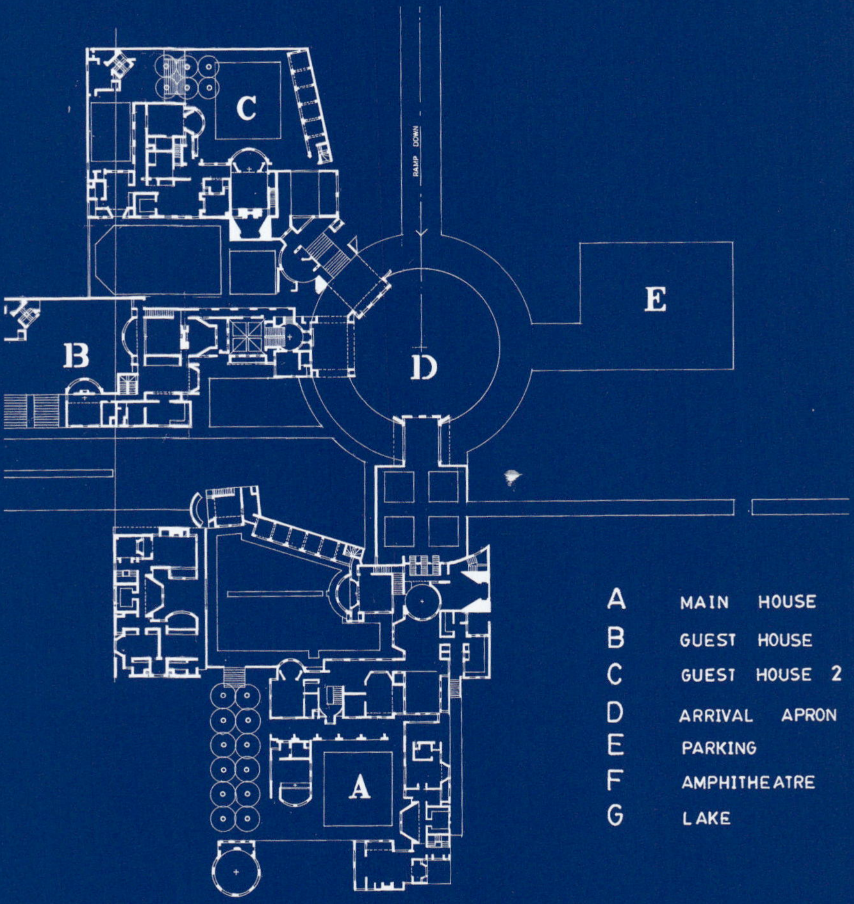

Harish Gupta House (Unbuilt) Mandi, Delhi, 1992

The private house mirrors its owner's image like no other possession. The design's public face reveals ideas of identity and image, conflicts between conformity and originality, expressions of idiosyncrasy, even aspiration. In it, social ideals become diffused, erased by scores of individual ideals, wherein people strive to promote and exercise individual choice. Yet houses reflect a more focused approach in the application of specific ideas. It is not difficult to extract something of the inspirational qualities in them, to see how, in each instance lies a quieter, perhaps conservative, suggestion of a personal or social utopia. In a house designed for a journalist in Delhi the focus shifts inwards, to court and garden, to an integration of space and material, so that no single image of the place is highlighted, and space is made in a string to facilitate intimate experiences. The building stands in a wide, rocky expanse of a real

■ Bedroom, pencil on paper, 2011

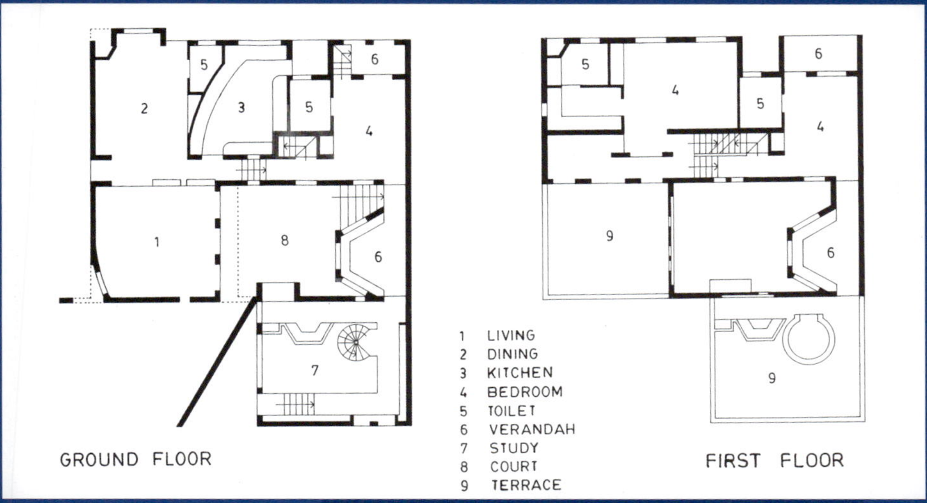

Arvind Das House, Gurgaon, Haryana, 1990

estate subdivision; a plot facing what may someday be, like all other streets of the big Indian city, a polluting, noisy road. In a setting with an uncertain environmental future, the public view beyond the house was hardly deemed desirable.

The external aspect of the undeveloped land surrounding the house made the architecture turn inwards, to its own inner resourcefulness, so that the private life of the house remained reclusive. The courtyard has been a constantly recurring theme in the traditional house. Its openness to the sky made it the symbolic heart of the home, and in shifting the focus of the design inwards, the plan made a clear separation between the house's public face—the stretch of an unadorned facade along the street; and the private core—the smaller rooms around the courtyard occupied by the family.

■ Bedroom, watercolour, 2011

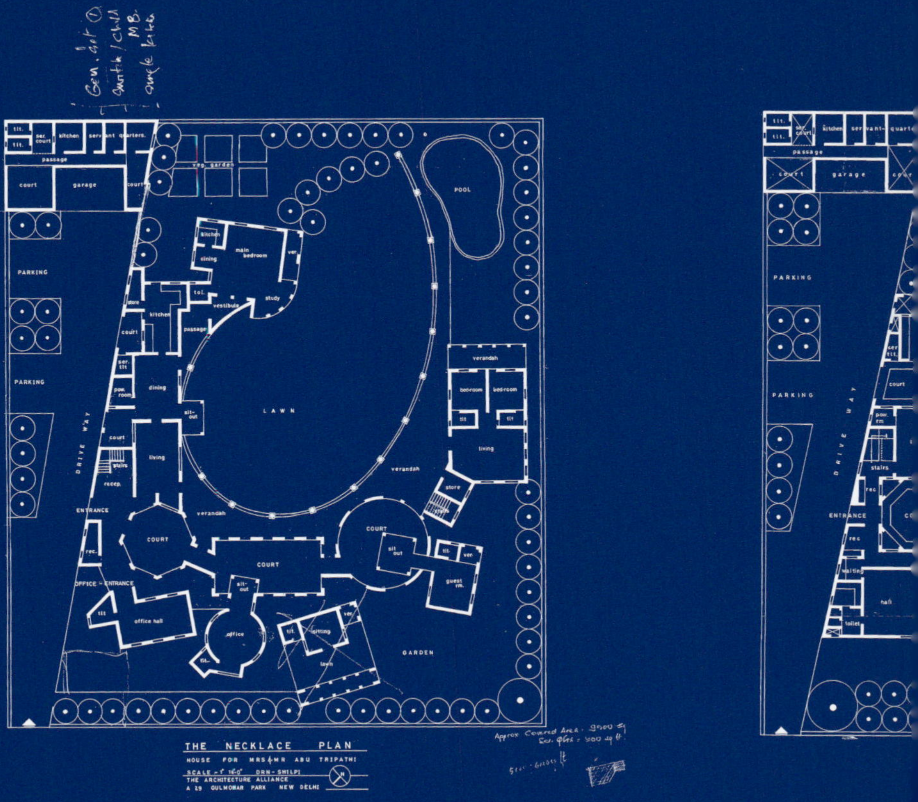

Jindal Farm House, Chhattarpur, Delhi, 2000

Of course a courtyard may have an uncertain function in an air-conditioned house or in one that is oriented towards the street, but the intention here was neither historical nor symbolic, it was just meant to use the isolating quality of the court to withdraw from the future blight of the surroundings. Consequently the house was designed as a linear procession, a movement from the outer public access of the living room to the dining room, to the bedroom, to the verandah, and eventually to the study. The plan turned upon itself, like a dog chasing its tail, stopping short of making a complete circle. If the traditional house acknowledged that coexistence with nature was a distinct and preferred possibility, I wondered then, whether the sensory deprivation that was the outcome of city living could be effectively reversed here through an introverted architecture. The

■ Cabinet, City, watercolour, 2004

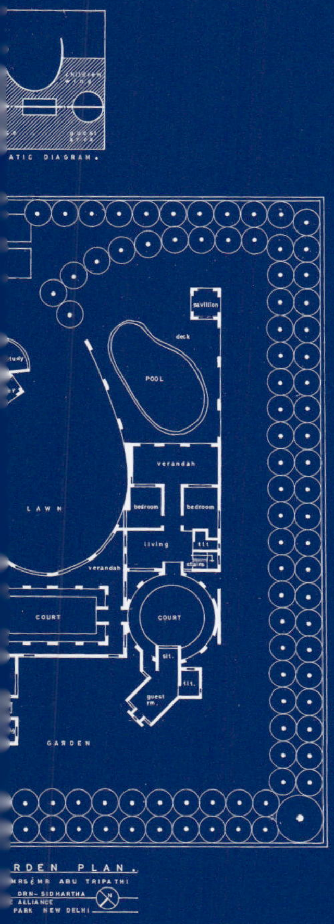

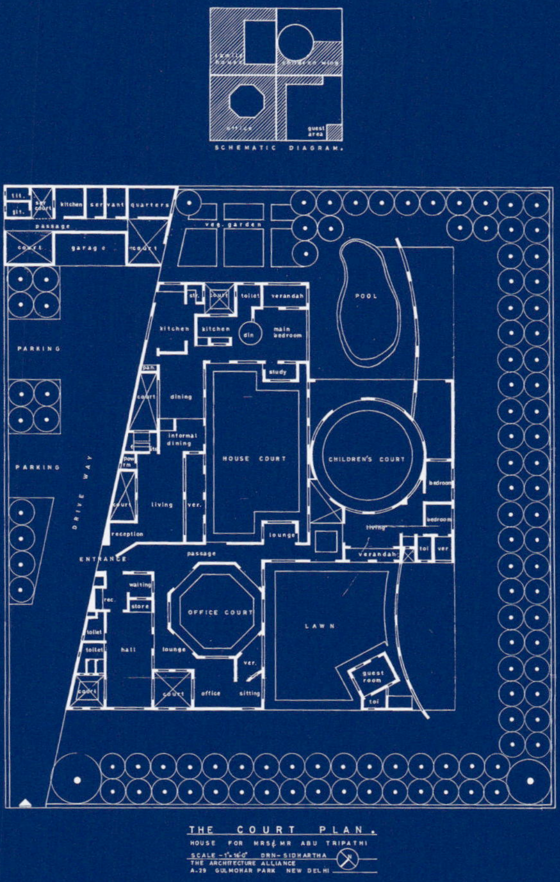

court that emerged from this encircling progression became the part of the outer garden held within the family's imaginative captivity. It was here, surrounded and overlooked by the familiar aspects of their own occupations, that the family created the home's outer life, gardening, reading or entertaining their guests within the self-prescribed boundary.

The court was a cocoon, a protective shell removed from the cacophony of any future real estate development in the area. The most important space off the court was a deep verandah set along the axis of the living-room, which was an entity in its own right. Its importance was due to its detachment, an independent room with a view, a place with an enclosing

■ **ABOVE** Cabinet, Home, watercolour, 2004
■ **BELOW** Cabinet, Country, watercolour, 2004

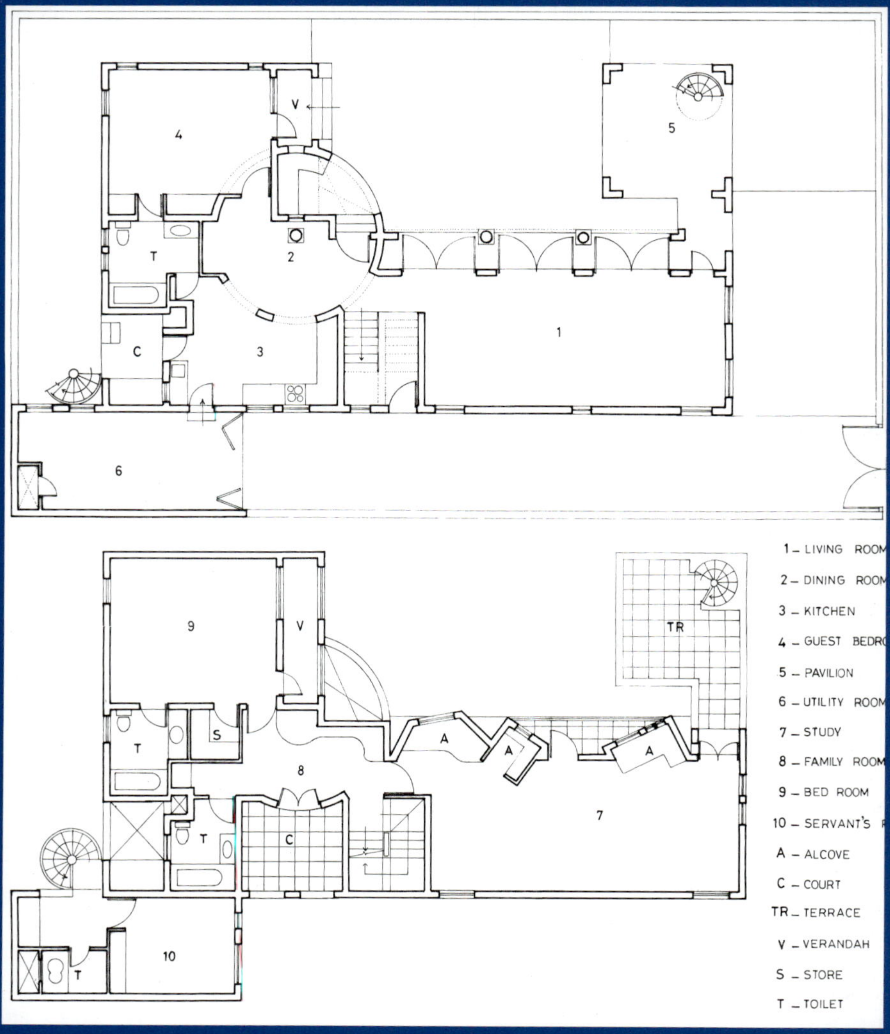

character that was different from the more conventional enclosures it connected. Yet the incompleteness of the wall around the court was an assertion of its link to the front garden. The ambiguity of the way the outside could be used was retained, indeed emphasized, in this tentative joining between courtyard and garden. The formal green of the lawn extended into the court; equally, the severely controlled familiarity and the personal accretions of the court leaked into the garden. Like a fluid creeps into all the crevices of a surface, the constantly shifting views of garden and court acknowledged the possibilities of their mixed or multiple uses. Separately, each was special territory; the court was a family compound, quiet and protected; the garden, with easy access to the outside, the public domain. But together, they set the stage for less confining uses, shifting moods, entertainment.

■ Suitcase Beach house, watercolour, 2011

Gita Hariharan House, Bengaluru, Karnataka, 1994

In a larger farmhouse project I had done for an actor, architecture was not made by just the addition of similarly varied elements to the scheme; gazebos, arcades, porticos and an amphitheatre. In a site that spread over 11 acres, the idea was not merely to fit a house on a spacious estate but to combine the liberating aspect of the openness with the building. A retreat, a country estate, a stately manor or a farmhouse, the nomenclature mattered little, but the design insisted on rambling across the manicured grass; the verandahs curved across the rooms and added ancillary porches, wings grew from the corners to enclose more garden acreage; arcades appeared around pools to provide shade to fountains and rippling water bodies. In a place that is overpopulated, the anxiety to possess valuable land becomes the most potent symbol of wealth. The open-ended nature of the rooms that looked onto the ground, owned but unoccupied, formed a display far more arresting than any singular object. No gold fixtures, no authentic Elizabethan sofa, no antique or family heirloom could ever compete with the sight of buildable land left unbuilt.

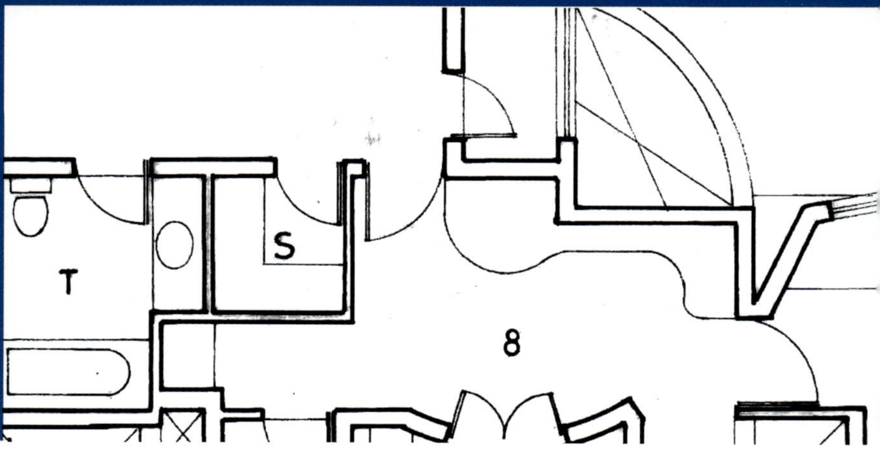

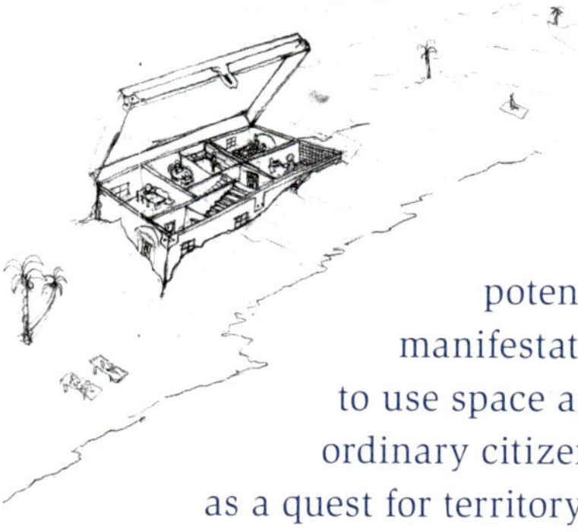

Objects and buildings and pieces of furniture endure, but measurably less than a piece of land. To the materialist, ownership of goods is seldom enough; once he reaches his limits he begins to seek acquisitions that are themselves potentially boundless. In a lucrative and subtler manifestation of acquisitiveness, the rich man learns to use space aggressively and less economically than the ordinary citizen. The public display of power manifests as a quest for territory; in the possession of the earth itself. With the extension of the house into the garden, the landscape to its horizons, the place took on a scale whose immensity was not just a matter of inconvenience.

The structure, in its spread, had lost something of the warmth and familiarity of a family dwelling. Home as a symbol of firmly bounded space, recognizable in its intimacy, had been abandoned for a willfully distinct reality. In losing its personal definitions, the house

■ Suitcase Home, pen & ink, 2011

Gita Hariharan House, Bengaluru, Karnataka, 1994

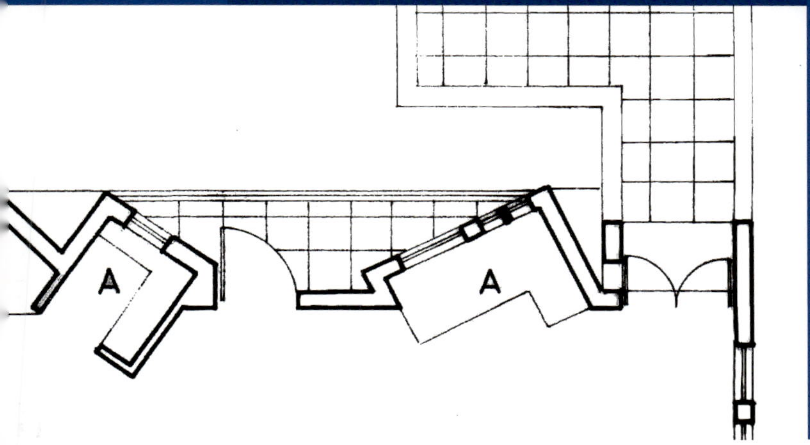

had become something of a family artifact, which only its members could appreciate. Domestic comfort however offers a range of varying sensations—pleasure, simplicity, ease, convenience, privacy and intimacy, all of which can only be experienced by the residents of the home. The shifting rhythms of family life were normal for a journalist client, whose peculiar lifestyle and daily routine necessitated these spatial variations, from solitude and complete withdrawal to one of meeting others and entertaining them. While the action of journalism was rooted in the exchange of ideas and information, its eventual resolution into writing required solitary thought. The nature of this solitary activity required a plan that convulsed into multiple shifts and orientations.

Whether journalist, writer, or artist, theirs was a private calling that demanded small spaces to think, react, sleep and escape

■ Home Delivery, watercolour, 2011

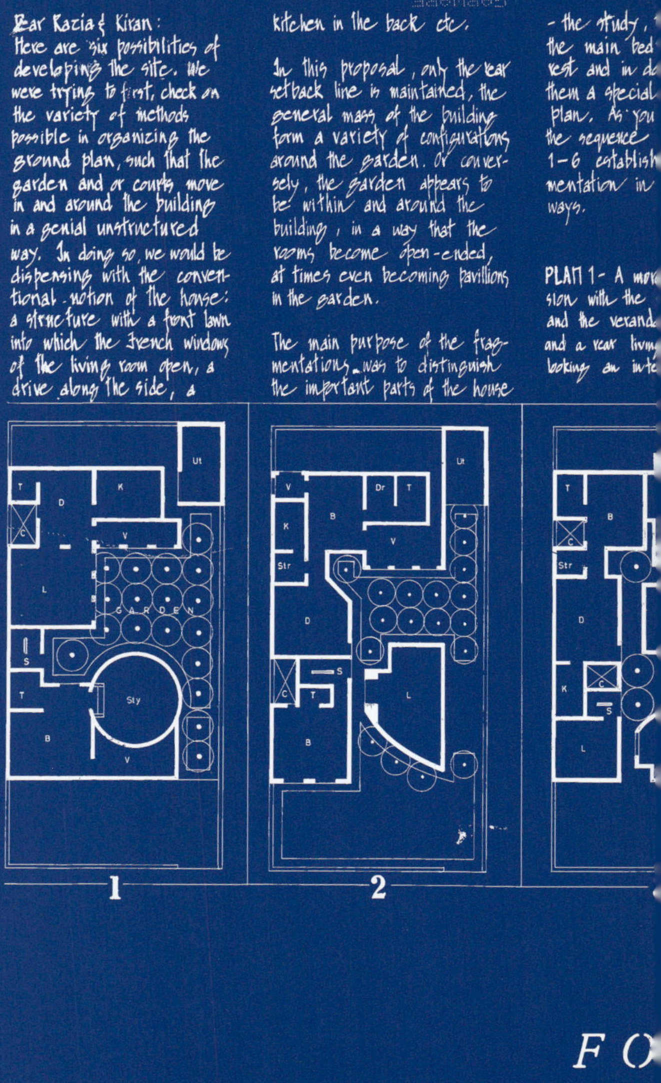

into fantasy. The architectural convulsions may be seen as oddities in the rectilinearity, but their presence does not mark confusion, rather an attempt to disengage with the plainer aspect of the house. There is the necklace of contortions, and the introduction of the sudden intrusion of disjointed private alcoves that have no relation to each other like marionettes that refuse to dance to the music. By adding to the usable dimension of the room, they induce a different and more

■ **LEFT** Den, watercolour, 2004
■ **RIGHT** Dining Hall, watercolour, 2011

Kiran Doshi House, Noida, UP, 1995

private state of play. A new appetite to the larger space within which they must co-exist. The distended wall with multiple alcoves was always bathed in new light; it drew you into its folds at different times of the day to perform actions that were not rehearsed or routine. I always felt it was a house I would build for myself someday; a feeling that ebbed and died with every house I built.

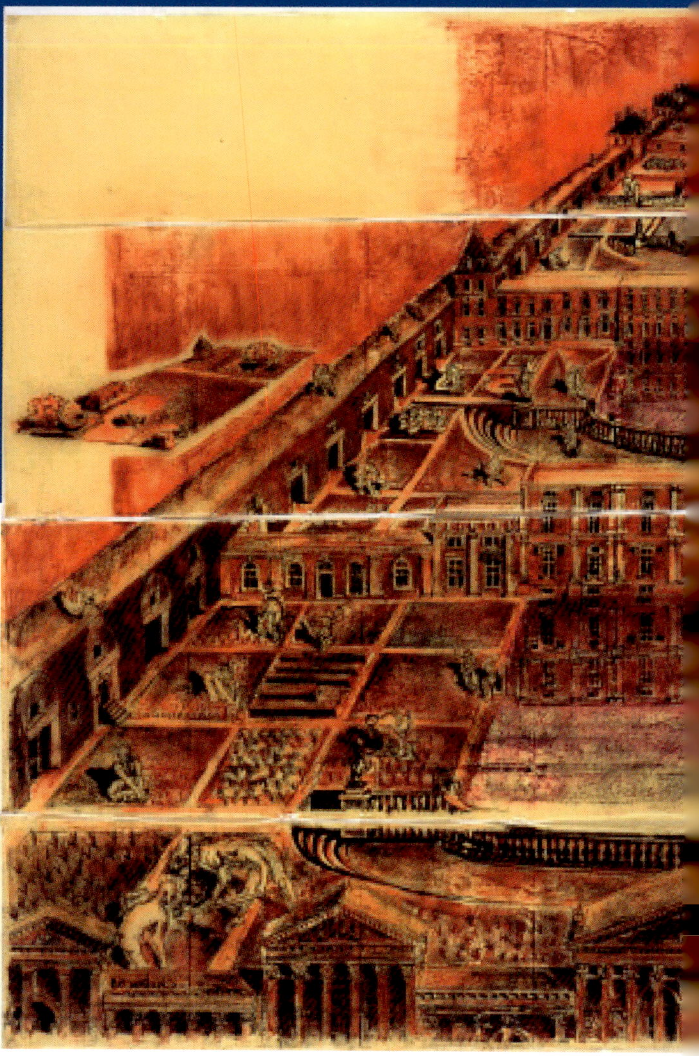

Country House, Conté Crayon, 2001

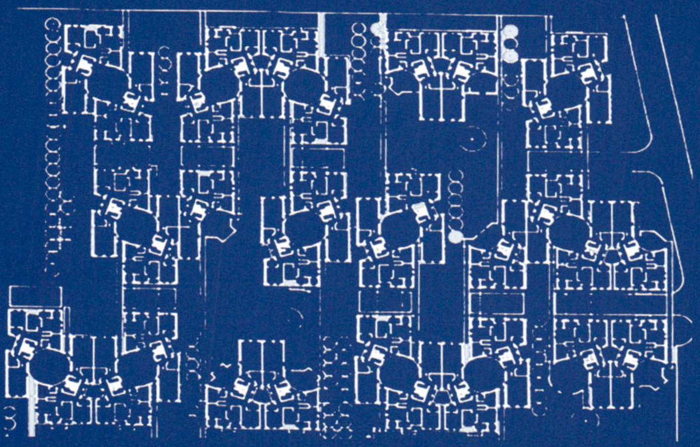

Apartment

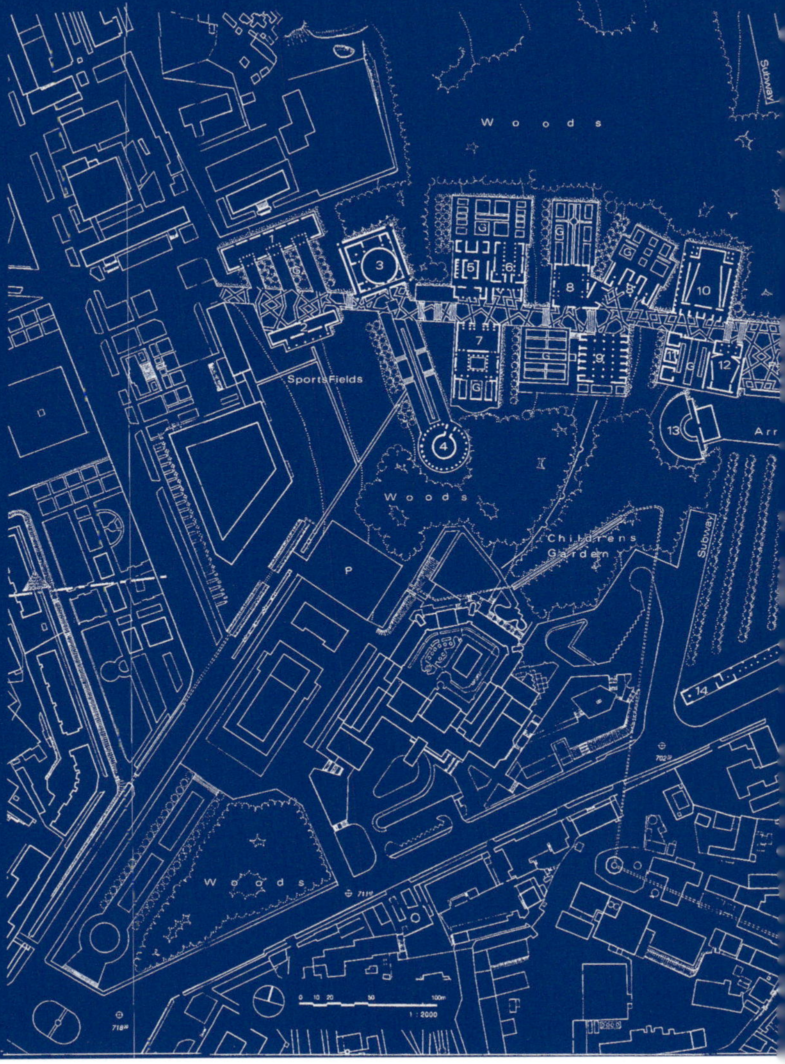

Does a consciously cultivated sense of the communal space that lies beyond an individual's house exist in India? Do we have an intuitive perception about how to design and occupy the city? Is there a particular Indian identification with public place? Without constructed form, there can be no sense of space. If there is no constructed form in the active public life of a city there can be no collective sense of community. Public places provide a social structure within which people's perceptions and experiences are modulated daily. Meeting, congregation, movement: the diverse nature of each of these activities is expressed in places explicitly created for entertainment and pleasure, work or living.

Every design affects the community in multiple ways. It controls what we experience in the public life

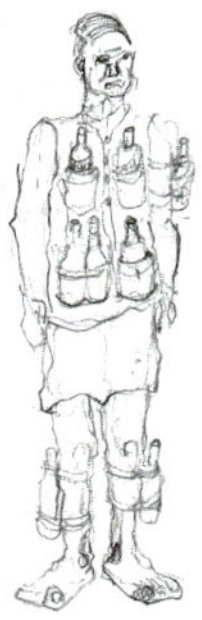
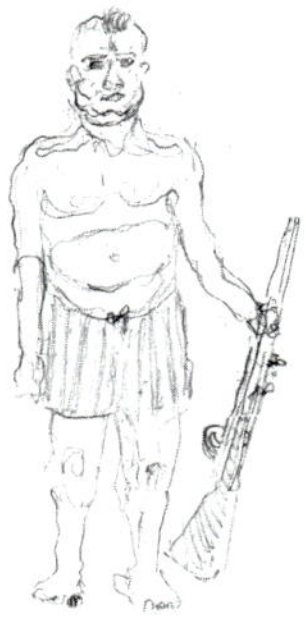

- **LEFT** Bootlegger, pencil on paper, 2012
- **CENTRE** Guard, pencil on paper, 2012
- **RIGHT** Policeman, pencil on paper, 2012

Cultural/commercial Development for Registan Square, Uzbekistan (Competition entry), 2003

of a city. The public or collective memory of the city which records the effects of demolition, renewal and reconstruction is directly linked to the environment buildings create and their location. They express a set of urban concerns—how we move between buildings, how that movement is perceived in sights and sounds, how it may be altered or modulated by intervening landmarks. How these come together—whether in a consciously designed way or as accidental encounters matters. Their physical appearance, metaphysical perception, relationships and proximities are all part of the scenarios that make community life possible and worthwhile. The architect had far too often neglected to inform the surroundings with his buildings.

The high cost of urban space dispelled the private design tendencies seen in individual pieces of architecture. What mattered then were urban concerns like physical connections, social relationships, spatial

■ **LEFT** Mali (Gardener), pencil on paper, 2012
■ **RIGHT** Bureaucrat, pencil on paper, 2012

focus and perimeters that buildings described, the impact on people's movement and the containment of their cultural lives. It required a blurring of the building's private design intentions and demanded a political assessment of architecture. But today, the appearance of walled compounds in the middle of the city marks a new kind of enclosed community. By its isolating nature, the boundary of the gated community acts as a marker, an anti-community sign; a reminder to those on the outside of their "outsiderness", the necessity for distinction, the maintenance of the differences of race, colour, caste, class, profession and wealth.

The boundary becomes a legitimate physical barrier, barring admission to some and welcoming others. In these places it acts as a sieve; a checkpoint for members, and an entry, albeit temporarily, for support staff. In the Indian city its primary, though unstated, function demands an exclusion of the impure. It not so much about establishing the hope of a higher purity for themselves, but about the active derision of others. This is seen as a means of enhancing one's status. The over-arching effect of such enclosures is neither wholeness nor an idealized community balance, but only an assembly of physical activities based on the developer's judgement.

■ Politician, pencil on paper, 2011

Cultural/commercial Development for Registan Square, Uzbekistan (Competition entry), 2003

The inclusion of seemingly incongruous elements in a place causes a psychic disturbance in the new resident. This is quickly replaced by incessant activity. The urge to sit under a tree or to be alone is a disturbance in the new order of designed community activity. It is replaced by opportunities to barbeque, swim in the community pool, pray together in the *puja* hall and meditate in the club. The ideology of exerting the togetherness of people of similar beliefs, likes and dislikes and desires is expected to be in force when people of the same caste, class and colour come together. The design inside the gate plays to the group's similarities, ensuring no one is made aware of individual differences. Capitalism's most delectable wants are made available inside a Communist prison camp: Manhattan miniaturized in Siberia. To question the believers is to question the defining ideology. The result may not be death or the Gulag, but exclusion.

If you stretch Thomas Moore's definition of Utopia, "the state where the residents are free from poverty and live in social harmony, with no probability of internal dissent, in a strictly planned town, surrounded by high boundary walls", you will land in many gated communities in India. Entirely disconnected from their specific locations, they could be anywhere. The division and high wall are essential because the insular community feeds on differences, and is conceived as a counter to its

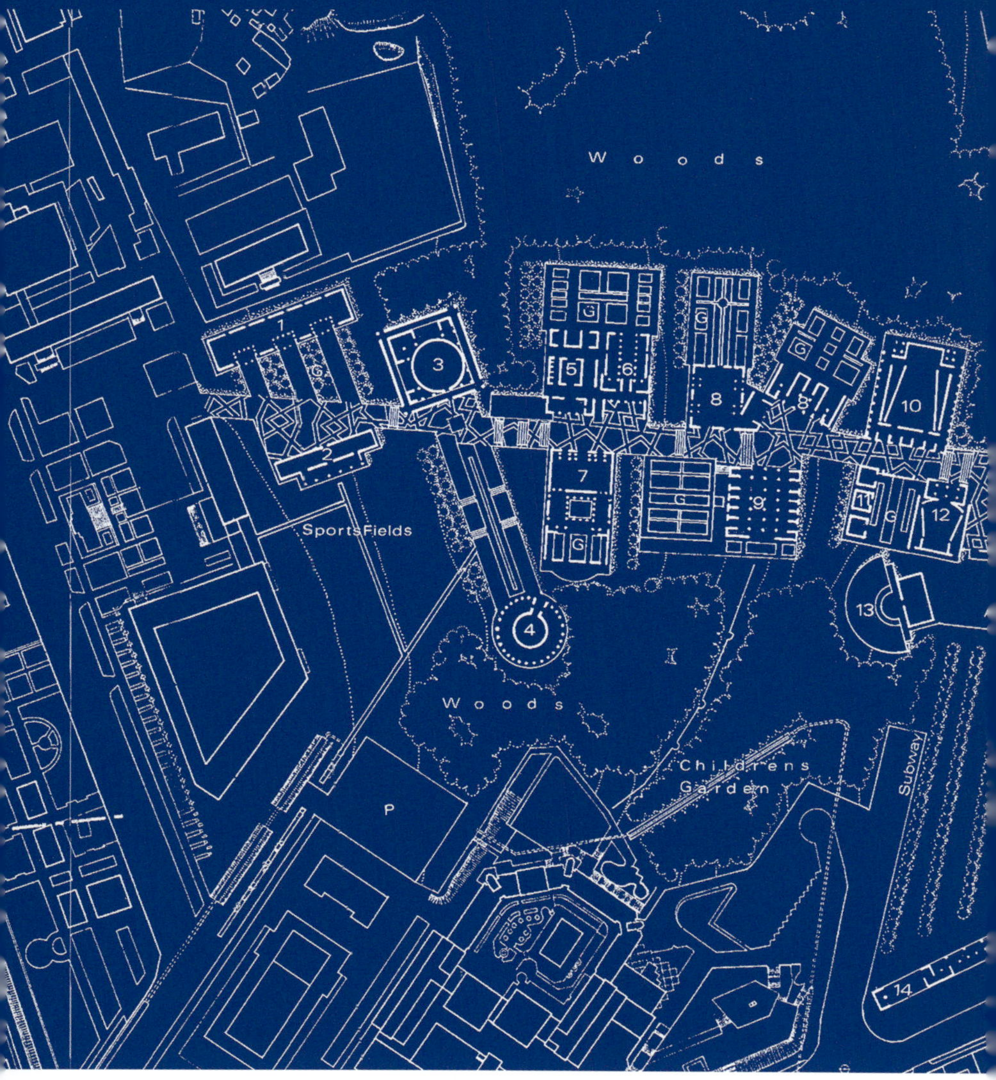

surroundings. Its closest architectural approximation, the Jewish concentration camp; with all the same shared privileges, the closely-watched life, the prison warden, the high wall and the improbability of escape.

In urban India, this is an outcome far more damning than death. The walled community casts a forbidding shadow on the city outside and fuels a long-standing battle. The entry into a rarefied enclosure comes at the expense of forgetting the past, and assimilating a new and more progressive future, a metaphorical death of the memories of the frugal bungalow life, so there can be a real rebirth into an orgy of loaded pickings. For many though, the embarrassment of riches is too sudden and without the requisite time for mourning and transition. It offends, and offends completely, leaving the resident in a state of psychic imbalance, lurching between old wants and new, untested

■ **ABOVE** Community Pool, watercolour, 2011
■ **BELOW** Community Barbeque, watercolour, 2011

Cultural/commercial Development for Registan Square, Uzbekistan (Competition entry), 2003

desires. The stuffy air of the large air-conditioned dining room is abandoned in favour of the more intimate kitchen and smoke-filled verandah; the pool, never used for exercise, is a trophy for visitors. The incompatibility of the accumulated assets defeats their functions and marginalizes all social activity.

If the interior supports material beliefs, its real purpose is segregation and the expulsion of foreign matter. The resident minority is formed out of their grievances with the majority outside, an implied threat, if never actually followed through, gives succour to the dormant idea that "their life is on the line".

- **LEFT** Band, watercolour, 2004
- **CENTRE** Civil Ceremony, watercolour, 2004
- **RIGHT** Civil Departure, watercolour, 2004

People in service temporarily are allowed to enter the compound at specified hours when cars are to be washed, vegetables cut, shirts pressed. Between those hours, a flurry of supporting activity takes place without fanfare. A silent march occurs past unseen gates and like sewage flowing out from pipes hidden below the neat hedges and hibiscus, the staff make a quiet exit.

At Treblinka and Auschwitz, the secretaries appeared in the offices to keep prisoners' records, for filing papers, making notations about new arrivals; the guards worked shifts whose timing was known only to them. At the rich Indian ghettos in Gurgaon and Whitefield, the routines are much the same. Here the similarity is the result of a reversal of social forces and tendencies. Like in the case of the 2002 riots in Ahmedabad where Muslims were targeted, the integrity of enclosure is a reasoned protective shield against the surrounding majority. Where the larger, integrated city acted as a means to disperse religion's identity, the new ghettos were a more resolute signal to the majority much like holding the cells of concentration camps on the verge of conflagration.

The isolation of these gated complexes was a measure enforced by the fear of the dominant community. Unlike the leisure practices of affluent enclosures—the pools, barbeques and golf courses—the

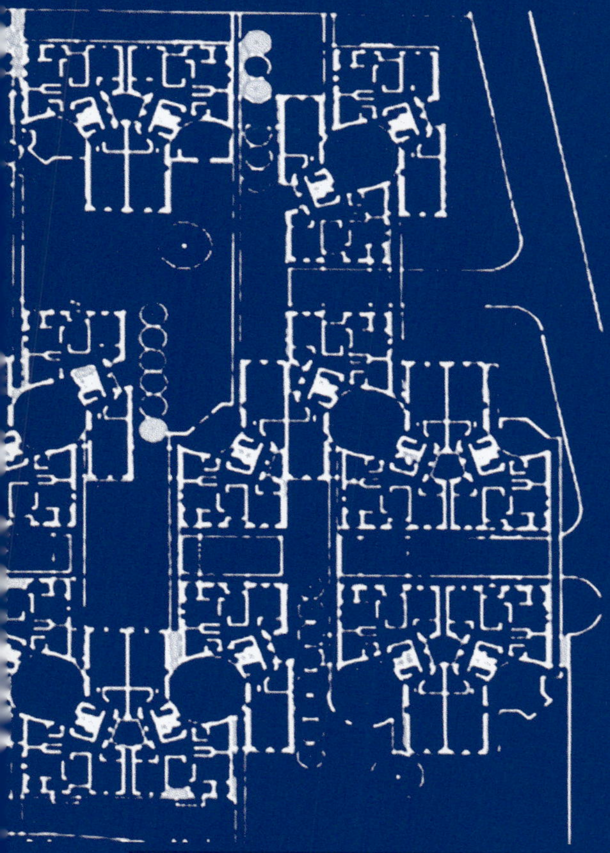

Type V Government Housing, Andrews Gunj, Delhi, 1995

space of the ghetto resolved into actual community acts. Mosque, *madrassa* and burial ground formed out of the necessity to live with a common cause. The ghetto gave people the freedom to practise without fear of reprisal from outsiders, under the supportive gaze of likeminded people. During times of peace, the enclosed minority was surrounded by the majority functions and ghettos existed as gated communities in isolation, with little interaction, and little or no contact with the other.

But both forms of architectural isolation are symbols of an uneasy peace, and they force the reading of "us and them", good and bad, and perpetually affirm the simmering tensions that erupt at the slightest of incidents. Bottled-up rage gives into easy violence knowing fully well that the enemy is easily defined by an architectural boundary. From both the *madrassa* which children attend in the ghetto and the couples gathered at the poolside barbeque in the gated complex, the eyes that gaze outward are filled with fear and uncertainty.

Is our loss of identity linked to the physical loss of identifiable and familiar places to live? Thousands of flats rise up every day across industrial wasteland. Bureaucratic citadels tainted by the monsoons, mediocre in design, they are the new public

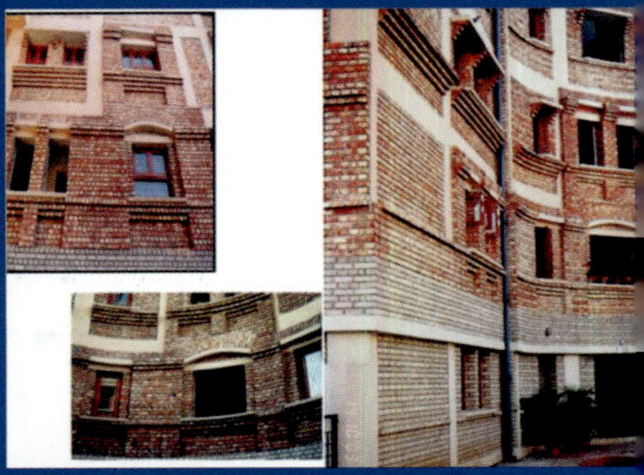

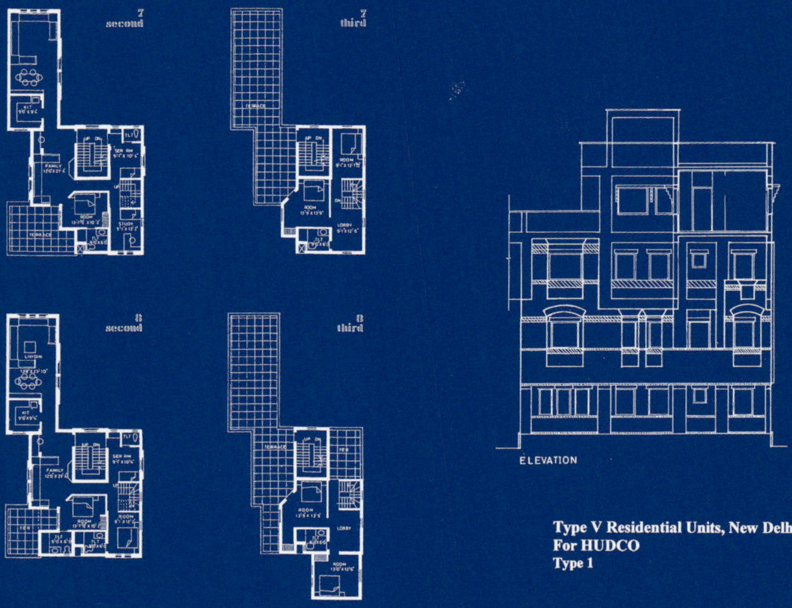

Type V Residential Units, New Delhi
For HUDCO
Type 1

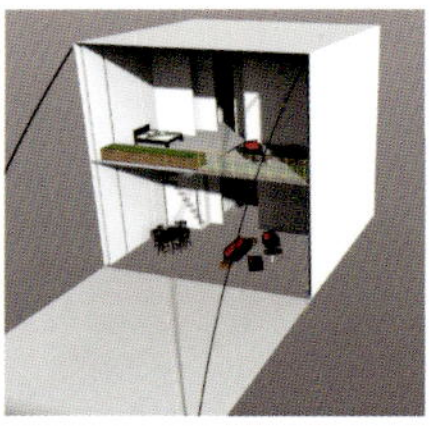

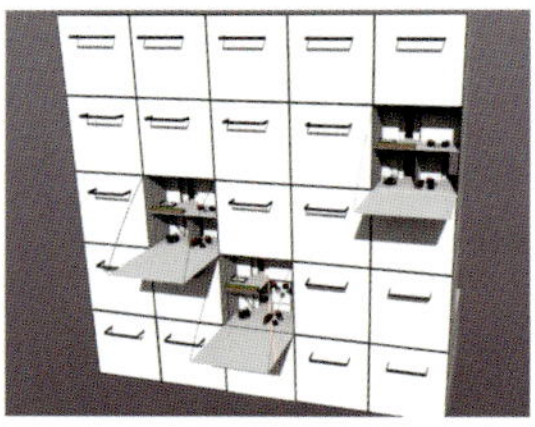

face of India. Is the imaginative impulse then no longer central to architecture? Or does the impulse to create public housing stem from other forces—mediocrity, mimicry, repetition, monotony, and eventually desolation? Habit dulls, and the mind builds without the awareness of choice. Home should not be where you have to go, but want to. Can the new architecture of housing revive our sense of identity? Is it possible to include in housing that which is cherished by the people who live in there?

Under this project, 99 Type V units were designed within a restricted urban site as part of a larger urban design scheme for developing housing, commercial and office areas. Free access to other parts of

- **LEFT** Office Cabinet, Apartment, simulation, 2014
- **RIGHT** Office Cabinet Apartment, simulation, 2014

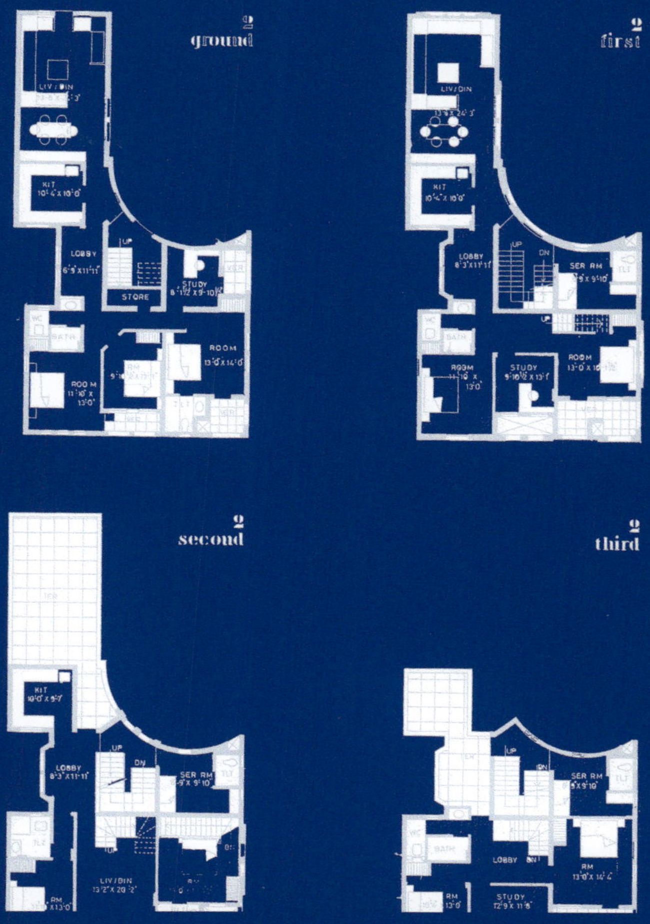

Unit Design, Government Housing

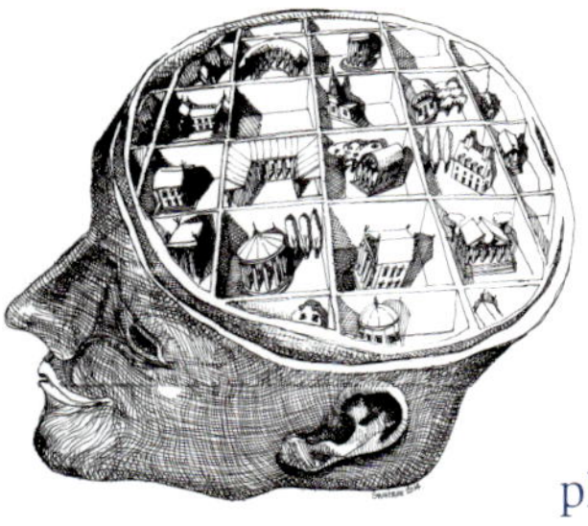

the site was the primary consideration. The plinth was raised at the centre to create an upper ground level and provide parking below it. Separating the vehicular movement from the pedestrians, the urban design created groupings of apartments around circular courts—places where privacy was more guarded, but also had restricted access to the play areas, meeting and community spaces. The architectural design of the housing negated the "apartment block" and created, instead, a variety of units plans in which rooms spanned across walkways and public areas. Consequently, the visitor moves under bridges, through raised terraces into the privacy of his own courtyard.

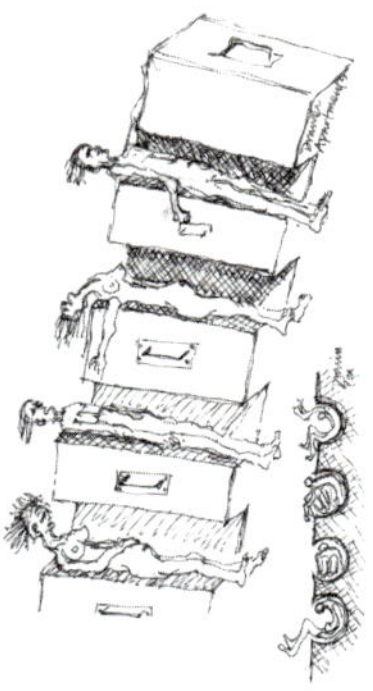

Internally, the apartments were conceived as duplexes, varied in plan, but each had its own set of verandahs and terraces. A vocabulary of exposed

■ **ABOVE** Gated Compound, pen & ink, 2015
■ **BELOW** Low Cost Housing, pen & ink, 2015

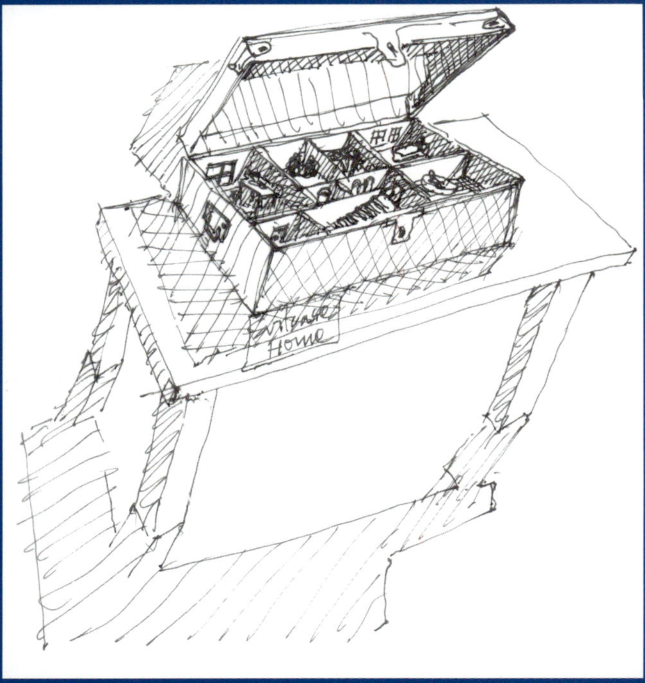

brickwork using arches and corbels was inserted within the concrete frame. For the most part, the "apartment's" singular identity for multiple families made for an awkward ideal. The building was neither an apartment house nor a private house; falling somewhere in the middle, a sort of "aparthouse". Within the larger frame of a collective life how was it possible to have individual expression? From a child-like perspective, it suggested single houses mounted one on top of the other, or an apartment composed of private villas.

The house was a private object, a solitary expression on a suburban street, which, due to lack of land, was lifted off its foundations and piled up in the air with others. The reasoning behind its new configuration takes on multiple forms and meanings, derived as it is from the absence of private land ownership, and from the need for shared utilities and circulation as well as from an altogether different kind of "neighbourliness" formed due to increased population densities. Was it any longer a matter of choice, or simply the obvious outcome of new urban life? From up above, the perspective stood changed; the relationship between house and land, or rather, house and air, established aerial rather than territorial connections.

The boundary fence of the private garden and the particular dimensions of physical ownership had been replaced by air rights,

■ Low Cost House, pen & ink, 2010

and the belief in the occupation of space rather than area. For a people used to the physics of touch and smell, and their perennial relationship with the climate, it was an uncomfortable compromise. But it allowed for a more telling experiment in confinement and exposure. Boxed in like caskets, piled one on top of the other, the apartment was a death trap, a closed, walled-in storehouse of personal possessions with the resident as a secondary occupier. The apartment was a place to sleep at night and escape from in the morning like a bank locker, a filing cabinet, a chest of drawers.

Were these allowed to remain open they promised a release from confinement, and a partial return to the memory of the house; an opening up that held out the promise of light and air. Despite the contradictions inherent in high densities, the new apartment was a happy restatement of the need for privacy afforded by height. Look in any direction, any time of the day. The drawer opens or closes, partly or completely, and leaves you in greater control of your architectural destiny.

I often use furniture as the first convenient design option to apartment life. A suitcase as a private home, or a beach house; sets of suitcases as a hotel, the lid as entrance and exit, a unit

■ Low Cost Housing, watercolour, 2015

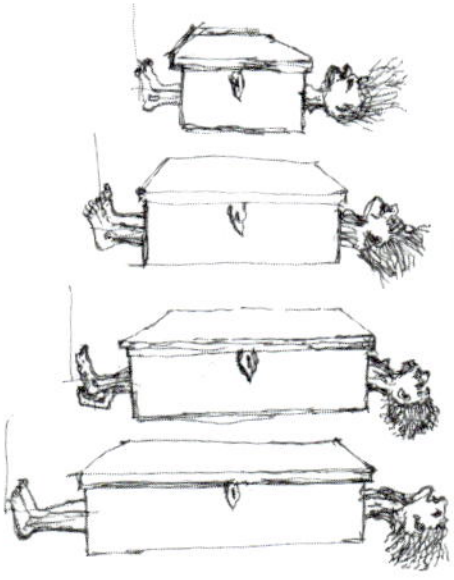

with a single movable part. Furniture has, and always will, act as the first source of inspiration for architecture. I have often wondered how a roll-top desk—the English kind, with pigeon holes for letters, papers and file holders, pen and pencil drawers—would function as a home. With its complex privacies and shared domesticities, the cabinet is an infinite provider of space, divided and multiplied; an anthill for an imaginative recruitment of family rooms made to custom order. Furniture used to literally box in life at different scales.

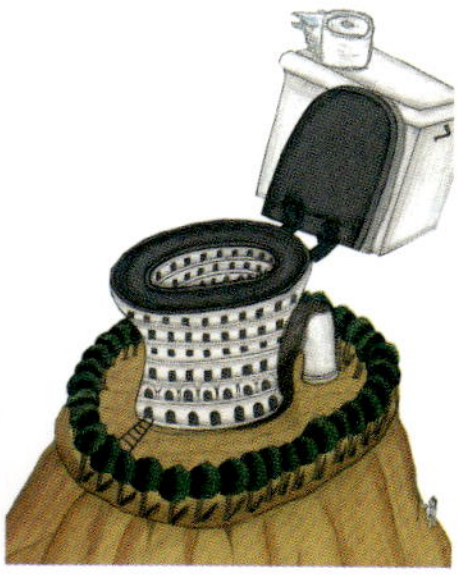

Imagine the individual in a suitcase or casket, dead or alive as space shrinks to envelop the body and lock it from the outside. Growing demands, changing, aging and dying inside; families joint and nuclear, couples with their own separate entrances and kitchens, garages, servants' quarters,

■ **ABOVE** Box Apartment, pen & ink, 2015
■ **BELOW** WC Belvedere Heights, watercolour, 2011

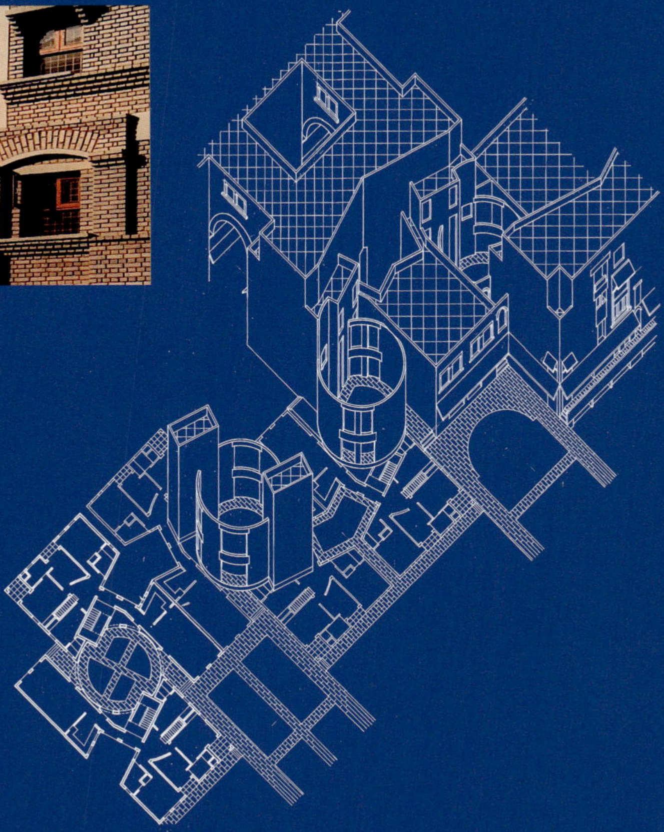

Type V Government Housing, Andrews Gunj, Delhi, 1995

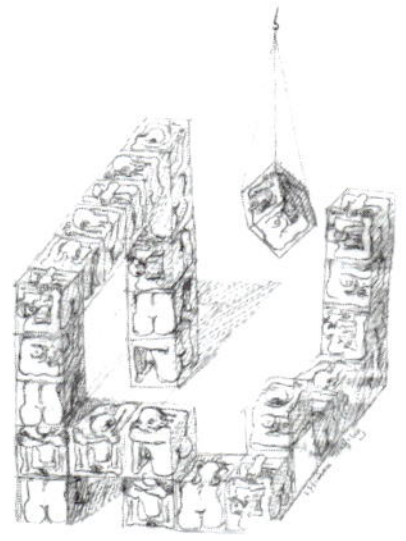

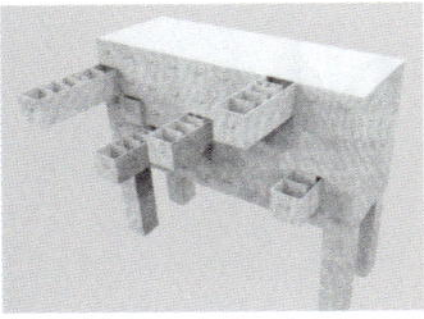

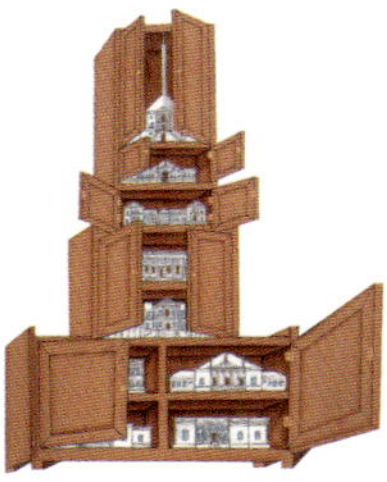

pantries and prayer rooms—all aglow in the summer light, when the roll-top is open by day. And as night falls, the building closes itself off to the dark. The house becomes a trunk or pill box, revealing only a blank face to the other trunks on the street. The architect was a cabinet maker with a longer measuring tape, replacing the act of storage with habitation. The new architecture had the additional capacity to breathe in air and light, and to fill the drawers with people packed closely together. Architecture risked being typecast as an interloper, a facilitator of urban savagery; and was no longer a provider of settled lives, but an improviser and instigator of new rivalries. The long-term psychology of its new configurations has never been felt so close to the skin, but at some point a future hallucination will show the wildly varied domesticities that once existed, separated only by a thin wall.

- **ABOVE** Prefab Homes, pencil on paper, 2011
- **CENTRE** Filing Cabinet Homes, simulation, 2014
- **BELOW** Cabinet Apartments, watercolour, 2012

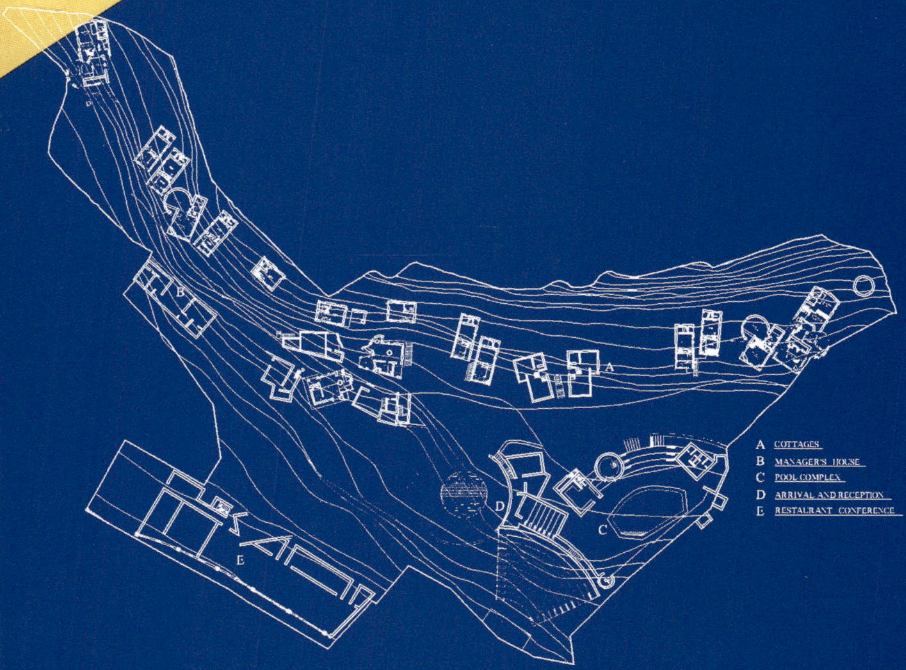
A COTTAGES
B MANAGER'S HOUSE
C POOL COMPLEX
D ARRIVAL AND RECEPTION
E RESTAURANT CONFERENCE

Hotel

I always understood leisure as something linked to the absence of work. Leisure had however, led most architects down the unlikely path of physical activity, actions that produce a collective play—the urge to go on vacation, the necessity of active participation in recreation, gambling, drinking. The search for indolence is a different and more difficult task that calls for withdrawal. Taking indolence as a measure of architecture, I began to test the thesis of the resort being a place of deliberate inactivity. Could the agitated nature of leisure be tested against the background of buildings that ensured only a lazy non-participation? A confrontation was obviously on the cards when the Indian perception of the vacation demanded a serious medley of family participation—in sport, in recreation, the ordering, sharing and excessive consumption of food and drink.

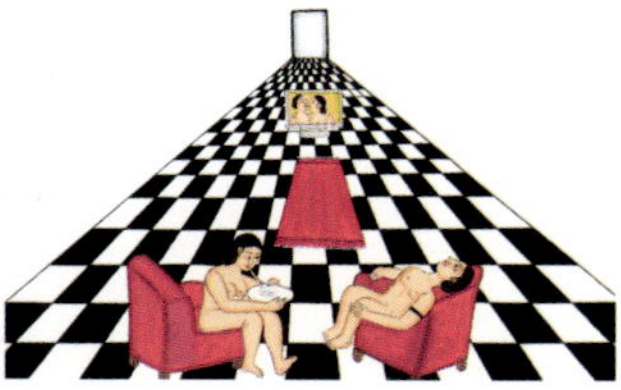

■ **ABOVE** Lounge, watercolour, 2011
■ **BELOW** Café, watercolour, 2011

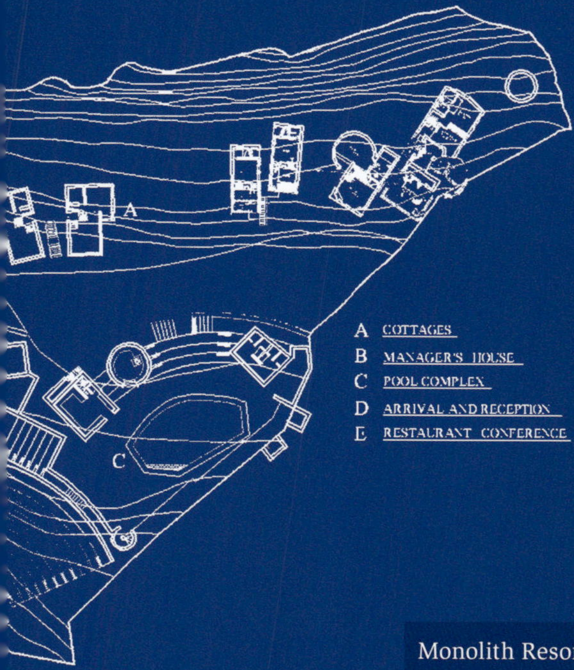

Monolith Resort, Bhimtal, Uttarakhand, 1998

The Indian tendency strays too often into hyper-consumption. At one end stands the family, the controlling arm of all public social discourse—involving marriage, routine social functions and annual vacations. The home is the natural guardian of family values—greed, intimacy, hostility, and acrimony—all practised within the rarefied atmosphere of an active compound that encourages a range of relationships between spouses, children, grandparents, servants and part-time workers. A vacation on the other hand is a renewal of family bonds and kinship, which were never broken in the first place. However contentious, dramatic, or emotional, the familiar atmosphere of the home is carried as it is to the vacation, whether on a beach paradise or at a hill resort. The most critical paradigm of the Indian holiday is the

■ Restroom, watercolour, 2011
■ Suite, watercolour, 2011

reproduction of the home's atmosphere in a new place—complete with every convenience, demand, object and person that is assembled in a configuration that gives people the sensation of never having left their homes.

How is it possible to achieve a happy state of mind and body if all the implements that assure this are not in place? The architecture that supports this definition of a vacation had to be supported by commerce—the opportunity to eat different cuisines, hand glide, bungee jump, go boating (with or without a lake on the premises). I was viewing the opposite extreme of this and clinging to the hope that architecture formed in seclusion and austerity could answer the call better. If escape from the control of daily routine was the aspiration, then the space inside and outside the building had to answer to the call for indolence. It demanded a conscious isolation of the body in its various states of "distress".

The building was to be the first reminder of a changed attitude. The construction using stone that looked as if hewed directly from

a quarry was perceptible on the buildings as you entered the sight-line of the resort, if only to make you believe that an old stone ruin was the farthest thing from the familiar setting of the home. I had seen old huts perched on stone outcrops on the way to Almora. They were made in a yellowing hue, cut and packed so closely that they required no mortar. The monolithic quality of the masonry came from the mason's ability to shape each piece and fit it in without air pockets—the art of the traditional craftsman that was increasingly being replaced by the brick wall and the concrete slab. Contempt for such traditional construction was due to the excessive time and expense involved.

It was always easier to build quickly and poorly, and then cover up the mistakes with an expensive veneer. Choosing instead to take the longer route, the rooms I built appeared from the ground as Roman ruins—heavy rusticated walls shaped by hand, stones fitted in and packed closely like a jigsaw. The willingness of masons to work with ancient tools was rewarded by a characteristically localized structure that addressed many

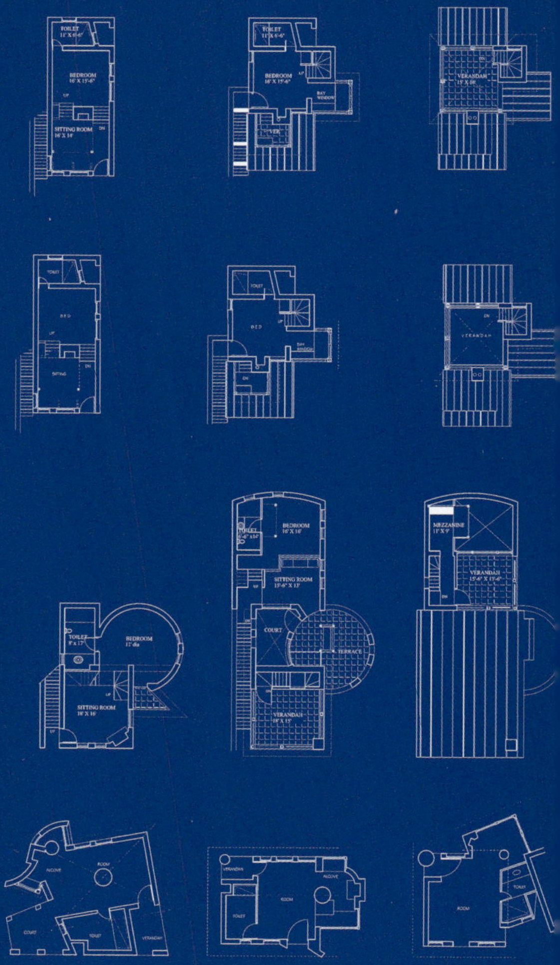

Cottage Plans, Monolith Resort

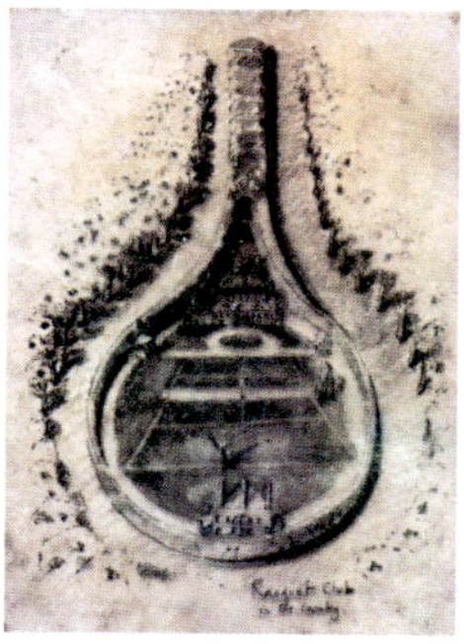

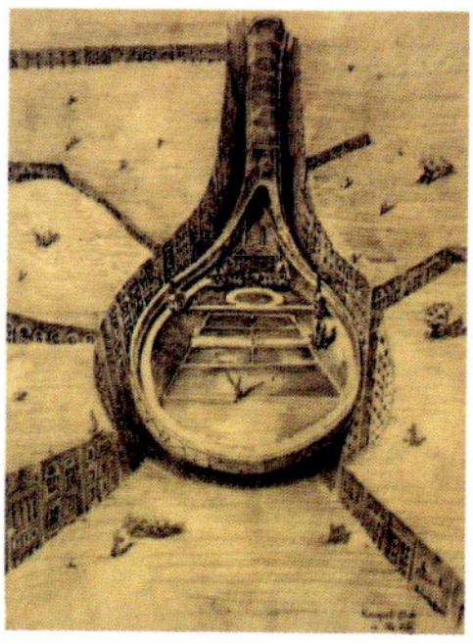

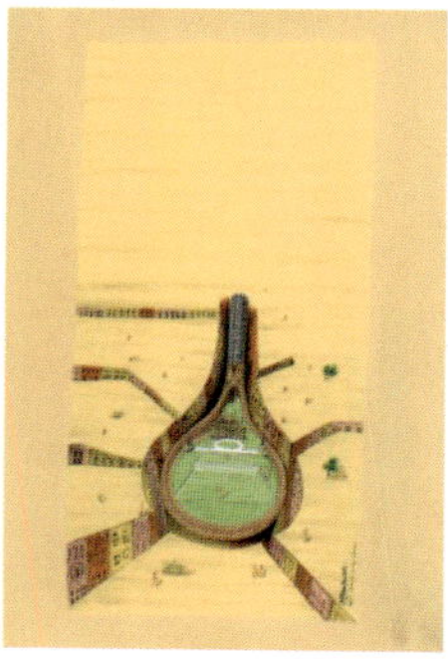

requirements simultaneously: enclosure, security, wall storage. Niches were built as the structure grew; doors and windows fitted, bays and projections incorporated.

The connection to the construction techniques was unintentionally symbolic — old, forgotten building techniques supporting a contemporary commodity. Relieving the structure of the burden of expressing the time in which it was built was an essential

- **LEFT** Racquet Club, charcoal on paper, 2001
- **CENTRE** Racquet Club, pencil on paper, 2003
- **RIGHT** Racquet Club, watercolour, 2001

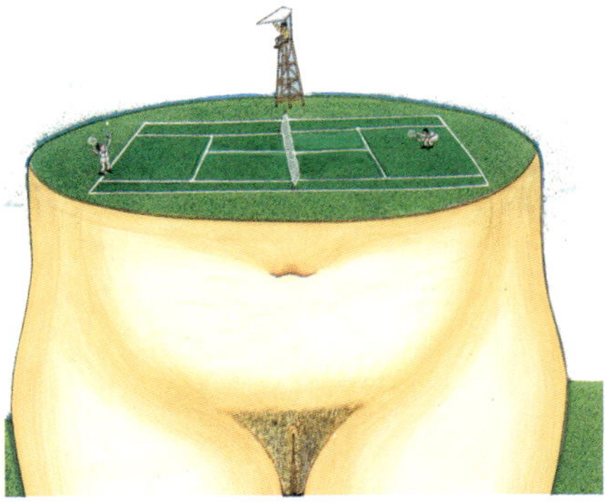

requirement of its "styleless" architecture. In the larger frame of the layout, the lake established a vantage point that was never going to change. Anywhere on the site you looked the lake was present. Only the reflections on its surface changed at different times of the day. The fixed nature of its constant sighting was at first the only alignment for the architecture.

In the rooms, or the garden, pool-side, or reception, the eye's guide to orientation was invariably the lake. The sheer scale

■ Racquet Club, watercolour, 2011

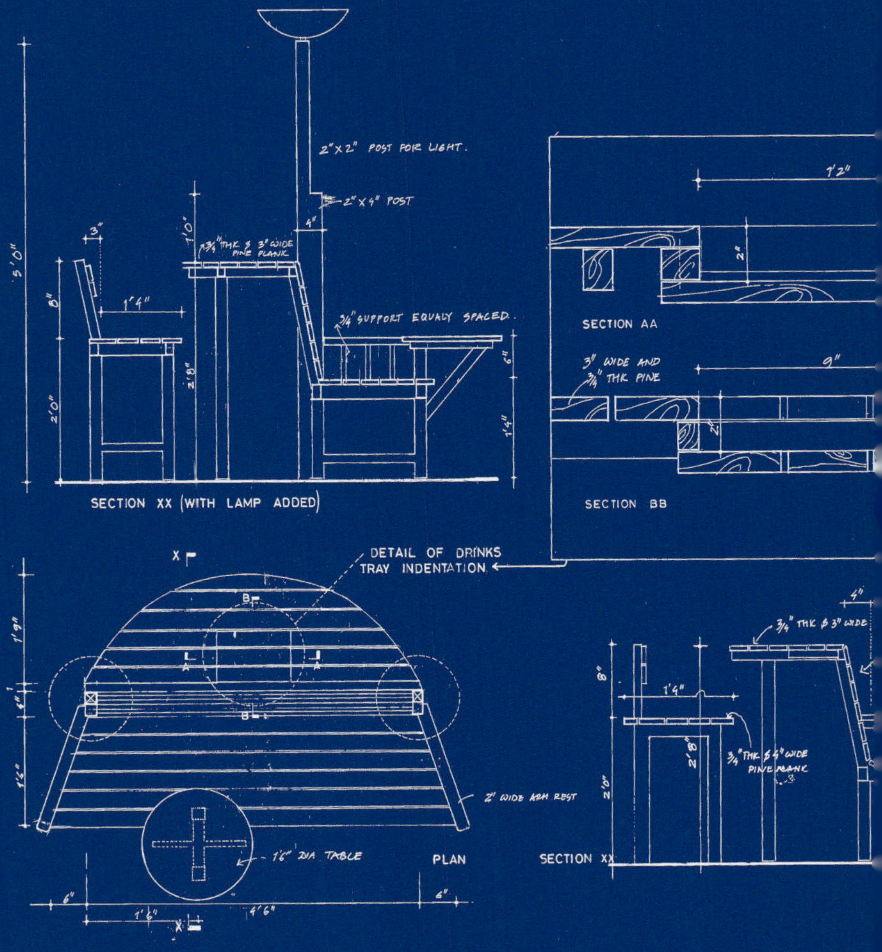

of the large sheet of water, smooth and unruffled, brought to mind the unfocused gaze of a five-day cricket match, where despite the inaction on the field, the beholder's gaze remains in soft focus, unseeing but entirely appreciative. To return the focus to more intimate frames within the architecture itself, other mechanics needed to kick in. An excess of planting would break the frame into a filigree, and fragment and conceal the distant view. Within the guest rooms, the construction of bays as self-contained rooms for lying down, sleeping and studying was a subliminal withdrawal from the expanse of the lake into moments of privacy. Social activities of the club, game room, bar, dining and barbeque were arranged in a passive ring around the pool.

People's engagement with the building and the landscape eventually made the lake into insignificant background. Over the years, as the treeline extended and the foliage massed around the buildings, the architecture altered completely. An introversion of shades and shadows replaced the geometry of building, changed its precise placements of shape and form, into an indolent maze of light and

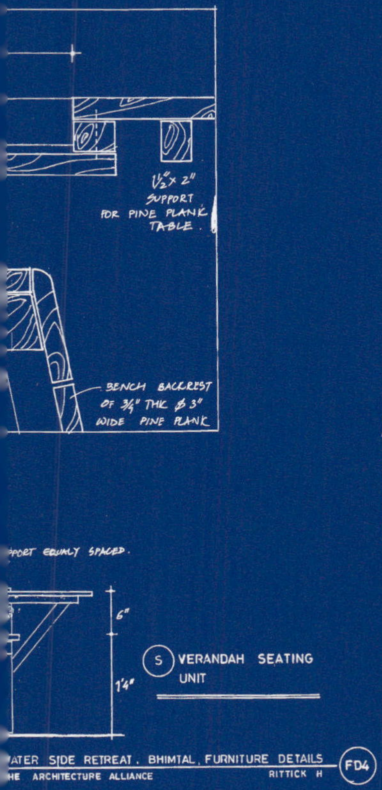

Furniture Details, Monolith Resort

■ Yoga, bronze, 2008

dark that lent no definition to place or movement, but allowed people to discover their own modes of engagement with it. The calculated necessity of using different forms for the same set of requirements grew from the varying conditions of social life itself. It had to express the differences among people themselves; their inclinations, posters, lifestyles and moods. Such cultural variations had to be contained in the possibilities of changing space and take into account what guests could do in, and with them.

Privacy, intimacy, play, sleep, whatever the form of engagement, the structure's projections and improvisations were an invitation to changing situations. The elasticity was made possible using a finite set of materials and techniques. Covered places were deliberately confined to isolated pockets in the landscape. Tradition was inverted by allowing the absence of roofs to cut into private rooms. I sat with the owner one afternoon in the shade watching guests struggle to express their vacation mood.

Elevation (top) and Interiors (above), Monolith Resort

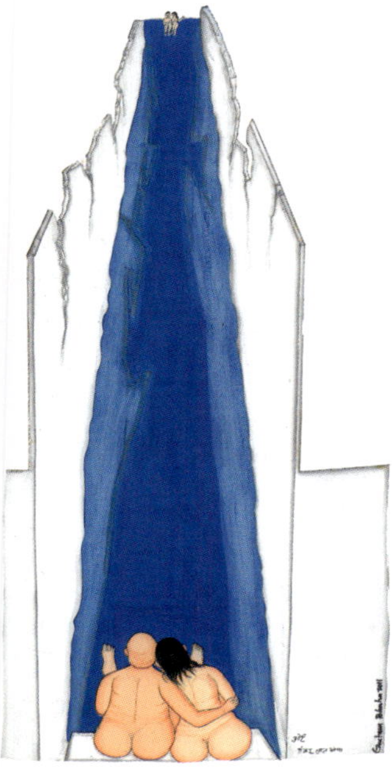

■ Pool, watercolour, 2011

A German couple had retreated to the far verandah near a blossoming peach tree and begun to browse through their Kindles. A large contingent of Punjabis had gathered at the pool—members, it seemed, of an extended joint family consisting of several generations. They were there to be entertained and to indulge in gluttonous revelry, something that was not possible in the regulated home environment. It was as outlandish and brazen a pursuit of happiness as any constitution would allow. They had paid up at the front desk. All their actions therefore had to reek of expenditure.

In full public view, the men stood outside the pool's changing rooms and relieved themselves of their clothes. Then they

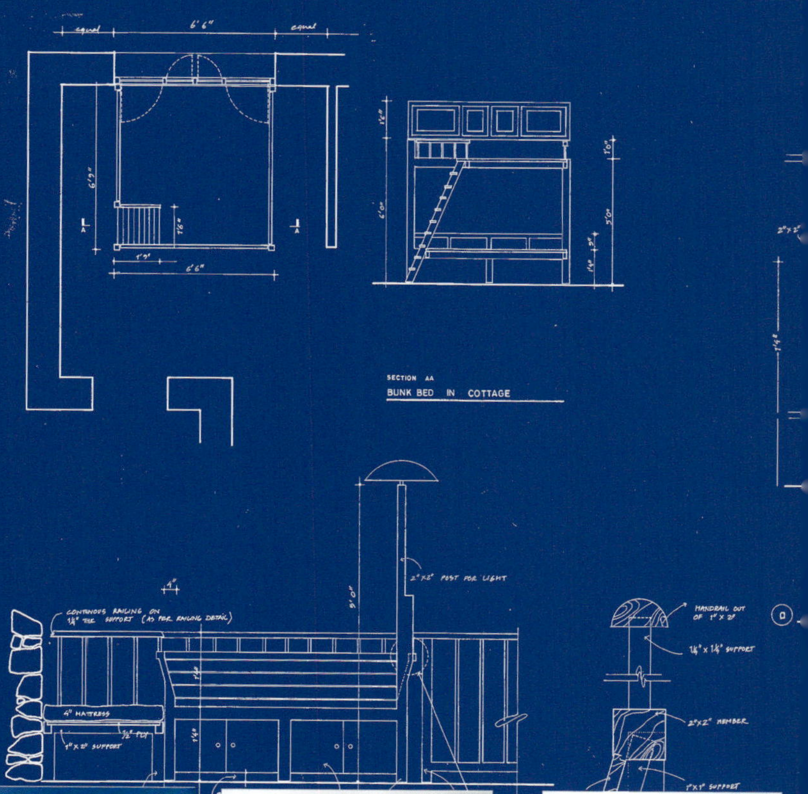

jumped, feet first, into the pool, with a splash that created a tidal wave for the benefit of the women watching coyly from the sidelines. The men sprayed water all around, the women shrieked. Water streaked their *saris* and skin; they struggled to keep their composure, imploring the men to stop the madness. Some of them approached the pool's edge offering the men plates of food. They were pulled

- **LEFT** Suitcase Hotel, watercolour, 2011
- **RIGHT** Game room, Charcoal on Paper, 2001

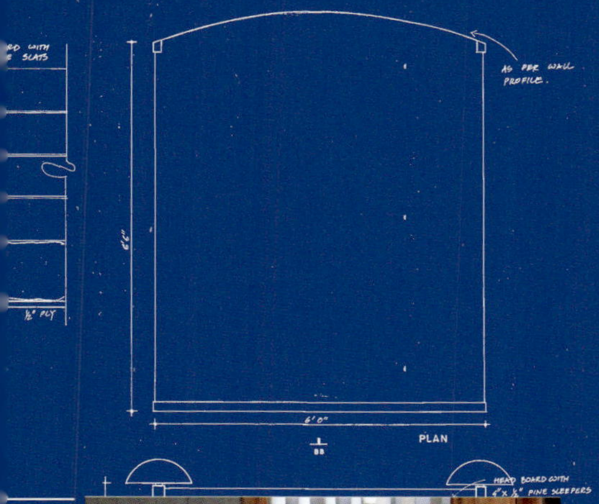

Furniture Details, Monolith Resort

■ Chess Hall, watercolour, 2004

into the water, fully clothed, till every member of the family was bobbing up and down in the pool. The water turned pink from tomato sauce, and half-eaten food was floating on the pool's surface.

The owner watched the scene with resignation. There was no tinge of anger or amusement to it. "Why can't we have more guests like the Germans?" he asked with a regretful expression on his face. "Why do they have to be like me?"

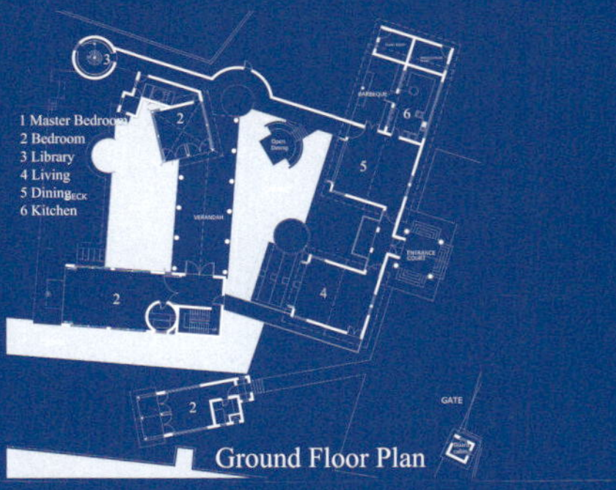

Ground Floor Plan

Lake House

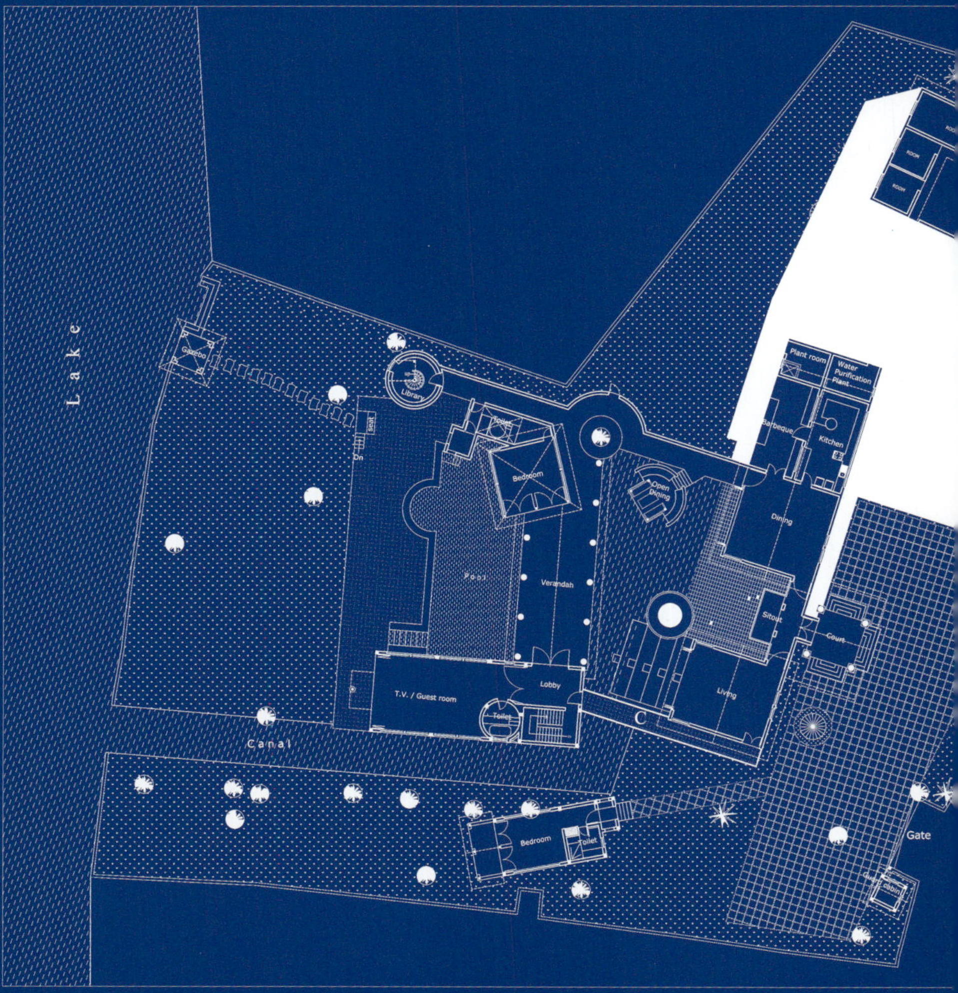

Among the many inland lakes of Kerala, the covered boats resting on the still waters conceal a life different from that of regular fishing routines. The frantic life of ordinary fishermen is seen in isolated pockets of the lakes where men desperate to get an early catch wade out, nets in hand, on single-oar boats into the shallow waters. The larger boats, however, covered in cane and thatch, often equipped with separate bedroom, kitchen and dining areas, are the real life-blood of the state's tourist activity. Across the site on Kumarakom Lake, the decadent life they promote appears and disappears in slow motion, a picture coming into focus and fading on the watery horizon.

The motionless lake imparts a similar sense of laziness to the boats and their short-term residents. The languid life of the watery landscape had appealed to the clients when they bought an acre of land on Kumarakom. The idea was that some day in the future, they would

■ Gateway of India in the Mountains, simulation, 2012

Site Plan, Lake House, Kumarakom, Kerala, 2009

retire and relax, sit back on their planter's chairs and watch life pass by. The result of the lake frontage and the view was an enlarged verandah that stretched the width of the site. Rooms gathered around it, bedrooms grouped in minor clusters fed on the edges of the verandah, yet they remained unlinked to each other. The verandah's openness was central to the plan. Free of building elements on its sides, its independence was assured by the presence of a pool in front and a canal behind.

Visibility across it was crucial though it was conceived as an island, and the rooms as boats leading to it. A visitor gets to the place in a series of layers that eventually connect to the roadside approach to the lake. The entrance presents a forbidding urban view—the long public face with living and dining, the lake entirely hidden. As you enter the house, the water is revealed, but only

■ Taj Mahal in a Wheat Field, simulation, 2012

through the frames of additional perspective and pictorial depth—first across a garden, then a canal, through the open verandah, its fronting pool and deck and to the lake beyond. The architecture of delayed gratification only enhances the value of the lake, and visually gives it greater distance. The desire to move towards it provokes the visitor to experience the middle ground that is constantly changing perspective and the distance to the water.

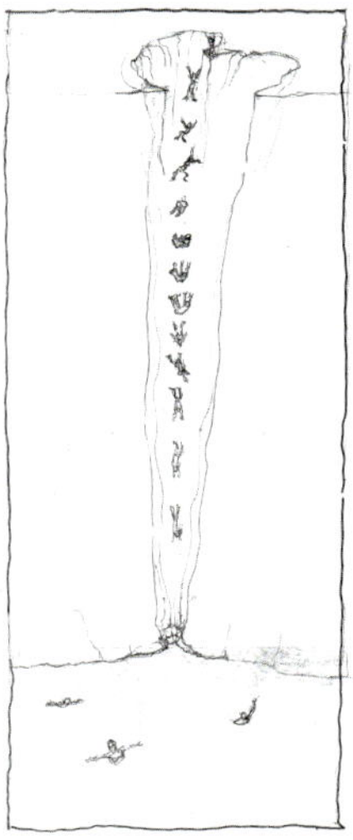

The filmed pictorial delay in the progression constructs an architectural disorientation where the framing building also becomes a participant in the deviation. The bedrooms, study and guest wing splay outwards, leading the viewer away from the original intention, and offering new perspectives on the site—aligning along the side canal, or engaging with a fishing pier. Each room moves away into its own independent landscape, but never strays far from the mothership of the veranda. I had begun the

■ River Fall, pencil on paper, 2011

Plan (top) and Interior, Lake House

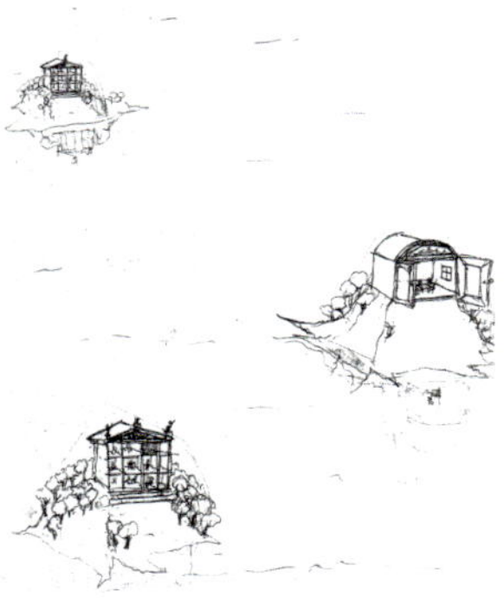

work from the perspective of the picturesque. In my mind's eye, long before the design began, the literal storyline had already been formed: this was the house on the lake.

People escape the city to be in a different surrounding like a mountain, lake, or beach. The building engaged with these in a detached, picturesque way. A limited, and limiting, architectural idea that was both conventional and professional, sanctioned by older stories about the vacation house in the same setting. I had failed to draw the story into a different imaginative plane and to see the lake as anything but a body of water with a picture-book surface. The architecture, however, was not just meant to display an engagement with nature, but to go a step further. The point of a building in such a location meant that it had to do both: present the physical situation in its design, and also do the things nature couldn't.

■ Island Building, pencil on paper, 2011

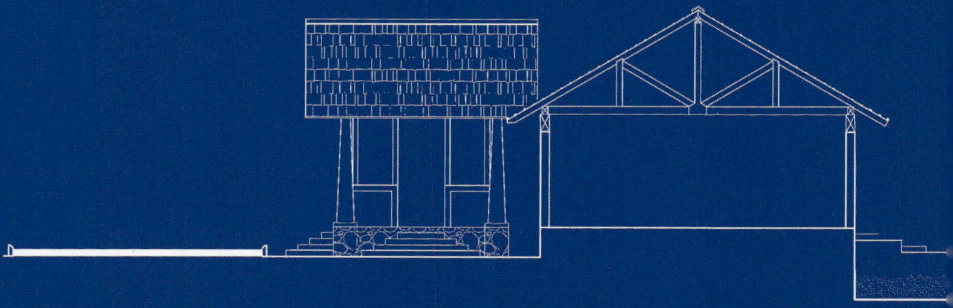

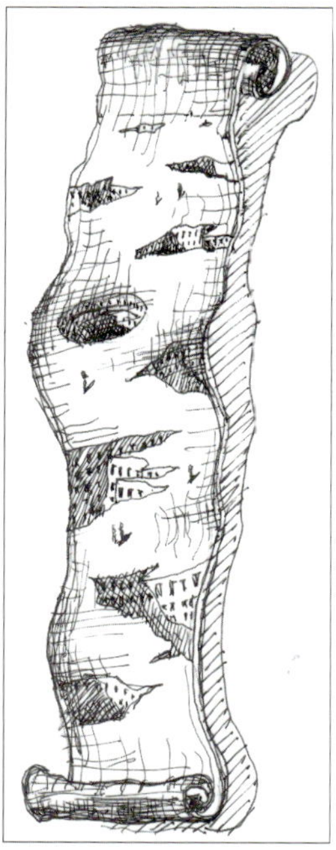

Architecture had to be a step better than nature, otherwise it made no sense constructing the building. In my attempt at a perfunctory visual coherence, I had failed the house its multitude of possibilities, and the landscape of other possible interpretations. On a clear winter day, I took a small boat out to the middle of the lake to survey the land. The shoreline, distant but outlined in a foggy silhouette, revealed little. Buildings withdrew into the green, their colours and sizes a smudge on the sight-line. The placid lake defined a muddy embankment, part earth, part rock, a gray line that rose up occasionally to define a building's silhouette. New structures stuck eagerly to the frontage, taking their seats as if for a ring-side view; the wooden jetty and stone church,

■ Scroll of Hollows, pen & ink, 2011

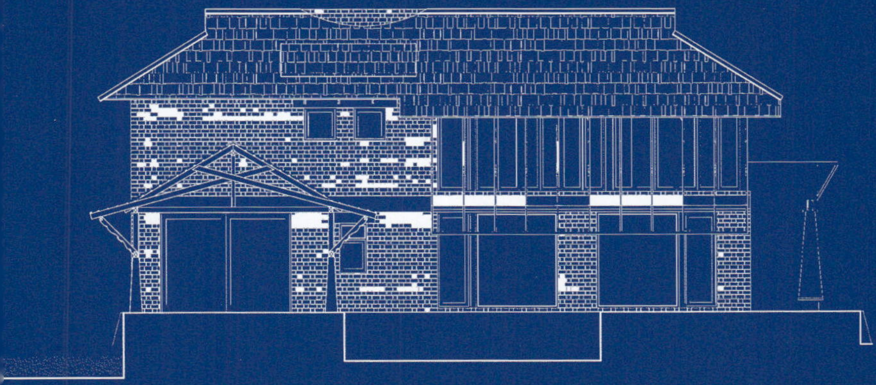

Interiors (top) and Sections (below), Lake House

faded and colourless, blended in. They watched the rest like grandparents resigned to a new indulgence.

I looked for the lake house in between the trees, distant from the larger hotels and the village of Kumarakom, but I could see only a dull brick red that disappeared into the retreating strata. Roland Barthes famously said that architecture's true value lay not just in the resolution of stated requirements, but also in the exploration of an impossibility. What is building if it doesn't ask the more difficult questions?

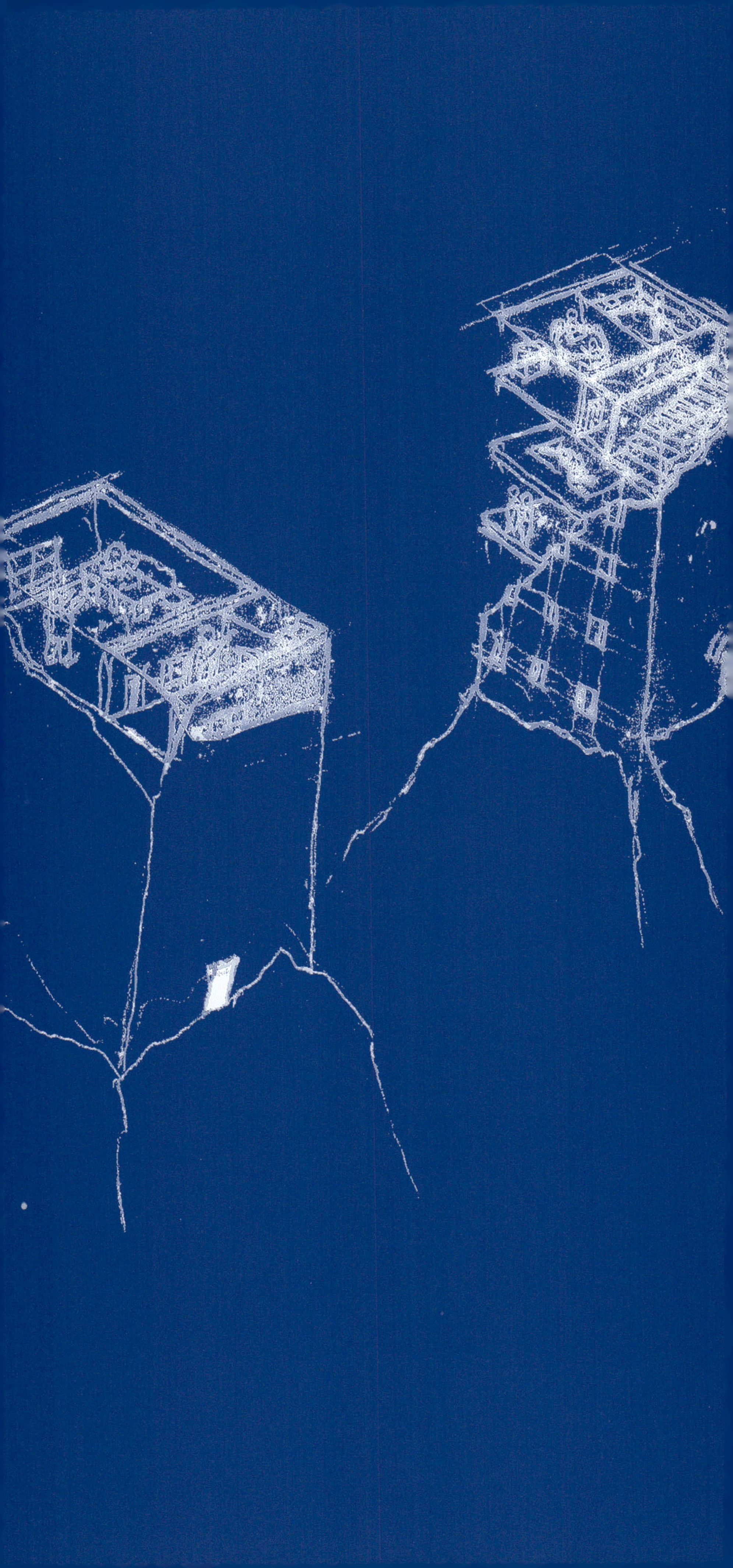

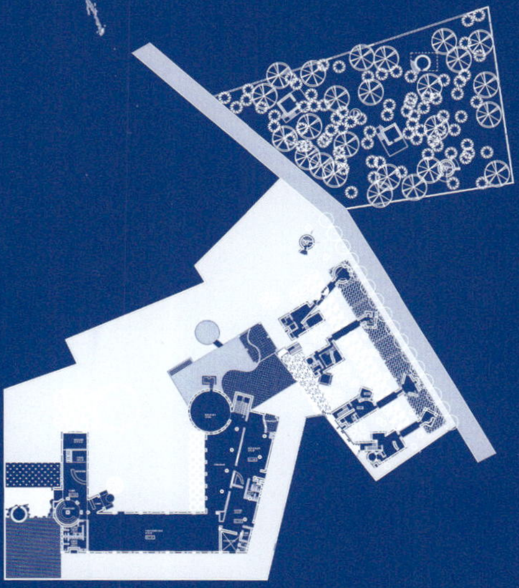

Lodge

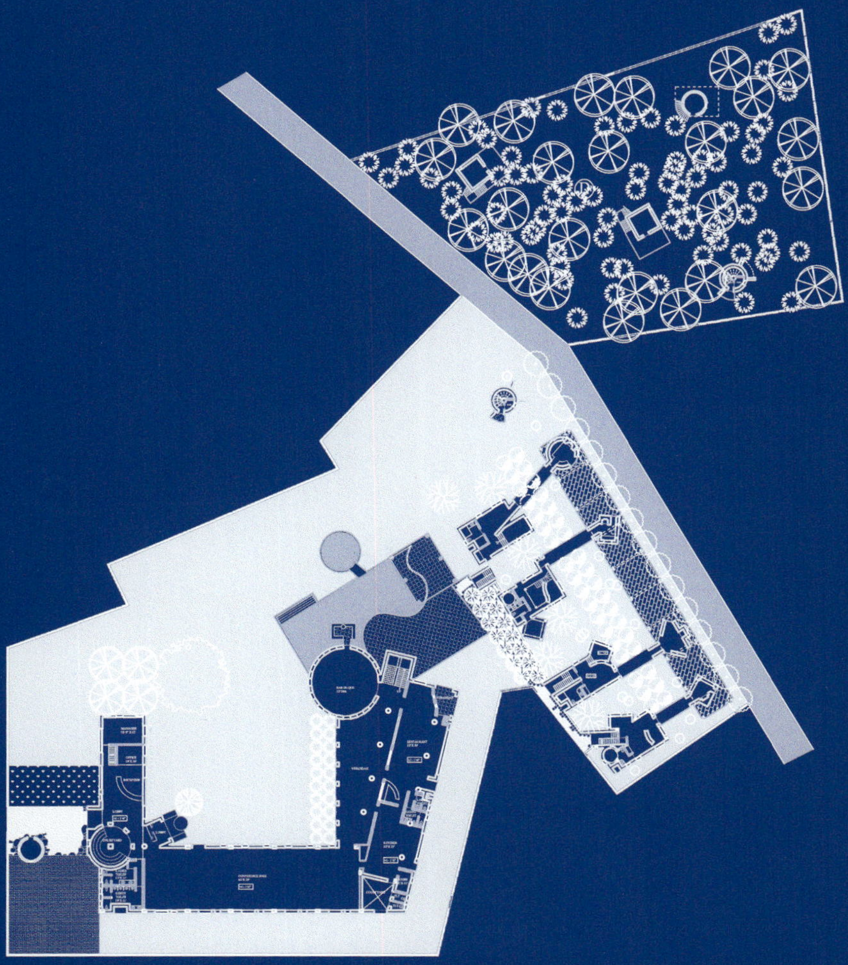

Plan (left) and views, Tree House Inn, Corbett Park, Uttarakhand, 2005

The forest as organic growth could never be conceived as a private entity. It was always larger than itself, always growing. The possibility of strict architectural control over its continually expanding entanglements and looming shadows drew building into benign relationships with its seemingly parasitic power. Architecture huddled in its shadows, scared and aloof, a bit unsure of its place. But there were multiple ways of engaging with it. The easiest was to stay outside of its organic gaze altogether and delineate a border between architecture and forest, the man-made and the organic, so the two could gaze fondly at each other without falling into each other's arms. Such a view only supports the architect's most basic fear: engagement.

■ Paradise 1, watercolour, 2011

This involves the desperate need to retain the building profile in an unchanging, unchallengeable future. It seemed the only way to

comprehend as well as state the difference between something entirely static and something that veers out of control. At the other extreme was the more risky task of overlap, the instinct to give in completely and allow a full-bodied encounter to take place. The building submitted wholly to envelopment. Alteration could become the centre piece of the architecture. The Corbett setting was the forest itself. Any construction then could only be made in a clearing. A small portion of green was hacked for the building to fit into its outline. The plan resisted the urge to die a slow death from its precise geometry and function. Instead it fulfilled the demands in a prosaic division into three parts; and a street frontage that allowed large groups to mingle in the hallway and the lawn.

Families staying in the suites stuck to the middle passages of pool and

■ Paradise 2, watercolour, 2011

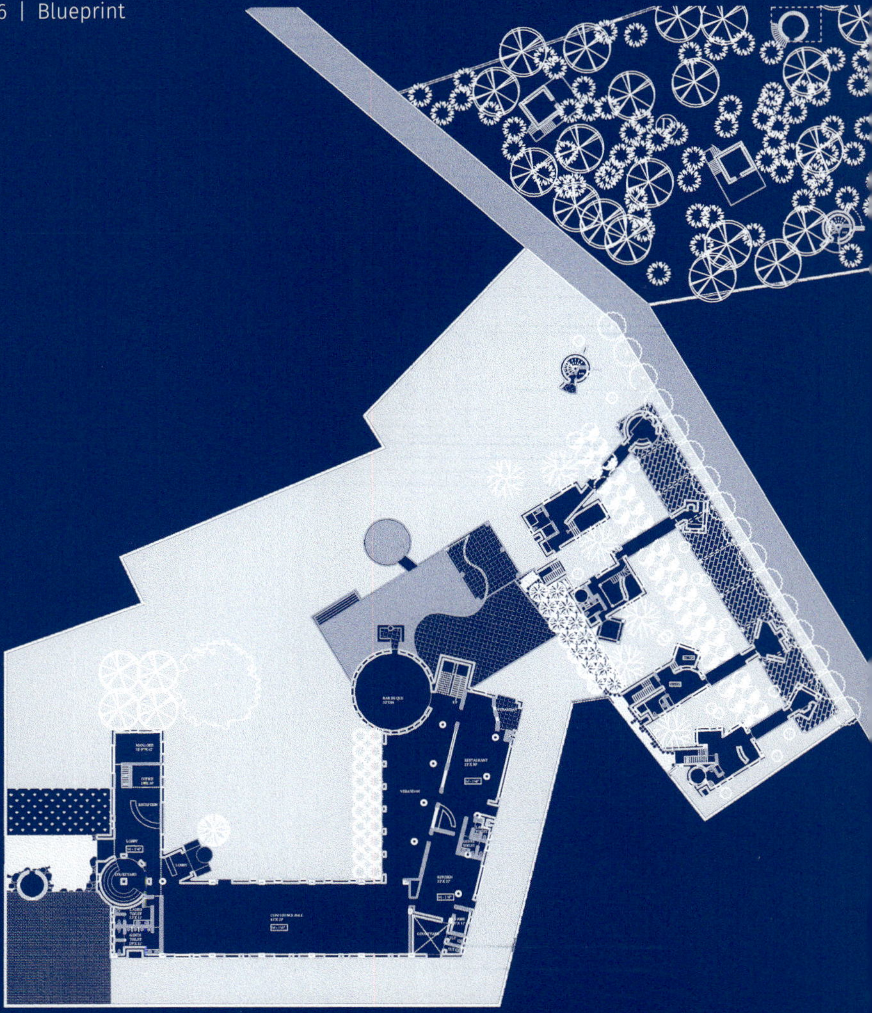

Details, Tree House Inn

restaurant, and the more seasoned traveller who sought the isolation of the forest chose the rear. The hotel was like a book, the deeper you delved into the storyline, the more likely you were to be rewarded by its passages. Over time the green was sure to take over completely. The bedrooms were built in isolation, near the main hotel, but the living rooms were constructed at the end of narrow passages within the forest grove. If part of the structure remained safely isolated, part of it was given to the forest as an offering. Change it, eat into it like into a ruin, run your tendrils into the walls, break the building, infiltrate it, cut it down to size...

The process of atrophy and willed change was slow like the enveloping dusk on a long summer day. You never know the divide between light and dark on such a day till you suddenly awaken to its reality. When architecture becomes a record of change, it seems to reflect the true nature of life itself. Similarly, in the mountain huts of Sikkim and Kumaon, no boundary existed. Buildings individually selected their tree and took root alongside it. Each distanced itself from architecture and sought a more integral role with the forest.

This was an imaginary role of two divergent things; a world of precise geometry, and another whose future had no recognizable form.

This was contradictory to the training I had received, but it seemed that a place possessed was far more relevant than one abandoned. The continually enveloping nature of the forest makes it harder to predict the future outcome of any architecture. The building's depiction of natural law as natural sensation was the unwritten requirement of architecture. The architect could be forgiven for the leaks in the roof, but never for denying its residents the expectation of celestial phenomena. The pleasure of sensory perception persists, and for me, the desperate scholastic and disturbingly intellectual path to resolving buildings is a loss for the

■ Paradise 3, watercolour, 2011

Magic Mountain Resort (Unbuilt), Nainital, Uttarakhand, 2004

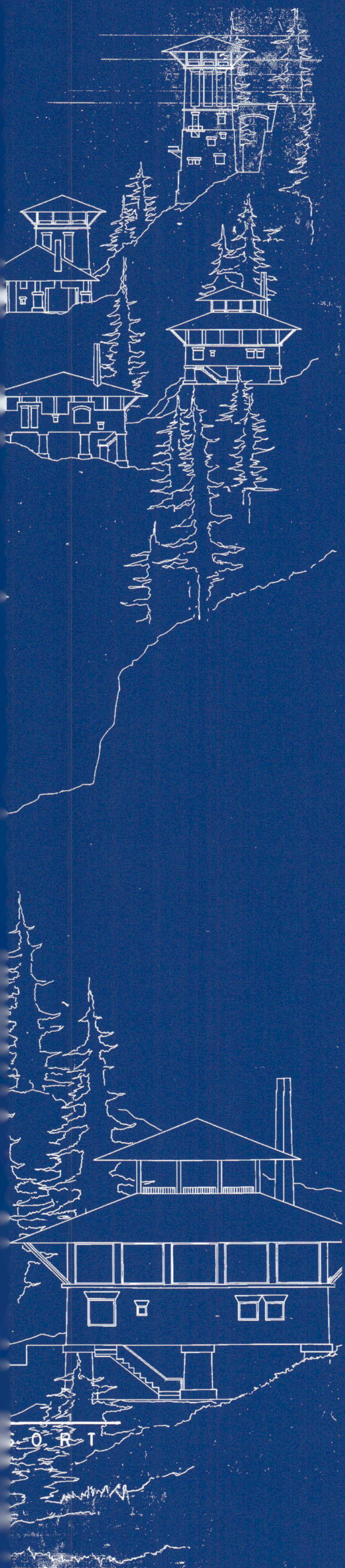
O R T

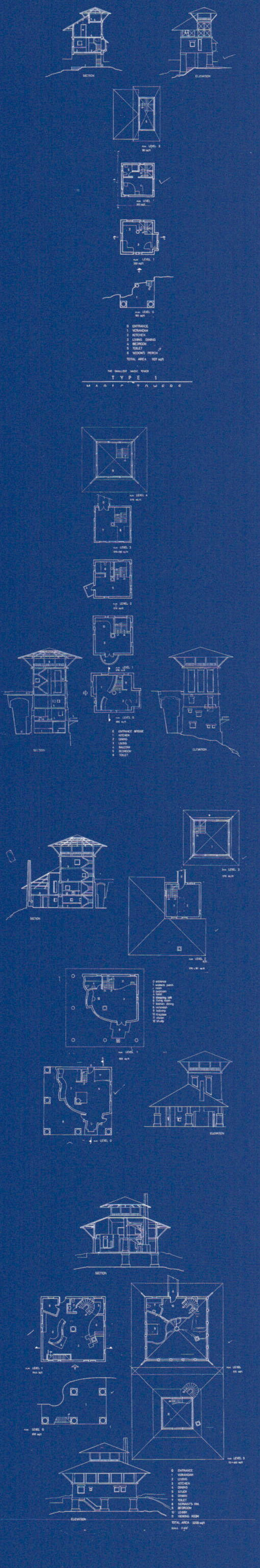
SECTION
ELEVATION
LEVEL 1
LEVEL 0
0 ENTRANCE
1 VERANDAH
2 KITCHEN
3 LIVING DINING
4 BEDROOM
5 TOILET
6 WIDOW'S PERCH
TOTAL AREA 1107 sqft
THE SMALLEST MAGIC TOWER
TYPE 1
MAGIC TOWERS

Tree House, Tree House Inn

profession itself. Not merely the visible and tactile sensations within, but the subtler traces of place and position. I began to notice how variations in the growth of vegetation in this place caused palpable shifts in architectural perceptions. There was no constant, only starkly divergent moods etched on the looming wilderness. At first, it grew as nimble shrubbery, a mild decorative green framing the new construction; a few months later, it became a generous, but skeletal, treeline. Within a year however, it assumed monumental proportions; thick branches loomed overhead, keeping the sunlight to themselves.

Eventually, the design's rectilinear geometry was subsumed by it. After a while, there was no struggle for supremacy between the two. The buildings huddled in defense, knowing that the battle was already lost, or won. It took a full five years for the architecture to be engulfed completely. I went there after the fifth monsoon to find that the masonry was shrouded in complete darkness; the parasitic growth gnawed and nibbled at the building's surface, trying to find a way in. Large sheets of plate glass were covered in tendrils; even at high noon, only a shifting patchwork of light was available as a

Forest House, Unbuilt, 2017

reminder of a brilliant summer day. Once the landscape had completely obliterated the architecture was there any reason to hope for success? A few months later I returned to find the owner had axed the forest to the ground.

When does a building lose its formal description as a physical object and become a phenomenon itself? The great effort of constructing walls and roofs is a practical denial of its spiritual allure. What would the forest lodge be without the forest? The exposed structure looked like a wreck.

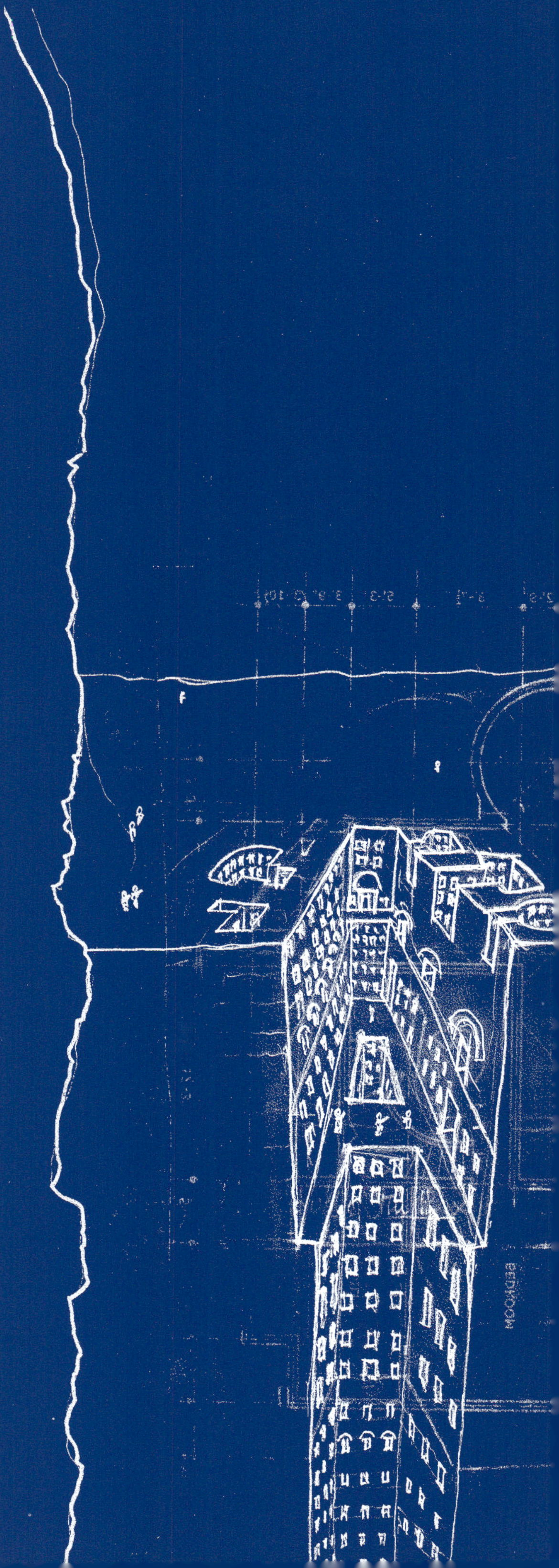

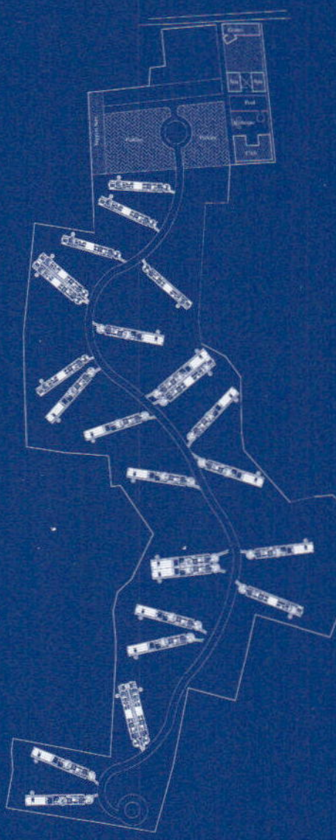

Floor Plan
House Type 1

Subterranean House

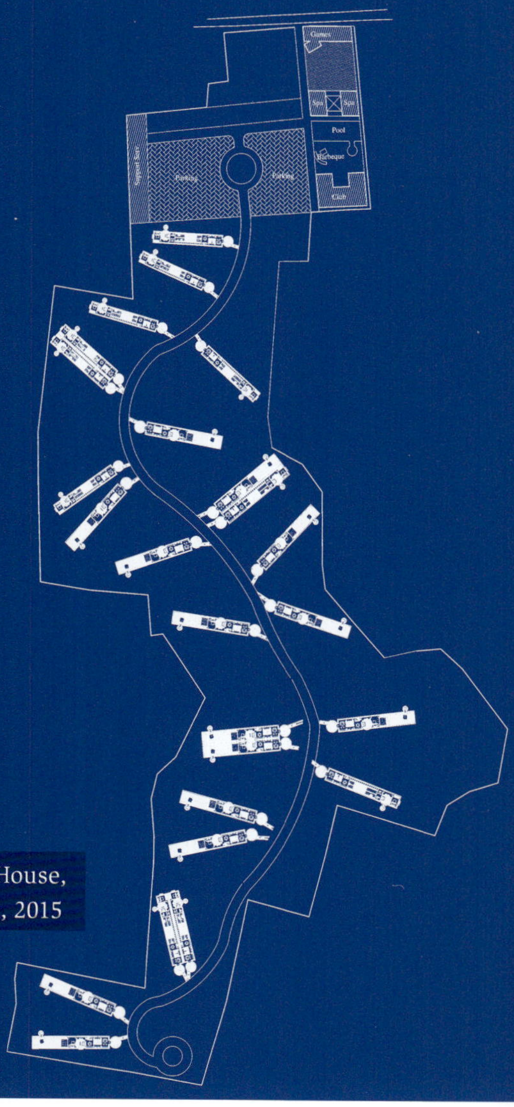

Site Plan, Subterranean Farm House, (Unbuilt) Shivpura, Rajasthan, 2015

It is hard to dispel the myths and misinformation associated with underground living. It is believed that the underground is unable to sustain life and that it is a detriment to the natural way of things. Many of these beliefs are patently false. Absence of light and air is itself enough to relegate the underground to the uninhabitable in people's minds. Basements and their association with parking garages or storage space is another stumbling block. The fact that the underground usually houses the innards of a building, the mechanics of air conditioners, compressors, home and water heaters, is another. In the course of the development of the Indian city, virtually all construction has been a phenomenon defined by ground surface. Even movement across it has been a ground-level experience.

Across road or sidewalk, on the ground including ground-floor entrances and lobbies, the connection between city

■ Underground Parking, watercolour, 2014

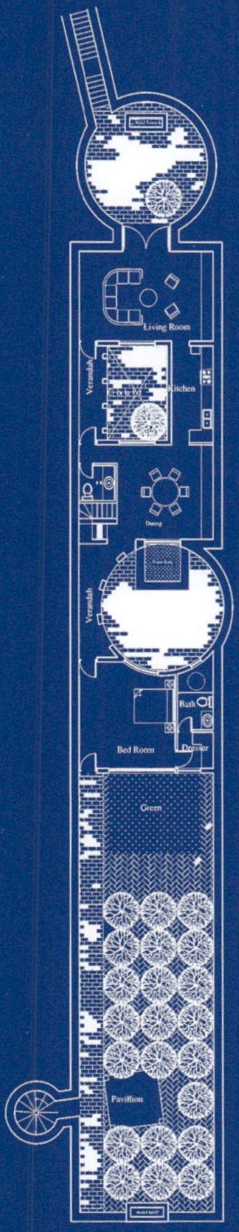

Floor Plan
House Type 1

Floor Plan
House Type 2

residents and their engagement with architecture has been a surface-level one. For the first time, the Indian Metro rail system has re-ordered the experience into another dimension. The underground and the above ground have propelled the daily sightline to a new and unsettling direction. Ingress and the movement of large numbers of people in the Indian city is a cataclysmic experience. An absence of public culture contaminates every public act here with uncertainty and perpetual despair. Boarding a bus or a train with others, parking a car in a lot, entering a public lift, accessing a subway entrance, or crossing a street, are all riddled with the prospect of unnecessary assault. It is as if the public is still not invested in a society that is shaped by family values alone, and everything outside the home is a battle.

Certainly in a city short of ground space, everyday confrontations are bound to be vigorous and often severe, leaving little room for courtesy. This is itself reason to consider the possibilities of moving away from the ground level altogether. Up in the air, or

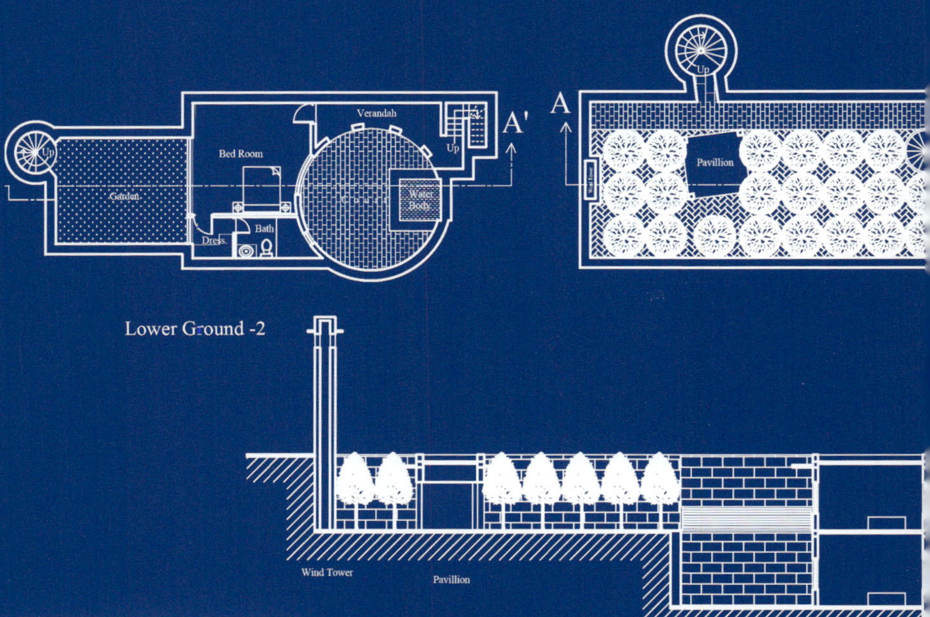

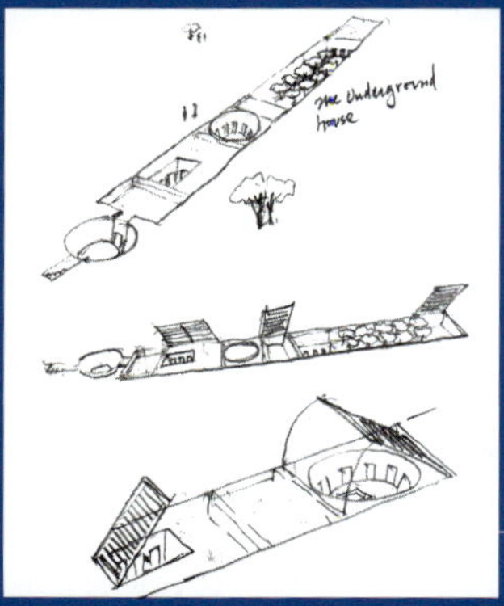

Plan (top) and section (above), Subterranean House

underground are good options. An engagement with the levels above or below is not just unusual, and it also provokes the viewer into a more comprehensive realization of the third dimension. It feels as if the dense earth below, and the rarefied sky above, are suddenly open for architectural discovery. Sadly this discovery is yet to be made by architects and architecture.

Any attempt to build within the earth or project space into the sky was a rallying point away from the familiar and a journey into an altered geography. The break from tradition, to recast the order of existing things was of value if it grasped the physics of its new mooring. The departure from conventional ground to a fresh imbalance. Unlike the skyward thrust which enveloped existing atmospheric space, the subterranean created

■ **ABOVE** Subway Entrance, simulation, 2012
■ **BELOW** Subway Entrance, simulation, 2012

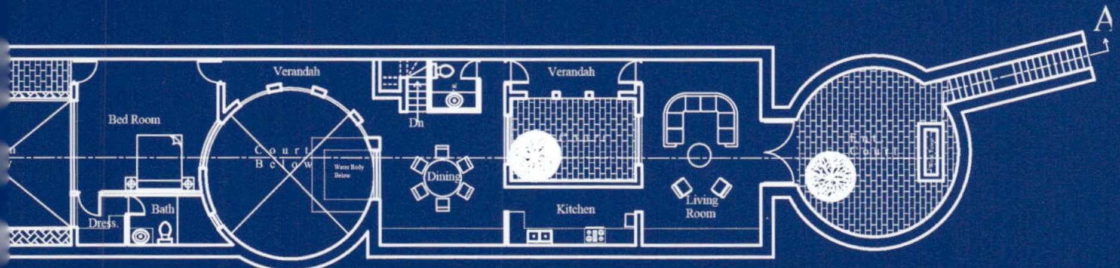

Lower Ground -1

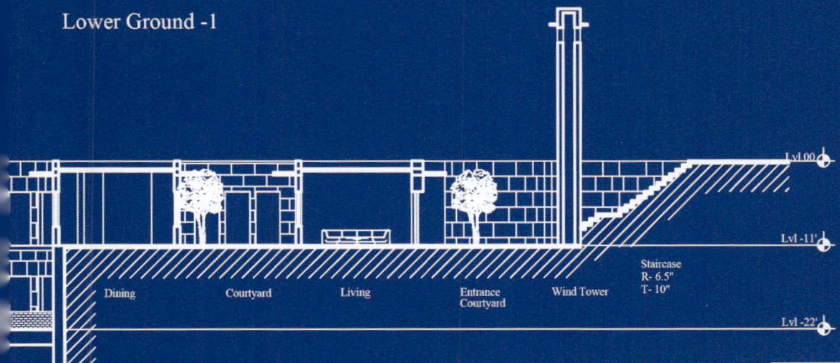

space out of matter. Is it a wonder then that sculpture despises architecture for its easy, selective formulation of space?

In a building below the ground, you intuitively begin to feel the great weight of the structure itself; the floors above increase the density, the framework of the concrete oppresses as does the pressure of the earth itself, the soil retained behind the thick stone walls is ready to compress you. By hewing the house out of the earth, it becomes a piece of nature itself that is physically bound to the soil and rock. In the geology below, the burrowing increases the sense of harbouring, and the buttressing pushes against the weight of the earth as if guarding against physical harm.

The underground house tells its own story. For a long time, architects have promoted subterranean structures for

■ Subway Entrance, simulation, 2012

■ Earth Apartments, watercolour, 2011

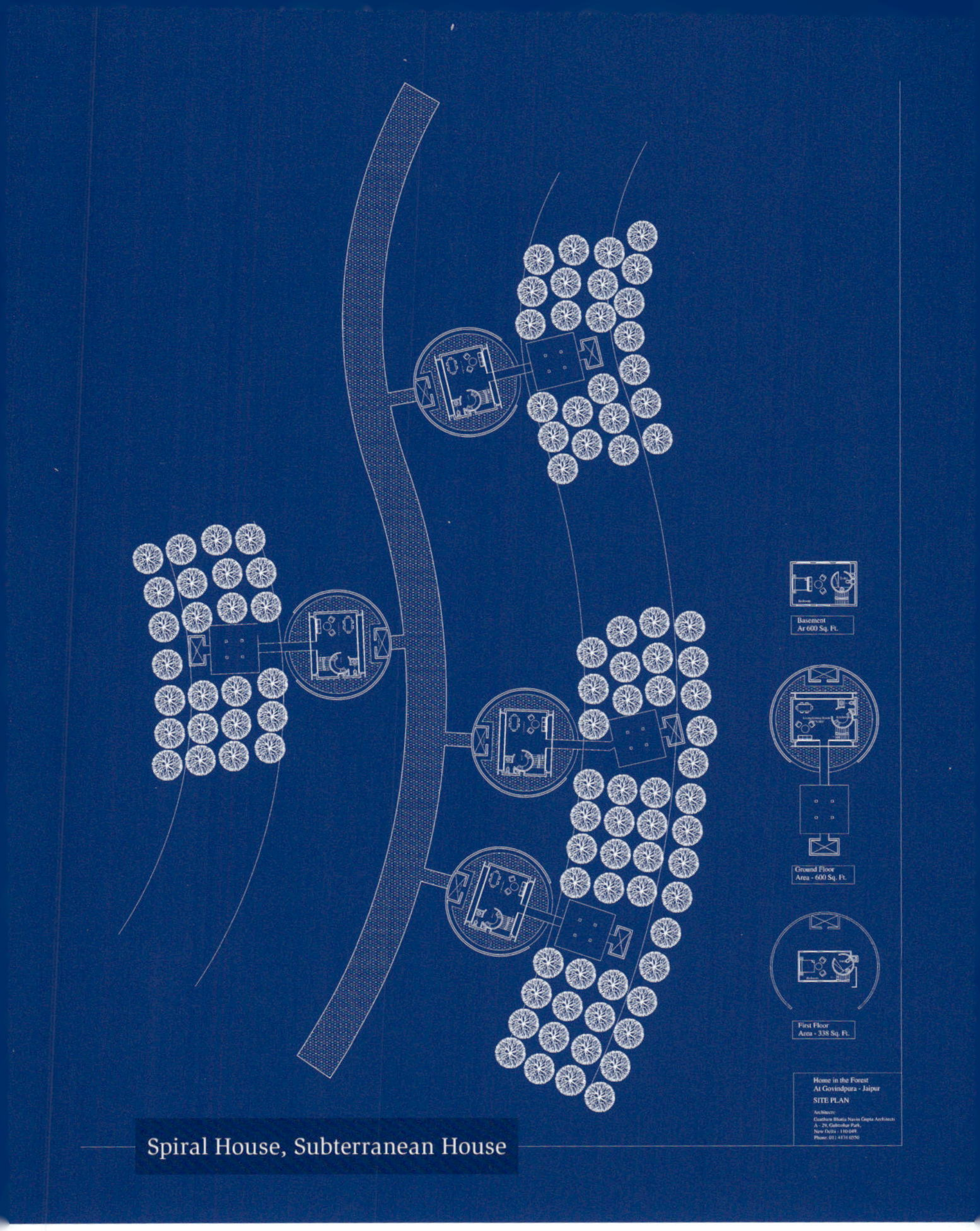

Spiral House, Subterranean House

environmental reasons. Over the years a great deal of convenient phraseology has cluttered their construction: energy efficiency, natural insulation, resistance to surface weather conditions, eco-friendliness, renewable and low-energy consumption. While all of this is true, the architectural reasoning is too often defeated by the incessant harping on ecology.

The spatial characteristics of the structure itself, its connection with the ground surface, the creation of open spaces—courtyards and gardens below—clearly affects the psychology of the inhabitant. How that density will psychologically influence people is hard to say. But there is a difference between living just below the surface and deep inside it. Wherever you happen to be, the physical and sensory qualities of the underground are themselves diverse. Distinctions in temperature, acoustics, the

■ Subway Entrance, simulation, 2012

Section AA'

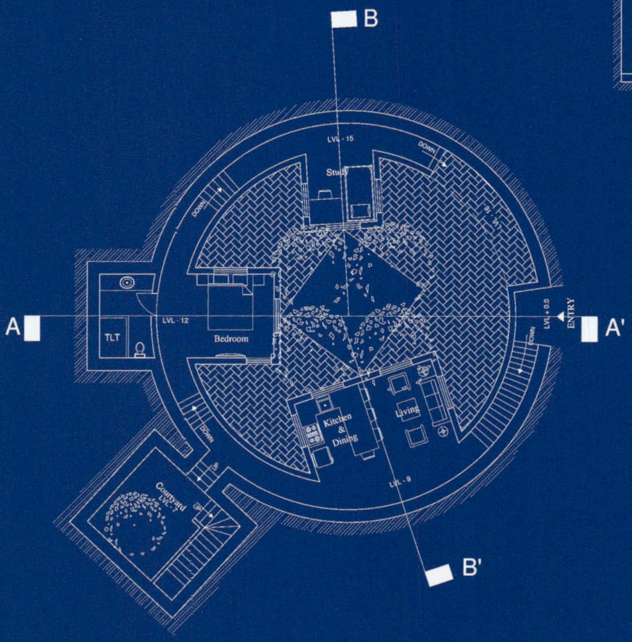

Plan

Spiral House, Subterranean House

Areas :	sq ft
Drawing, dining, kitchen	202.6
Bedroom	128.4
Toilet	112.6
Study	88
Circulation	390
Total	921.6

The Spiral House
At Govindpura - Jaipur
Option 3

Architects:
Gautam Bhatia Navin Gupta Architects
A - 29, Gulmohar Park,
New Delhi - 110 049.
Phone: 011 4174 0550

quality of light entering from above, the insulating levels of the earth itself, all these are felt and easily sensed as the depth changes.

I had lived for too long in a dark, damp, unlit basement to ever wish the underground house on anyone. So the exercise began as a hollowing out that set out to establish first, a visible and approachable connection to the ground, and second, to ensure enough open ground space at varying depths of the underground. Down below the house fragmented, creating wide swathes of open courts and gardens—both essential to make life possible underground. The only way to achieve the freedom to create the space within which the house spreads was to consider the house not below ground but its opposite; on top of a hill.

Openness became relevant only when it was without constraints and physical barriers as if the house was open to the weather and the wind, the rain and the sun. Its exposure was the only guide to its design. To begin with, every room disparaged the gloom of the underground and sought the open horizon. In keeping with this,

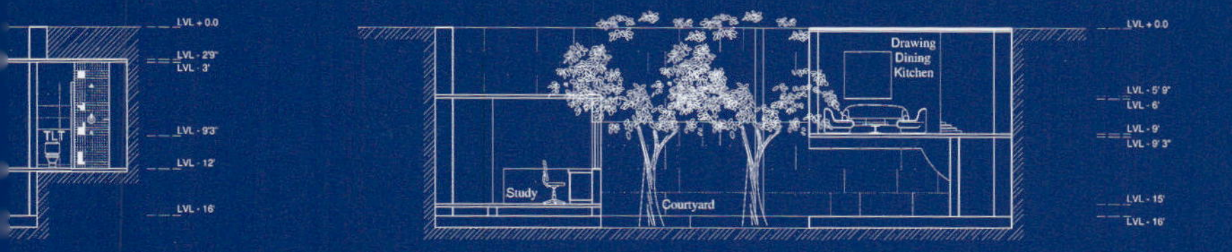

Section BB'

all the ground-level places—the garden, the terrace, extensive patches of green and intimate enclosures of courtyards—crept below the ground and attached themselves firmly to each room. Every room became a breathing, living thing, entirely unaware that it stood several storeys below the earth. The room's awareness of the outdoors was also the resident's awareness of it—an understanding that comes from a careful manipulation and apportioning between exposure and enclosure.

Wherever possible the roof disappeared and revealed a landscape sculpted into an underground form. The landscape was the essential, unclaimed territory that made life possible below the surface—the "wasteland", like the breadth of the pressurized bubble between a spacecraft and the emptiness it orbits in. The sun enters the deep wells of courts and gardens, perhaps a little later in the day than it would in a surface house; in protected seclusion, it casts a long shadow and leaves the house earlier than usual, but to everyone inside it, the graded light is a critical reminder of the day's passage. Every element in the house assumes a different cast that is invariably linked to its relationship with the ground. Because the house is not linked to the surface, it luckily misses the sights and sounds of the ground level. No car horns, no screech of traffic, no distant voices or dust cloud raised by trucks on dirt tracks.

Inside, the acoustics of the quiet amplify—and because the outside world is missing—every incident, every physical occurrence resounds with greater intensity. Once the social networks of the outside disappear, the resident becomes acutely aware of the home, its map and orientation, the people around him, his own actions and the sound of his own breathing. The stimulation of the underground is then its very isolation, and the resulting concentration enables you to observe life differently. When you walk down the staircase, from ground to underground, the light changes with every step and causes a shift in your awareness. It is not merely a transit between two floors; the stair is a means to a new psychic state.

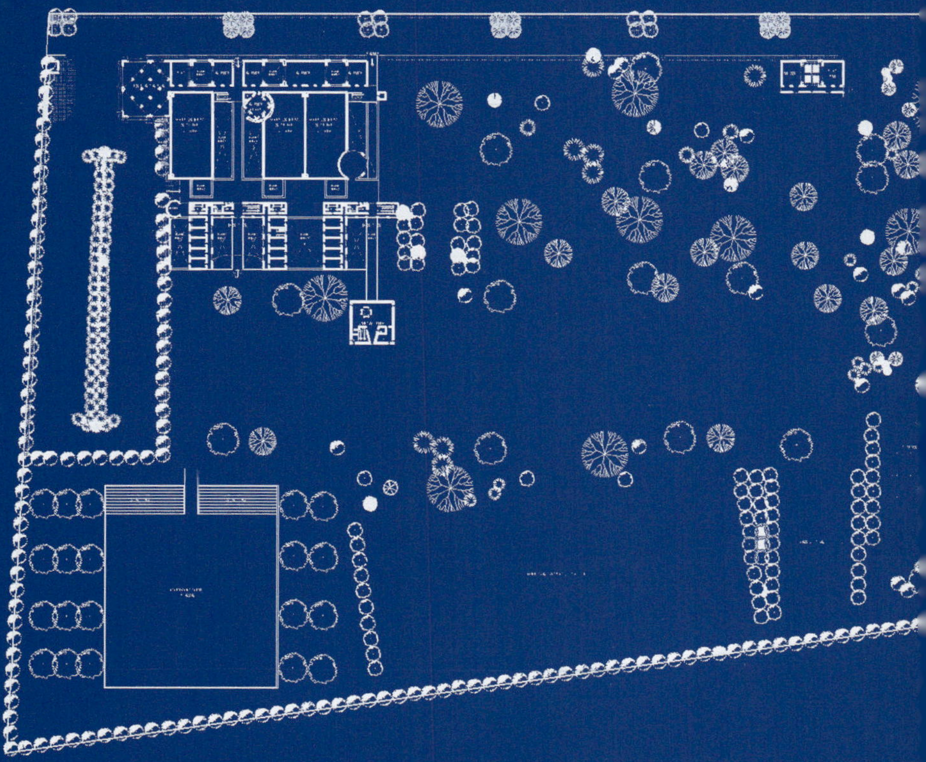

GROUND FLOOR AT + 1.2 M 1:400

The quality of islolation magnifies the silence of the underground as does the depth and the essential solitude that comes from the absence of a neighbourhood. However close underground houses are to each other, their nearness is never felt. But the disconnection with the surface affords the house a more engaging relationship with the sky, a setup that is at once intimate and cosmic.

Devoid of the tireless clamour of surface sight and sounds, the small courtyard of the house I built was open only to the stars. When you entered the house, the descent was first a descent into darkness, and into the hope that lies in the unknown. I saw it as a form of sensory drowning where the eye was no longer the trusted guide and therefore the expectation of experiencing something different was even greater. The intemperance too often came with the wish for extremes in which the engulfing hold of the surrounding earth let you remain alone.

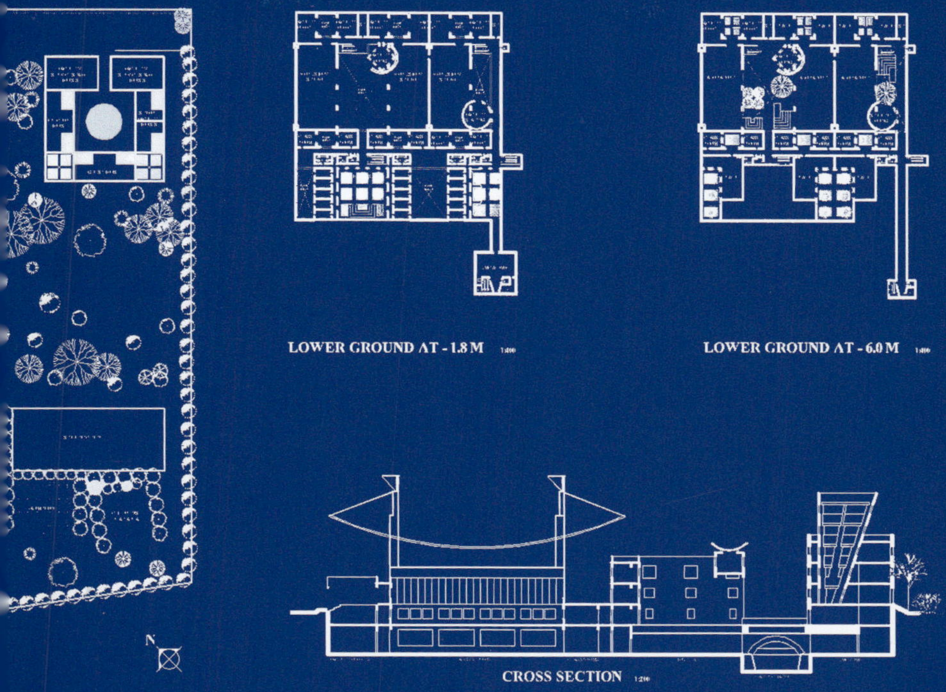

National Institute of Design (Competition entry) Gandhinagar, Gujarat, 2004

An idea that is much more difficult to execute in a collective space, the workplace for the National Institute of Design (NID) campus was thus a record of that collective institutional isolation. It was meant to provide a more deliberate programmed canvas for conceiving, thinking, making—all within the warm glow of one's own initiative; a space to cultivate an intimate relationship between the mind, the hand and the object one was making. Visual and acoustic relief from the reality of life on the surface would enforce a private solitude that could resurrect old thoughts, or drive a person mad. After all, the eventual impact of the underground lies in perception and interpretation—a confining prison with the contradictory message of liberation. Architecture's most formidable challenge was to provide both exposures.

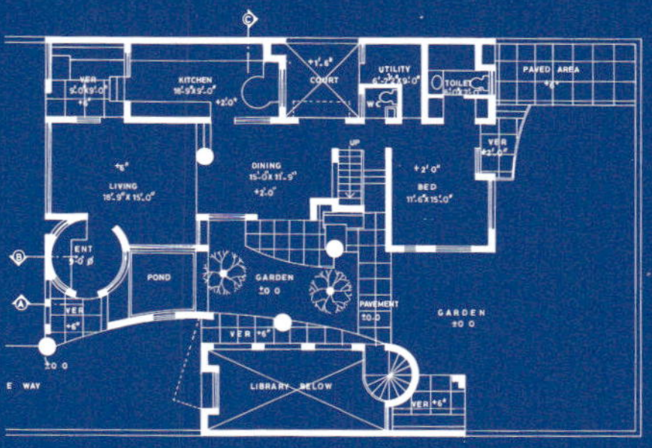

Ground floor plan

Adobe

Campus Plan, Nambikkai Foundation, Palavoor, Tamilnadu, 1991

The oil crisis was a significant prick of conscience that left the Western world rudderless and in self-doubt. When thirty-foot-long cars came to a grinding halt on the highways, the American idea of architectural space found itself in jeopardy. No longer a matter of access to abundant fossil fuels, the cavernous space of building was in inexorable decline. Non-insulated walls, vast stretches of glass, black-top heat radiating parking lots, air-conditioning tonnage and design that scoffed at natural ventilation, the history of the profession was a full throttle proclamation of support for the oil industry. Without a hint of unease, the architect and planner had gone on a spending spree, giving visibility to their exaggerated enterprise.

The spreading city, the sprawl of bloated buildings, spaghetti formations of roads and highways, architecture was in constant denial of its escalating relationship with energy and excess. The sightline of sprawl and exaggerated materialism was part Roman splendour, part Indian picnic. The thrill in consuming within a foreshortened time and leaving the remains of the feast behind.

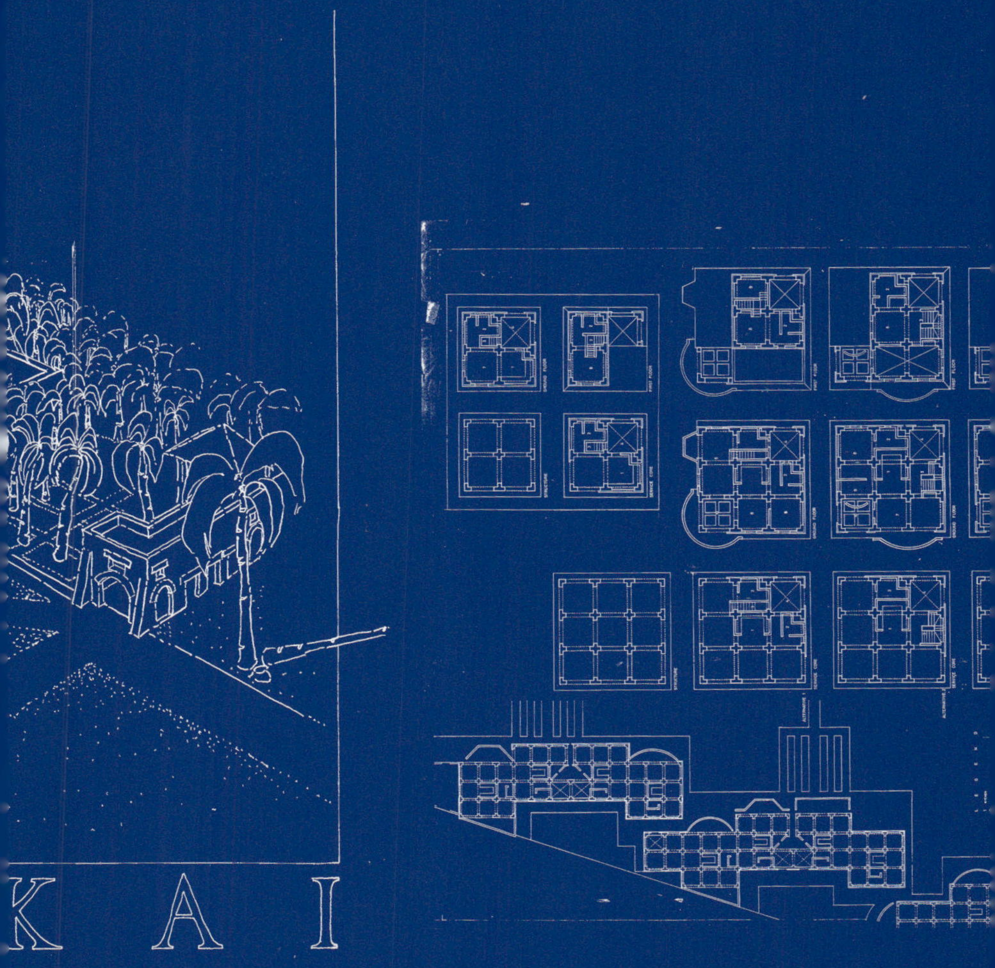

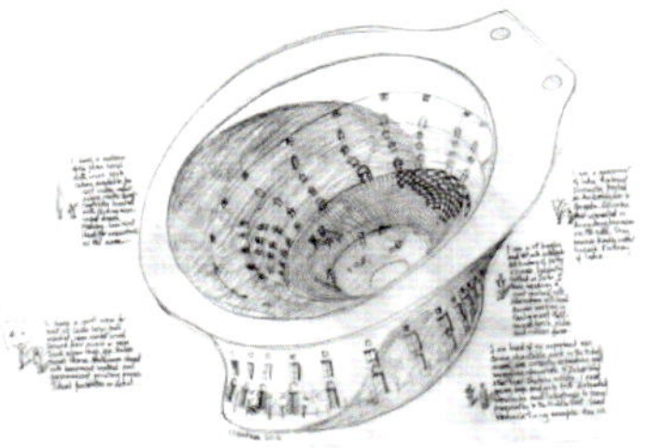

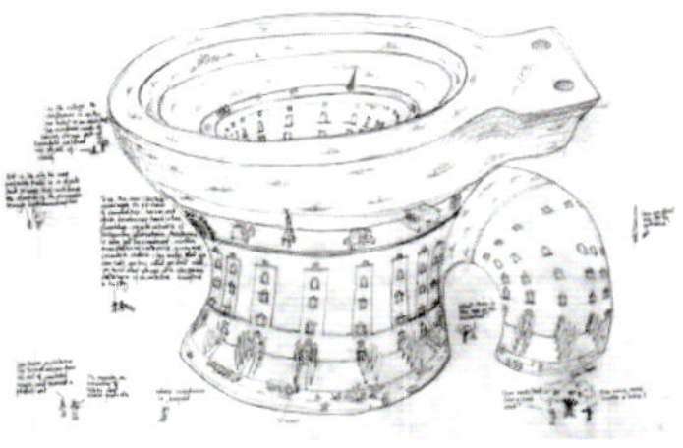

In the cannons of hallowed architectural thought, these new memorials were not the sites of ordinary routine, but expensive retreats made as masterful afterthought. The Barcelona Pavilion, Fallingwater, Villa Savoye—all replacements for the homes of the Vanderbilts, the Astors, Hadrian and Nero. The unfortunate history of affluence was merely a representation of excess and style.

It was in the nature of conquest to use architecture to betray a singular mistrust for the rooted life, and establish these expensive camp grounds. The vacation house was the most potent symbol of architecture, but also the most attractive sign of its failure as an instrument of building settlements. To sustain life

■ **ABOVE** Falling Water, pencil on paper, 2011
■ **BELOW** Falling water, pencil on paper, 2011

Institutional Building, Nambikkai Foundation

over the long term was part of the unwritten oath of architecture. Into it were woven in the subtexts of culture and community. The modern ideal of excessive mobility was derived from the changing view of citizenship. Home was everywhere; where work was, across the street, or beyond national boundaries. Its place as a symbol of family and the resting place of generations had altered in space and time. Without guardianship, the place could hardly be expected to develop roots. Without the home as a microcosm of the biosphere, its sustainability was suspect. And without a settled view, even architecture was in doubt. It had forgotten its own organic ancestry, simpler formulas and applications.

A question about keeping a building cool in the hot season had appeared in a university course that I once took. The course was titled, "Advanced Thermal Comfort". Potential architects like me and my fellow students were

■ Earth Homes, watercolour, 2011

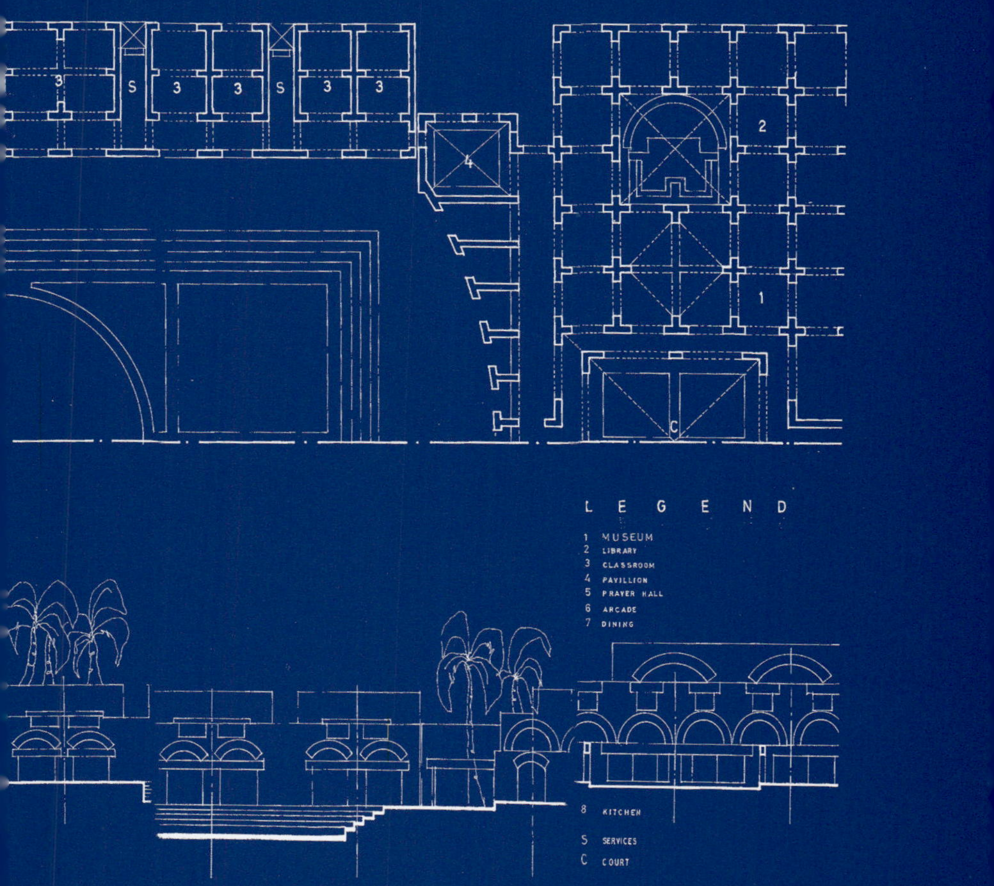

in eager pursuit of applicable ideas regarding comfort. Moreover, since this was an advanced course, it was assumed that we already knew about the basic and intermediate levels of comfort and were searching for sophistication. We wanted mechanical devices that would cool, heat, humidify and pressurize buildings—devices that could be operated by buttons that were conceived by astrophysicists and nuclear scientists after years of testing in germ-proof laboratories. They also had to be produced by a difficult, expensive and laborious industrial process.

We wanted contraptions of sophistication whose mere mention would leave the client dumbfounded. The course and our instructor seemed just right for such critical inquiry. The teacher was a respected Israeli engineer. On the first day of class, he said, "The most effective device for cooling is the rolled blind on a rope

■ Earth Homes, pen and ink, 2011

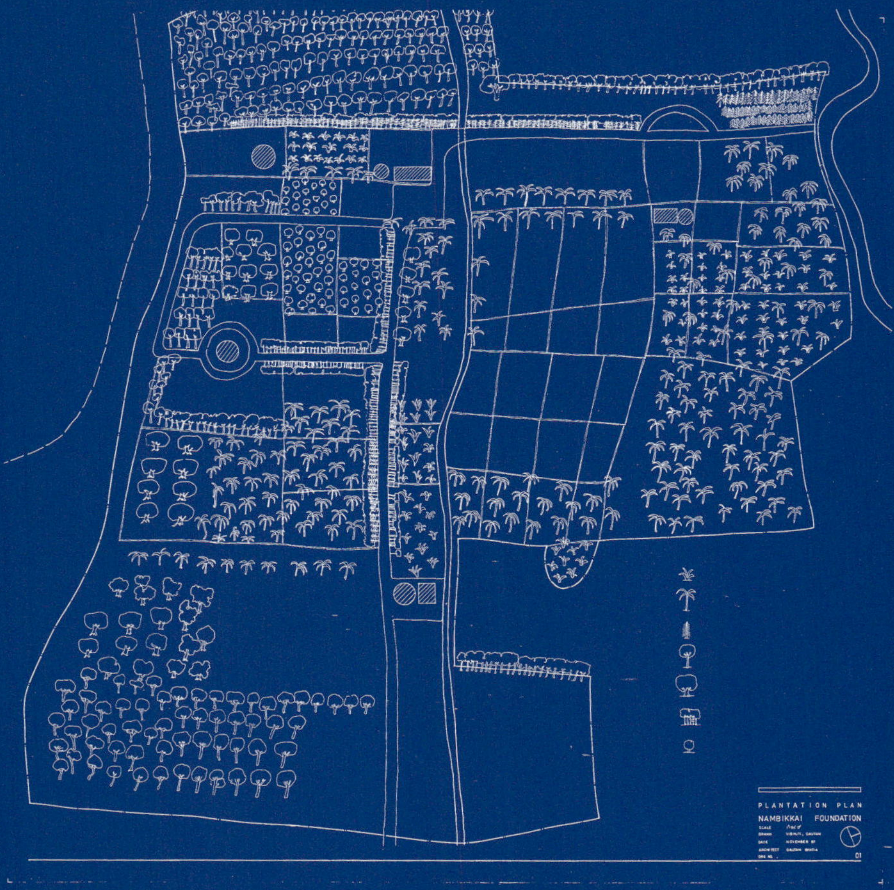

Planting Plan, Nambikkai Foundation

pulley. It has been in use for 700 years in virtually every tropical country to shield windows from the sun. If you want the building to be even cooler, just use a lime wash and paint the walls and the roof white."

The natural way to heat water is to pour into a black dish and expose its surface to the sun. In winter the south wall of a house should be painted a dark shade to absorb the sun's heat. "In any case," he continued, "you must wear warm socks and a sweater if you need additional warmth." We sat back aghast. This was a Harvard professor and an engineer from a country that had changed the

Uses of wood, pencil on paper, 2001

perception of the desert as a dry, fallow place to being one of fertility and perennial orange groves, a man with 40 years of building experience and four books on the subject to his credit. The real lesson of the day was in his outright rejection of useless technology—to dump what may be achieved in the future by some mechanical, electrical, or electronic device. To understand what could be done easily and quickly by engaging human labour and common sense.

Solar buildings that aligned correctly with the path of the sun made more sense than those that shifted on elaborate electronic solar trackers. Water distributed by the forces of gravity was preferred over any mechanical pumping system. Architecture based on smaller initiatives, intent on local situations and resources called for no proclamation. Much of it exists without public acclaim. In desert huts designed to keep out the hot winds, in urban houses that harvest monsoon rain water from their own roofs and store it under their courtyards, in buildings that use wind towers to cool their insides, the instances are far too many to recount. But if, as in the past, architectural problems are approached in direct, practical and responsible ways, instead of using superfluous theory and abstraction and futuristic technology-based solutions, there are ideas worth examining.

In this context, Russian writer Leo Tolstoy once asked, “How much land does a man need?” American architect Buckminster Fuller asked a century later, “How much does your house weigh?” Both questions were intrinsically tied to the environmental logic of limited resource and land. And both came well before the modern ecological crisis hit us. Yet so complex is the measure of ecology when applied to building that the architect’s logic is often prone to over-simplification. The complexity draws not just on the design of the building but also on what materials are used, how they are manufactured, the efficiency of their erection, their longevity, their reaction to the environment, and the availability and quality of the material used.

At the Nambikkai Foundation in Kanyakumari the quest for building was further complicated by the lack of conventional building materials in the locality and the need to devise new ideas and techniques. It led to an unfortunate mining of the earth; dredging up mud from ponds on the site to make shallow mud bricks and build walls with a mud slurry. Local wood and bamboo was used as scaffold and window frames. At the time, the building was seen as a triumph of conservation and thrift. The material was excavated from the land, made into building blocks and erected using local labour and skills. The sustainability of the site was linked directly to the evolution of

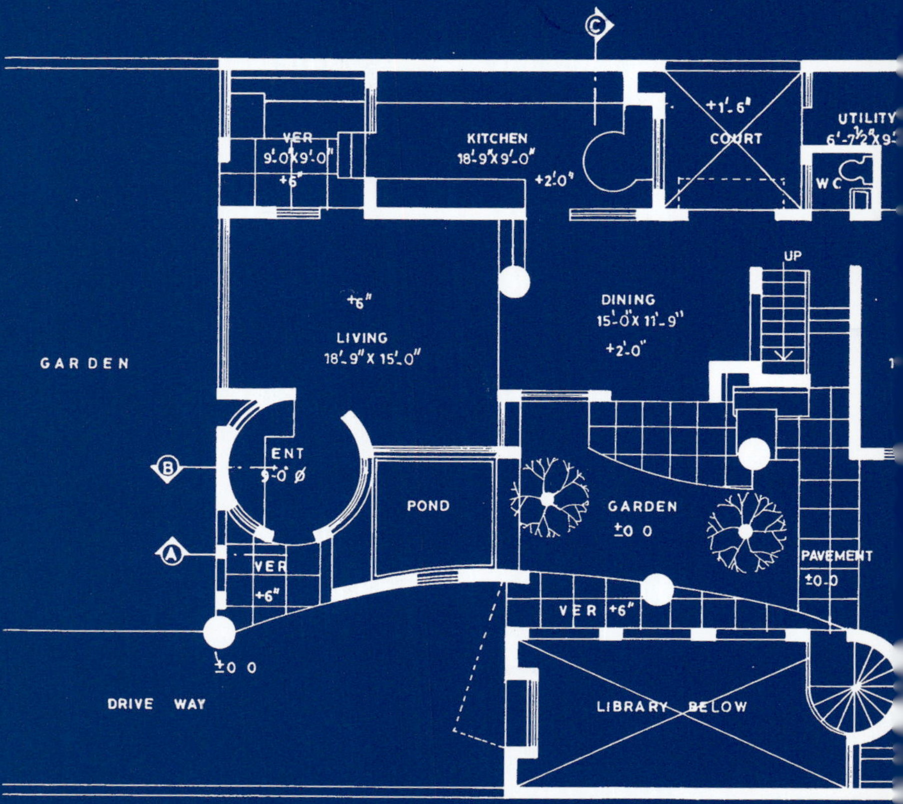

Sarkar House, Gurgaon, Delhi, 2002

a certain construction medium and process. Yet the temporal range of such a perception was limited when measured along a wider time span and considered in terms of the implications on a national scale. It was destructive terrestrially and, because of the mining of soil, only partially successful.

An architect's blinkered vision that effectively neglects the long-term affects of construction, and the destructive processes of material manufacture make green building a hollow victory. A measure of all the destructive forces of construction, if fully accounted for, will profoundly change architectural conceptions. The things considered external to the design process need to be wholly viewed if the building's value in the environment is to be correctly assessed.

■ **ABOVE** Green Car, pencil on paper, 2001

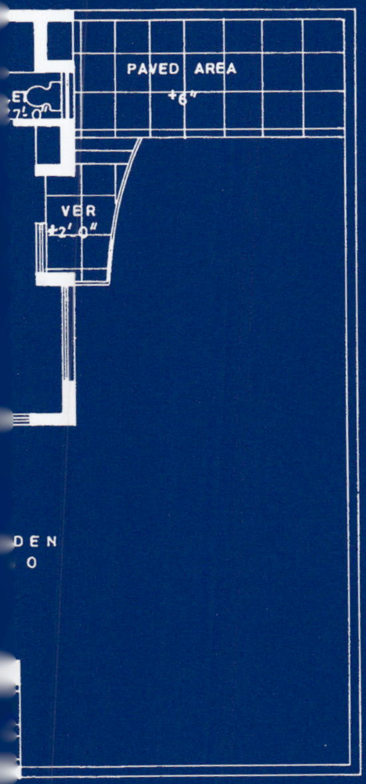

Benign ways of producing building components, the material and energy used in erecting a building, its chronological age and the methods of its eventual decline and death, are the more critical subjects of architecture.

More than ever, intelligent design of any sort that affects environments on a large scale is now being studied in terms of bio-mimicry. Not just by looking at anthills, spider webs, or leaf formations, but by looking to nature to provide clues to efficient materials, coverings for buildings, or solutions for enclosure. The vitality of such future technologies will snuff out toxic and high-energy methods. We will move away from the partial, cartoonish attempts that camouflage conventional buildings in green clothing. For now though, the Indian home, whether house or apartment, luxury or low-cost, seems destined for some misinformed cyclical changes and muddled perceptions, emerging as it does from the confusion of crossed cultural purposes—borrowed Western design and technology, and the 2BHK/3BHK of builder terminology.

FrontElevation

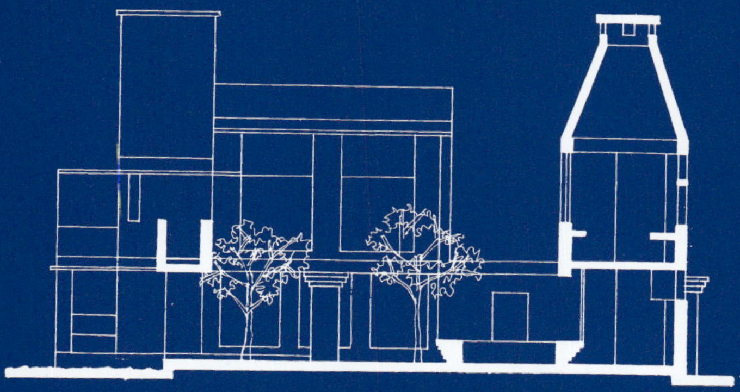

Section B

Do these trends signify an altered architectural belief in the Indian family? Caught in the current crossfire of green building, reduced carbon footprints, environmental consciousness, low-cost, user friendliness, the design process is confined to a set of convenient categories. Tried, tested and rusting models of change spring up coated in the superfluous sheen of newness.

The suburban brick house I built outside Delhi was a similar incomplete test of partial theories. It grew in part from available models, in part from a decoding of middle-class inhibitions. The necessity to make the house look different from the rest was there, but there was also the need to lay down a scientific basis for its appearance. The brick bonds, underground cooling vents and roof-top

Section C

Elevation, Sections and views, Sarkar House, Gurgaon, Delhi, 2002

air funnel were literally borrowed from tradition, and the prevailing professional techniques assembled the house's introverted courtyard layout. Garden space leaked in and around making you aware of closure, and compaction, without literal divisions.

The antithesis of streamlined space, the house attempted to suppress its modernity by encouraging the messy overlaps of family rituals and cultural idiosyncrasies that are allowed to develop in an informal enclosure. The greenness of the building sought dimensions beyond technology so that in the long term, the house would descend into a subconscious state helping the residents absorb the eternally familiar: the culture and nature that exists around them. Without a direct relationship with the reality beyond the building, the architecture of it becomes a self-conscious bag of technical tricks whose magic remains in the instrument panel and the instruction manual: the glossary of heating and cooling techniques made available to the residents. Where does this leave larger projects?

■ Greener Car, pencil on paper, 2001

In the many decades of work done on low-cost housing projects across the country, there has never been an attempt to define in clear, simplified architectural terms the kind of lifestyle possible for and desired by the average Indian family. The solar-windmill housing project attempts to create altogether new definitions and nomenclature for the home. It is not a middle-class definition of home life reduced for low-cost consumption, but a new form of architecture that embodies a return to collective action in aid of a unified place. The project attempts to reduce construction cost through two means: first, through alternative materials and technology, and a rethink of all the elements that go into the making of a house like floors, walls, roofs, and services. Second, through alternative design: to redefine home life by re-structuring the planning and architecture that had been missing in conventional low cost projects so far.

One of the serious debates surrounding building for a section of society whose main concern is low cost is about not creating a building reduced to its lowest common denominator, its sole

Sarkar House, Gurgaon, Delhi, 2002

attraction a cheap and ready roof overhead. Part of the loss of cultural integrity lies in the minimalist nature of modernism itself; the excessive paring away that eroded historic and ecological connections, and left the resident bereft of the psychological structures of place and community. The importance of understanding and clearly stating a differently-enabled lifestyle is a crucial first step in defining a low-cost home.

In taking the first step, the design then re-states precise attitudes to privacy, community, possessions, family life and services. The notions of privacy as defined by separate rooms is a kind of sub-division created by a Western middle-class attitude. Whereas the low-cost family tends to create privacy as a moment in shared space; within the larger compound, the low-cost house shares a courtyard or frontage with other families. Sport, leisure, recreation and entertainment are shared instances of family or community life. The design was moreover based on the idea that reduced number of private possessions allow for a greater openness and physical security. In the urge for a more cohesive

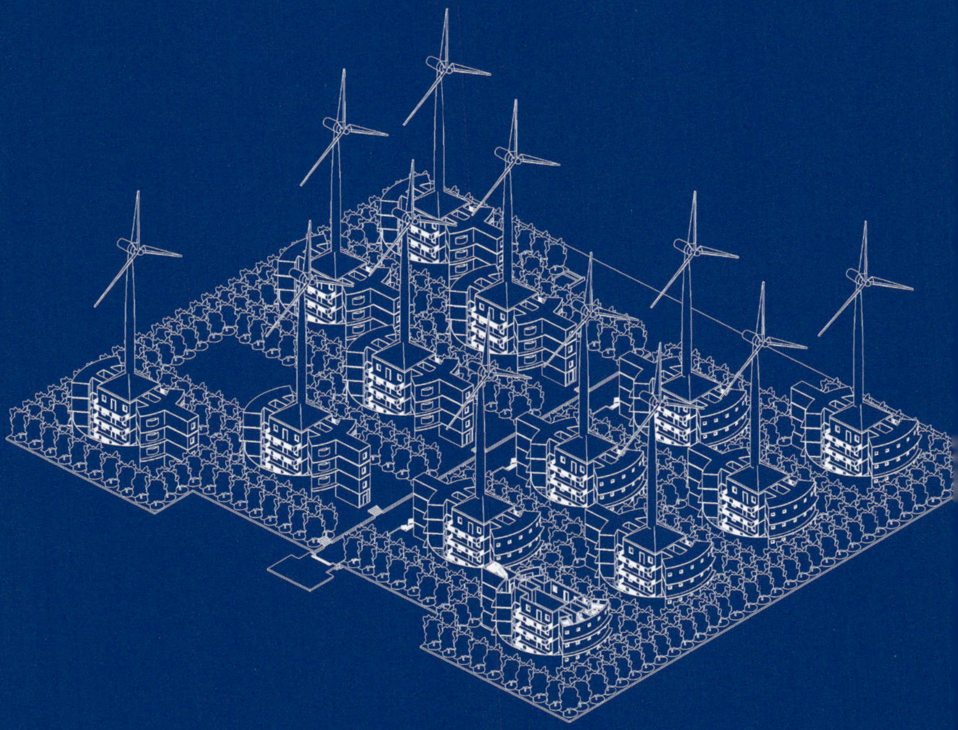

family life; eating, sleeping and meeting others form part of an unselfconscious matrix that occurs as and when required.

Moreover, the primary need for any form of dense housing is landscape and site-planning features that are entirely ignored in low-cost work. In this regard the design takes into account green areas, paving access and entrances, and parking. Central to any design for the low-cost house is the necessity for a set of efficient and compact services. Kitchen, toilet and bath—all requiring water and sewage connections—are compressed into an efficient unit to be shared by the family. Built-in furniture is inserted wherever possible. The structural walls and flooring themselves form the finish of the home. Frameless doors and windows of bamboo mat and compressed natural fibre are hung on wall brackets.

The primary feature of the home's greenness comes from passive and active approaches to architectural ecology: a dual system of water supply, a rain water collection tank, a windmill mounted above each complex, a "green wall" on the periphery of each unit, a

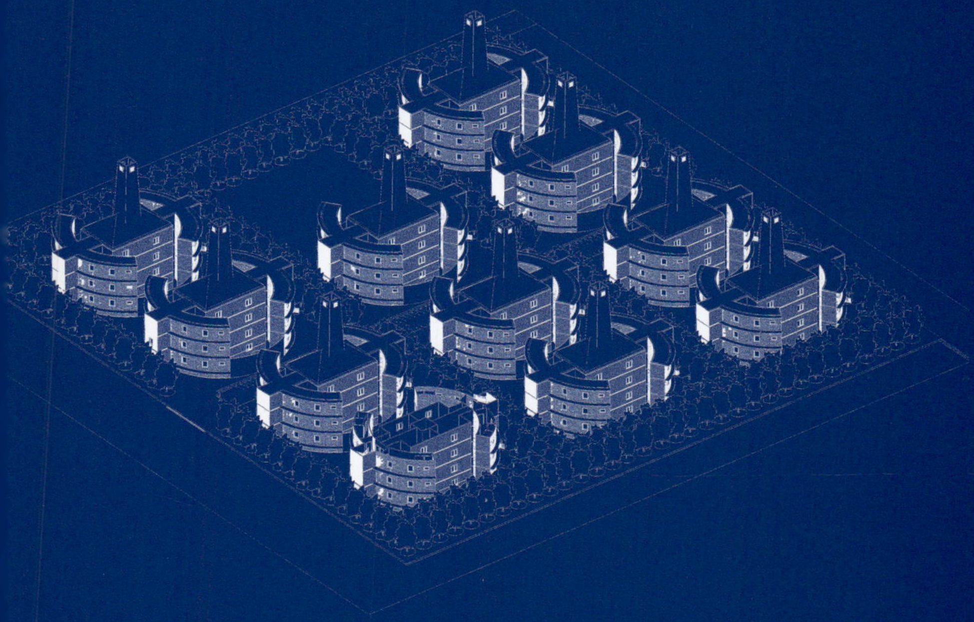

Windmill Housing, Chambal, MP, 2008

clay refrigerator, an open ventilating vegetable storage, a solar cooker mounted in the kitchen, a two-stage bio-gas plant... The crisis of green building has turned a deeper ecological and cultural equation into an engineering problem. The simple target of crossing a river requires a range of solutions and methods of infinite complexity; in contrast, the method of architectural mechanics is relatively simple. But the eventual goal involving cultural, social and environmental complexities is more taxing and ambiguous, and certainly not simply charted by technological facility.

The conception of windmill houses was an admission that the architect was incapable of ever foreseeing the final result. The acknowledgement was stated in significantly open living areas and utility cores that refused to address the complex issues of domestic privacy, ownership, possession, etc. Sometimes the extension of an idea to the extreme is an essential condition of an architecture that had begun to display a blatant disregard for cultural norms. Building designs swung to such awkward

NATURE'S GREENING

Can the current state of global architecture – gla
– be made responsive to the needs of climate ch
Burj Khalifa, the world's tallest structure. For two
aware of the design directions of architecture, an
it sits in an extreme climatic situation, clad in

5 million sq ft of space raised to 150 stories, makes the Burj Khalifa the tallest mixed use structure in the world. While its structural achievement is laudable, the building creates an impossibly harsh ecological footprint in the desert environment. Its greatness is measured entirely by height. Is this then the final measure of a building's greatness? Is design merely a display of structural facility and the conquest of air-space?

Dubai's location on the coast of the Persian Gulf gives it climate variables from hot-dry to hot-humid and sub-tropical with daytime temperatures as high as 115-120°F

Atmospheric pressure over the course of 150 stories itself alters the temperature by 12°F from the ground level to the top, despite direct solar radiation on the glass facade.

A peak cooling load of 13,000 tons is required to offset the demands on the exposed glass

At peak capacity the building uses 250,000 gallons of fresh water

Electricity requirement stands at 40,000 kilowatts

In the current global imbalance of climate change and finite resources, architecture must ask the more difficult question of design: What is the value of design if it does not consider the following factors:

- Climate, location and environment,
- Consumption of energy
- Water requirements
- Building micro-climate
- Solar radiation & heat absorption

The idea is to create a model for architecture that is informed by ecology – the by product of a dynamic natural system rather than the static design perceived by the architects. The greening of Burj Khalifa is conceived as an active exercise of vegetative germination and growth brought to bear on a designed object. The intention is to transform the building's inert surface into a constantly changing living system that eventually transforms the structure into an active complex organism. The exterior wall is a cavity curtain wall throughout; it maintains

transparency
views of the
this feature
essential in
atmospheres,
note in Dub
sea-salt aer
matter make
proposal itse
glass facade
that – over ti
structure, con
symbol of 20
idea for the n
– if over a
with its ow

(1) TREE ROOTS ACT AS PART OF ITS INTEGRAL LIFE SUPPORT SYSTEM.

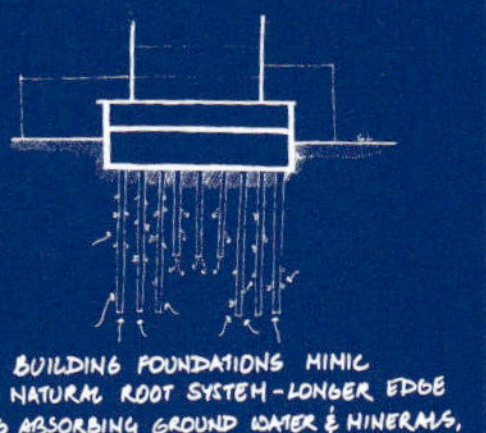

(3) THE BUILDING FOUNDATIONS MIMIC THE NATURAL ROOT SYSTEM – LONGER EDGE PILES ABSORBING GROUND WATER & MINERALS, OTHER PILES FOR DISCHARGING WASTE WATER.

HOW THE
MADE
NATURE'S

– USING TH
BURJ KH
OUTER
STRUCTU
ITS CAPIL
THE PRIM
MINERALS
AND DISTR
OUTER GLA
SELF SUSTA
PLANTS &
WHOLE ST
INDEPEND

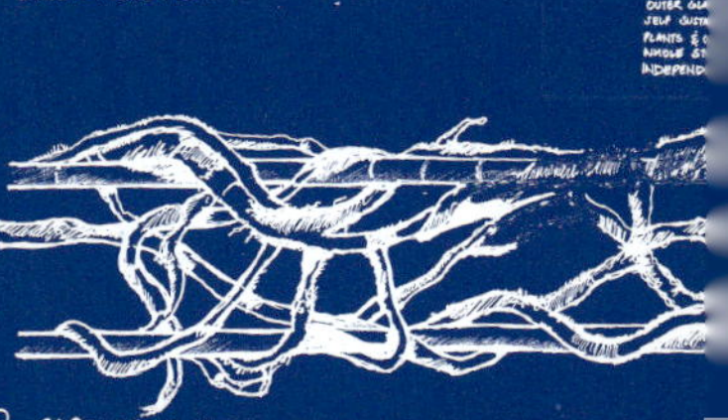

(5) CAPILLARIES

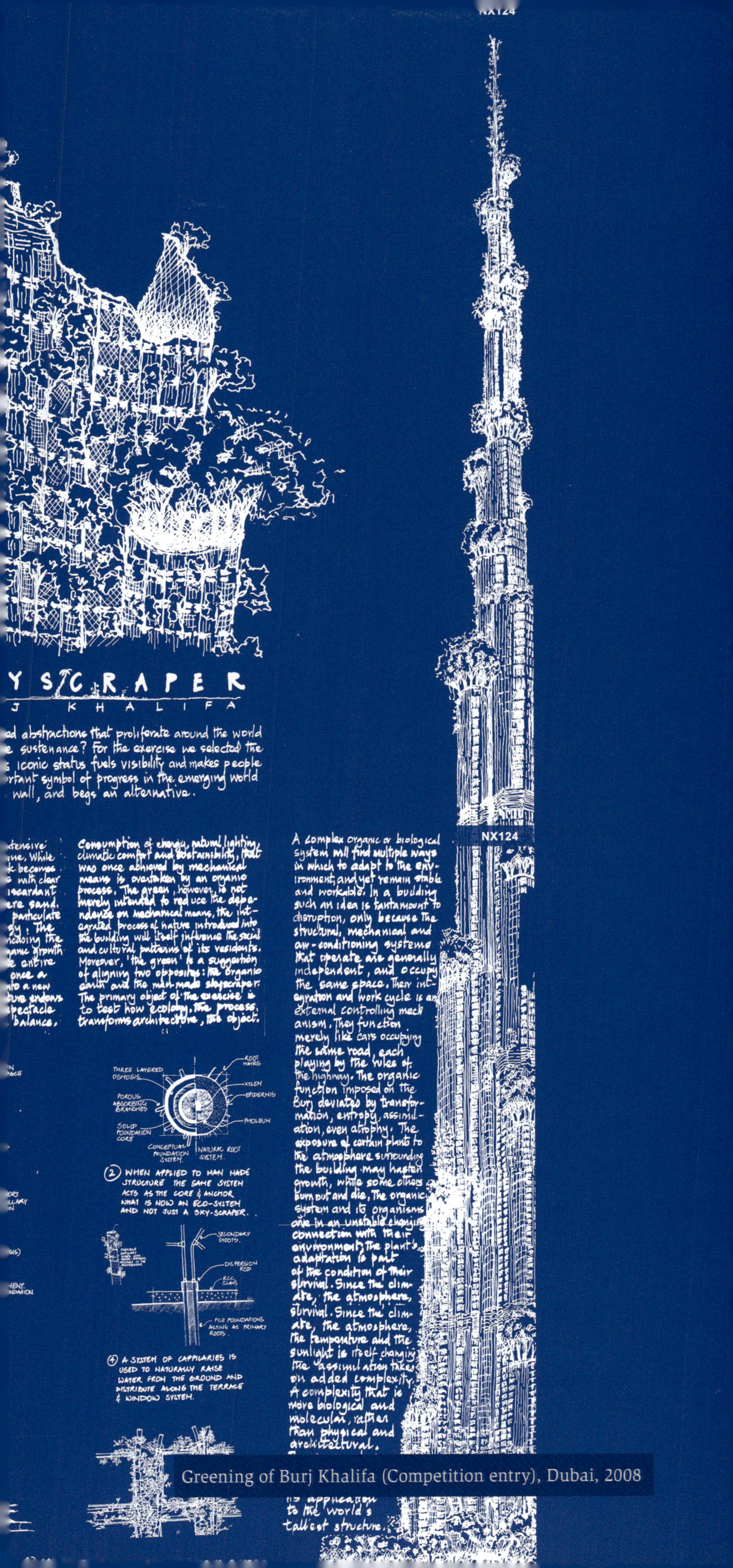

Greening of Burj Khalifa (Competition entry), Dubai, 2008

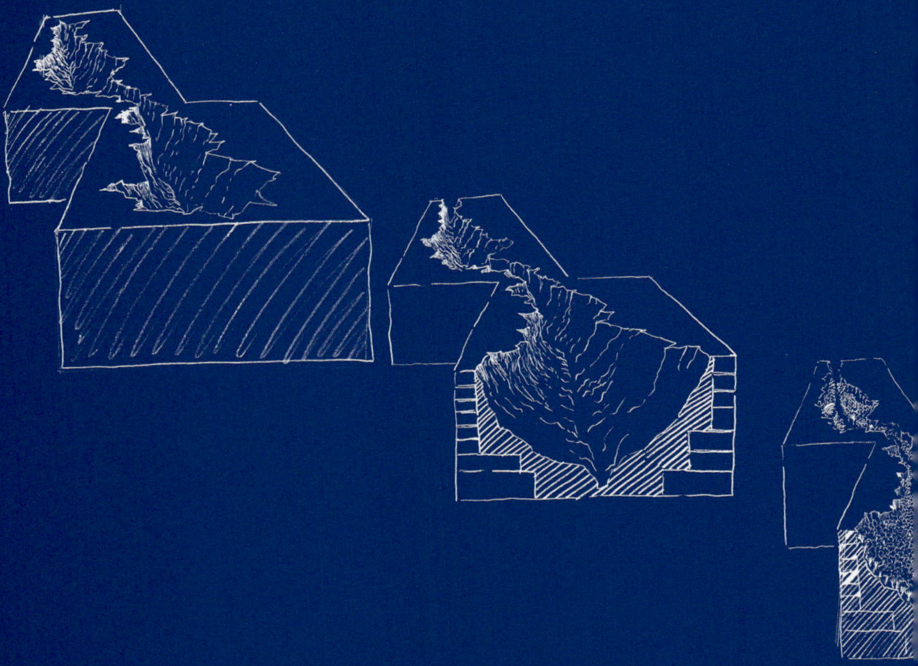

Development plans, Earth Office Complex, 2008

economies of scale and dimension that the only method lay in extending the madness to the other extreme.

In the desert kingdom design was the instant recognition of success. The Burj Khalifa in Dubai not only celebrated its technical virtuosity in size and height, but also in the supporting mechanics that outraged the economist and environmentalist when it sprung up. The only answer to its mega-consumption lay in violating its glossy synthetic beauty with an organic from of clothing that hid all 132 floors from public view, an attempt I knew was too outrageous to be taken seriously. So the vines grew; every time the building process slowed down, a new set of plants took root and began to vend their way up the outer glass frame. This went on till the structure was completely shrouded, and looked, as one of the jurors said, "like a tree on steroids".

On a day like any other, I rode up the electronic elevator of the Burj Khalifa. From ground zero to the 132nd floor, the black, soundproof box of the lift gave nc indication—visual, tactile, acoustic—of this

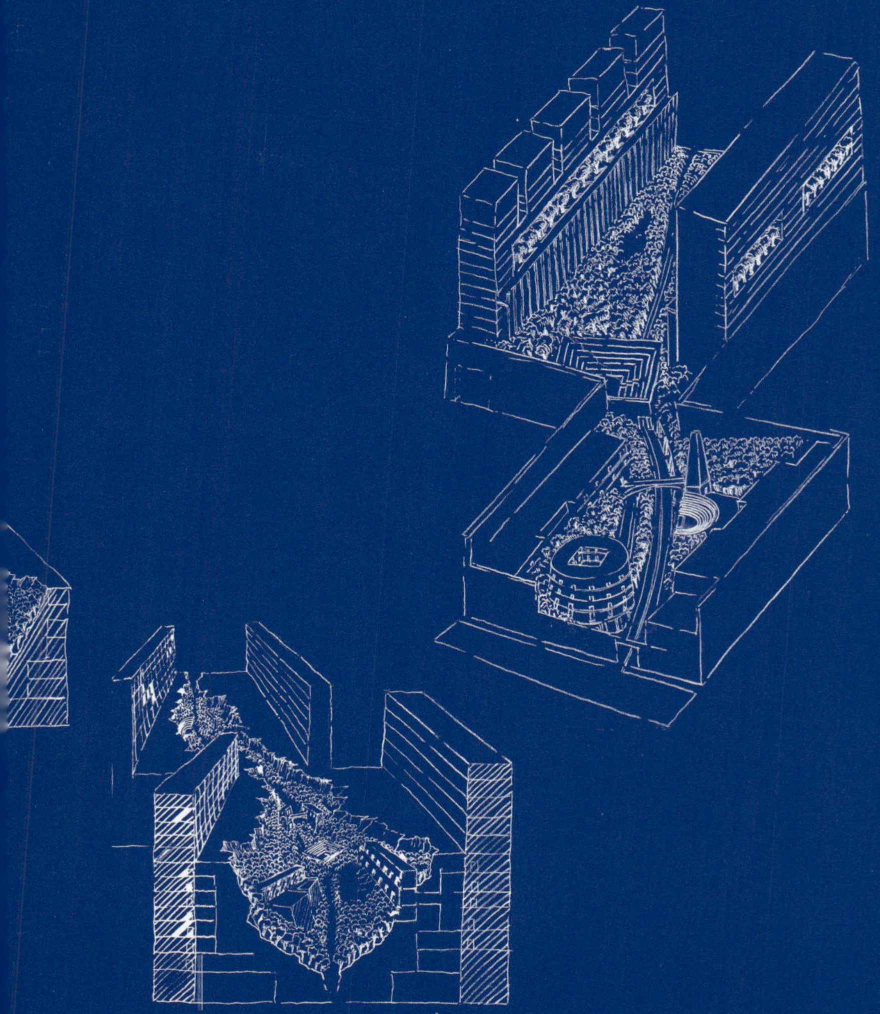

enormous height. I was deposited soundlessly on the observation deck. Looking down from my perch, the other glass towers below appeared dwarfed, and grounded in yellow dust. Dust remained suspended around the glare of mirrored glass and the brown extended all the way to the horizon. It looked like a miniature city swirling in a muddy water tank. Far away on the Dubai shoreline, the old courtyard houses with wind funnels were an awkward apology for a culture that was being ignored. Their age was more than a significant reminder of the fact that without cultural collaboration, the deeper narratives that describe architecture will go missing. The longer they stretch back in history, the greater the ecological connection to things outside of the buildings themselves.

From this great height, Dubai looked like a grave mistake. An unfortunate marker of one man's folly. The city was a model that the Sheikh should have first tested after taking a more serious look at the old city. Perhaps then he would have said, "Let's not do it. Just leave the money in the bank."

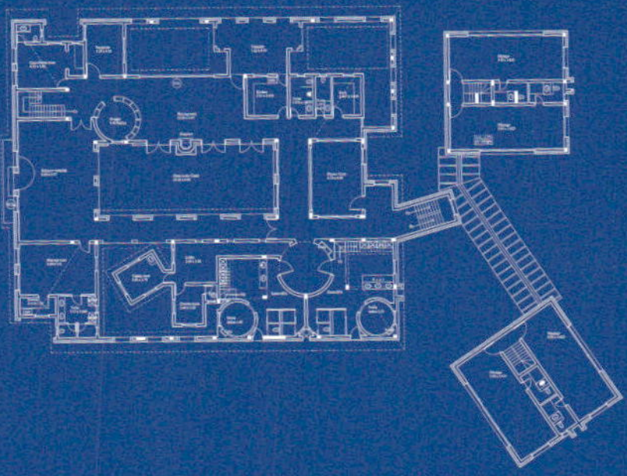

Spa

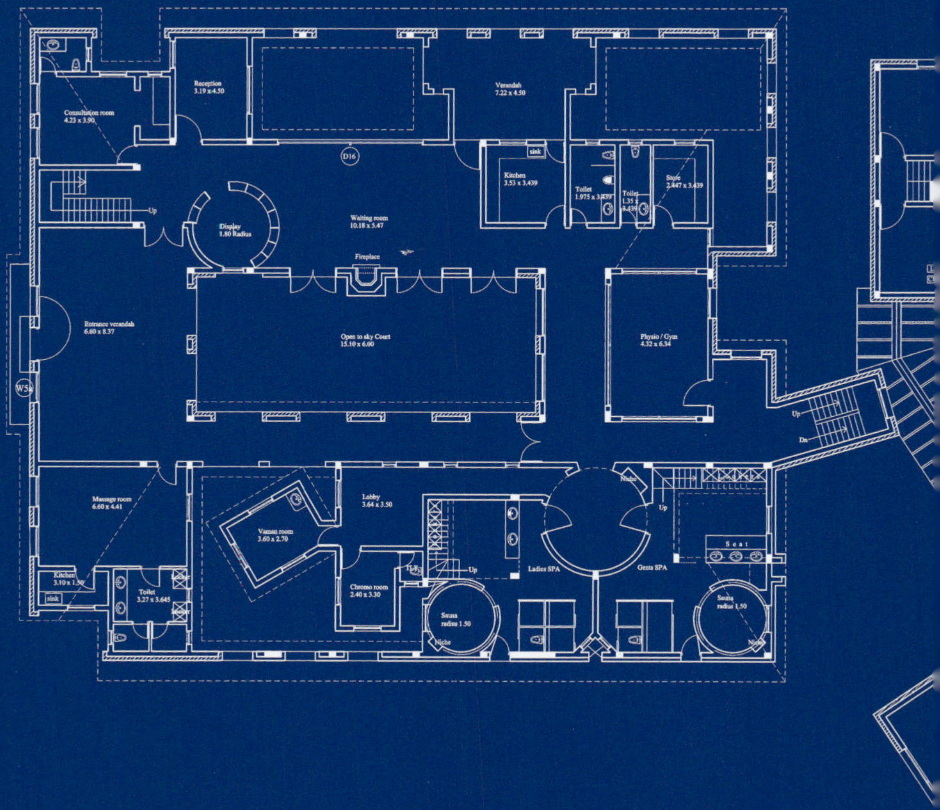

Plan and exterior views, Kalmatia Sangam Spa, Almora, Uttarakhand, 2015

On a grey hill shrouded with winter mist, the vantage of a long ridge stretches into the fog. The land, fertile and forested with deodar and pine, gazes at the ridge of the snowy peaks of Thrishul and Nanda Devi on sunny days. The twenty-acre site also looks down onto the valley at the district centre at Almora, a town so distant that no smoke or sound from it reaches the height. The way to the top of the hill is a narrow path through a rhododendron and sal forest that clears to give space to building. The spa occupies a place that had an old colonial footprint—a stone and mud bungalow that had stood there for over a century. The owner's sentimental attachment to the structure suggested a plan that emerged from the existing foundations.

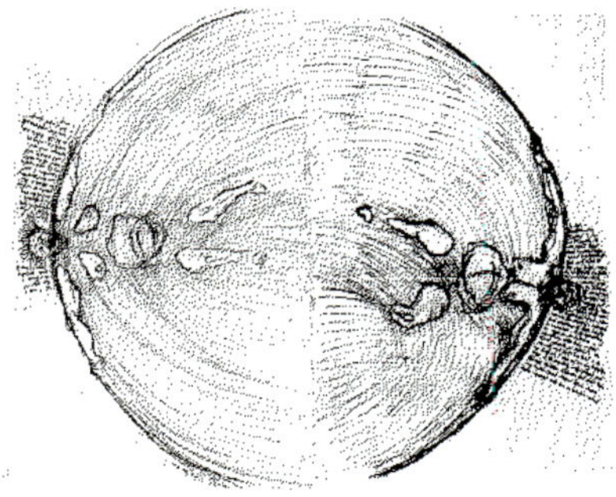

The long, oblong building with a slate roof was assiduously

■ Tub 1, pencil on paper, 2011

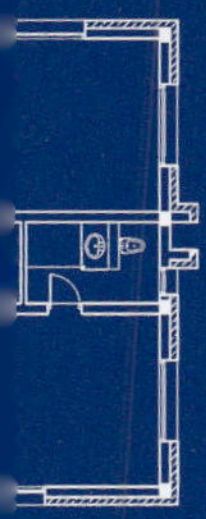

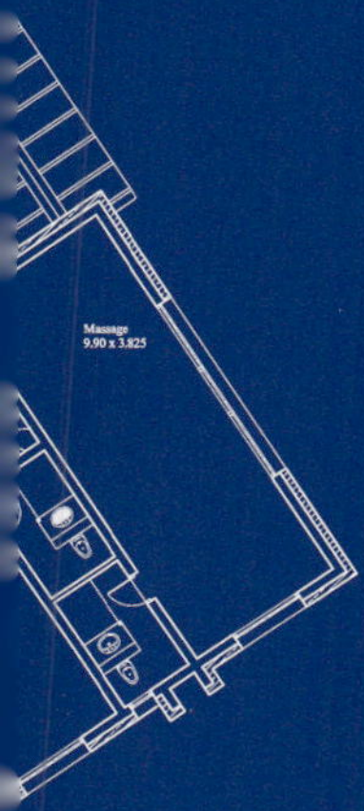

demolished, fragments of doors, windows, curved beams and fire places carefully stacked, decorative architraves and stone slates piled up for use in the new construction. The architecture became an exercise in salvage and reassembly, a method of conservation all too familiar to the local masons and wood workers. The new requirements for a full-fledged Ayurvedic spa however called for a substantial addition to the floor space. Besides the office, reception, changing rooms and bathing areas, the need for holistic healing stretched the building envelope beyond the footprint of the old structure. The design became a deliberate and visible clash between the old and the new.

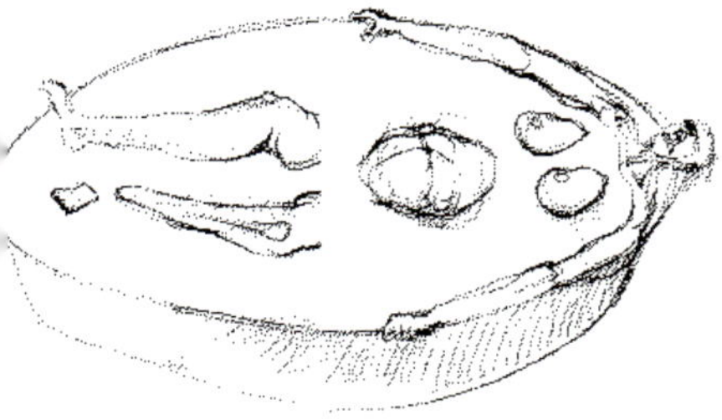

One suggested a conservative closure to space in the masonry; the other demanded a new glassy openness to the landscape. On the ground a partially dressed

■ Tub 2, pencil on paper, 2011

Solarium, Kalmatia Sangam Spa

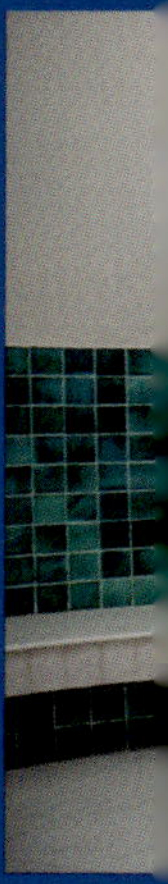

Bath and changing rooms, Kalmatia Sangam Spa

stone masonry supported the low roof that began its ascent much like the profile of the historic bungalow. As it moved inwards towards its central ridge from the four corners, it was interrupted by the steel and glass structures of a modern intrusion. The solarium, yoga hall, meditation and rooftop bathhouses appeared as independent entities that thrust out of the masonry. The combination of a stone ground floor topped by projections of glass was intended only to delineate and inscribe the divide between the old and the new.

The spatial experience too was reflected in the move from a dark ground floor of insular walled enclosures and few windows to a sudden exposure to light and views above—a rapid movement away from the confinement of building to the trees, sky and distant mountains. In such a setting architectural

■ His & Hers, watercolour, 2011

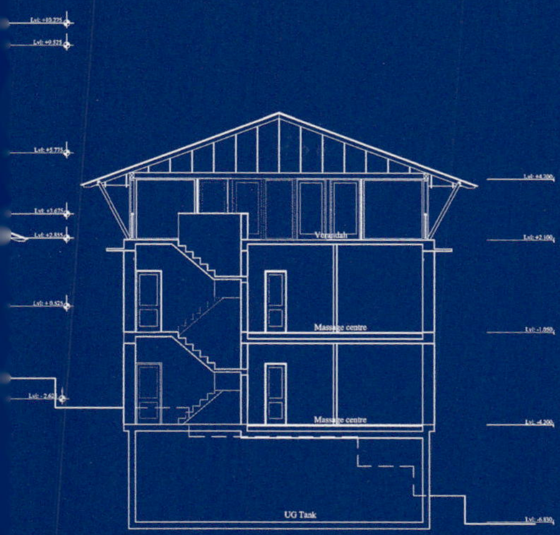

considerations can be nothing but the building's own enlargement of the mountain experience. So conscious is a visitor of the natural surroundings and the intense play of celestial and climatic phenomena that the body, mind and vision are always in a state of conscious vigilance. When the wind picks up, its play against the pines, the rain and the sun, the changing light and fog, all reverberate and affect the spa. When the hill is soaked in sunlight, it is light so charged there is no escaping its intensity. It felt like the sudden disappearance of a 150-year-old tree whose shadow was taken for granted. When it was gone you were left disoriented in the sudden light. Daily weather and seasonal changes are themselves part of the natural treatment in the spa. Affected by natural forces, the architecture becomes another form of therapy.

■ Car Wash, watercolour, 2011

Infinity Pool, watercolour, 2015

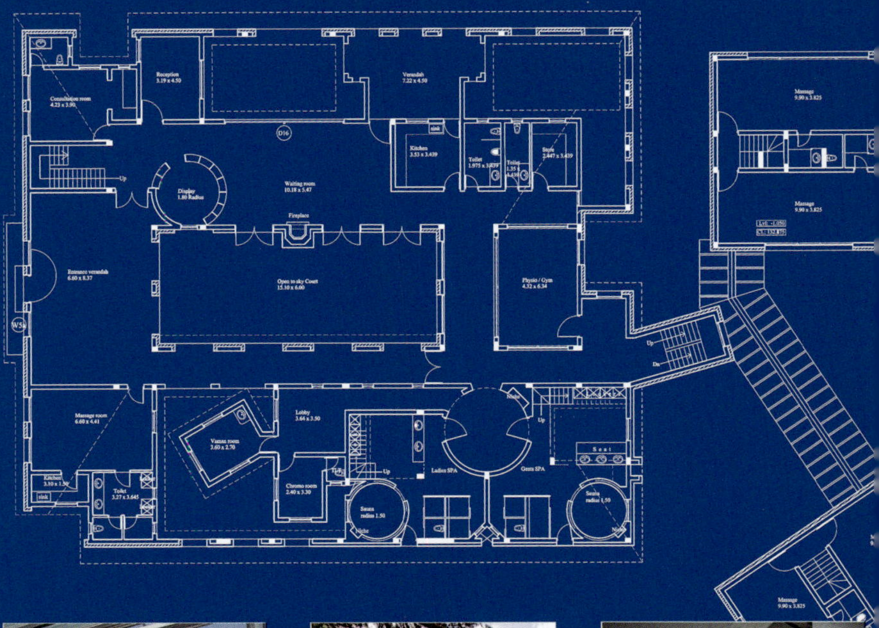

The design began as a device that removed clutter and the self-consciousness of defined space; so too, the absence of heavy furniture. The description of each room and its purpose was intended to spark spontaneity between people and the surroundings as if the users were presented a blank canvas to fill in. In a place devoid of the social complexities of relationship, the body is a solitary presence placed in the receptacle of reform. It is to be pummelled, coaxed and cajoled in space. The isolation of intent is supported by the isolation of space itself. To be alone with the trees, the distant mountains and sky. For reasons of privacy the massage therapy building was built along the lower slopes and it was left open on the wooded side of the hill. The two blocks were oriented away from each other and housed a roof-top recuperation room overlooking the valley.

■ Bucket Bath, watercolour, 2011

Roof Top Baths, Kalmatia Sangam Spa

Throughout the building a combination of flooring inserts were used to define movement and rest. The floor varied from rough to smooth to polished, intended as it was to give directions to the visitor in a place that had neutral white-walled interiors. The independence of the glass enclosures was displayed in the distinctive roof geometry, and precise alignments that linked their exposures to cardinal directions—meditation along the east, solarium and yoga on the north–south axis, baths along the warmer western side. The dual nature of the building called for both group activity and meditative isolation. Within the complex arrangements for Ayurvedic traditions, the architectural scheme

■ **ABOVE** Private Soak, watercolour, 2011
■ **BELOW** Public Soak, watercolour, 2011

posed a simplified rationale that gave each activity an independent identity within a compact layout.

Paradoxically, one of the essential conditions of architecture is its value as a magnifier of space. Architecture invariably begins with an act of confinement, and then moves outwards, towards the horizon. Every opportunity to connect physical space to eternal space is an enhancement of building; a way first to connect the physical to the visible, and then the visible to the metaphysical and cosmic; an idea that ties in with the persistent human need to be forever hopeful and optimistic. It is like the prisoner confined to the four walls of a cell for whom the small, barred window is the view

■ Public Bath 1, watercolour, 2011

Rest room, Kalmatia Sangam Spa

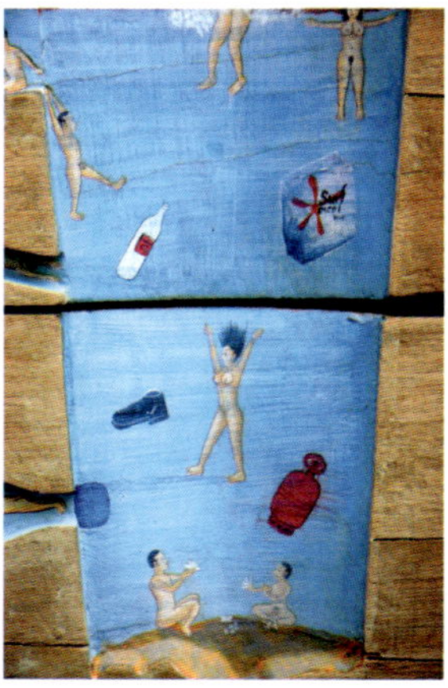

into infinite space and freedom. It is similar to the mountain hut whose small dimensions are compensated by the immense valley beyond. Human comprehension of space is necessarily small, and bounded by architecture. It is just enough to feel secure and protected, but not so large that it cannot be guarded.

The extension of these measures beyond architecture, into landscape, past the window of a house into a courtyard, beyond lakes and mountain ranges, was part of the boundlessness of architecture itself. The only way to affect that in the design was to view your own architectural intrusion into the scene in geological time. You had

■ **ABOVE** Car Wash, watercolour, 2012
■ **BELOW** Public Bath 2, watercolour, 2011

Massage Room, Kalmatia Sangam Spa

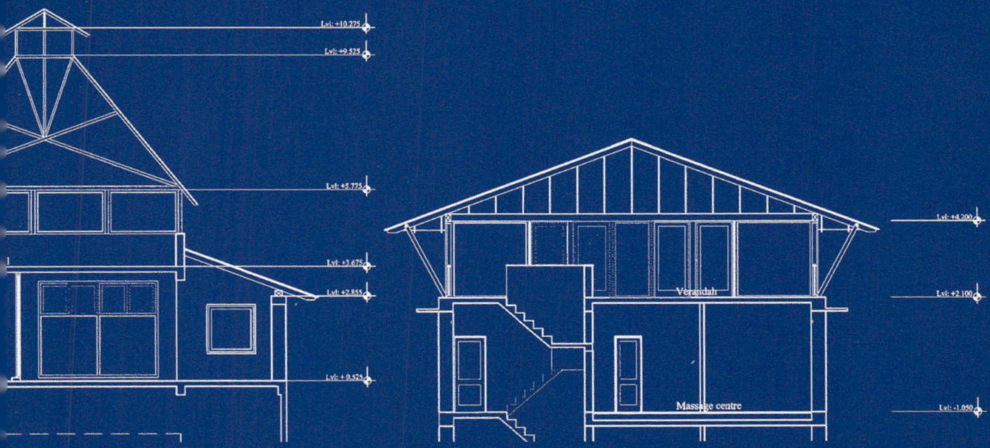

Roofscape, Kalmatia Sangam Spa

to consider if the stone hewed for the building was part of the rock encrustations that grew on the uneven ground, when the weathering of the masonry would condense the rubble walls into a monolithic mass and become, over time, a part of the valley. This would extend the vision from the shallow perception of private space to the far horizon and the blurred remoteness of mythic time. The attempt may seem impossible, but it was a necessity into which architecture always hoped to escape.

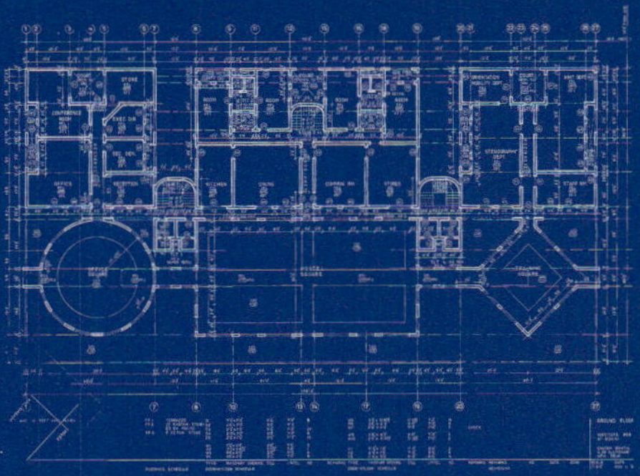

School

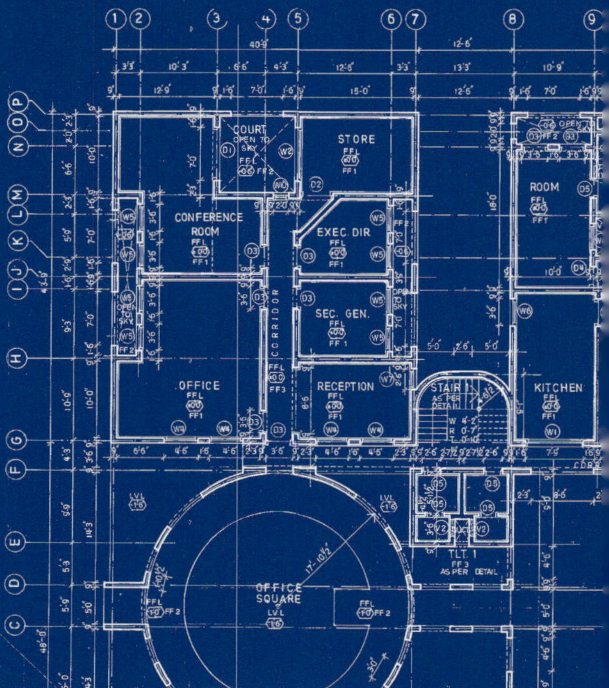

School for the Blind, Rohini, Delhi, 1988

The courtyard stands as a reminder of the penalties of overbuilding. So the centre is hollowed out, and even though the construction all around it is man-made, and invariably over-done, the missing centre provides much-needed relief; a bit of nature and sky held in private captivity. Like an urn, the hollow is held in thrall. The useful part is the emptiness that fills the architectural void with light and plants and air, and distributes its bounty to the rooms that surround it. It is in the nature of building that it doesn't shout out its function to the users, but acts as a mere background to daily life.

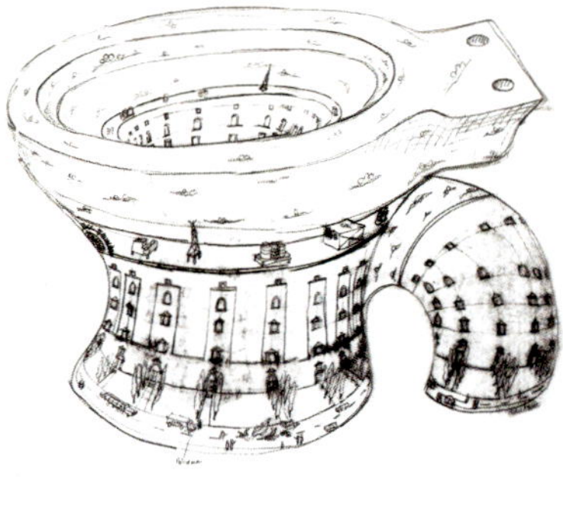

A church or temple is a call to prayer without drawing attention to its details like its spires or stained glass; a library designed for study provides a place for reading but elements of its containing structure like the windows and lighting are almost invisible.

■ Public School 1, pencil on paper, 2012

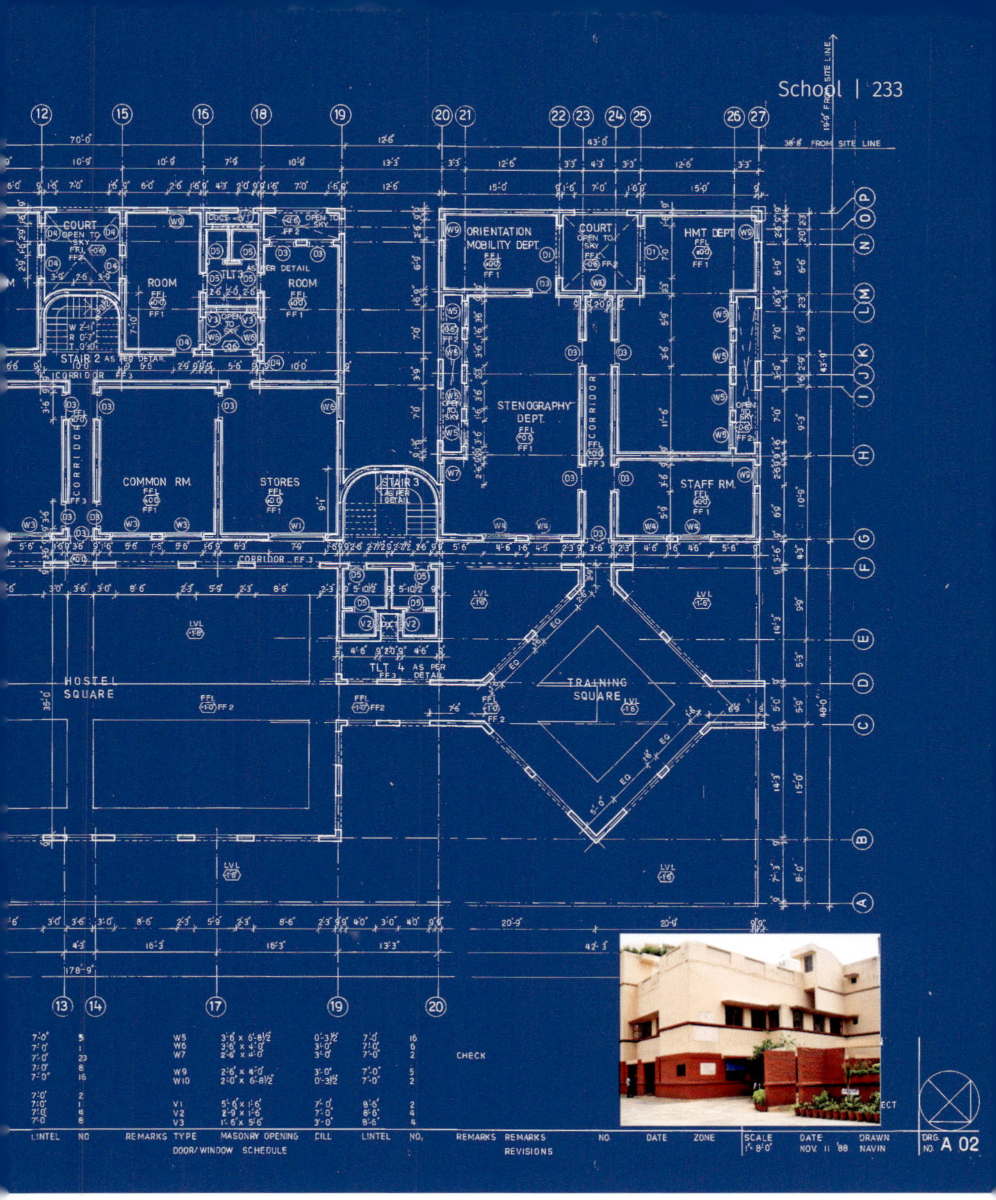

But a school that is invisible to its students confesses an all too different response to its users. It demands sensory attention rather than a subconscious reading of the landscape. In a design exercise for a school for the visually challenged, the structural provision for auditory and sensory responses had to be given great priority along with the visual enhancement of the building. The plan generated for the school not only attempted to meet the difficult condition of designing for the visually challenged, but also tried to make the sensory solution a feature of the scheme.

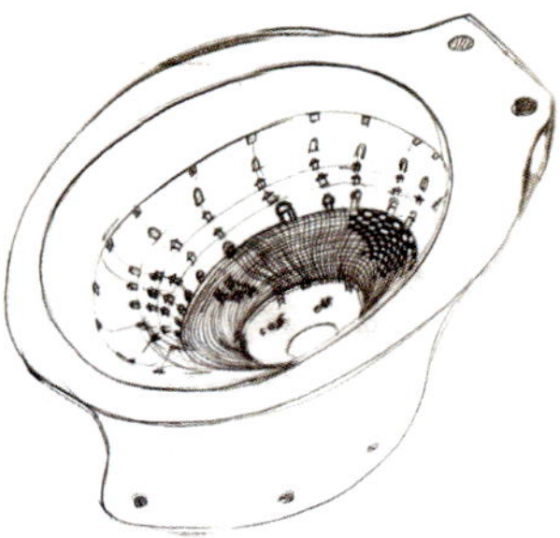

Blindness offers new realization to space. Devoid of boundary, ceremony, or visible intent, it reconfigures life as a continuous activity; a culture that merely spreads activity so that architecture's only device is to enforce movement towards it.

If conventional structures are physically and psychologically damaging to the handicapped, it is primarily because

■ Public School 2, pencil on paper, 2012

School for the Blind, Rohini, Delhi, 1988

in the design process, that sympathy to their handicap is missing. When the place itself does not offer any coherent sensory clues to movement, orientation or location, the blind person begins to feel incapacitated. The sensory difficulties with the school project were additionally compounded by the fact that the building's users were not all similarly handicapped; some were completely blind, some only partially so, others, involved in administration and teaching work, could see perfectly well.

Designing for varying sensory impairments and disabilities, it was difficult to propose an entirely barrier-free environment in which all three kinds of users would feel completely comfortable. Yet all these handicaps had to be addressed and provided for in the kind of manoeuvres that were required in moving through the building. In simplifying the plan for ease of circulation, one of the more urgent needs was to make clear the separate identities of the building's various functions. This necessitated the easy identification of three distinct blocks of administration, training and residence. So the identity of each individual block was heightened using colour. Red, yellow and blue in their most primary shades were used on the door surfaces and window frames, while a more subtle display of these on the corridor floor also helped direct movement from one block to the other.

Since the partially sighted have the ability of distinguish hues, colour became an essentially architectural ingredient in suggesting orientation. Through the murky haze of reduced perception, the partially sighted person could view these colours as signposts; red gave way to blue, the administration section receding into the training block, the blue of the training block changing into the yellow of the hostel. While moving around the person was always reminded of his place in terms of the larger perspective of the building.

A school for the visually challenged belonged less to a world viewed as a fixed object, rather as a changing state of experience and stimulation. To see architecture as an entity that is not fixed and one in which there is no visible distinction between one

■ Field of Action, watercolour, 2004

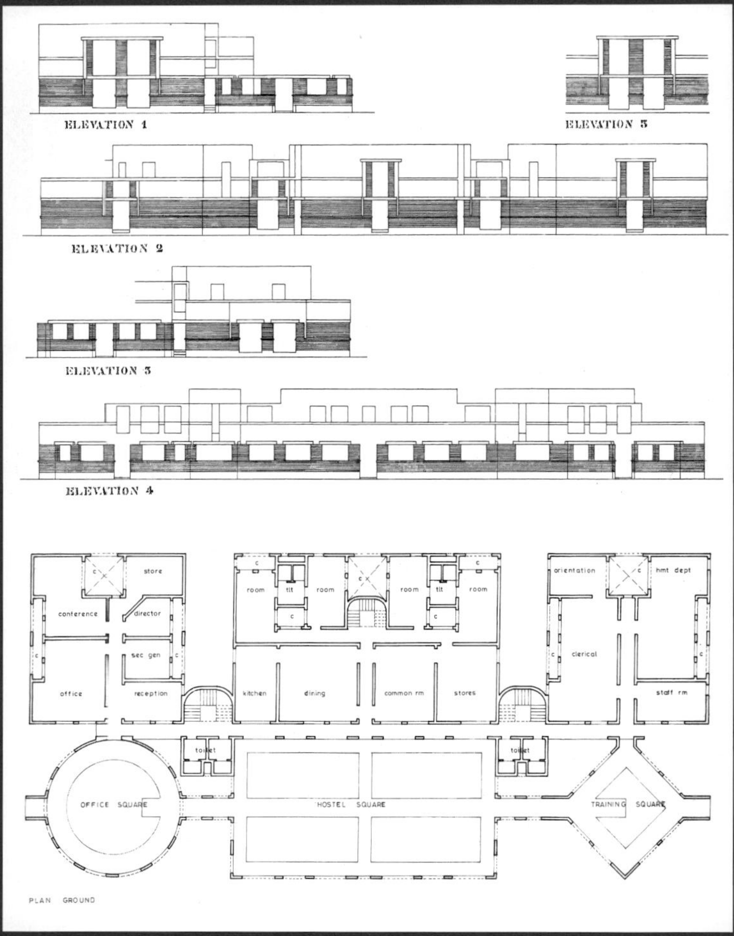

School for the Blind, Rohini, Delhi, 1988

place and the next. For the visually challenged, architecture's profiles were experienced in movement, and not, as in ordinary building, at rest. The lack of sight also eradicated boundaries between the self and the other. People too didn't occupy fixed positions or space but were similarly objects of experience.

The visually challenged also depend heavily on sound perception and on olfactory reminders to some extent, so certain fixed landmarks became crucial for orientation in the building. The rigidly orthogonal scheme of the building broke away from its confining regularity into a set of courtyards—circular, rectangular and square—which attempted to become olfactory benchmarks. Positioned as landscape extensions parallel to each block, the courts readily identified with their function without altering their internal circulation. To those walking down the building's corridor, they appeared as mere brick enclosures, open to the sky and built for no immediately perceptible purpose. But to the more sensitive nose, they were important as containers of aromatic shrubs and flowers, each of which gave off a distinctly identifiable smell. Though they were landscape appendages

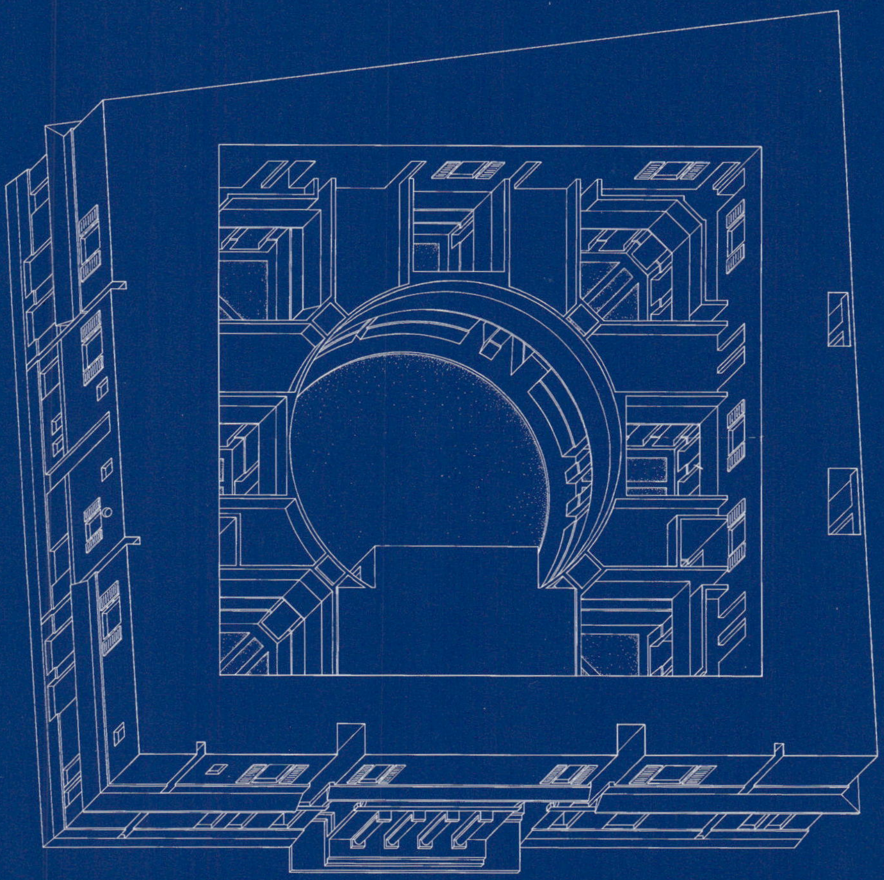

Joint Family House (Unbuilt), Sarahanpur, UP, 1989

to each building, they served the more critical purpose of providing orientation through the sense of smell.

Even with the difficulties that accompany a confusing handicap, the space of the landscape was seen as a series of connected places. They were aromatic rooms that prescribed a boundary to the landscape, which was too often viewed as limitless. The construction of walls to contain the landscape was meant to suggest its importance in the scheme of things, and to say in no uncertain terms that scent, like sight and touch, had a claim on architecture. After all only buildings had walls, landscape often did not. But the definition of nature's enclosures as in Italian piazzas or New York's Central Park, or indeed in the circular garden in the joint-family house mentioned above have all gained from the surrounding walls something of their own history.
In the confinement of the school yard, the containers are but segments of space held in momentary captivity like the passing whiff of scent they offer.

Office

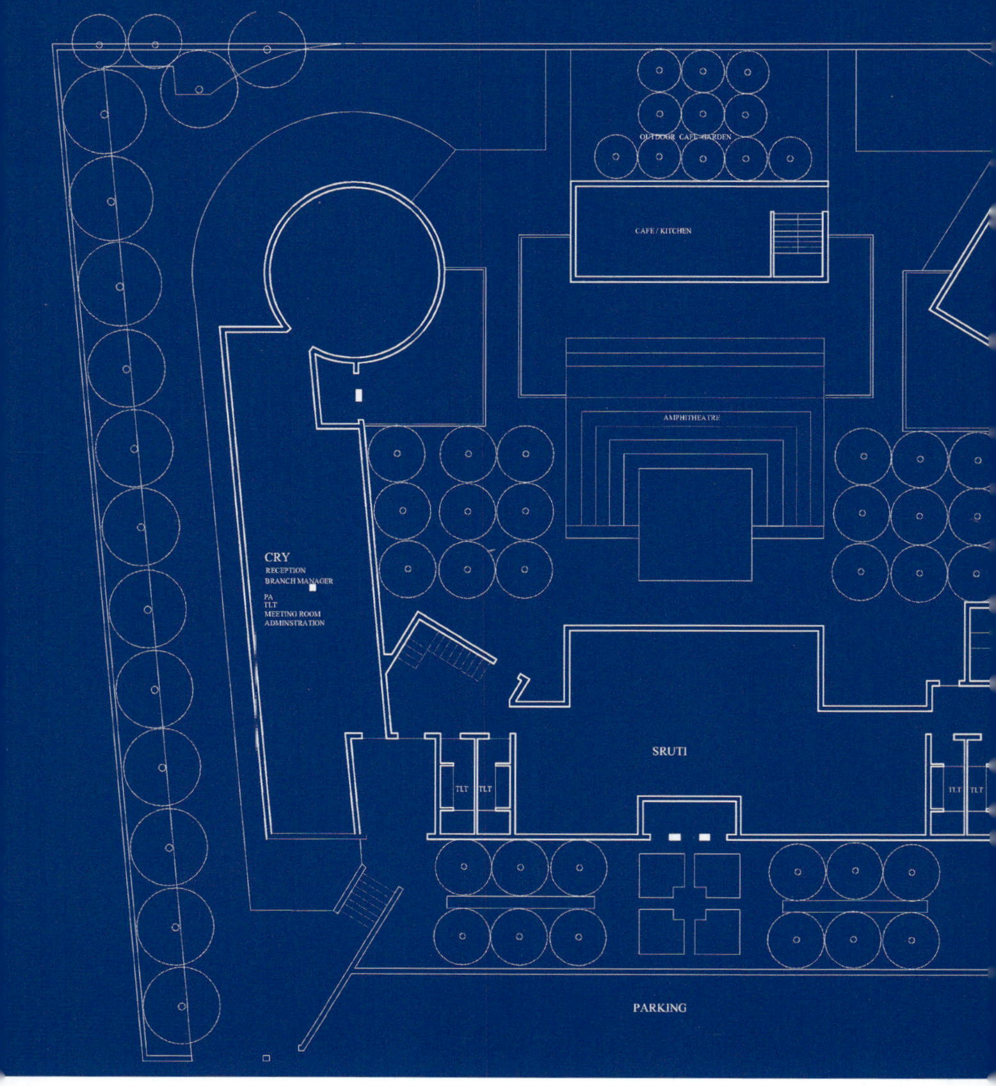

I have always felt that architectural secrecy is a mode of operation essential to any building committed to the idea of research or study. Secrecy is the essential condition of thinking; it elicited space that could be privatized for the moment, whose elements of enclosure overwhelmed those of exposure. The CRY-Oxfam headquarters in India was additionally challenging because the building shared that enclosure with five similar organizations. How could one turn the repetitive layout of shared office space into a more secure and intimate arena of privacy? Was it possible for people to work more effectively in smaller spaces, secretive and personalized as they are, than the standard open office plan?

Much of that secret life emerges as an offshoot of memory, and remembrance of forgotten times. The illumination of the building's inside was less important in the use of natural light than the demands that familiar shaft of sunlight placed on remembrance, to times when similar states or times of daylight intimately connected you to some incident in your own past—something that illuminated your mind's eye and made the present relevant all over again. The

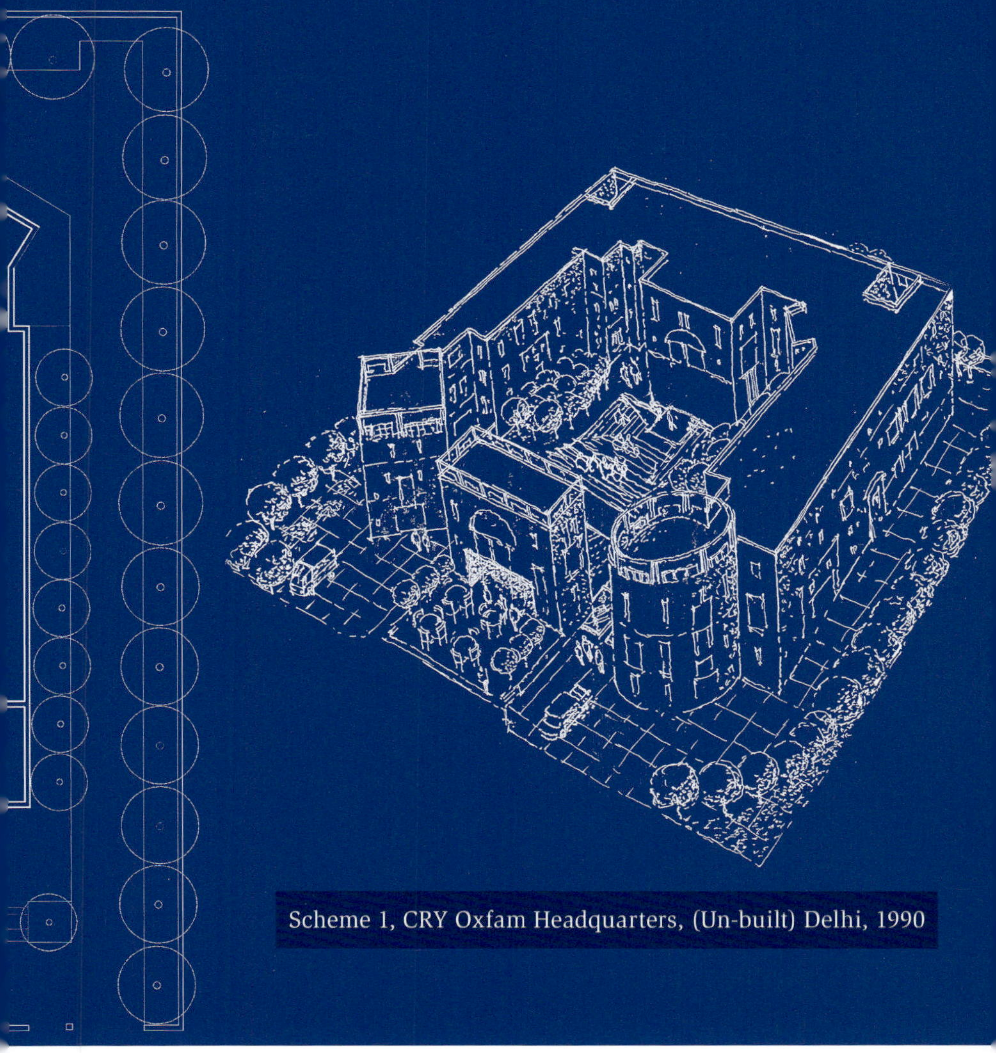

Scheme 1, CRY Oxfam Headquarters, (Un-built) Delhi, 1990

anonymity of shared space has too often been likened to willful detachment. I had begun to see in the idea of collaboration between unrelated institutes, not a meticulous, rigidly defined prescription of space that is divided and conscious of function, but a recognizable image that belonged to everyone. A subterranean darkness that was as much mystery, as workplace.

The reasoning behind my thinking was two-fold: first, by confounding space and diffusing the divisions between the various parts, the idea was to enlarge by deception using darkness, narrowing alleyways, sudden bursts of light. Second, the intentional blurring of institutional divisions would also make the whole building belong to all five owners. A place confounded by constant confrontation between people, moving through tangled passages, secret walkways and courts, could only elicit

Office Secret, watercolour, 2010

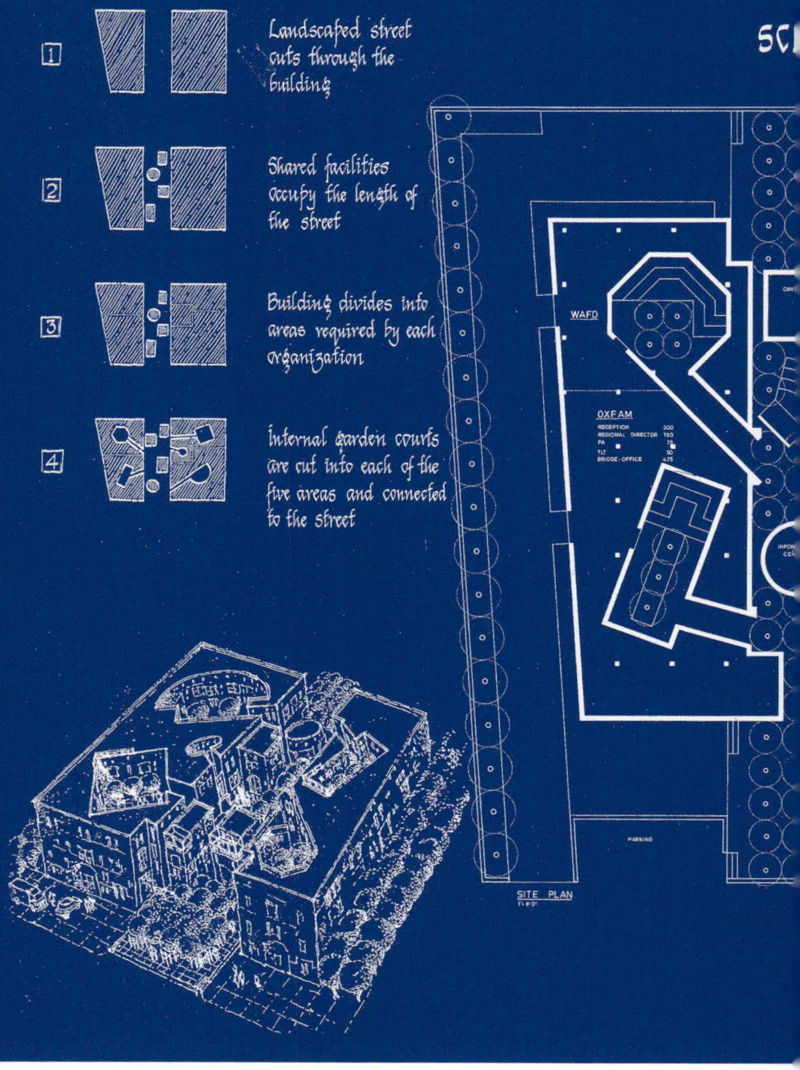

equally unexpected exchanges among themselves in an architecture entirely devoid of conventional order.

The irrational side of life remains inhibited too often, yet allows us to function within a multitude of randomly related ideas. The building takes on regulated but differing forms of geometry. The circle, the square, the rectangle, the hexagon, all collude in attempting a different captivity of sunlight, giving to each office its identifying stream of light, and the inferred logic of orientation to the visitor that each time he would feel he was in a different place, and at a different time. I began the design using the open space within buildings as a way of imparting an identity to each of the five offices that shared the complex. It was a polygamous building that relied on multiple relationships for its complex personality. The street at the centre was shared by all five, along with its library, canteen and information centre. The rationale behind its shared external life grew out of the need to balance their private ideologies, given that their work was compelled by similar intentions to foster the good of society.

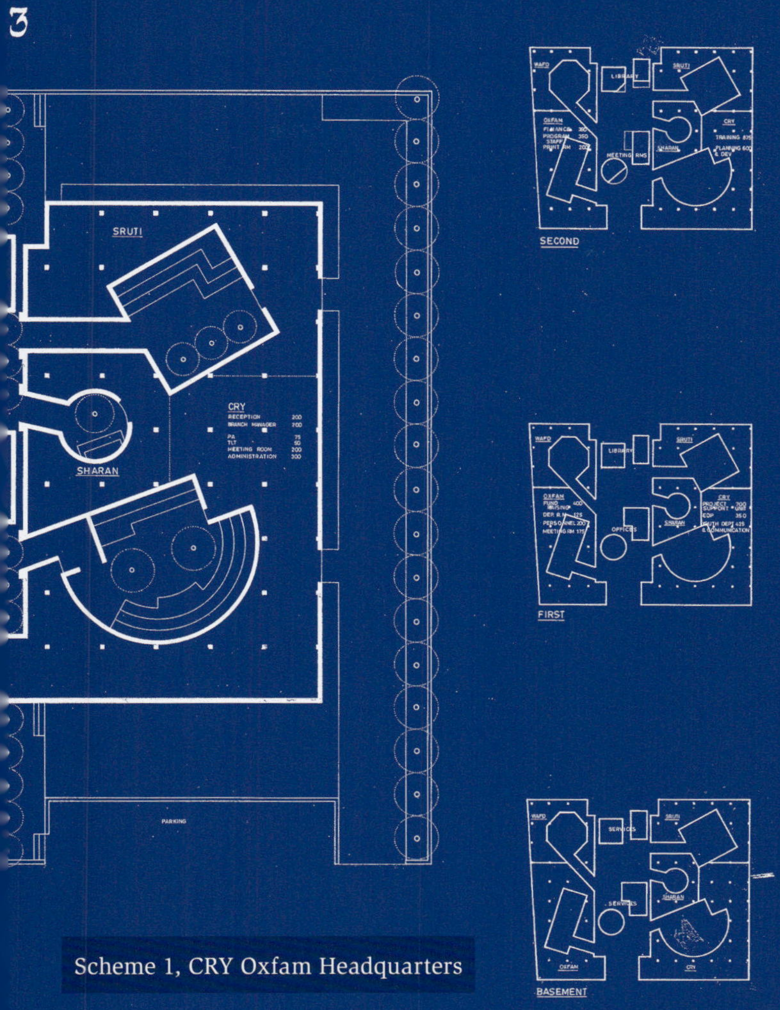

Scheme 1, CRY Oxfam Headquarters

Yet, the element of secrecy persisted throughout. It expressed itself in the transport of the visitor from the public outside across stretches of trees, down narrow, shadowed lanes into private courtyards and building interiors. The architecture lengthens the transit, using light and dark, open and covered, to connect the visitor to his intimate moments; pauses and movements that themselves depict the secret geography of the building. Part of the absence of knowledge of places is the pleasure of discovery. The unknown here doesn't amount to disorientation, but creates a pleasant imbalance in the mind akin to healthy curiosity. By concealing space within the undiscovered depth of shadow, behind walls or the convoluted geometry, the risk of despair outweighs the more despicable fear of not being noticed.

The secrets of places prompt the mind to quite literally work at visual clues, forcing the viewer into an unintended game plan that proclaims that reward lies in discovery. In larger projects perhaps the clarity of orientation is a necessity, but the experience of the circuitous path, the deliberate misrepresentation of

Resort at Mashobra, 2017

architectural sign and place confronts the possibility of an imaginative sustenance, where the building is itself proactive in confronting its resident. There architecture must concede that it is not content to merely state commonsensical reality.

Eventually work has to be done within the building, meetings held; the withholding is only a short-term disturbance to future actions. The undercurrent of disjointed movement through tunnel and shrubbery follows an intentionally illogical pattern, devised to confuse only so it achieves its architectural objective: to bump into a colleague or a stranger, rest under a tree, feel the stroke of a shadow. So too on the inside.

Architecture following the repetitive order of an office plan cannot avoid the disturbing emptiness of grey space. When desks are placed in the precise row of an open plan, the standard layout comes with the unshakable belief in the industrial assembly line when production was a matter of repeating the same task for eight hours, and starting over the next day. The uneasiness with misunderstood

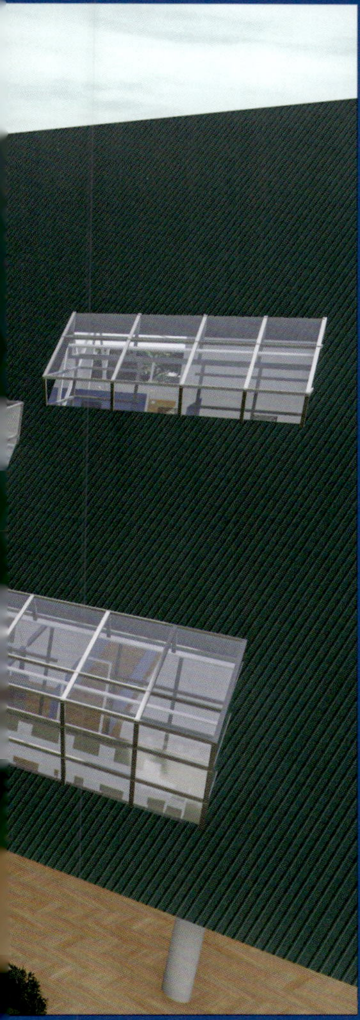

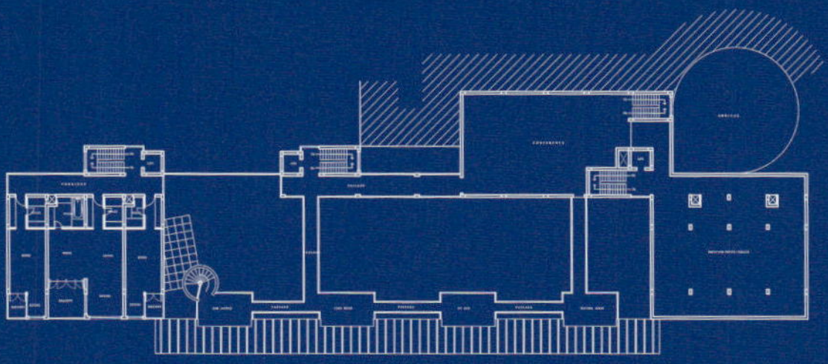

LEVEL 6 (+116.5)

space was meant to evoke a fresh sense of disorientation every time; unmarked and unclear entrances, no distinction between lobby and office, a territoriality unaided by map or plan, a distortion that would, over time, begin to make clear to the long-time resident or user the power of spatial incoherence.

The intimate secrecy of buildings in such overlapping proximity acts as a foil to confound things further, dispelling ideas of ownership and privacy it brings together the daily struggle, ambitions and corruption, and reveals the surface tensions and intrigues. These are not far from the truth of the incestuous and polygamous relationships in a joint-family house. Every member colluded in secret within the larger household. They have to. The mother-in-law is always watching!

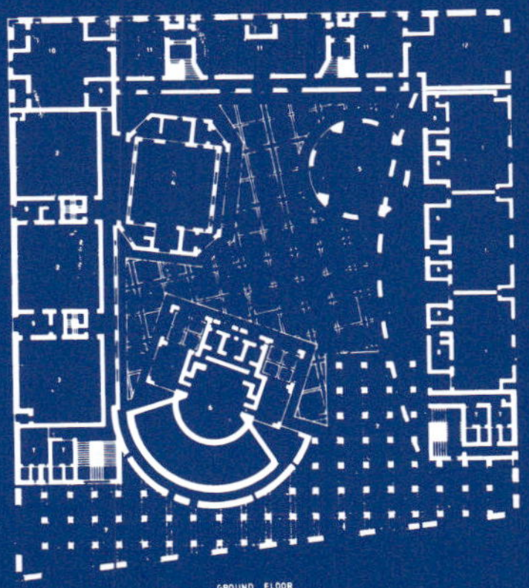

GROUND FLOOR

Theatre

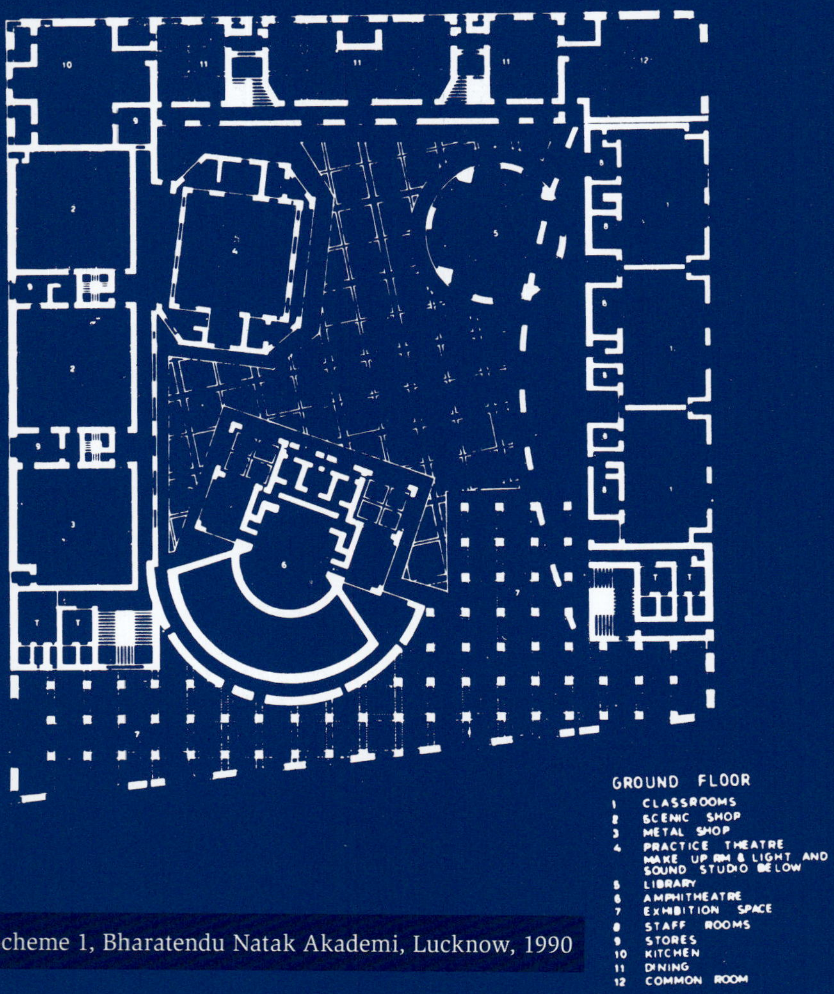

Scheme 1, Bharatendu Natak Akademi, Lucknow, 1990

The integrated life of the theatre was best expressed by the English playhouse in which the life of the performer was built into the performance hall itself. A belief in such fusion is rare in other professions. Only stage actors, of Shakespearean drama, could live with such daily rigour. The intrusion of daily living—sleeping, eating, etc.—into the work ethic of the theatre—acting, practice and performance—required a new design approach. The conscious integration of areas of the theatre with those of domestic use was the norm. Students ate, drank, practised, slept, performed, studied, made sets, all in an unplanned sequence during the course of an actor's day.

Architecture relented and re-stated its position not as a distilled product, but as one contaminated with overlap and variety. It grew simultaneously as classroom and bedroom, practice hall and dining hall, alternating space for its users between sleep and performance, making room for the public play and student night life. It was easy then to think of the building as domesticated office space or a factory where the workers lived on the industrial floor. Would accountants live and learn in an Accounts House and Dormitory? Could lawyers domesticate the Law Courts? Unlikely! The Natya Akademi was conceived to counter some of these separations that are evident in urban life. A place of residence and work, its self-containment was meant to reflect the partnership of the two ideas, ideas that were traditionally bound to a single place. Students live, learn and perform within the same building. The architecture consequently was viewed as an Indian version of the Shakespearian playhouse.

The design was meant to suggest a place where transitions between acting, learning, stage craft and sleeping were deliberately obscured, where students and teachers caught up in the self-created obsession with life in the theatre lived and worked on a kind of set of their own making. But, for me, it was an uneasy reading. When I began to think of it as an educational building, the theatricality of the performing art would intrude on it. When I considered it a place for large-scale public gatherings, the student dormitories and domestic living spaces would complicate the equation. Architecture's capacity to incessantly organize and divide separated functions into predictable, unrelated and seemingly unnecessary categories. For most, the profession had become a necessary encounter with division and the need to put up walls everywhere.

The result of viewing building as a set of plans meant that the line was a representation of a wall, and as the plan developed, it boxed it in and created more precise realms of privacy and isolation. In the playhouse such thinking was anathema, especially when measured against the props of a theatre, architecture was an impregnable theatre of fortifications and finite walls. The answer lay in endorsing the connections between disparate functions, and initiating spatial surprises through overlaps and proximities. It was possible to connect the student bedrooms to the practice theatre, home life, classroom, lecture hall and performance. Because of the sudden juxtaposition of entirely unrelated functions, the building transgressed into an imaginative reverie. The disturbing effect of extreme variables—sleeping and teaching, dining and workshop—all worked in its favour, and architecture gained strength from the opposing ideas.

As in art, the mind draws relationships where none exist—a lawn mower on a double bed, a woman asleep under a steam roller—the mere act of improbable juxtaposition gives them meaning. The absurdity of the proximity may have destroyed the original intent, but it subsumes the objects with new meaning. So too with space. When rooms are shaped by mismatched intentions, their paralysis produces new relationships. It allows room for the

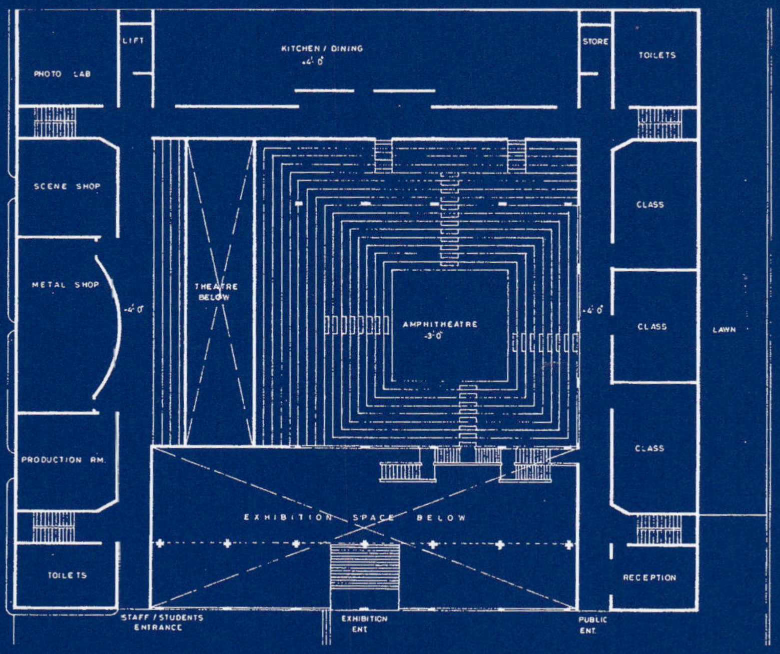

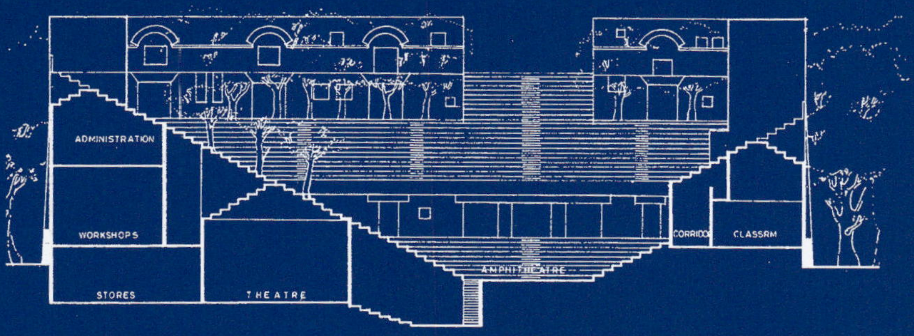

possibility for architecture not to be taken literally. The interweaving of space was attempted in play. At first, the central, special position of the amphitheatre received the added theatrically of an alignment different from the orthogonal rhythms of the other components of the academy.

But then the overlaps demanded the building be designed in sections. The formal space of the educational institute rose upwards and transformed into an amphitheatre encompassing the entire building. The amphitheatre in turn grew homes on its upper edges, regaining both a sense of enclosure for the amphitheatre itself, and privacy for student domestic life at its border. The seeming incongruity of private residence, educational institute and public theatre grew into a structure that defied local zoning regulations. The willful clarity of the internal idea lay in the confounding overlap of its multiple requirements, and revealed nothing of itself to the public eye.

As in art, the contradictory quality of awkward relationships between keenly divergent functions is a step towards an energetic revival of

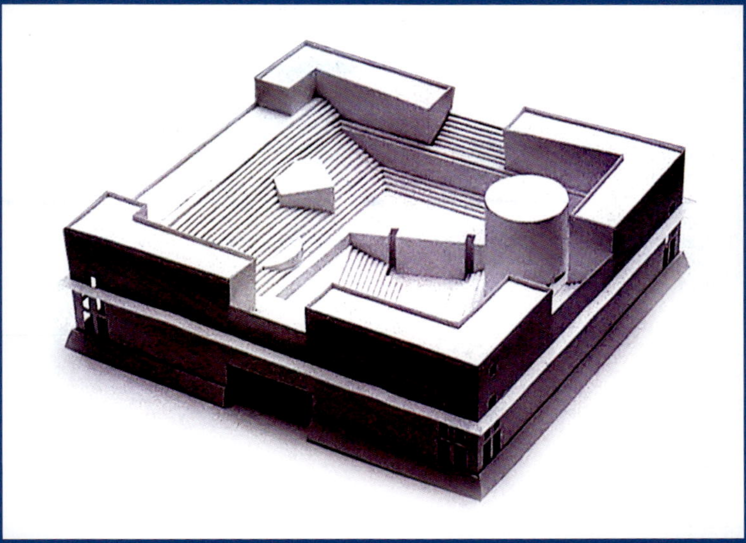

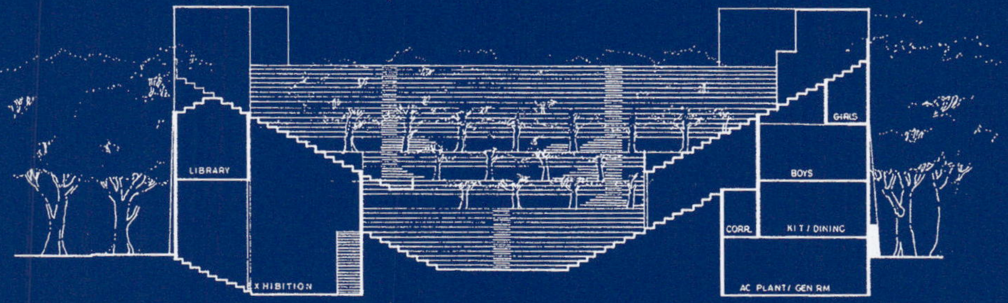

Scheme 1, Bharatendu Natak Akademi

those functions themselves and not a step towards chaos. They are to be seen together in a fusion of various forms that unify and enlarge the architectural experience, and not to be analyzed as a science with each part being a separate distinct entity. It is a cohesion of orchestrated chaos. The ambiguity then comes not from the set of requirements, but the experience itself. For a long time I had believed that collaboration between the various disconnected parts of the building would be successful only if it could not be represented in architectural drawing, neither as plan nor section. The answer lay elsewhere—in a time-lapse film, a model, or a rapid fire three-dimensional sequence, maybe a collage of sorts.

The eventual building was designed in the image of a theatre with multiple levels and orientation and a formal meeting ground at the centre. Though this central space of the building was conceived as an amphitheatre with a directional stage, its upper tiers were fragmented into landscaped areas that corresponded to the functions around them. Classrooms, student residences,

library and dining hall—the relative position of each suggested unstructured methods of space utilization. Even though the plans themselves segregated the formal and institutional functions from the teaching and the residential, they were all contained by their overlook into the larger space of the amphitheatre. Classrooms, workshops and the library that fulfilled the stated requirements of a teaching facility occurred at ground level and were located along the side-wings, while the student and staff residences stayed on the upper levels of the building, thus forming a series of small houses that occupied the roof terrace of a formal, symmetrical institute that was in fact, neither formal nor symmetrical nor an institute.

The implicit theatricality of the open roof space was meant to effect a landscape of discovery, where people found places suitable to their changing needs and desires. As real life personalities within a school, and as imaginary ones in the theatre, they could invent, subvert and enact a variety of uses and roles at different times of the day. While a play was being staged in the main amphitheatre, students could watch from the hostel terraces above. The terraces could themselves become the setting for rehearsals. A class could be conducted in the interior of a practice hall where the light and acoustics were

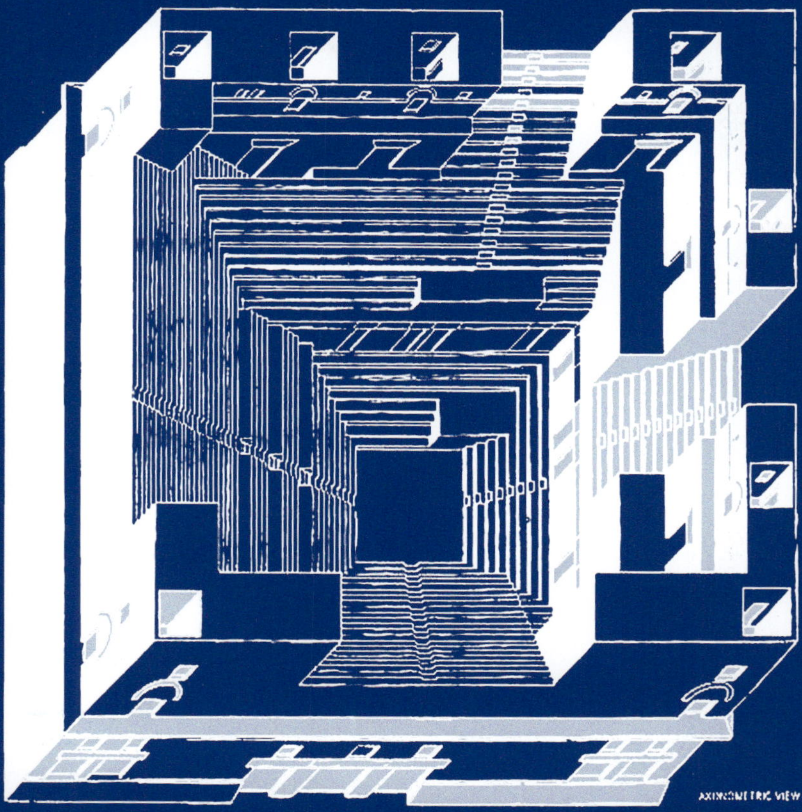

Final Scheme, Bharatendu Natak Akademi

controlled, or move to the openness of a roof deck. Students could perform Mullick or Shakespeare or Ibsen centre stage, or choose to sleep within the amphitheatre's masonry fold at night. The architecture merely accommodated and allowed the realization of such shifting notions. The intent was to create a stepped, garden-like setting, with covered spaces where students could meet in groups, or isolate themselves.

The building became a theatre in real life, intruding onto the stage set. To the performers within the complex, there was little difference between the real and the theatrical—an actual meal consumed in the dining hall, or one enacted as part of a play; a scene studied in the classroom, or played out in the practice hall. The outer profile of the building was forever attempting to eradicate the boundary between illusion and reality, the theatre of dream and of daily activity. Student dorms broke through the confluence of steps; workshops invaded the back wall of the amphitheatre. Home, classroom, or mess hall, the space on the roof only encouraged contradictory and messy opposites. When the improvised imaginings of students mingled with the realities of day-to-day living, the entire complex would turn into a play.

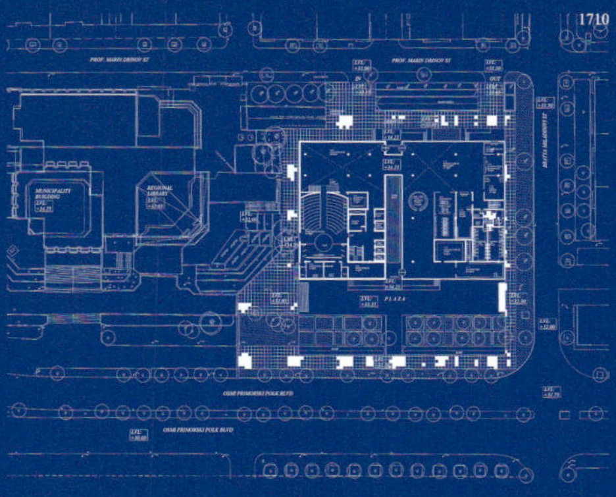

Library

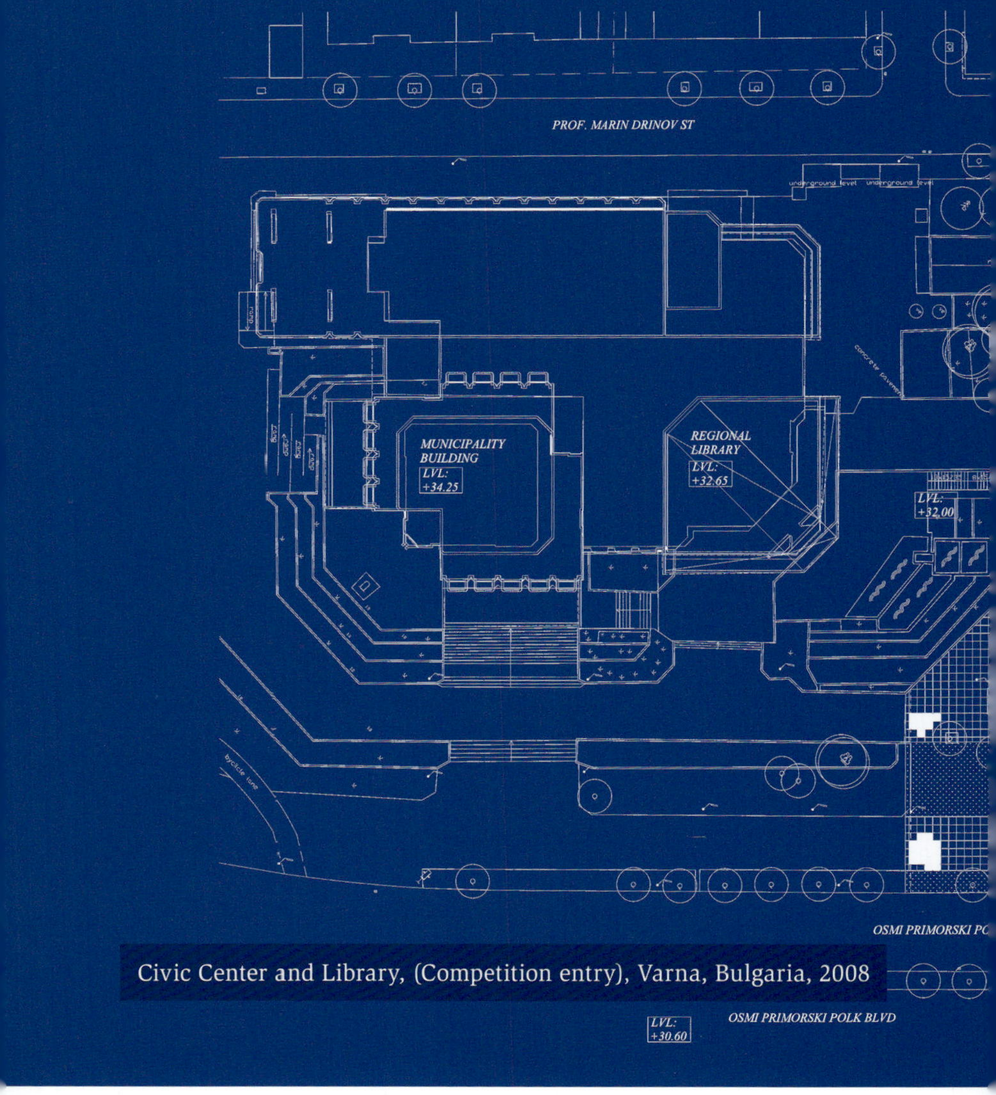

Civic Center and Library, (Competition entry), Varna, Bulgaria, 2008

The size of large structures has long been derided, especially in India, which promotes the Gandhian vision of simplicity, self-reliance and craft as the ideal to dispel poverty. But, in the West, size mattered, not for sheer gigantism, but for "bigness" of resolve. The real visionaries of size expressed and proliferated their ideas soon after the Garden City sprawl of the late 19th-century. Suddenly technology and the urge to think big mobilized the profession to come up with some real innovation. At the turning point, even Frank Lloyd Wright, despite his agrarian tendencies, suggested the Mile-High Tower. A combination of engineering, electrical power, a vertical multiplication of floor space and the invention of the elevator, all this mutated into an organism of thrift that sought to reshape a new social order of space: the high rise.

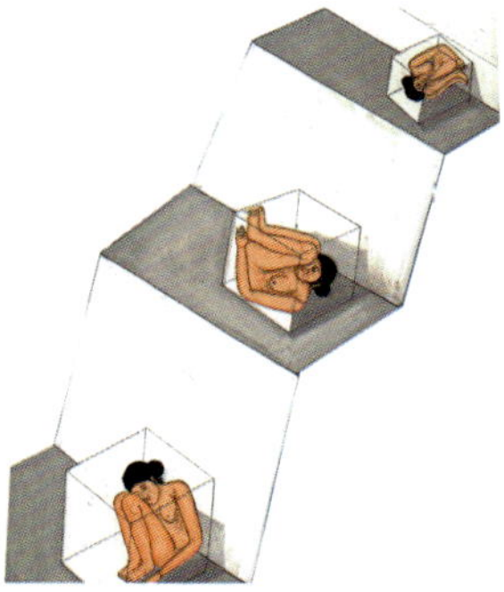

Land parcels could be hung in the air rather than spreading out on the ground.

■ Escalator 1, watercolour, 2011

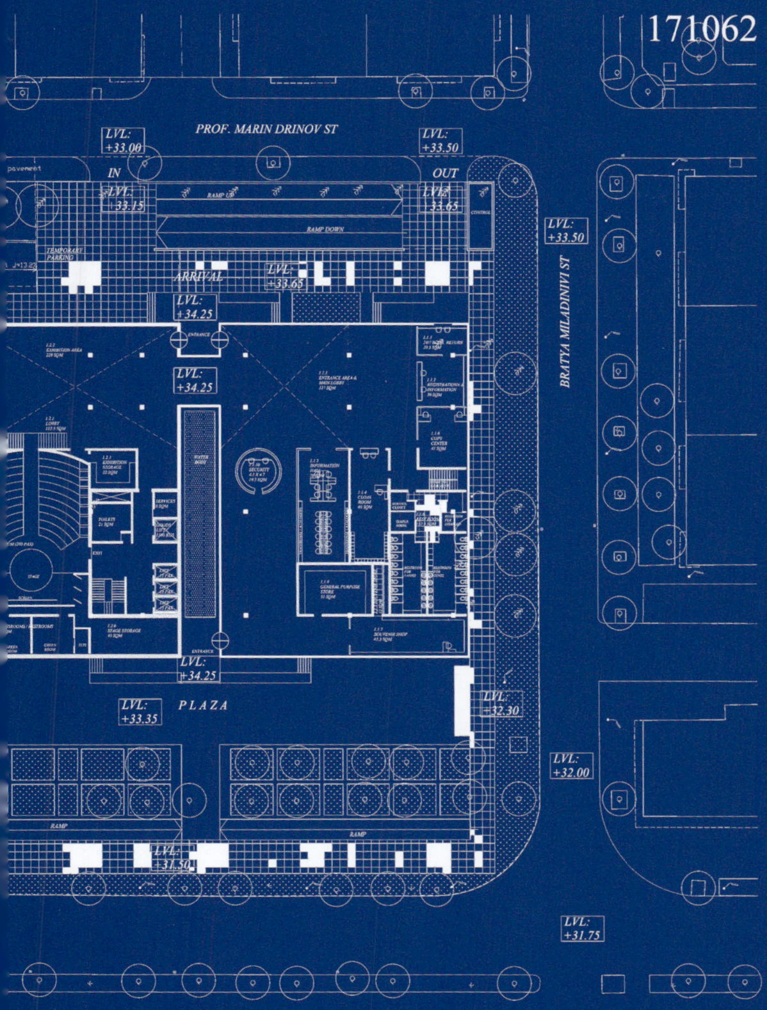

The common feature of the shared neighbourhood was the tenant across the corridor, not on the street. The invisibility of neighbourly exchange occurred on the building's private highway, the lift, as it passed local streets on its way to a viewing platform; the great *maidan* or open space; a bright stage of new architectural energy that festered for so long on the ground. The brave new world could not be approached with timidity. Sheer size was a form of architectural liberation; the snail in an earthy crawl now in flight. The building was a bewildering perplexing behemoth, a stone mountain that only the brave-hearted and foolish tried to scale from the outside. A special team of window washers who were paid better than the executives inside it were trained in the psychology of vertigo suicide baiters. The idea of "bigness" contaminated the pond with the larvae of more growth, more height.

As a single high rise on a street of low houses, the building atoned for its sins, for bringing the surrounding ground into shadow. It wept in the rain, shedding rivers of tears that slid

along its surface and filled the streets with a mud wash. It destroyed the old Greek fabric of proportion and scale, and formed awkward relationships of the parts to the whole—elongating cornices, filling entrances with colonnades and capping ungainly pediments. So untrue to the old dictum of revealing the inside on the facade, the widening gap between entering the building and entering your apartment in the building was a long sequential erasure of memory.

The sum of so many fragments no longer created a whole. So its presence disturbed, adding nothing to the eternal fabric of location, the edges and textures of streets and neighbourhoods willfully destroying the exposure at eye-level—trees, parks, people, shops, houses, and with it, the larger picture of settlement. Its presence questioned the inflexibility of the traditional city, and invalidated all personal identity. Identity, in fact, contaminated the singular dictate of the state, the Soviet-bloc like expression of the collective. People mattered in only as much as their presence fuelled a larger ideal.

Throughout history architectural symbols have been used to designate cultural significance. The church steeple, the big house of a chief, the Greek colonnades on a government institute, all stood apart at one time. Modernism's anonymity decapitated the symbols into a democratizing sameness that declared that the mere exposure of the building's function to the street was adequate to confer differences. Yet more and more of that characterization was merely a requirement to reconcile the building with the urban culture of the street and the city. It was in that defining moment that turned spectator into participant that the building's influence became critical in creating atmosphere, and the possibility of some indirect communication. By stirring emotion in the observer; expectation, possibility even disappointment; the architecture expressed its urban intention.

Library, (Competition entry), Varna, Bulgaria, 2008

At the city library for Varna, I was looking to explore the connection between intimacy and urbanity. What happens when the insular, private activity of reading is stretched to the monumental scale of a city? To connect private study to the vast city horizon demands dissociation with the immediate surroundings. No bookshelves or study tables or stacks, just two complimentary images of loneliness; the page of the book with its characters and narrative in which you are immersed when you look down, and the immense plane and distant horizon of the city when you look up. The strength of architecture relies solely on the connection between two extreme sightings; the literal focus of the page in your hand and the soft unfocussed gaze of the city at your feet. The design attempted to free the reader from the awareness of physical attachment to a building and set up an isolated vantage between the act of study and its place in the city.

The value of the library wasn't in the various stacking and study areas, but in the absence of enclosure at the edges of the building—the capacity of the readers to read and absorb the words as they sat in the seats along the outer glass; the most public face of the building. The library's structure was a personal reading of the building's size and its relationship with the immediate neighbourhood. The anonymous skyscraper in an unknown Indian city however was a different matter. Somewhere along its evolution, the image fell flat. Its genetic neutrality evolved into an awkward, visible reminder of changing cultures.

Neutral was a four-letter word that had no place in the sensory expressions of a people born to a different set of

■ Higher Rise, watercolour, 2012

public routines. The building was always a cesspool of emotions—recorded, felt, made in stone, obliterated, spat and urinated upon, and worshipped with oil and incense. The Indian was always traumatized by innumerable associations—historic, traditional, the belief in religious, ethnic and professional identity, appropriation of modernism and the hankering for global standards. This was a life that expressed its wholeness by fragmentation. To the unkind eye the erosion of small-scale towers in Indian downtown areas appears as a complete collapse of the system whose eventual renewal can happen only through a rebirth and reconfiguring. It feels as if all criticism is futile when the culture is on a steady path to self-annihilation. Buildings looked old and weathered even before they were completed.

The Indian high rise had none of the idealism expected of architecture being built for the first time. It was no experiment in design and no test of technology. It was only a replication of urban fatigue that looked as if the pieces of the ramshackle landscape had been mounted on top of each other. The seed of the new structure carried with it the root of a previous habitation. Houses—bungalows or cottages—were grafted like new pieces are tagged on to a dying tree. They were fully-laden boughs of fruit hanging low and giving private meaning to a public deal. But often this was a critical misreading made by outsiders and people like me whose physical world had evolved from over-simplification and classification, and for whom movement in a building or a city was a privilege, not a trespass. It was a modest achievement that attempted an immodesty of scale.

From a distance the structure melted into the distended chaos of urbanism; up close, its details retained the symbolic illusion of chaos, and the hope of private disorder. Though left without a clear expression of that disorder, the structure was at sea. At Varna, the design explored the contradictory and paradoxical nature of the public library itself, and expanded on the idea that a building could have both, the formal layout of a public library as well as the secretive privacy of a home study. I have always thought of reading as an intimate, possessive act. The physical possession of a book is the first step towards a possession of its contents.

A public library is an oxymoron like a public bathroom. The act of reading is just between you and the page. So other than being a storehouse, what is the public dimension of a library? On the lower floor, the formality was expressed through the standard layout of Orientation and Information procedures that opened up into the formal reading hall. The visitor was duly made aware of the library's literary offerings, their extent and exact whereabouts, and given directions about how and where to go. However, the upper floors of the library drew visitors into a distinctly different narrative. Here the library block began to curve upwards, leaning towards the concrete warehouse. In so doing, it exposed a large area of the north-facing glass to the sky, turning the wall into a roof and allowing natural light to fill the reading space.

Along the incline emerged a roof garden, an outdoor reading area. Further up, the glass structure was divided into private reading compartments—study carrels along the wall that integrated with the roofscape. The upward movement of the library was as much a discovery of informed knowledge as an encounter with the structure and its changing spatial parameters. The building's dispersed space—open or closed, monumental or intimate—allowed the reader a greater variety of spatial experiences as the building rose. From these upper levels, as the glass structure narrowed, the open library plan offered a wide perspective of views across the city. In this way, the library made a literal and visual connection with the city. How the library functions as urban study space is one thing, but the discomfort with anonymous and monumental size remains.

We approach all environments as scavengers, beating away barking dogs and apprehending all wilderness as our own. The mistaking of the public urban dimension for wilderness too often collides with private sensibilities. It is either one or the other, never both. The conflict between mega-structure and intimacy is never resolved and this leaves a blind spot in the architectural retina. The growth of the city, the apartment house and the street remain afflicted with the private vision of size and scale—an anthill or Disney world—where additions and subtractions are strategies of private organization. There is never a moment in time when the creators can stand back far enough, and declare, "yes, it is complete now". Consequently the whole, whatever it might be—building, city, or neighbourhood—is always read as a collective of small parts, disjointed and unrelated. The climax of all construction is a state that is ravaged and seemingly incomprehensible. It has the quality of craft's artisan formula that makes small, tactile displays that overlay each other but contribute nothing to the order of a larger dimension. The Varna project similarly set itself private parameters in a wholly disjointed scale of public space. The frame of the larger picture was continually contaminated by the inarticulate picture of ceaseless private activity that, however hard you try, can never be confined to a single blueprint or intention.

■ Chess Players, charcoal, 2001

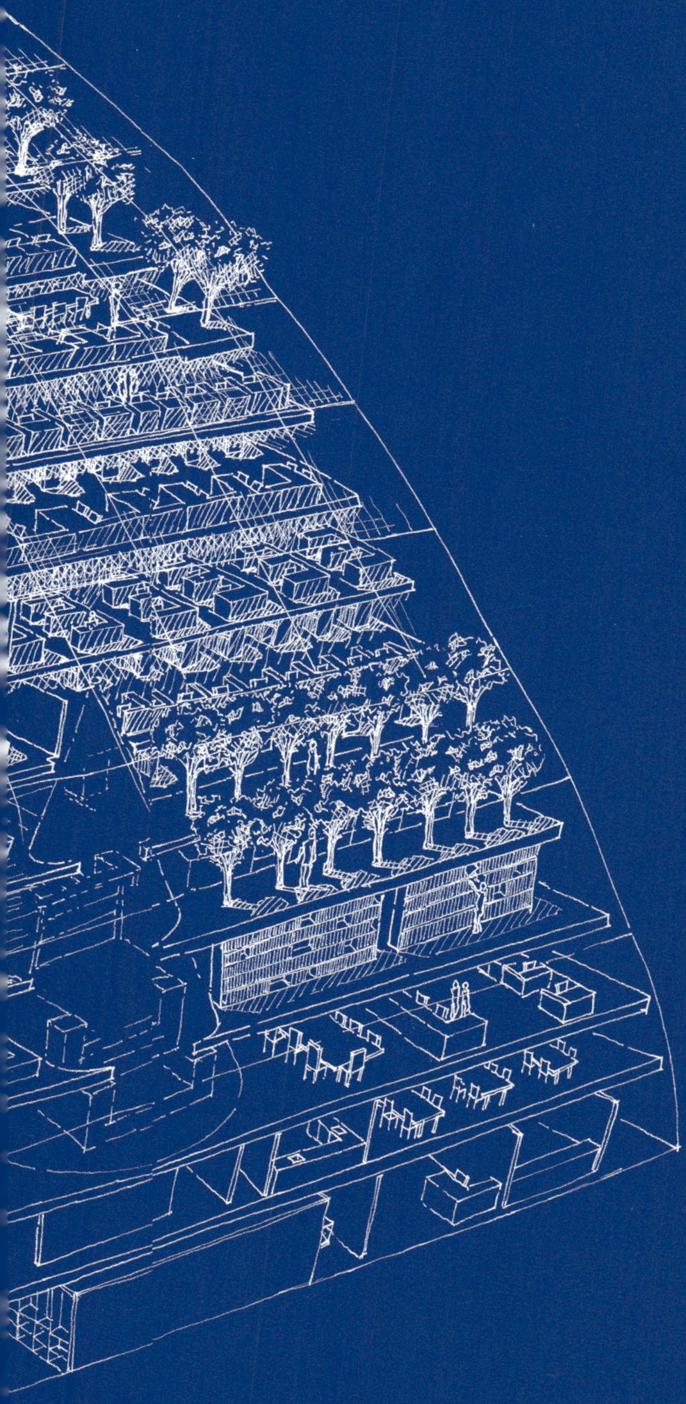

Library Building, Varna, Bulgaria

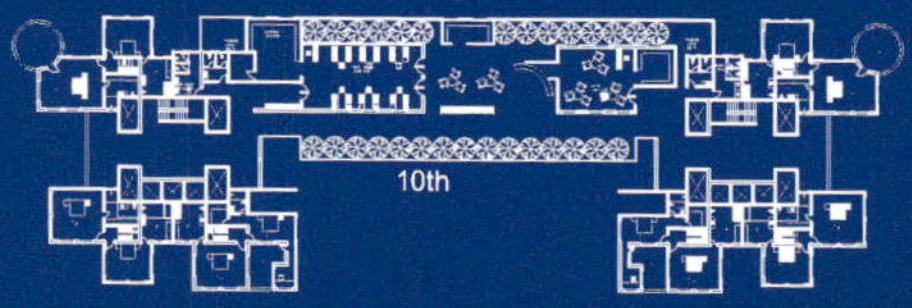

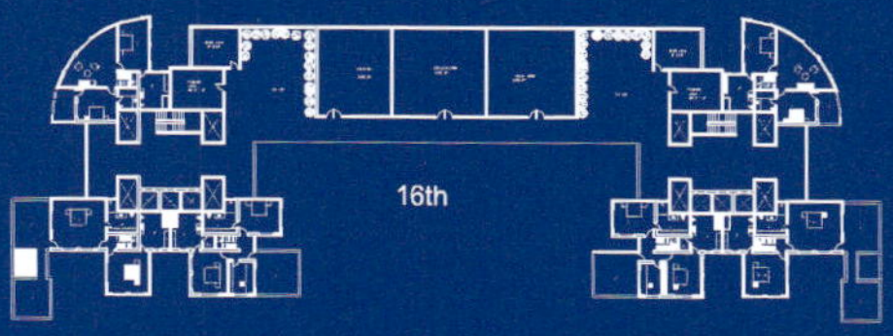

Tower

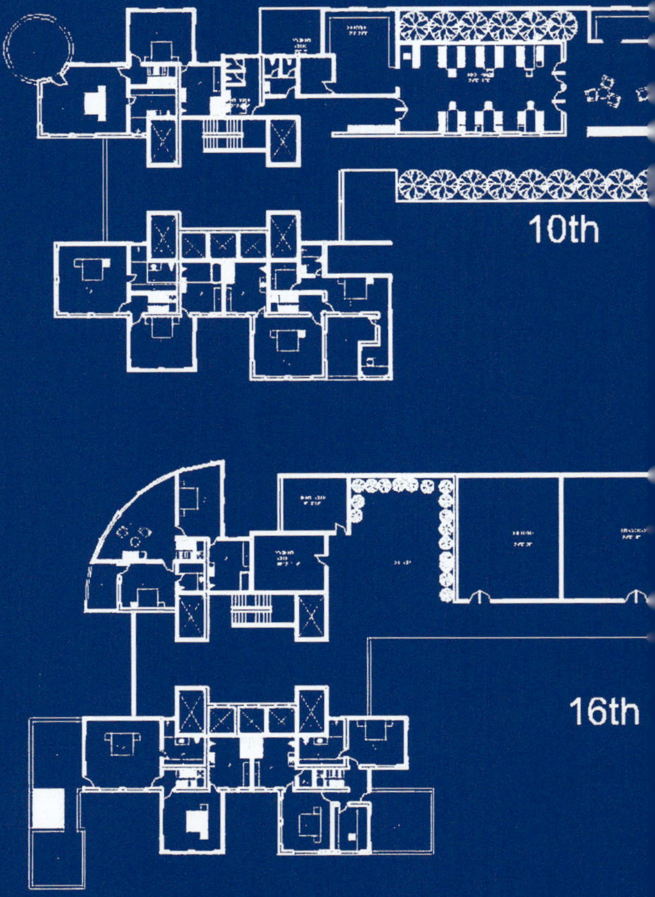

Plans, Apartment Tower, Patiala, Punjab, 2008

The terrestrial nature of human existence throughout history makes life in the vertical dimension a completely new experience. The growth of cities has been related to sprawl, the continual occupation of land—the usurping of agricultural terrain for residential purposes. The move below ground or high above has been largely necessitated by human density and made possible by technology. Architecture begins from a state of weakness, as an empty instrument of provision, rather than reform; its programme and space determined as a consequence of convenience. The rigid non-variables of vertical space force the inhabitant into new, evolving symmetries; practices similar to that of a ruin inhabited to new purposes.

The elevator's efficient run up the hollow core of the structure surrounded by utilities, leaves the wider frame free. As you walk ahead inside a bus, ringing the bell for your stop and clutching your briefcase, you are programmed to a new architectural form of public life, an uncomfortable, theatrical closeness that most recognize as a cultural invasion of privacy. The unchangeable form, altered to suit private life, draws and makes visible the creative potential of both

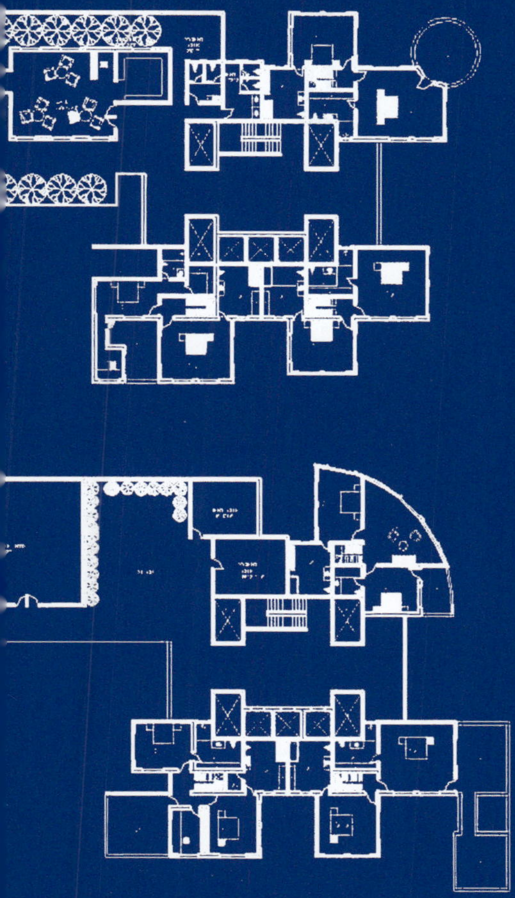

the building and its user. It gives the freedom to inhabit the space behind the glass at will, and still reveal nothing of the interior arrangement to the outside. So it follows that the vertical dimension, when fully exploited, first, leaves greater manoeuvrability on the ground, and second, gives a physical unity to the clamour for mixed use—a desperate human imperative that seeks to lessen the distance between home, workplace, shopping and recreation.

It is hardly a radical view, and in small measure, the thesis was tested time and again in the high rises of Manhattan in the 1900s. The impossible mechanics of the city's land made the architect seek a revolutionary answer within the tight fabric of the ground's congestion. Rem Koolhaas called Manhattan an "archipelago of independent entities consisting of 2,028 islands". This maritime model depicts the typical city blocks of the Manhattan

■ High Rise, watercolour, 2011

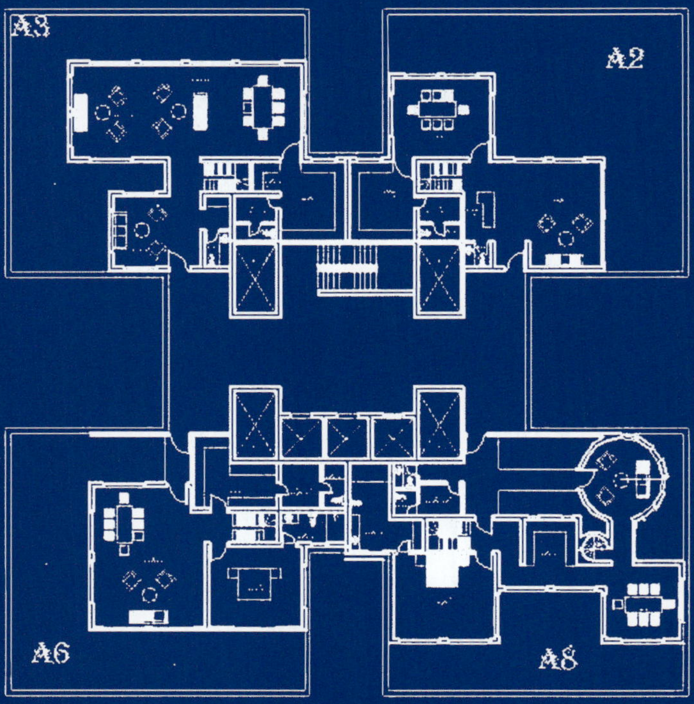

TYPE2

Ground floor

grid floating in a sea of traffic. The city's congestion created an unprecedented mutation; a building that grew multiple uses inside its elevated slabs of unrelated land.

The distillation of disparate social actions condensed into a tower produced a programmatic variation that gave the city a new foreign type—an encounter of such diverse variables in one structure that resembled a social theme park on architectural steroids. McKim Mead and White, time and again offered to condense and distill the outdoor life and infuse it into multiple strips of high rise design: an outdoor club located indoors, but absorbed in spatial dimensions so surprising, architecture lent a totally new perspective to the activity itself. The swimming pool, Oyster bar, golf course, barbeque patio, wrestling arena, squash court—the full spread of conventional club functions came together in intense exchanges and overlaps.

The culture of sport that crackled against its inner skin emboldened the fuselage of functions to a new dynamic performance, an act that combined personal will, the physics of recreation and the wider connections, to the agitated street and the distant river. The divisions by floor separated functions, but the member was free to construct his own story and move at will. The only way to test the thesis of an emerging confluence was to give in wholeheartedly to a vision of improbable performance. It asked for architecture to be subjected to

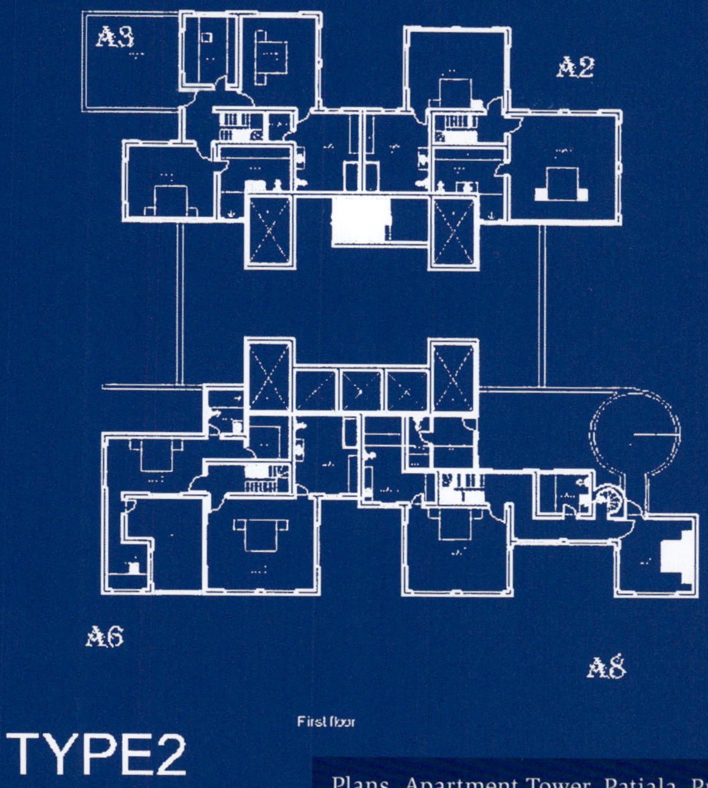

Plans, Apartment Tower, Patiala, Punjab, 2008

multiplicities of fragments that either sustained or destroyed the ideal. So the architect continued relentlessly, separating places too similar to each other, heaping ceremonial space on utilitarian ones, making groups, then breaking them apart, superimposing differences, placing open next to closed, play against work.

The skyscraper was an attempt at a new homeland, a vertical one that had never existed before. In order to assume real space and dimension it necessarily destroyed classical convictions, and was deaf to contemporary life and traditional knowledge; becoming a whole without prescribed form. The real value of the mixing of infinite activities lay in the accidental collisions that occurred when two opposing forces were housed side by side. Initially the confinement produced anxiety and restlessness. At the same time, it also induced new experiences, human interactions and sensations missing in the rarefied privacy of life on the ground.

In every form of work there is a utopian tendency, the human wish to alter the norm. The high rise has the potential not just to alter itself, its surroundings and the view from its ramparts. The disconnection from earthly confines and the innate ability to make buildable slices of earth in the sky formulated a new metropolitan instrument that was at once a mounting assembly of floors not linked to each other, and a complete composition

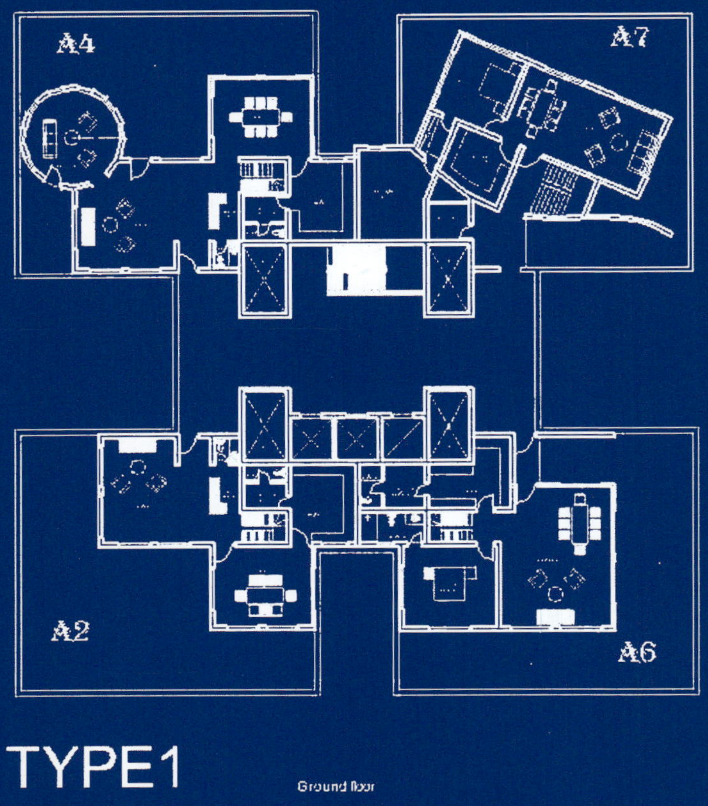

itself. The building's unerringly democratic arrangement made architectural control and division impossible.

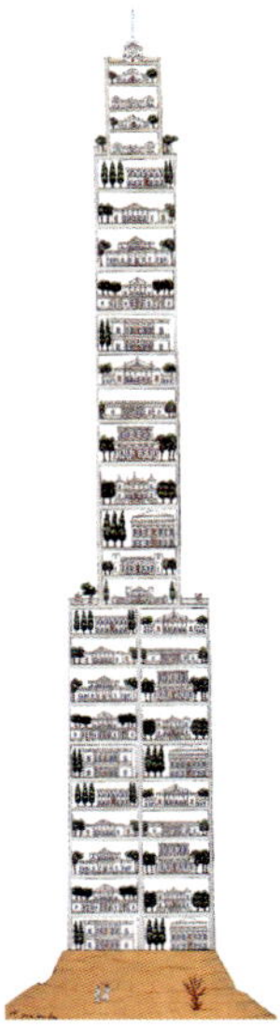

People mingled in the elevators, collided in lobbies and verandahs; the close packing and movement in circulation zones were a source of intense discomfort. People shared treadmills in gyms, arranged marriages in community halls located between apartments and a park. The messier the exchange, the more sensory and invasive the overlap, the more successful the social intent of the vertical life. Without the choices of lateral movement, the confinement in limited space spelt only two choices: mix and live, or commit suicide.

Life on the sixtieth floor produces only the unprecedented and the exceptional, creating either heroes or martyrs. The building is a revelation of mistaken conventions: tower, town house, apartment, office, home; it rises downtown, in business district and suburb. It can exist alone or

■ High Rise of Bungalows, pencil on paper, 2011

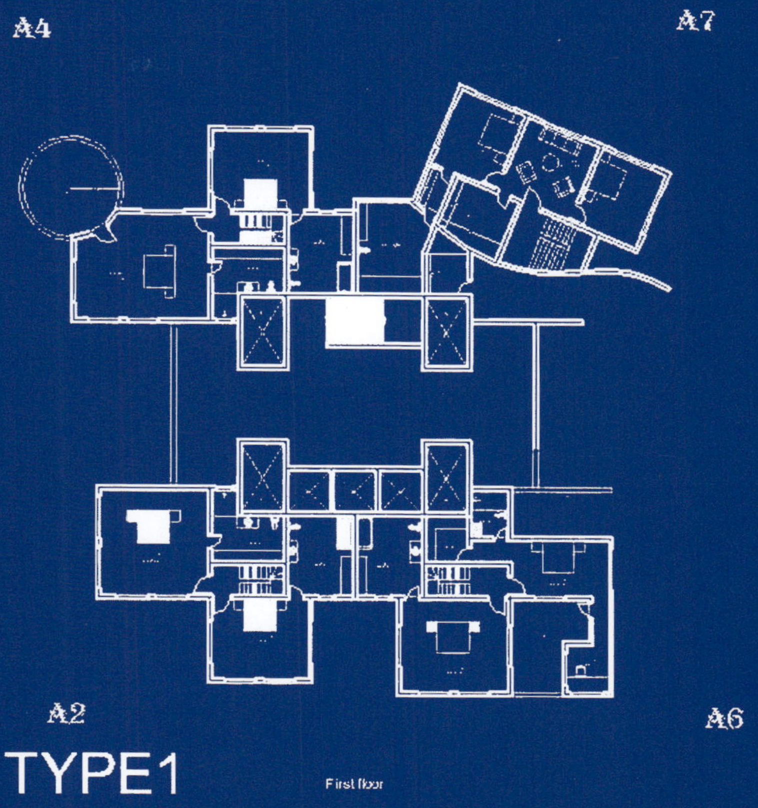

Plans, Apartment Tower, Patiala, Punjab, 2008

with other skyscrapers, defining its margins in narrow glass or thick stone. If you move the Empire State Building into the mountainous countryside of upstate New York, or the Chrysler Building into the Grand Canyon, it would make little difference to the type, function and architectural intent of the structures. The long bands of string window, the lower floors of masonry replaced by the glassiness above would remain intact and entirely inscrutable.

The view of the seventieth floor will exact the same revenge from its surroundings; the internal diagram of floor to ceiling height, the depth between window and elevator core, would all stay fixed. The outer skin of the skyscraper has a life entirely separate from the inner arrangement of floors, the division of plans and the placement of objects. The rising face visible for miles performs for an urban audience, entirely unaware of the families held in lonely confinement in sixtieth-floor bedrooms. In this unintended paradox of its schizophrenic existence, the building is cast as a mental patient hiding its paranoia on its inner shelves

Interior (left) and exterior, Apartment Tower, Patiala

and only exposing its sunnier sociability to the street. The division of states, like the advertising slogans printed on a breakfast cereal box, further the conflict between the box and its contents.

The current picture of the city in the Indian subcontinent is made up of multiple factors: Shortage of buildable land, increasing migration and densification, the divide between the rich and the poor, shortage of services and utilities and cultural and social inequities. The positive aspects of such a diverse mix must be sought through new planning and architectural assemblies. The complementary nature of this diversity can only be harnessed through mutual support of differences and a belief that proximities in lifestyle and daily routines will remove the suspicions and unrest that make Indian cities divided and lifeless places.

The unity and close packing of the skyscraper can nourish the connections and promote better working and social relationships. There is of course the standard argument against the vertical city: we have an earth-linked culture, we value street life, the country is prone to earthquakes, high rises require greater building resources, Indians

wish to derail anything new, but the most obvious of them all is the urge to keep all experiments at bay. It is well known that high-density living makes for corresponding reductions in pollution and energy consumption. People travel shorter distances, save time and generally live healthier lives. Standard of living surveys place high rise cities like New York and Hong Kong above more spread-out cities like Paris and Los Angeles.

Moreover, controlling, and even restricting the movement of people in urban centres can only be done through high-density living. We are not talking about the cosmetic addition of a floor or two, but the challenge of 60-70-storeyed structures. In such a scheme, there would be obvious questions about infrastructure, parking, the drain on utilities, etc. But if thoughtfully conceived along with a design that combines an Indian sensibility and new technology, the great middleclass skyscraper is likely to succeed. The current imagery of the luxury high rise is only a squalid reminder of urban India's architectural class distinctions. And despite the neon wasteland that immodestly

■ **FOLLOWING PAGES** Khajuraho Towers, charcoal on paper, 2001

claims to be Shining India, the country's architecture can be truly heroic if it claims a place in the minds of ordinary people, where the unworkable model of perpetual growth is replaced by one of contentment and neighbourliness.

The daily life of a town—home, work, recreation, commerce, pleasure—could be combined in a singular framework, providing the space of multiple neighbourhoods in one structure. A workable model of a complete green city inserted into a single structure will have to be dense and urban—without driving, and unnecessary commutes, more modest homes, no private land ownership, and a citizenry that engages with each other. I had begun to view the city skyscraper in a similar light. Not as a controlling mechanism for functions diagrammatically filled into its framework, but as something with potential for a new kind of behaviour, invigorated by the proximity of varying social environments.

Unprecedented in its multiple allocations, the building was a potential zone of conflict of functions. It held the promise of an

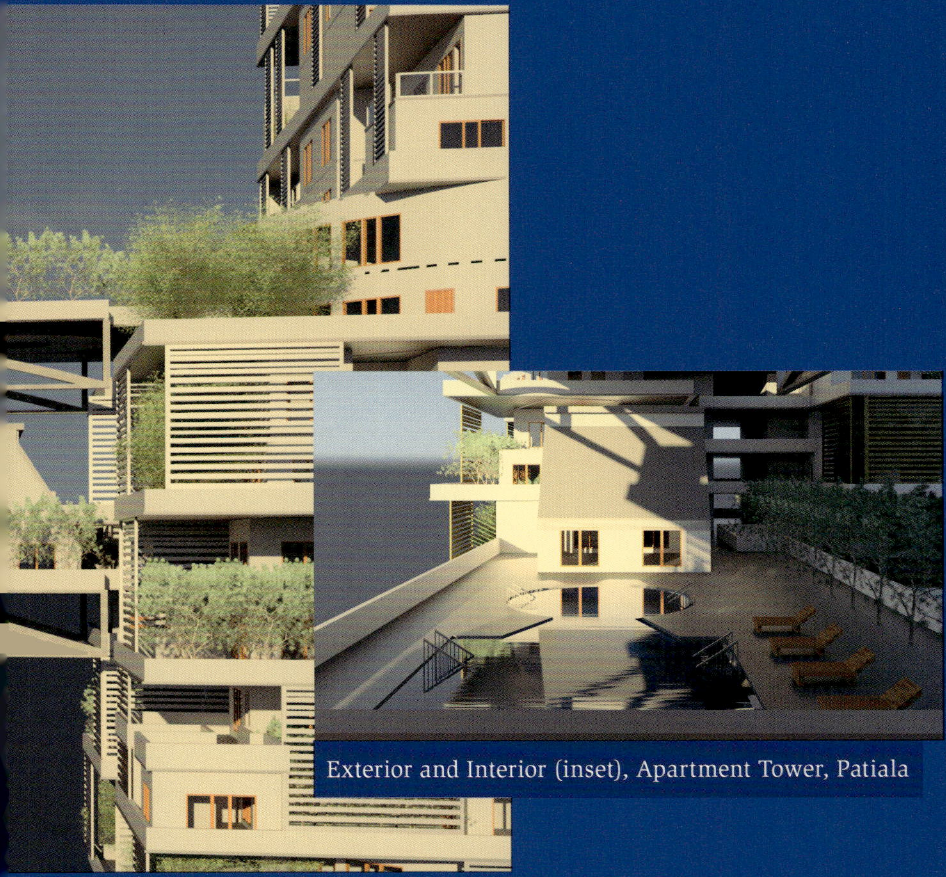

Exterior and Interior (inset), Apartment Tower, Patiala

altogether different work ethic, and consequently a different work day. It questioned long-standing ideas of travel, distance, the concept of place as building on land, individual choice, commuting, the notion that landscape was ground. The presence of constructing contrasting situations in such close proximity produced a new perception. If architecture got out of hand, if people's behaviour became too adventurous, the building authority would have to issue a restraining order—the bar could not come within 50 feet of the swimming pool; the spa had to maintain its distance from the library.

The unprecedented nature of the bloated exercise required a new set of zoning laws. These would need to permit overlaps and restrain activity. By itself the building survives on the limitless contrast of reactions brought about by decisive overlaps. Architecture lays bare topics for colluding performance in which the architect's role is limited to that of the shadow director. The production of stress, despair, delight and disgust are dependent on the nature of the visitor's involvement and the visitor's own

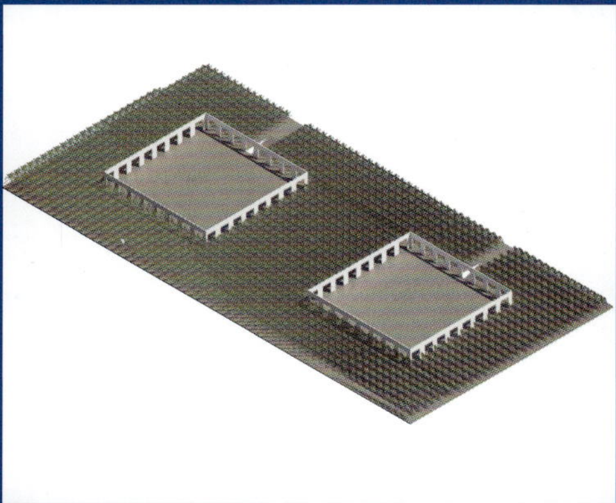

Development, Apartment Tower, Patiala

inclinations, and not on some centralized monitoring system. The history of the tower, rising with advancing technology, left the Classical architect in a visible state of distension and despair.

The building's long and steady relationship with the ground and sky had marked the facade with a characteristic assembly of classical elements—entrance portico middle ground of colonnades, and a topping of pediment. Technology had blown the scheme apart and left a disturbance in the mind's eye and the question of how to reconcile the limited measurable ground with the open sky as the building rose up. The early steps were a tentative mounting of earthbound structures, mounted saddle back one upon the other, creating a facsimile of the repetitive homes of a suburban sub-division in the ungainly pile of a domestic skyscraper.

My own inability to employ the skyscraper merely as a tool to erect domesticity at a height led to formal exercises with the Indian bungalow, long since considered an urban ideal. First, the recognizable single and double-storeyed bungalow from Lutyens and Palladio is carefully packaged in a similarly recognizable wood cabinet. Each shelf acts to store one family compound, complete with arrival porch, fronting verandah, a servants quarter and a vegetable patch. The drawers of the cabinet open and close with the time of day and change of season. Such a scheme offsets the misuse of un-built urban land, and paradoxically bogs down a building type designed as a spreading, lazy offshoot of wasted land; its boundary wall shrouded in green behind hedges and creepers. The economic basis of the original was always suspect.

Up at a height, piled one on top of the other, land was once again useless, repetition happily distorting its ground value. The final imagery can hardly be tested for its real estate value, and the juxtaposition of furniture and architecture is riddled with a mindless

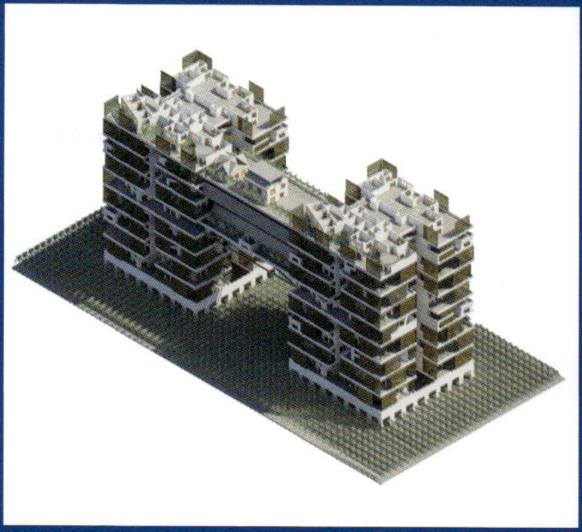

sensibility somewhere between the insolence of trial, and the pretence of invention. The biggest fear is of being read as ironic, theatrical and whimsical, and being misread as "unserious". The architect then has learnt to live in an ultimate hyper reality. When everything around is a lie, and tests the imaginative grasp of the viewer, it falls upon the architect to resurrect another form of physical fiction. The deadening forces of advertising, the patented structures of mass appeal, the product launches and celebrity testaments, the sales pitches of the politician, the sponsorship of daily news, the ready sale of journalists and artists, the borrowing and selling of a foreign lifestyle, the eventual retreat into building is itself a blatant and unflinching device of commerce now.

The sum of the high rise's many parts rises to denote a new form of monumentalism and because of sheer size, the building denotes a noticeability above all else. It is no longer monumentality like in the formal representation of an established landmark, but a gigantism of volume enclosed in what Koolhaas called "the symptom of automonumentality." The Qutub Minar's height draws more tourists than formal monuments like India Gate or Humayun's Tomb. The necessary message that human will is capable of creating such a physical effect is enough to give it a profound and lasting significance.

I was at a complete loss when once asked by a builder for a "high-end" design for a skyscraper apartment complex in Patiala. In the eyes of the builder, air conditioning, valet parking, pool, roll-out bar, electronic security, barbeque, were all necessary requirements and expectations for anyone paying above a million dollars for a flat. Luxury was something else. Luxury was the magic that separated the super rich from the ultra rich; the merely elite from the super elite. For a long time,

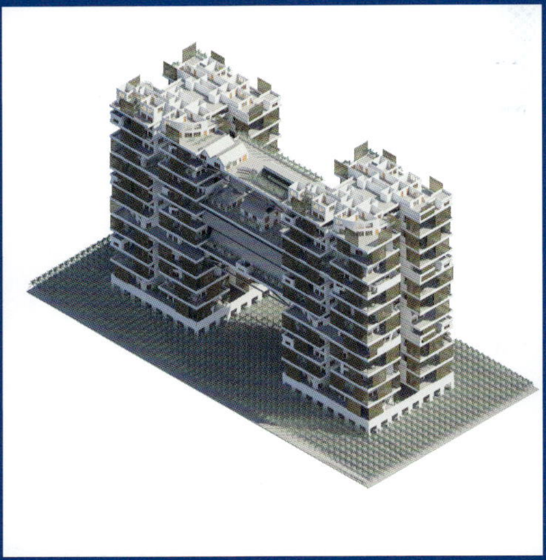

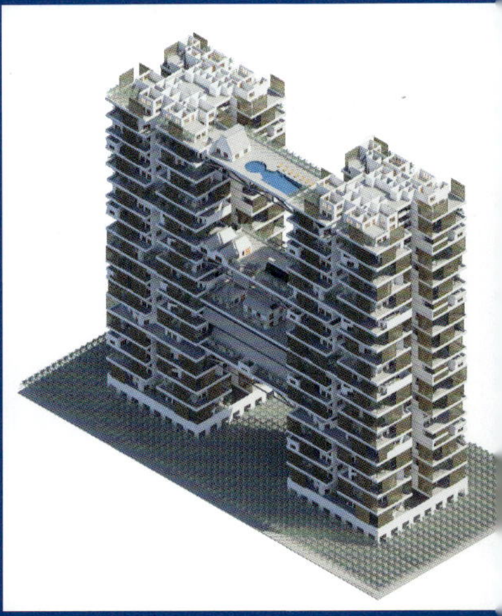

Development of Skyscraper Apartment Tower, Patiala

my colleagues and I wracked our brains, read Brazilian vacation magazines and scrolled through Mediterranean holiday websites. But there was nothing out of the ordinary there. Just a lot of bored people lying around half-naked on the sand. We needed a gripping new irrationality, some mindlessness that would renew rich people's faith in luxury.

What emerged from the design discussions was the basic flaw in the location of consumer facilities. Most golf courses, tennis courts, swimming pools and parking lots are built directly on the ground thereby disturbing the natural flora and fauna, and consuming precious land. So in our new scheme, they were lifted up into the air at considerable cost, and made into extensive bridges between two towers of apartments. You could walk out from your sixtieth-floor living room, as if you were on the ground and play a few holes of golf. Or you could do an easy breast stroke as the evening lights of downtown Patiala glowed in the distance, below you.

The Indian obsession with the car meant that apartment owners were unhappy with the idea of leaving an expensive and beloved family member in the parking lot. So individual garages were inserted with each apartment and owners could ride up the ramp and pull into their private porch high up. Instead of the panoramic view of the landscape you could be watching your own Jaguar from your entertainment den. Since the basement was now left empty, and airless, dark and damp, it was ideal to house the servants and generator sets.

The expression of luxury in part was related to added facilities; but in large part it also lay in the belief of ownership of an original

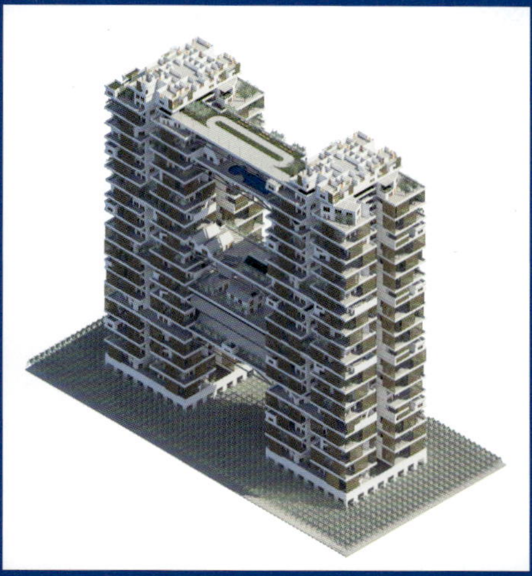

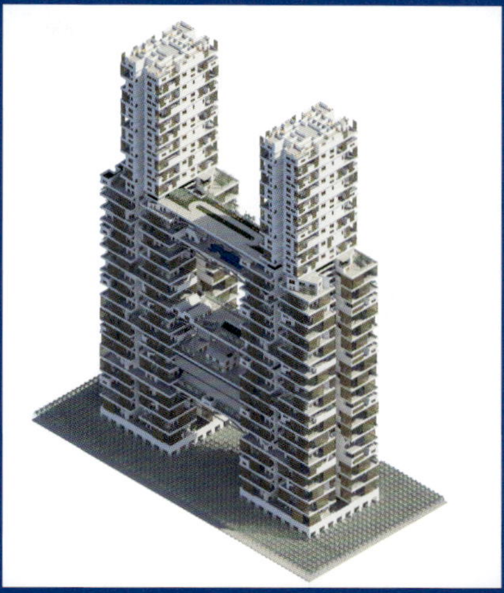

architectural artifact. Each home resolved in multiple variations fitted into high, pre-determined aerial space. Such an unravelling of different elevations on each floor was also defined by the inherent need for disorder in a high rise envelope repeating endlessly across 70 floors. In the desperate human need to mark the home by constantly personalizing institutional space, the apartment complex was likened to a furniture cabinet in which every shelf was a different residence—a house, a villa, a bungalow, a cottage—with its front garden, kitchen vegetable patch and servants' quarter.

The only difference from the home on the ground was the relationship to the horizon. The need to achieve complexity through private variables was an impossibility in a structure sold as a series of finite, repetitive commodities. I had always sought such contradictory reconciliations in architecture—with the spreading privately stylized country house at one end, and the builder flat, sustained in small pockets of air space at the other. The conflicting nature of their design when seen together would only produce unusual hybrids.

My exchange with the builder went something like this: "Lakshmi Mittal has a squash court in his house," I'd say. "Then we must have two." "His garage has wall-to-wall carpeting." "We'll put it in our driveways as well." "Mukesh Ambani has a snow-making machine in his house." "We'll have a full-time resident fortune teller." "Dubai has a ski slope in a mall," "We'll have a beach with sand and waves… Everything."

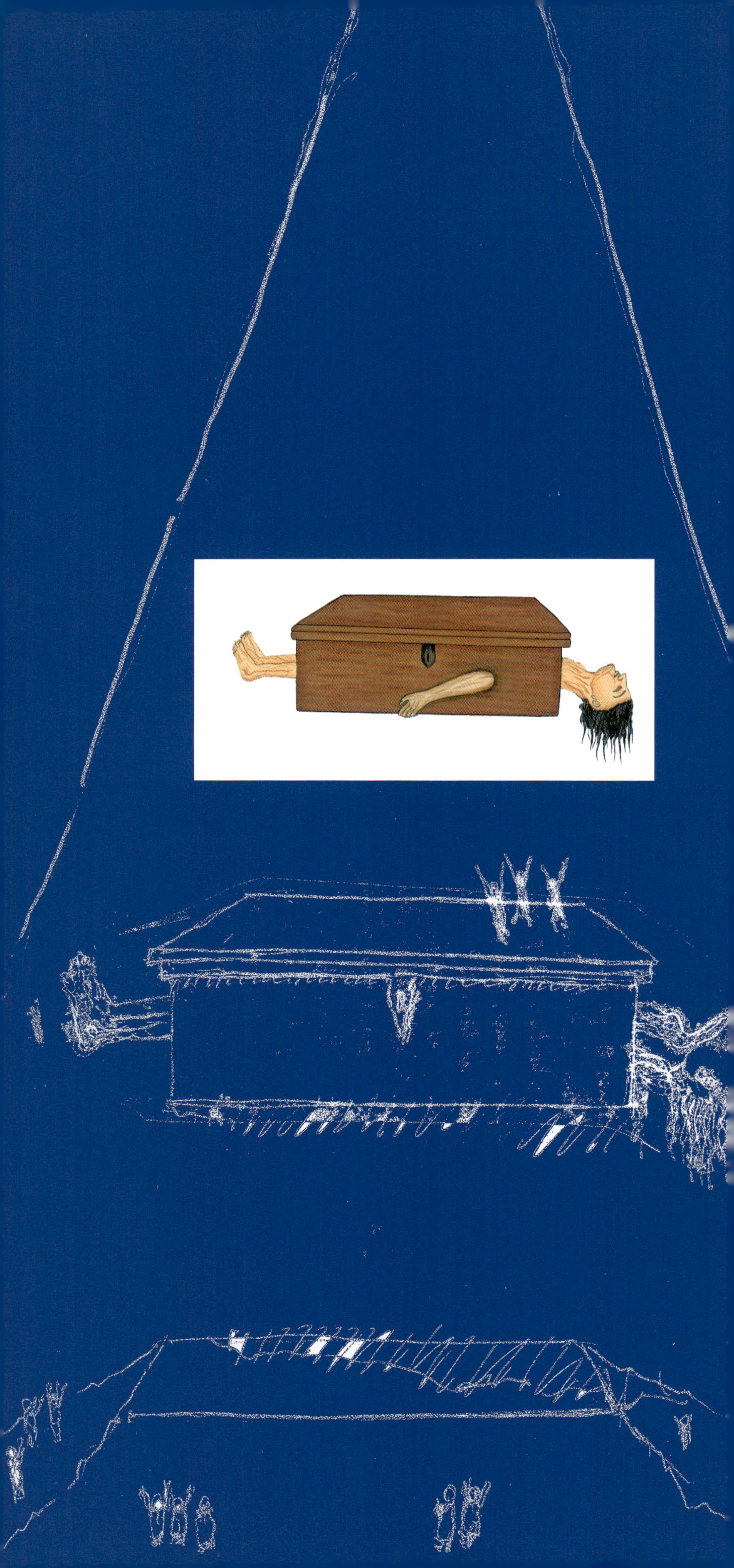

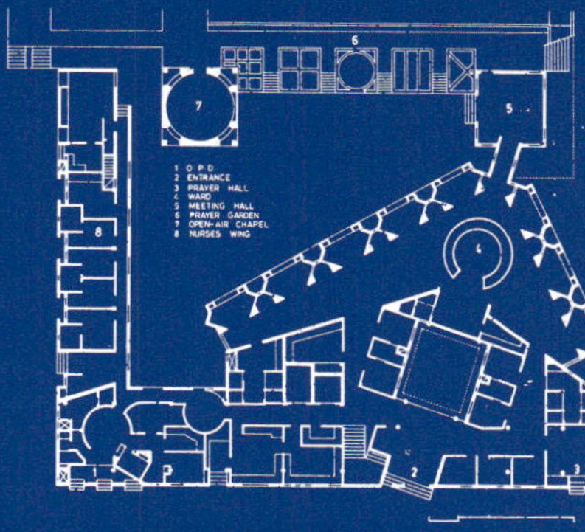
1 O.P.D.
2 ENTRANCE
3 PRAYER HALL
4 WARD
5 MEETING HALL
6 PRAYER GARDEN
7 OPEN-AIR CHAPEL
8 NURSES WING

Hospice

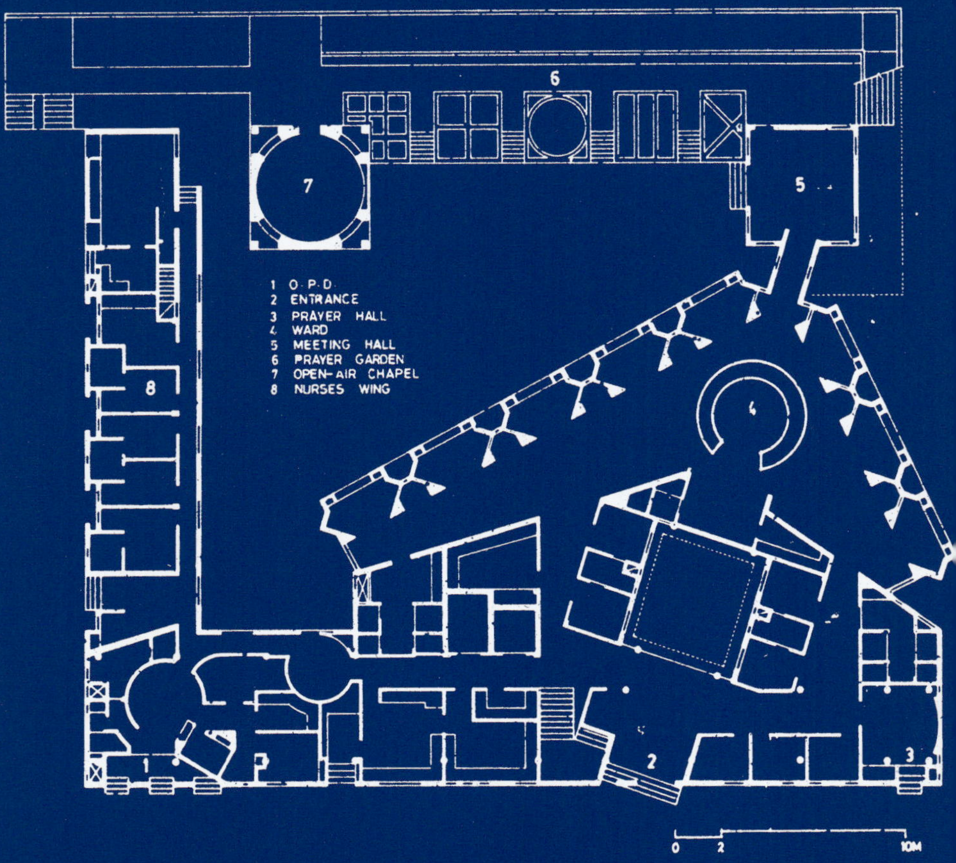

Cancer Hospice, Ring Road, Delhi, 1993

While on a visit to a hospice in Mumbai, on the insistence of a client, I watched a young girl waiting to be wheeled into the ward. She must have been 14 or 15, but her frame, wasted by disease, shook with a kind of inner violence which only she could experience; her cries gave us no clue about the reason for her distress. Was it the certainty of death implicit in the admission to a hospice, or the pain caused by her disease? It was difficult to tell.

In the hospice structure, the orientation of the wards to the open ocean, away from the confining mess of the roadside shops of Bandra, remained the most crucial decision in the building's architecture. In its two inflecting arms towards the Arabian Sea, the design stressed on the uninterrupted view of the seascape as the most important criterion for the well-being of its short-time residents. The sea view was an architectural gift of the site given to every patient, to be seen through his own picture window, from his own personal balcony. Sitting in

■ Escape, watercolour, 2011

stillness, viewing his own private sky and ocean, he would be instinctively given to meditation and reflection. If life is short, the scheme seemed to suggest, let its final moments be sustained by the more enduring natural environment outside.

Unlike the pleasing circumstance of the Mumbai location, Delhi presented a difficult and more unkind situation. Other than ease of access, there was little to redeem the site on the city's busiest road, made noisy by non-stop, aggressive traffic. Even the few trees that lined its precarious edge were reduced to sparseness, their shrivelled leaves coated with the rising dust. The industrial pollution in the area had reduced the visibility, shrouding the place by evening in a mist of gloom. The plight of cancer patients constrained to lie on a line of beds overlooking this grim, choking pall of urban blight, and the dim-lit street outside, struck me as a strange, cruel irony.

■ Burial ground 1, watercolour, 2011

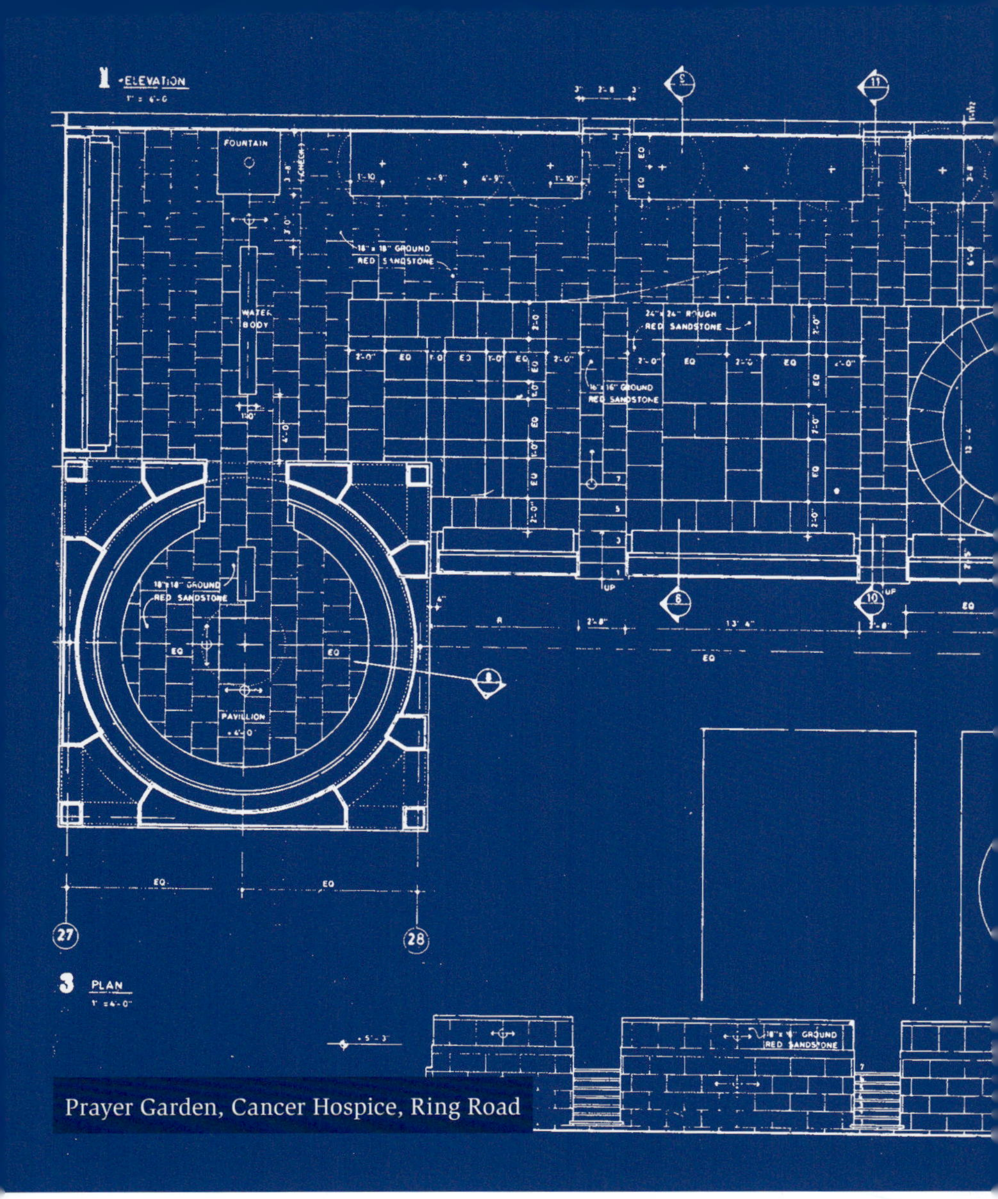

Prayer Garden, Cancer Hospice, Ring Road

Under such a darkening spectacle, any building providing care, love and promoting a sense of hope would necessarily have to look to its own inner reserves for sustenance. The only method was to enact a reversal in design. In the final scheme, the front service wing rose three storeys and they contained all the facilities that required easy public access—the out-patient clinic, administrative offices, conference rooms, kitchens, storage areas and common facilities. The building's long, undifferentiated volume served as a formal entrance as well as a shield for the more important wards behind it. With its minute, reticent windows, the front was not designed for any great visual impact, but merely provided the backdrop, the white palette, for the sandstone portals that suggested entrances into the institution's three main facilities—the out-patients' clinic, wards, and viewing chapel.

The names of individual gates—Peace, Hope and Eternal Love—were suggestive of the varying conditions of its patients: those who only required periodic treatment, the terminally ill, and the dead. In the facade, the sandstone portals attained varying heights

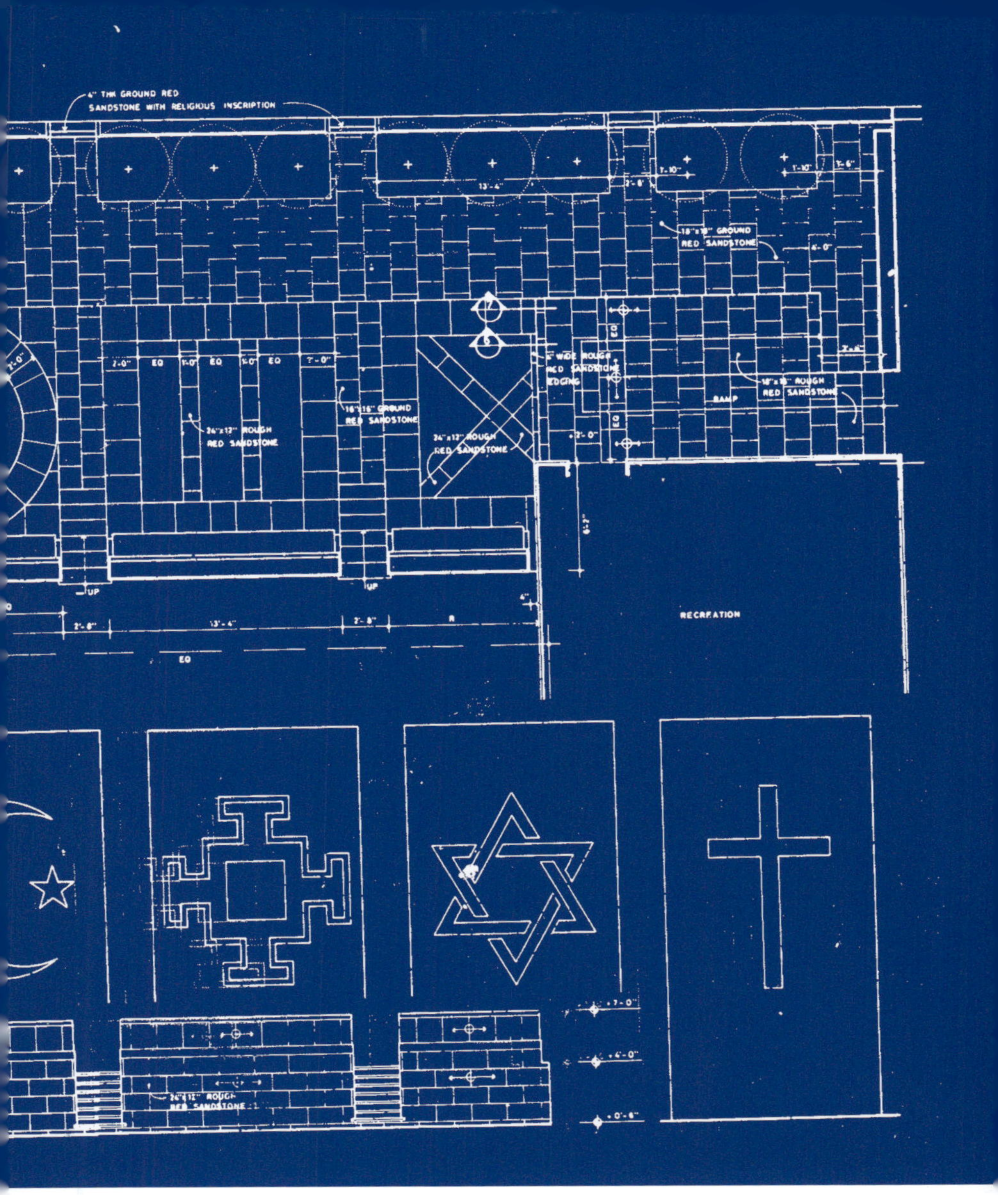

and proportions, concealing the larger windows behind their stonework, and stood as architectural markers of these three distinct functions. There then occurred a symbolic separation of the service areas of the building—treated as a simple foreground—and the introverted patient areas, which became a more idiosyncratic background. The high wall of the northern street edge was chosen for offices and facilities that required little sunlight, while the more desirable southern exposure was given to the wards.

Central to the organization of the plan was a formal prayer garden, a substitute for the sea view in Mumbai. Concealed from the buildings that were part of the noisy day-to-day running of the hospice, it allowed a view and access only to the patients

■ Burial Ground 2, watercolour, 2011

who would gain something from its affinity. At the time it felt akin to the landscape of a cemetery, its half-built, overgrown nature used to draw the patients away from the restlessness of death into an organic uncertainty. It was a place in which both death and life were present. In my mind the cemetery, its unkempt garden and tomb stones, has the curious contradictory quality of withdrawal, solitude, even escape. Moreover in a ward shackled by pain and restlessness, I hoped the private circular enclosures would work like personalized confessionals, and induce a quieter state of mind.

With all the ordinary services of the building relegated to areas beyond its sensory periphery, the garden's very orientation afforded an experience of tranquility, which was heightened by its introversion. Only those places of special ceremonial or symbolic significance, such as the open-roofed prayer hall, were allowed to intrude on the sanctity of this special place. The building sought to project itself as a place of comfort in the hope that familiar surroundings would help the residents to adjust. Besides making a subliminal connection to a large house, the building had other more desirable attributes: adequate

Detail, Prayer Garden, Cancer Hospice

ingress for light and air, a sense of enclosure, the privacy of individual bedrooms, the well-judged placement of shared living areas and a view of the outer garden. These conditions became the controlling values of the building's architecture.

The patient was the primary consideration, and the close-knit architectural sequence allowed the free movement from the bed to the prayer garden to be a natural progression from the private to the shared landscape. Such transitions were seen as the ordinary inclinations of day-to-day human behaviour. To this end, the public spaces of the hospice were treated in textures, material and lighting, distinct from those of the private wards, where the sensory and the tactile became far more critical. Within the large public movement of the wards and hallways, the bedrooms receded into their own private alcoves. Differing in material and texture, and affected more directly by the outside light and air, they became tiny sanctuaries, withdrawing from the circulating anonymity of the ward and the controlling gaze of the nurse's viewing station.

A parallel condition was created outside. The raised plinth of the rear garden, the deep bands of low trees and sandstone seats all recreated a dense, manicured geometry of landscape; a setting that encouraged solitude and prayer and allowed the patient to withdraw inwards.

INDIA

Institute

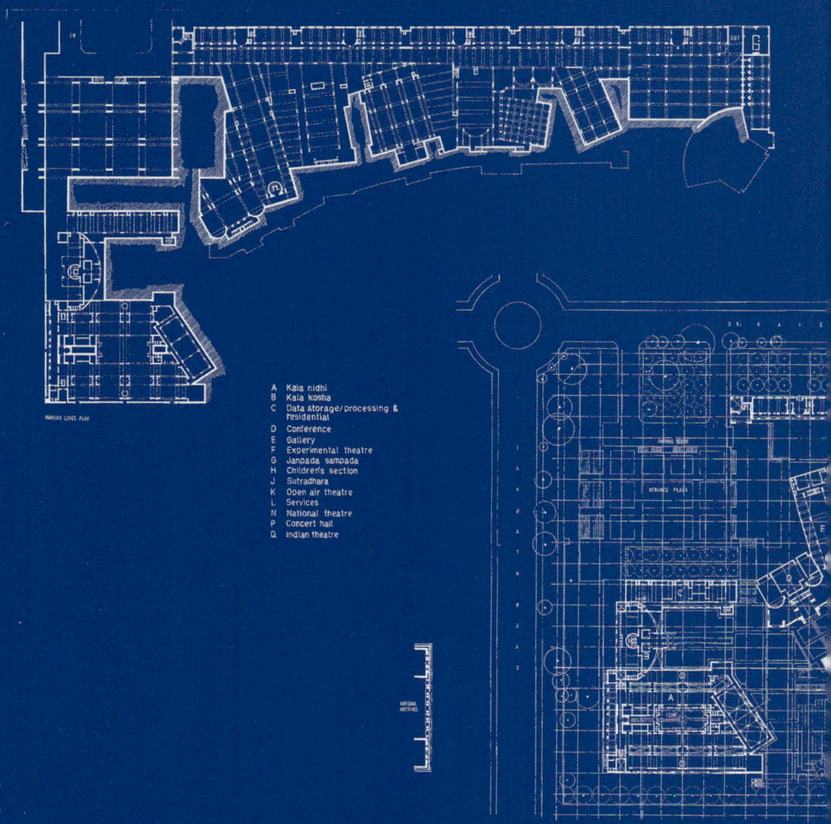

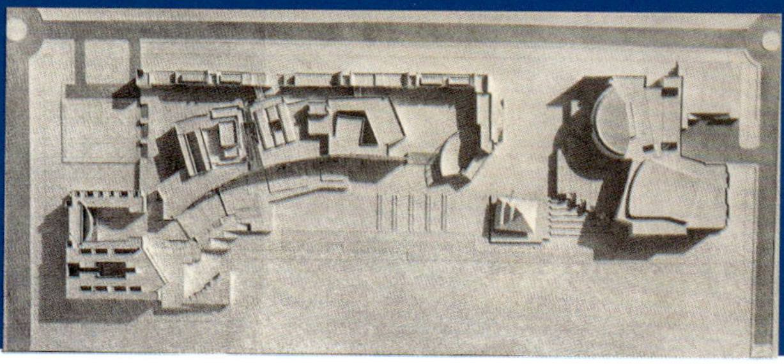

For two years I lived and worked on the campus of the Indian Institute of Management, a complex designed by Louis Kahn. My room in one of the dormitories was a monastic shell, a closed space open to the light. It was a safe room surrounded by brickwork. Every day, it woke to a new light—red, then yellow, and even white, reflecting the moods of the sun. There was the sound of birdsong outside, and the sweep of brooms on the walkways and grass. With each passing day, I learnt to recognize the changing light by the way it moved across the plain walls. In the morning, on the way to work, I walked down the high corridors, traversing the deep hollows and shadows of the building. And in time, I began to detect a certain resonance in the stillness. The brick walls drew my attention. I began to examine the way they were made and noticed the darkness that enveloped the high arches above me. While I walked, I became aware of the somnolent space around. Drawn into the monolithic rustic character of the place, I began to see something of the colour and preciousness of the architecture.

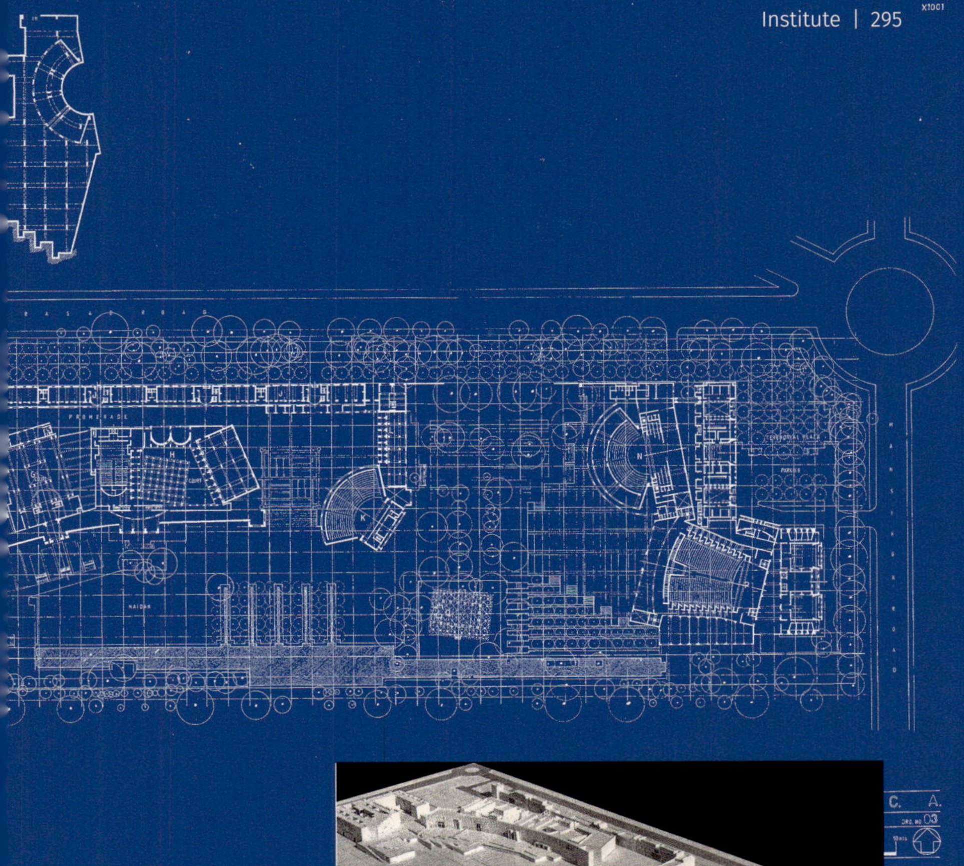

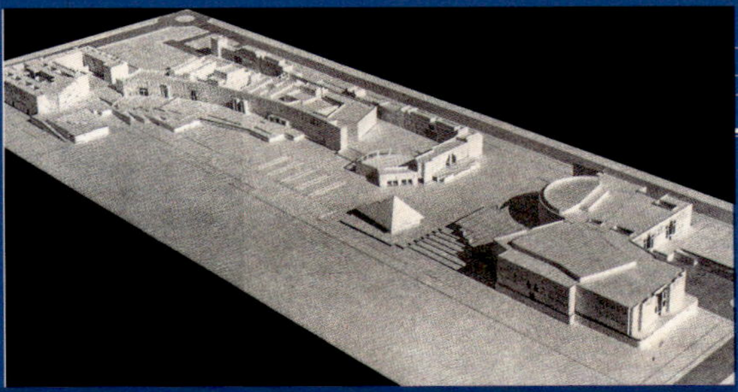

Indira Gandhi National Centre for the Arts (Competition entry), Delhi, 1986

Conventional roles of the student and the teacher become diluted. Both are returned to the original purpose of teaching: sitting under a tree and talking to each other. In the late afternoon with the sun high above the building and its halls, the place seemed like a world crouching under the summer light. Some days, I stood at the edge of the encircling brick parapets and gazed out, away from the building, letting my eyes slowly work their way to the horizon, and saw the shallow, treeless setting on which the building had grown.

This was the same ground that Kahn must have seen when he made plans for the building. Trees barely rising out of the ground, spread so low it looked like they were trying to hide under their own shadows; a bald stretch of earth covered by thorny bushes, bathed in a hot whitewash of sky. It was a dry, airless place, without depth, without volume, capping a sweeping, open plain. Beyond it, along the stretch of road that ended in the cluster of low whitewashed dwellings were open

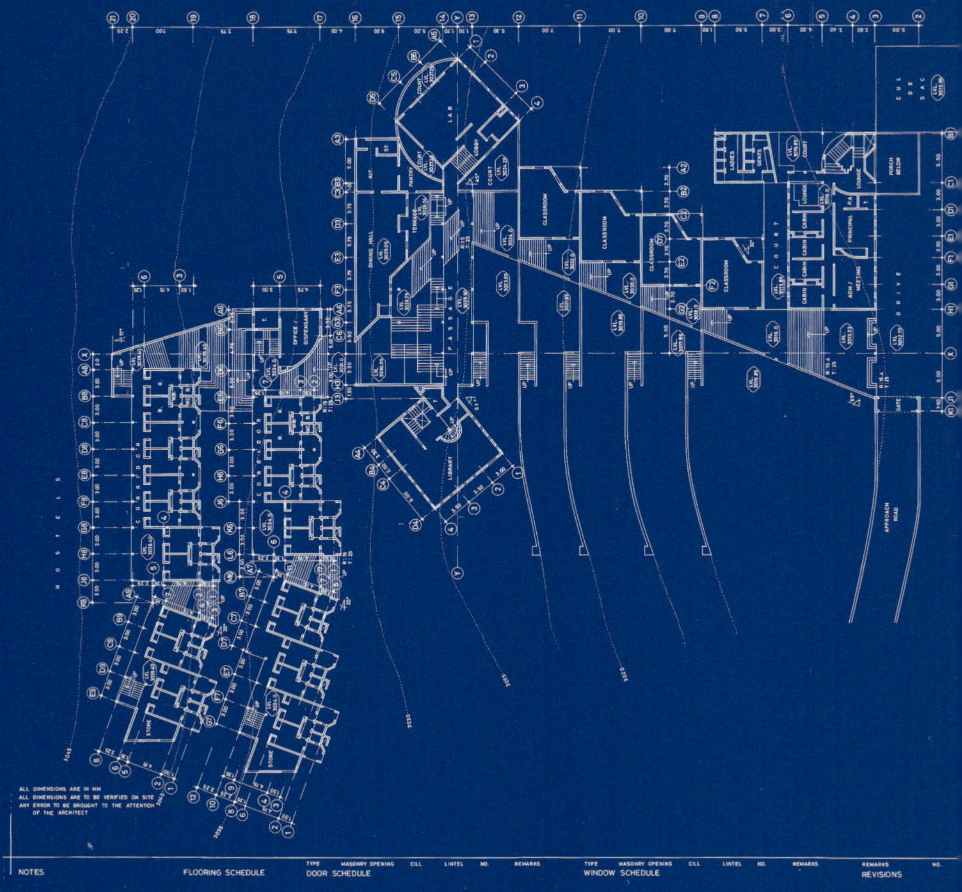

District Institute for Education and Training, Gangtok, Sikkim, 1990

fields. I walked in the evenings through one about half-a-mile away, just so I could look back at the building. And the profiles of brick that rose out of the scrub. These were black circles in red-yellow washes of watercolour. The whole complex had the look of a ruin—massive walls, fortress-like, the circular openings in them reduced to the utmost simplicity. Their alignment and repetition were the result of a primary ordering; a hard-line geometry so precise and sharp-edged it cast an impenetrable glow on the surface as the sun fell away around the brickwork—this was what Kahn called “the building’s share of light, a slice of the sun”.

Like the landscape that it occupied, the building’s position only amplified that space, that silence. Day after day, as I walked past it, I

Conference, watercolour on silk, 2004

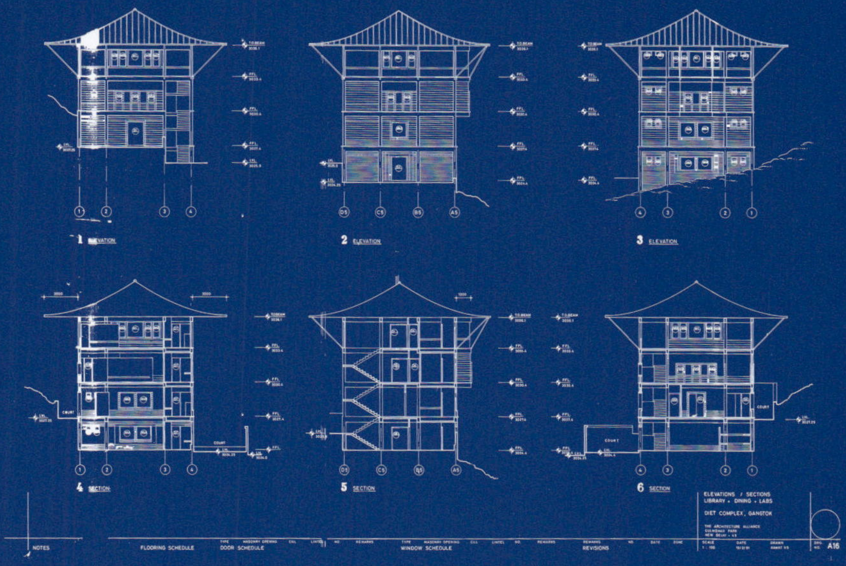

began to understand something of its underlying message—truly great architecture stank of a sort of despotism, a despotism of scale and size and a frequency of structural repetition. For a building to be good, it had to display its elements in continual progression. At the Institute, there was a forbidding aspect to the design, an architectural severity which, surprisingly, I began to see as a positive attribute. The student dormitories were planned in an austere distillation of the barest essential elements—a bed, a table, a window—sleep, study and light translated into physical terms.

The library's halls and portals also appeared in stark, monumental confinement of light and shadow, the unrelieved expanse of brickwork offering the monasticism essential to academic life. There were none of the conventional images of comfort associated with a reading room to be seen. No stuffed sofas, no lounge. This was architecture expressed as the primal condition of existence. I also sensed how important repetition really was. It was critical that the same window was repeated from the same

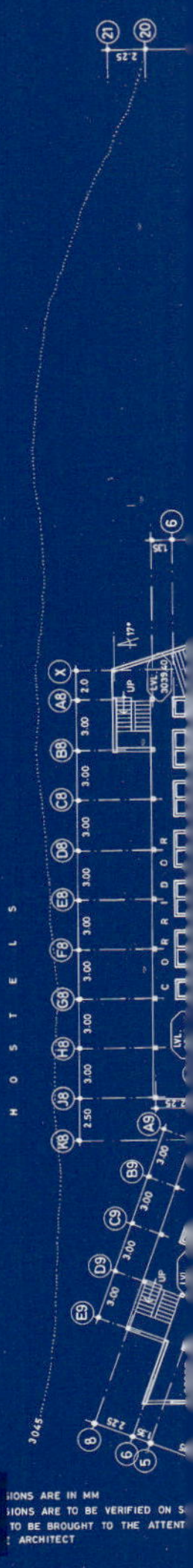

District Institute for Education and Training, Gangtok, Sikkim, 1990

brick wall. How futile, how senseless, design and inventiveness were to architecture! Throughout the structure, repetition persisted. As a sensation first, and then slowly conveying its reasons.

I realized that during my daily walk through the grove of neem trees into the brickwork of arches, my mind had perceived nothing. No aspect of building, nothing of the landscape. I saw no change of material, detected no change of texture. Repetition of the most ordinary kind was creating the visual absence so necessary in the experience of architecture. The unifying aspect of the experience was only the shadow-line of trees that gave way—without sound or deliberation, without even a change in step—to the shadow of the building. The same neem tree repeated, one after the other, and another, till the repetition dissolved the individual entity of the tree into a line, the line into a grove and the grove into a thick smudge of shadow on the ground. I began to see the building in exactly the same way, as a series of reminders of the daily and seasonal changes of light. The building was part of everything else; part of the weather, the atmosphere.

Just as you lose all sense of boundary in the desert, so it was here. Every time I looked at the building, each time I walked through it, I saw less and less of it. My eyes were still open but their focus had disappeared; they perceived the structure as a continuous passage of shadows similar to the rhythm of things you see out of a train window, a rhythm that lulls you to sleep. It appeals to you because the subject doesn't matter. Whether trees or electric poles, bushes or sugarcane plants, the monotony of their continual passage is so hypnotic that it draws you along a deeper meditative path till the mind feels truly liberated and alone. Is that really the purpose of rhythm, the method behind boredom? To steal you away slowly from dissonance and lower you into a deepening chasm of silence? To lull you but keep you suspended in a prolonged moment of contemplation?

The perception of such rhythm occurs daily in actions that catch bits of stillness. In states, perhaps of perfect harmony, but realized for just a fleeting moment. The mind dissolves the pattern of light or sound into hazy twilight, without memory or

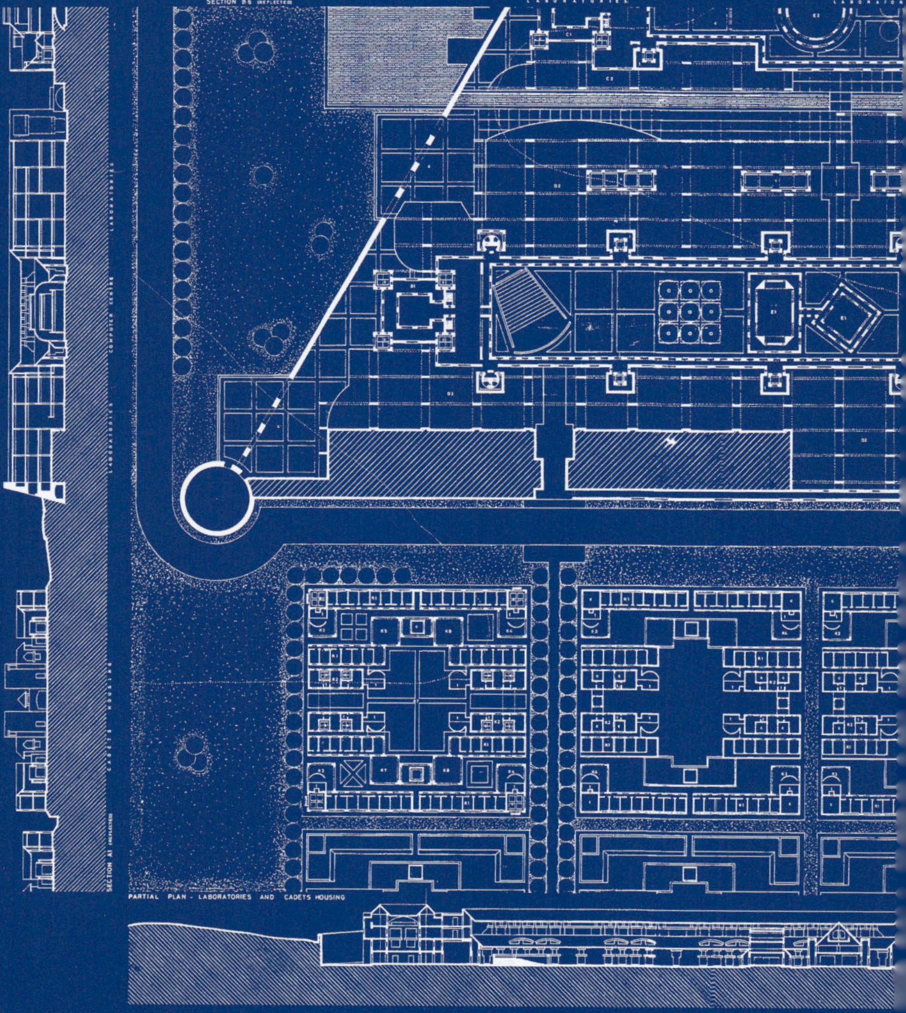

analysis or judgement, into a threshold below wakefulness. As that moment has eradicated the past and the future and it now allows you to exist for yourself, in the moment. Over the course of two years, time spent walking past the walls of offices and classrooms, along dormitory bays all exactly the same, the building and its details slowly sank into the background. With every passing month, a sense of quiet repose began to build, an image that was entirely free of sensation, visual delight, or disgust.

Despite the precision of the brick planes and the sharp edges that ended the buildings, the mind began to perceive a boundless landscape. There was always something beyond it. The building was more than what it was. It offered the sort of clarity you sense only in the dark when you know the sky is there, even though you can't see the stars or the clouds. There were shadows in the building, layer

■ Business School, oil on canvas, 2004

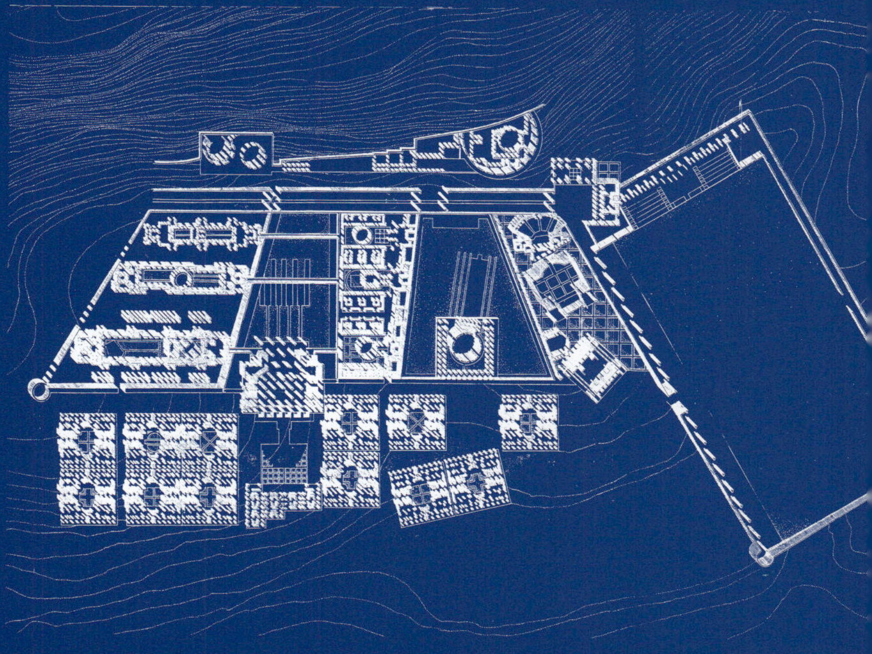

Naval Academy (Competition entry) Ezhimala, Kerala, 1990

upon layer, but once you entered, they fell away quietly. They peeled away like coats of skin and when you looked again, you recognized the light hidden within them. There was a permanent wind blowing in the dark; air currents not perceptible in the open, constantly skimming and sifting against the brick like sand on a desert tent.

Always there was raw light, pouring down, thick as cream and creating the full-faced pattern of a circle. It repeated the geometry of the sun on the floor and walls, rendering its passage across the sky in space. But there was never any colour in the light, only an intensity that grew and died around the brickwork every day like water across the bow of a ship. It did not affect movement or impede progress. The architecture it described reverberated, exercising a gentle pull, making me aware only of myself, my insides. Free of style and history, and even of the materials of which they were constructed, the buildings bared no logic, no expression, denying even their own existence as large, physical entities.

N A V A L A C A

Naval Academy (Competition entry) Ezhimala, Kerala, 1990

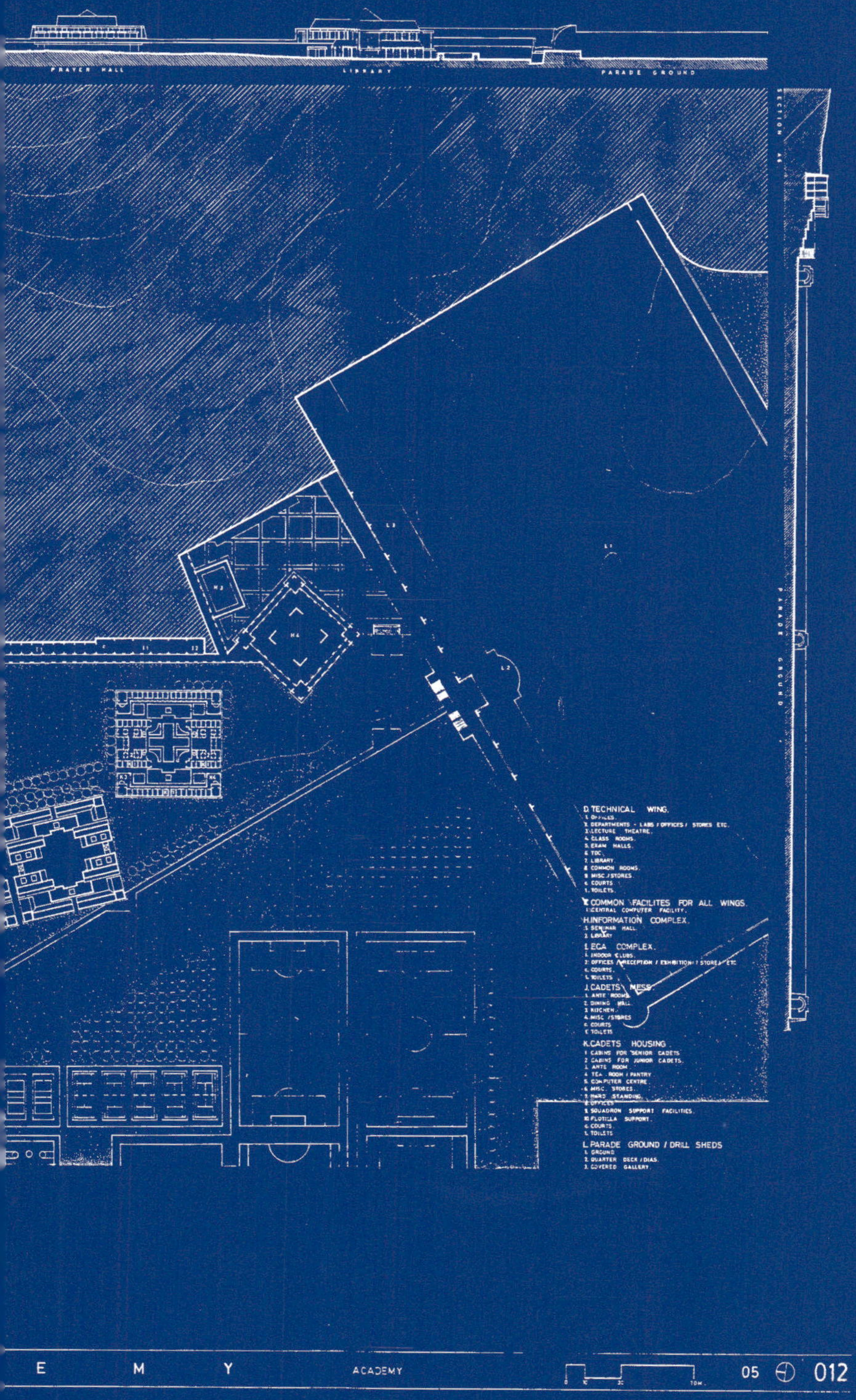

PRAYER HALL
LIBRARY
PARADE GROUND
SECTION AA
PARADE GROUND
D. TECHNICAL WING.
1. OFFICES.
2. DEPARTMENTS - LABS / OFFICES / STORES ETC.
3. LECTURE THEATRE.
4. CLASS ROOMS.
5. EXAM HALLS.
6. TDC.
7. LIBRARY.
8. COMMON ROOMS.
9. MISC. / STORES.
c. COURTS.
t. TOILETS.
COMMON FACILITES FOR ALL WINGS.
1. CENTRAL COMPUTER FACILITY.
H. INFORMATION COMPLEX.
1. SEMINAR HALL.
2. LIBRARY
I. ECA COMPLEX.
1. INDOOR CLUBS.
2. OFFICES / RECEPTION / EXHIBITION / STORES ETC.
c. COURTS.
t. TOILETS.
J. CADETS MESS.
1. ANTE ROOMS.
2. DINING HALL.
3. KITCHEN.
4. MISC. / STORES
c. COURTS
t. TOILETS
K. CADETS HOUSING.
1. CABINS FOR SENIOR CADETS.
2. CABINS FOR JUNIOR CADETS.
3. ANTE ROOM.
4. TEA ROOM / PANTRY.
5. COMPUTER CENTRE.
6. MISC. STORES.
7. HARD STANDING.
8. OFFICES.
9. SQUADRON SUPPORT FACILITIES.
10. FLOTILLA SUPPORT.
c. COURTS.
t. TOILETS.
L. PARADE GROUND / DRILL SHEDS
1. GROUND
2. QUARTER DECK / DIAS.
3. COVERED GALLERY.
E M Y
ACADEMY
05
012

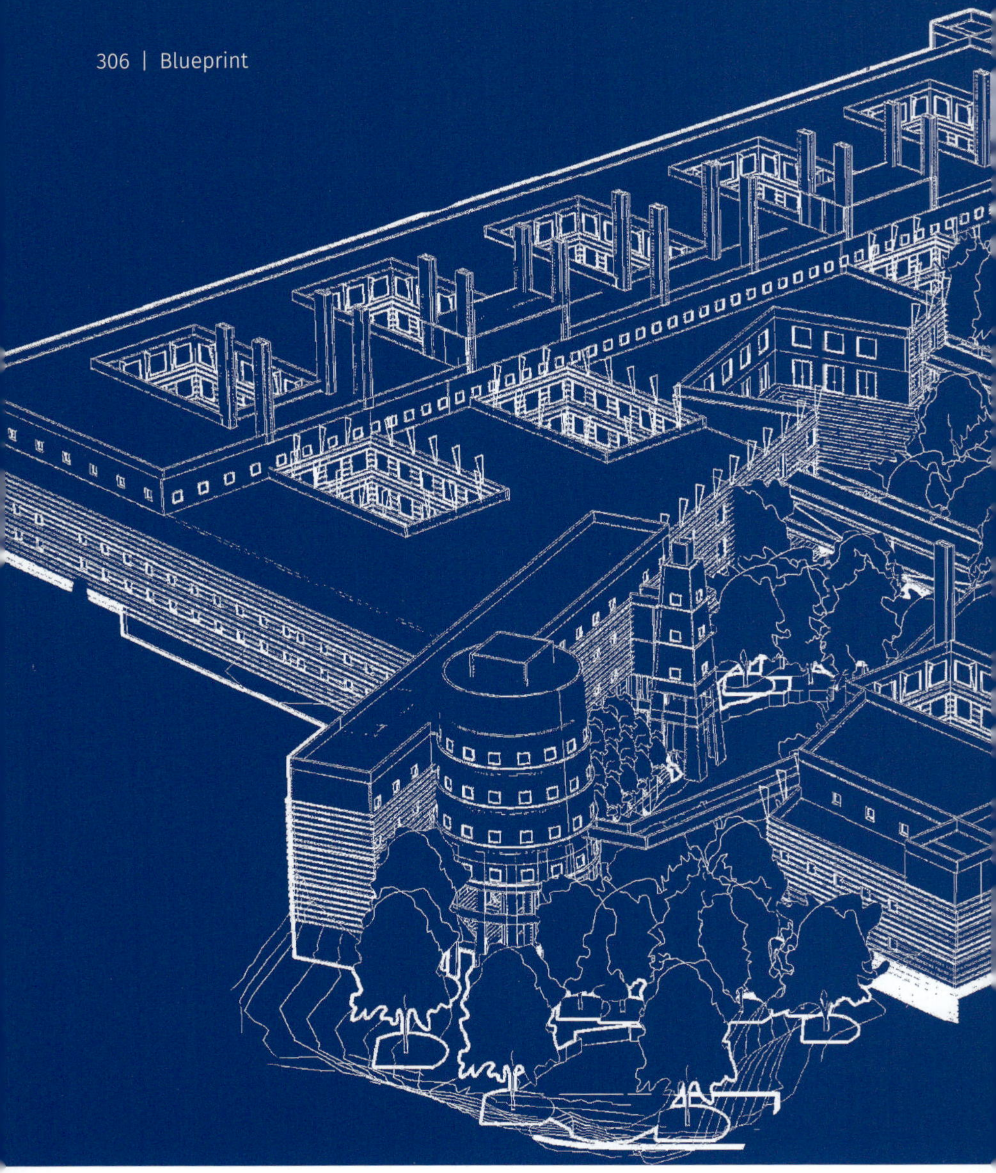

Yet, this simplified perception of the building was a carefully controlled deception. Within its outer skin and primary geometry lay a host of complex layers that hid the order of movement and occupancy in subtle inflections of wall and building elements. I had tried to understand something of its repeating, shifting complexity in the plans for the Indira Gandhi National Centre for the Arts (IGNCA) competition. But I had always been wary of buildings that strayed off the grid without reason. The move away from order to another form of order, not disorder, required intentions that explained the shift in relation to the wider extent of the plan. The scheme's attempt to contain the shifts of individual buildings was seen in the light of a harbour with a fixed geometry of containment; as if within it, the individual buildings were boats that continually altered their positions in the water, but did not stray off their mooring.

The shifts were so minor that they only caused a slight disturbance. They were in no way meant to be a dramatic realignment and because of the shift, they only reinforced the grid. It was planned imbalance that restored balance through opposing tendencies. Trying to repeat

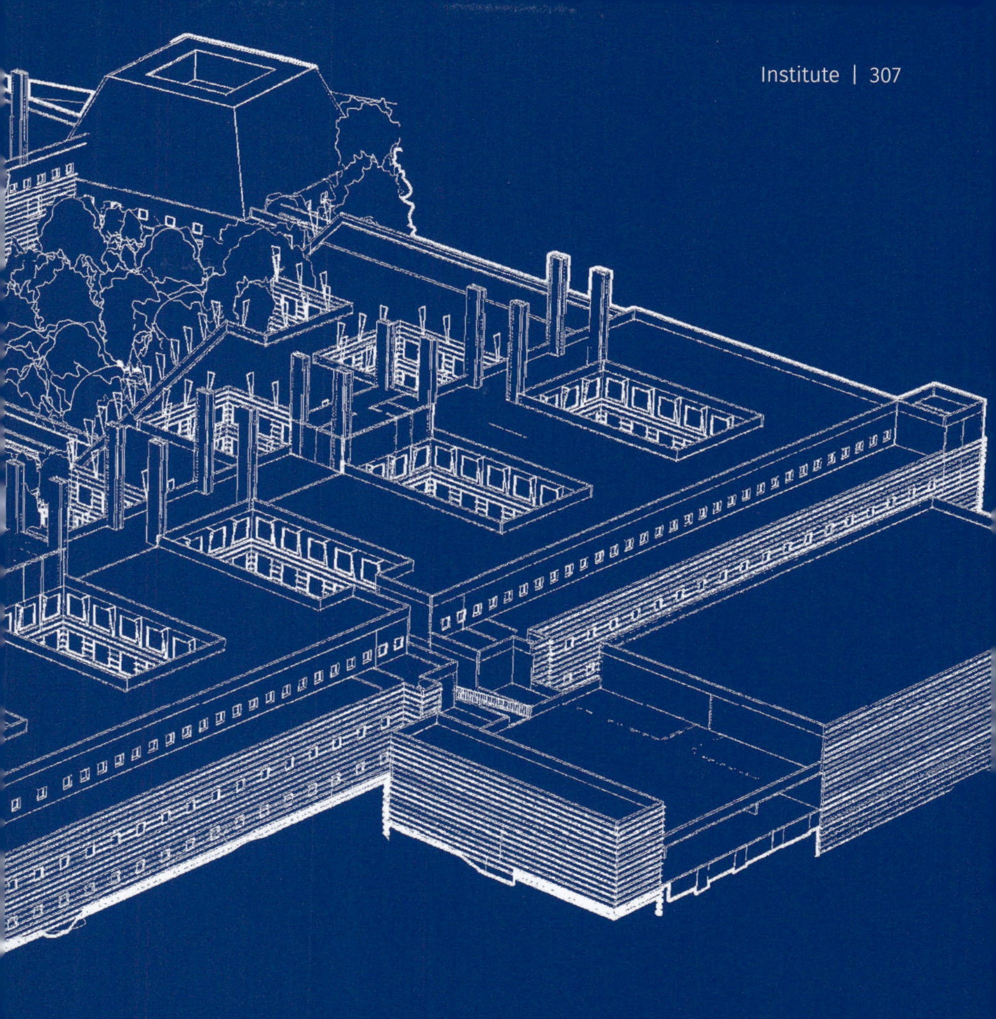

School of Planning and Architecture (Competition entry) Delhi, 1998

a similar march of structure at a training complex in Sikkim, the steep rise of the hill appeared not so much an obstruction but an added factor of displacement. Movement was guided through stepped corridors where teaching areas became points of rest along the rise. The institutional layout was determined less by a structural grid than a series of repeating retaining walls that were integral to the architecture. In developing plans for institutional projects at the complex, the layouts attempted something of the same somnolence in the geometry.

The collective of functions was lost in a repeating grid that conveyed the intentions directly to the user. The logic of constant dimensions perceived in measured steps allowed people to immediately comprehend the layout, and engage more easily and briskly with it. Within the perceived structure, as the body and mind began to subconsciously recognize the repeating orthogonal dimension, other shifts took place. The repetitive state of structural order defines only an optimal condition, the space that results seemingly naturally, correct and positioned

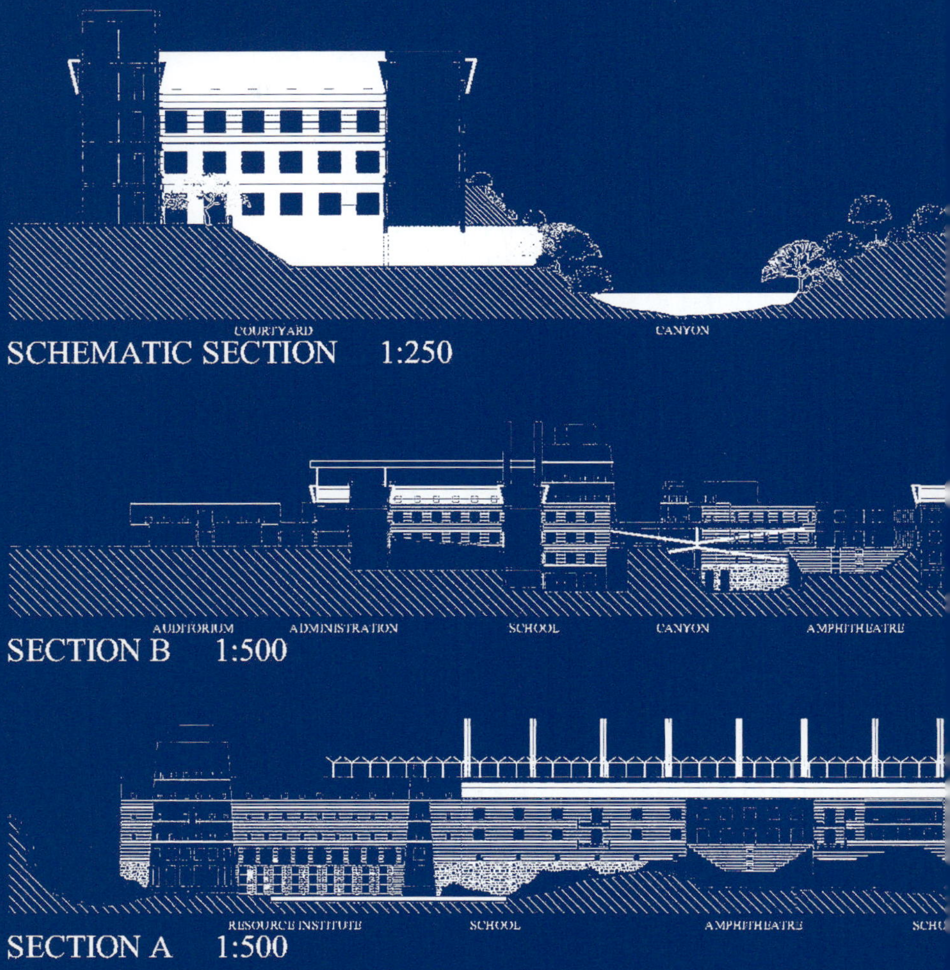

by engineering formula. In the wake of the academic placement, the urge to connect elements that may be incongruous and disjointed becomes a necessary disorder imposed within the framework of symmetrical geometry. The intentional disorder, however, does not destroy the lucidity of the grid, but offers a competing defying arrangement that only further reinforces the original syntax. The relocation is not an afterthought but a heterogeneous consolation, a more poetic description of what exists in the first place. The plan's performance is enhanced by the ensuing logic of the intrusion and its new relationship with the simplicity of the original geometry. A disturbance, an uneasiness and an anxiety that mentally dissolves the insurgency and returns to the simplistic reading. It is as if the newness of the modern structure, straight jacketed and comprehensible, is trying to engage with an ancient ideal, flexible and remote.

Sudden inflections of structures within the grid announced the importance of one space over another. Against the backdrop of rigorous, unrelenting geometry, the turn of buildings on their own

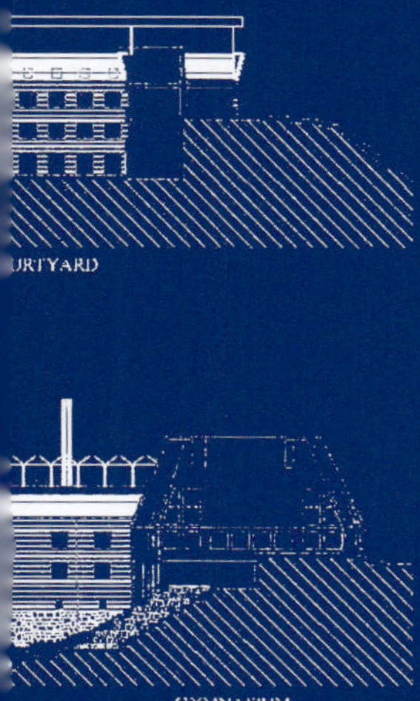

School of Planning and Architecture, Delhi, 1998

axes was a Romanesque tendency that illuminated the special room within a gridlock of masonry.

In larger works like the plan for the Naval Academy, or the repeating modular structure at the Architecture School, the distortion of plan was an obvious presence of natural intrusions; steep drops at the Academy, and a deep ravine that sliced through the School. The insertion of distortions in the mix was a much-needed disturbance that rejuvenated the space through carefully planned collisions. Such manipulations and angular fusions altered the prosaic demand for institutional repetition and created moments of identifiable space like focal points in an elaborate novel, an intentional displacement in the mind's eye. It was a completely different way of looking at building, and it produced a larger frame of philosophy to which design and architecture could conveniently attach themselves.

That state of architecture falls somewhere between real and abstract notions of happiness, the kind of philosophy that doesn't

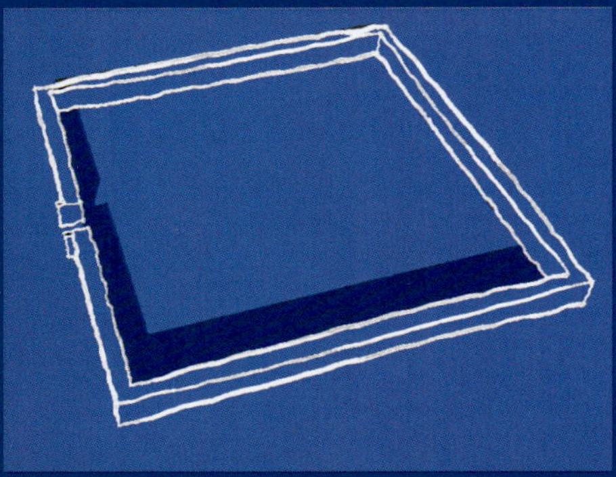

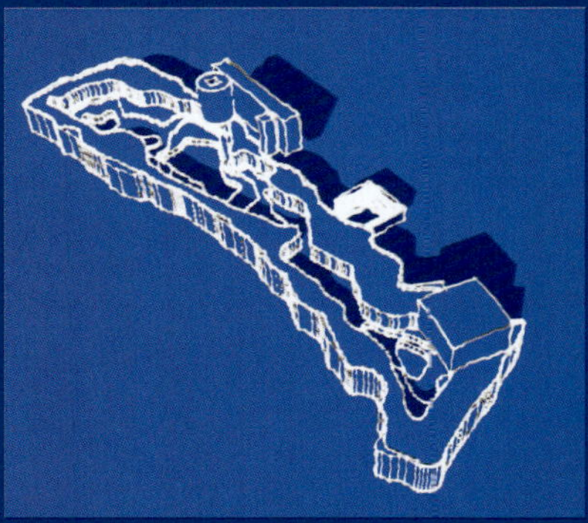

have easy "how-to answers". It is not formed out of felt or describable emotions like joy, pleasure, familiarity, or comfort, but has a larger unformed dimension that encompasses all these and much more. It has much to do with the seeming rightness of things, the overall quality you perceive over time, an invisible picture of a place that steadily grows in the subconscious and only comes into focus there through a long-term experience of a place. But it is never complete. The final comprehension of architecture only works like a series of synchronized imprints; overlays that don't produce a formal picture, only a pleasant disturbance at the back of the mind, something that lingers and fades.

Unlike the standard measures of building, the image is not composed of explicit structural, cultural, historic, or design ideas, but an indecipherable compounding of all these. It is almost like a piece of

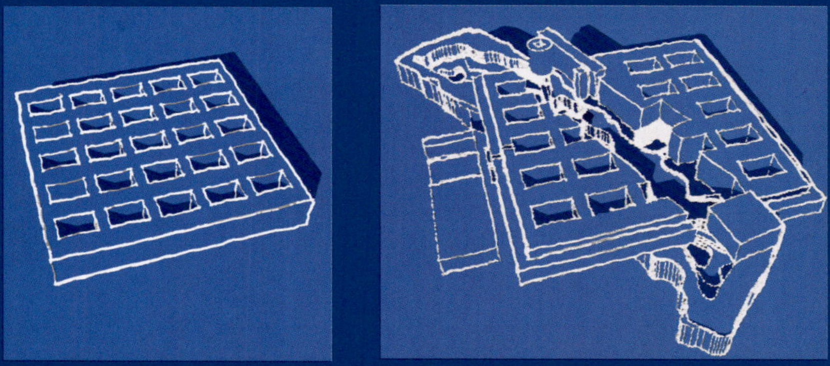

School of Planning and Architecture, Delhi, 1998

music heard across the distance in a valley where the precise notes don't matter. It was all about memory and recall, the persistent refrain that reminded you that you were, in that short moment, in its thrall. It was part of something wonderful, something that made you feel whole again. I think its greatness lies in the resonance, the remains of experience that survive long after the experience is over. Whatever it is, it exists without physical form or description. In fact, if it takes on a visible physical form, you immediately become suspicious and aware of its falsification.

Memorial

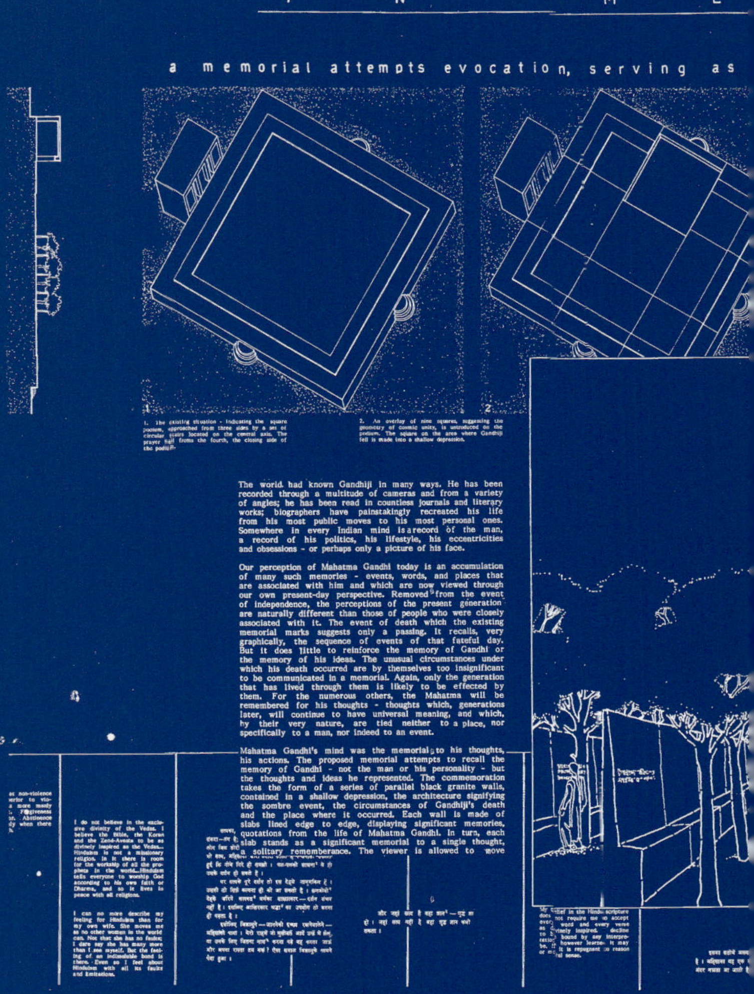

It is one of the more persistent ironies of our times that protests around the construction of a mosque in America came at the time of a judicial decision on the demolition of one in India. In both cases the mosque was seen by many as desecration; in one, a violation of the private memory of the dead of 9/11, and in the other, the public myth of Lord Ram, firmly ingrained in the Hindu mind after 6/12. While much of Indian life is the setting for daily religious ritual and offerings, American rites are more controlled. Remembrance in America seems to follow a cycle of ten years. A decade after the 2001 attack on the Twin Towers, New York unveiled the new scheme for Freedom Park; two fountains pouring a continuous line of water into the hollows of the Towers' foundations. In the mid-eighties similarly, the testimonial wall of the Vietnam Memorial opened to public view a decade after the end of the War.

In both, the sentiments of national grief were absorbed in an architectural abstraction, a collective catharsis that could be shared by the sight of thousands of private names on public view. The personal and private nature of American memorials is part of a

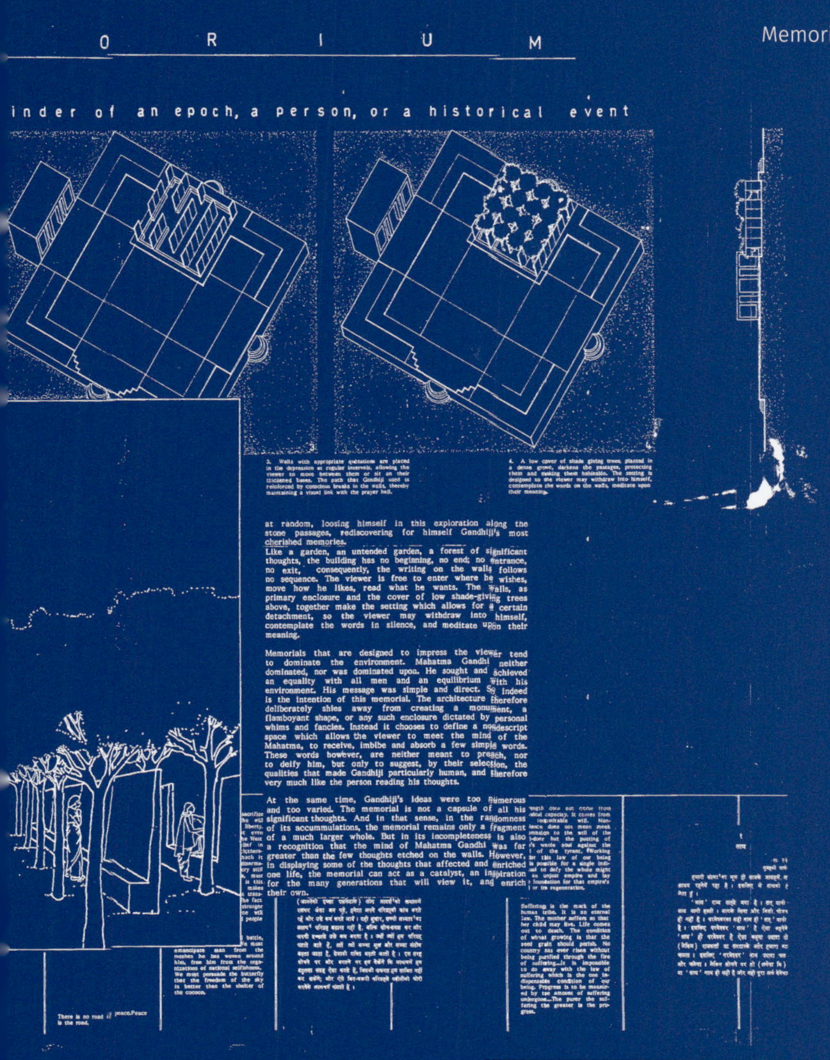

Gandhi Memorial, Delhi, 1988

tradition which publicly celebrates history as a living memory. Vietnam, Korea, 9/11, become deified in public memory through time and the passing of generations. Indian memory however has a mythological dimension that often makes the physical memorial a distortion. Disconnected from the present, statues and structures are literal rather than imaginary or abstract reconstructions. Along Mumbai's shoreline, a 30-metre-tall Shivaji on a horse will soon ride the waves; at Tees January, the site where Gandhiji was assassinated, his footsteps are painted in red cement. The Ram Mandir, if built, will doubtlessly be the physical representation of a perfect structure, as are the larger than life memorials to the leaders Ambedkar and Mayawati.

Unlike the American view of remembering ordinary people facing difficult circumstances, the Indian vision is heroic and elevates the remembered into giant, mythic proportions, removed from the puny humanity they represent. Yet the wider American debate on the proximity of the mosque to Ground Zero propels the country into contradictory social positions.

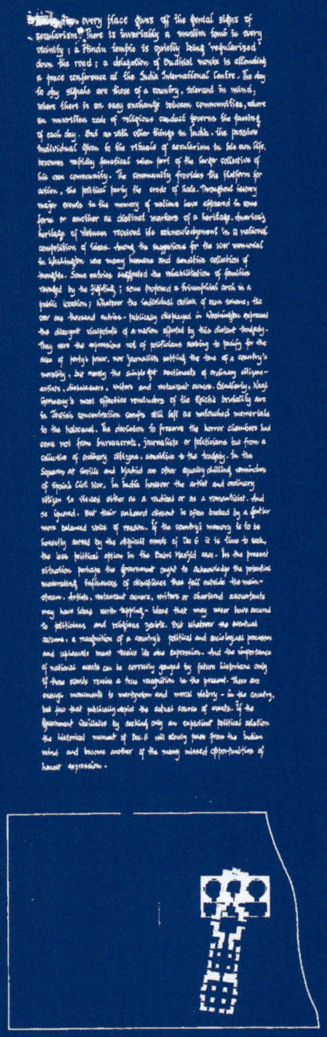

Church congregations in small Southern and mid-Western towns, usually affronted by anyone that is not White, Anglo and Protestant would doubtlessly protest against something as alien as a mosque in their midst. The more liberal coasts and big towns, with a wider experience of ethnic and religious diversity, maintain that the Constitution allows all religious practices. The widening arc of these disparate views is encouraged in a country that prides itself on its freedom of speech while viewing people who voice too liberal a stance with suspicion and typecasting and rounding up those whose skin colour matches that of the 9/11 plotters. Yet at the time of the 9/11 tragedy, during a period of high emotion and grief in America, few raised objections to the idea of a memorial to the dead.

Maya Lin, the architect of the Vietnam War memorial, was the lone dissenting voice that explained with a chilling clarity that without the value of memory, the place did not warrant a memorial. The memorial to Franklin Roosevelt opened in New York City 67 years after the president's death. It is a roofless granite room built on a five-acre site. A contemplative place in the midst of the noise and bustle of

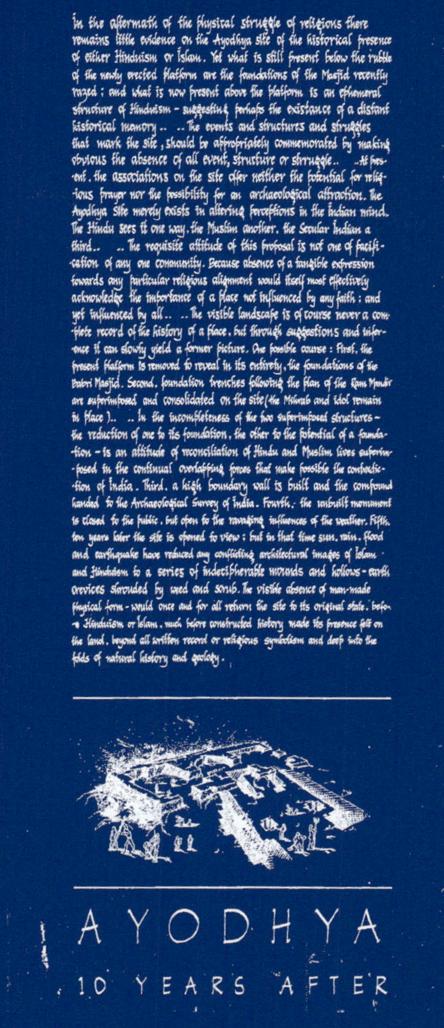

Memorial for Ayodhya (Competition entry) Ayodhya, UP, 2001

the city, the memorial has little to do with the worship of the man as a political figure, but is a reminder of his historical ideals at the time of War and the Great Depression. His four freedoms: the freedom of speech and worship, the freedom from want and fear are etched on the walls of the memorial. They combine with the stated thread of Roosevelt's statesmanship and create a floating, contemplative circumspection with the surrounding river. A subtle enactment of the memorial's intention drew its architect into an act of monumental generosity that opened up the enclosure to the river, leaving the viewer as much in contemplation of the message as of the watery infinity in front of him.

In contrast, the Indian view is often a pictorial rendering of memory. Delhi approved the construction of a National War Memorial, an underground structure planned around the canopy at India Gate with the names of those who died in the War since Independence inscribed on it. While the Indian soldier's bravery certainly deserves recognition, such large-scale public pronouncements of martyrdom are a strange form of

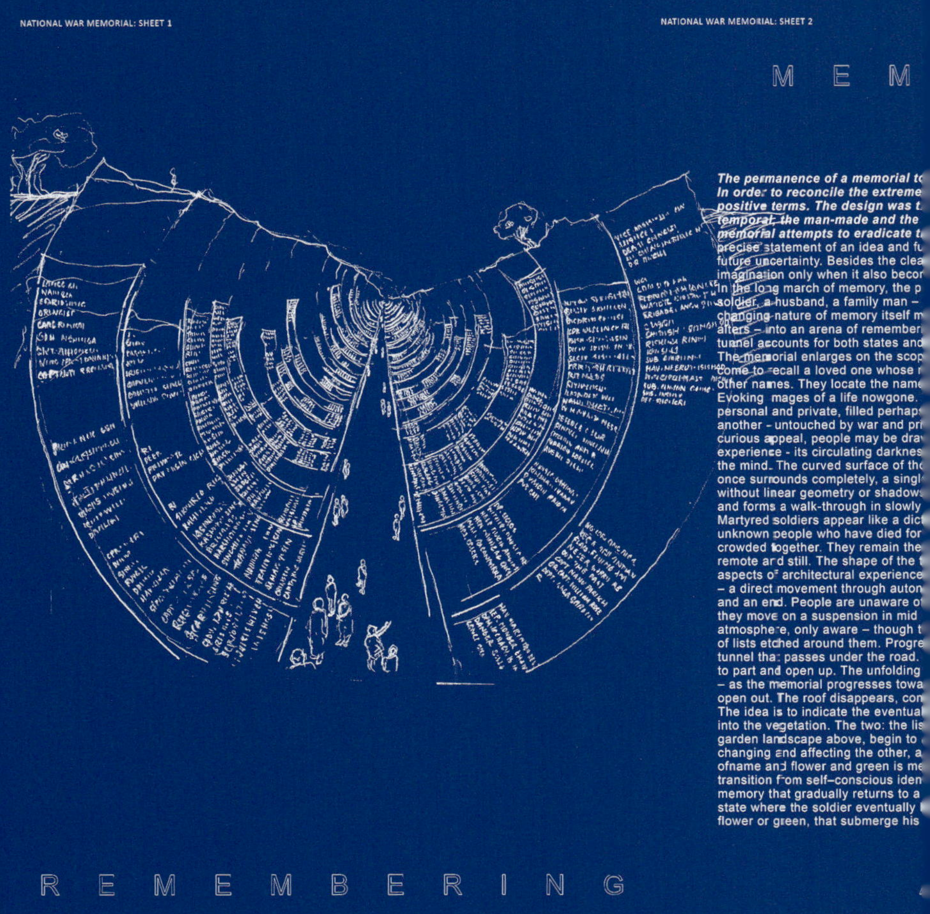

National War Memorial (Competition entry 1), Delhi, 2016

commemoration in a country where little of public life—or death—is ever deified. There are no great memorials to the Independence Movement, or the Partition, none to those who died in the 1984 anti-Sikh riots, or the 2002 Gujarat riots, nothing to remember those killed in police operations, or Naxal attacks. Jallianwallah Bagh is itself the memorial to the massacre. Rajiv Gandhi's death is commemorated at Sriperumbudur. The absence of Gandhiji's footsteps at Tees January Marg is the only reminder of his murder.

The Delhi War Memorial imitates a Western ideal of deification and follows none of the instinctive dictates of Indian eulogies where the place itself evokes memory. The open competition for the Memorial made us examine the nature of memory itself. Since the permanence of a memorial too often contradicts the impermanence of memory itself in order to reconcile the extremes, we saw the eventual dissolution of the memorial over time as a positive attribute; a way in which architecture slowly decays and destroys itself. The design was envisaged as a fusion of the two: the permanent and temporal, the man-made and natural, a mix of architecture and landscape. The design attempted to eradicate the border between the two. If the memorial is a precise statement of an idea and function, it must simultaneously also convey a sense of future uncertainty.

NATIONAL WAR MEMORIAL: SHEET 3

Besides the clear elucidation of intent, the spot gains a place in the imagination only when it becomes an imaginary deposit of possibilities. In the long march of memory, the permanence of loss of a loved one; a soldier, husband, family man, requires a visible marker. Yet the changing nature of memory itself makes recall difficult, and over time, alters into an arena of remembering and forgetting. When conceived as a tunnel, it accounts for both states and follows the course of memory itself. The memorial enlarges on the scope of human experience: people go there to recall a loved one whose name is etched on the wall along with other names. When they locate the name, thoughts run through their minds, evoking images of a life that has passed. The experience of recall is a personal and private one, filled perhaps with emotion.

For someone untouched by war and personal loss, the tunnel could have a curious appeal; people may be drawn to it for the architectural experience; its circulating darkness that induces a different state of mind. The curved surface with thousands of names on it, all visible all at once, surrounds a single surface without breaks or edges, without linear geometry or shadows. A progression from dark to light, it forms a walk through

National War Memorial (Competition entry 2)

slowly unfolding panoramic space. Martyred soldiers appear like a dictionary of names, a chronology of the unknown who have died for a purpose, marching in columns. They remain there, suspended in geological time, remote and still.

The shape of the tunnel defies all conventional aspects of architectural experience. Its primary course is processional; a direct movement through autonomous space that has a beginning and an end. People are unaware of wall, floor and ceiling. Instead they move suspended mid-air as if floating through the tunnel's hazy atmosphere, only aware of the despairing chronology of lists etched around them. Progress through the memorial begins as an enclosed tunnel whose roof begins to part and open up. The unfolding takes place as an act of dissolution where as the memorial progresses towards the lawn, its circular section begins to open out. The roof disappears, connecting the tunnel to the sky and landscape. The idea is to indicate the eventual dissolution of the list of names on the wall into the vegetation.

The two: the wall's lists of names, and the garden landscape above, begin to reach towards each other in a slow timeless crawl, changing and affecting each other, and fusing in a future time. The eventual synthesis of name and flower and green is meant to signify the altering state of memory itself, the transition from self-conscious identity to a collective anonymity; the final resting place of memory that gradually returns to a formless original. The move towards anonymity is a positive state where the soldier eventually has no identity at all and is seen only as the fluttering white flower or

green that submerges his name and preserves it for posterity. In another option, the Memorial to the Fallen was literally seen as a rendition of the fallen soldier.

The architectural idea created a series of monumental stone plates that incorporated the names of the martyred on their surface, the composition of plates were set in dynamic collision. Some were fallen; some in the process of falling; others supporting the fellow soldiers. A comprehension of the conventions of gravity: the erect, leaning, inclining, collapsing plates create a visible disturbance in space, generally understood in rectilinear terms as vertical walls and horizontal floors. The imbalance of a battlefield—of soldiers in a state of war—standing, fighting, falling, dying is an unsentimental reminder of their collective belief in the protection of their homeland, and the unforgiving call of self-sacrifice and martyrdom.

With the names of the dead written on the angle plates, the visitor is able to walk between them, through a space that is often narrow and constricted, and made in accidental play between the leaning, falling plates. The idea of the severe confinement makes the visitor strain for clarity in the constantly changing theatre of the memorial. The falling plates erase any definition of a clear pathway and access, and confounds the viewer into accidental moments of dark and light, leading them to into interpretation and contemplation of the state of war, the value of human life and the fear of death.

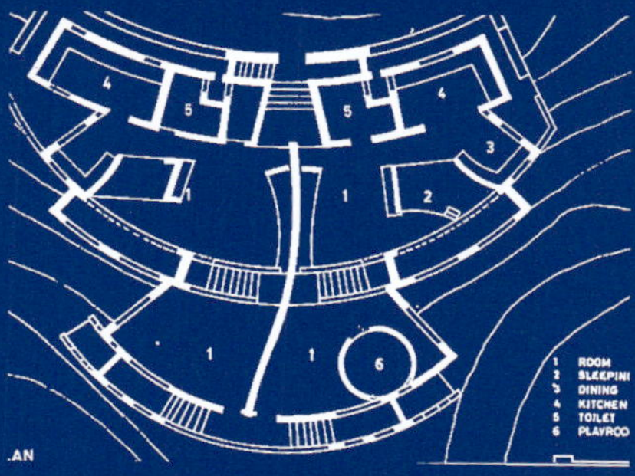

Mountain House

The site for my own home was a barren promontory of agricultural land in Ranikhet, 400 kilometres north of Delhi. Less than a quarter of an acre in size, the land faced a panorama of the Himalayan snows. It was a dry farming terrain that had lain fallow long enough to develop its own form of wilderness. Pine and oak, the natural species of the area, had taken hold of it after tenant farmers had abandoned the site. Behind it, on its southern approach and perimeter, were the Forest Department's rows of deodar groves.

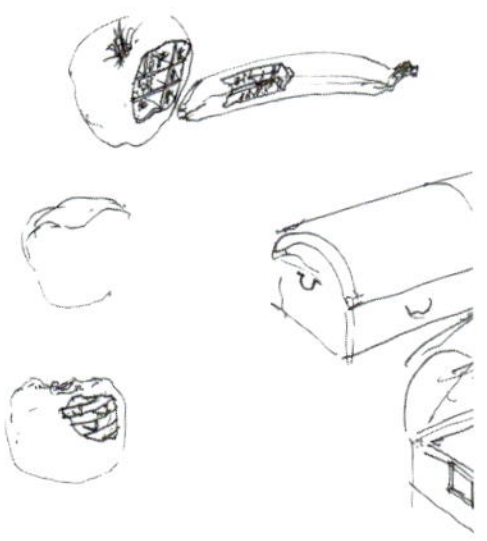

Along the site, at the edge of the promontory, stood a rural hut. I saw it every time I visited the site. Huddling below the mountain range, its solitary and regulated form was the simplest and most fundamental of human habitations. The accommodation seemed barely adequate with two rooms, stacked one on top of the other. The stone building's timber frame was filled in with mud. A narrow staircase rose through a hole in the floor

■ Organic Houses, pencil on paper, 2008

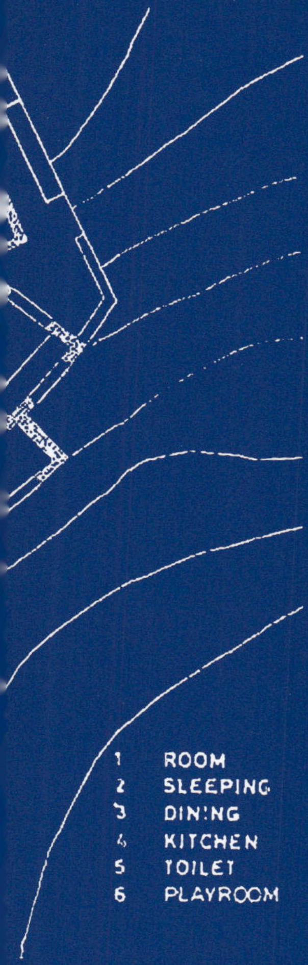

Home for Self, Ranikhet, Uttarakhand, 1990

to the room above. There, under a trussed roof the family sat, slept, cooked and ate their meals in a place they had themselves shaped.

The house succinctly expressed the values of the local culture, the collective intelligence of the people who had built it. Their instinctive command of material and technique was something I could never equal as an architect. It was an architecture entirely unselfconscious, which was born of necessity, its refinement over seasons and generations of builders had evolved a building type that had become common in the whole area. While considering a design for my house, it seemed important to me to indicate something of the surroundings in which the structure was to be placed. The

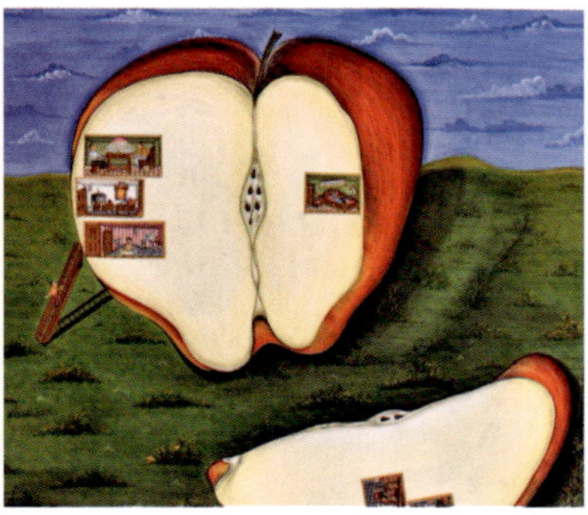

■ Apple House, watercolour on paper, 2004

Interior, Home for Self, Ranikhet

house was after all an organism, and the particular relationship it forged with the environment would make it of the landscape. Consequently a distinction between inside and outside would deliberately obscure the plan with the intention that the house, in its own way, would naturally lay claim to the landscape.

Sadly though, when the house was eventually built, it said nothing about Kumaon or the hills. With the strict bans on quarrying and felling it could not be built of local stone, that patchwork of randomness which goes into making the walls of houses in the hills. Instead brick trucked from the plains and assembled in tidy, structured courses of masonry was used. But the orientation of the walls was distinctly different from those of the house's urban counterparts. It was difficult to think of a conventional rectangular enclosure on a site that was stepped down in irregular agricultural terraces. So the plan was conceived as a series of layers, each opening wider as the volume of building descended in the direction of the mountains.

Walls were built to retain the agricultural terraces in their original irregular form, and the house was constructed simply as a natural occupant of the land, the walls following the curved terraces. The house's reciprocal relationship with the site was meant to transform the existing state of nature into a habitable place. Given the site's scarcity of building area, the structure (although designed for separate families), preserved its identity as a single house, under a single curving roof span. Within the confines of its brick shell, two different designs were developed for the internal container, each

allowing for the necessary adjustments to be made to suit the specific requirements of two families.

Our neighbour, Ramesh, required a separate room for an aged parent, so a mezzanine level was inserted. We wanted a small, secluded study, so a brick drum was built within to loiter, lie down and read with a measure of privacy; Ramesh had a pair of dogs, we had a child. And so the single house became two distinct homes with all the identifiable quirks of both residents. Of course, a house designed by an architect for himself becomes the most unwitting biography of the designer, for it carries within it learned, acquired and remembered notions of how personal space is to be made.

The architect in me had learnt to express pleasure from abstinence and the practised phrases from architectural school—simplicity of line and space. Space was precious and had to be displayed; it could move around the house in dramatic sweeps, rising two storeys above or going down the terraces with no furniture to impede its movement. All that was messy and vital and essential to the running of a home—my wife's decorative designs or my son's personal possessions—were whisked away or kept behind white walls; the idea was to create a background of almost monastic simplicity. All signs of human frailty and idiosyncratic delight were absent, all vestiges of the past denied. Even the materials were joined with utmost severity, details rough and local, but painstakingly flush. Space was indeed the final luxury

for those who had everything else. But the architecture looked strangely out of place in the frugal mountain setting.

It was a point that had been raised by a visiting relative. "Your house looks too different from all the others around," he commented after spending an afternoon walking down the narrow paths of the forested ground behind the building. I detected a disparaging undertone in his voice. What had disturbed him was the fact that the structure didn't display any of the familiar signs expected of a mountain home. There were no entrance porches, fireplaces or chimneys, no verandah in the front, no shuttered windows, no gable roof or dormers. The progression from drawing room to dining room to bedroom could not be traced. You couldn't even tell the front of the house from the back. The place had none of the coziness expected of a cottage in the mountains.

My relative was not an architect, and I took his comment to be a layman's observation of little consequence. But his words rankled. Architecture was meant to create different looking buildings, not something that replicated an age-old pattern. But his questioning of my assumptions of design got me wondering why the house should

■ Traditional House 1, watercolour on wood, 2003

Interior, Home for Self, Ranikhet

not look like the other houses in the area. After all the traditional role of the architect was not invention, but refinement; in this respect perhaps my own perception of architecture was flawed. I had been taught that originality and uniqueness of form were essential in producing distinctive and innovative architecture.

For the city dweller on an occasional mountain visit, it was more important to turn outwards to the sights and sounds missing from his life in the city. The temptation to orient the building to the unrelieved expanse of snow naturally seemed irresistible to me. It was by far the most persuasive consideration in the design. Eventually, the day-to-day functions of the house were incorporated within parallel layers of walls opening to the Himalayan view; the kitchen, toilets and entrance in the first, most secluded row formed the service layer; alongside, a parallel layer of living, sleeping and dining; and on the lowest terrace, a place of study and recreation. A circular drum, as a smaller room within the hall, served both as a contained study and a place for withdrawal from family activity—essential in a house that was really only one large space.

■ Traditional House 2, on wood, 2003

Each area within the house achieved, through platforms and screen walls, its own level of relative privacy, something that was additionally created when the rooms began to fill up with possessions. In a house that was by dimension very small, the need to create levels, platforms, screen walls and even entire rooms within a single space seemed crucial to me. They were built to suggest the sensations that come from a discovery of opposing architectural notions realized within close proximity of each other—high and low, in and out, small and large, intimate and monumental.

Study nooks, storage lofts, window recesses for lying down or reading or sleeping. The way in which one moved and occupied these elements blurred the distinctions between the specific and assigned functions of the house. Alcoves, courtyards and screens were the devices that offered a multiplicity of variable definitions. The court was delineated enclosure and yet open to the sky; the screen, similarly, was made of brick, but also by an absence of brick. In a similar vein, areas within the house too began to suggest an ambiguity of use; the recessed window alcoves projected beyond the protective bounds of the house, but they were also part of the room.

The study slab was an uncomfortable part of a noisier living room, but its placement behind the curving wall gave it the intended isolation. Such architectural incidents may appear entirely whimsical

to the outsider, but for the resident, they help to define moments of privacy. A sunny morning area, a dark study corner, or a wide expanse of window suffused with an evening glow, the architecture changed their uses with the changing seasons and time, and I would move from one area to another, seeking the sunlight or retreating to the darkness of a corner alcove, gazing into the valley from one vantage or shutting it out from another.

The Himalayas, however wonderful as a passing frame of reference for someone temporarily in their midst, may not always solicit the same yearning from the permanent residents of the place. But for me, the architecture had to be a matter of setting up desirable proximities to the snow and view as well as creating effective distances from them. Along the final perimeter of the house was mounted a massive window, stretching in circumference, and providing the reason for its orientation: a jagged line of white peaks set, like the house, in layer after receding layer into the far horizon. Here, when the sun was good and snow heavy, a steep staircase inserted within the outer double wall carried you to a seat under the picture below. Each time the fog lifted and revealed the distant whiteness or when the evening sun coloured the snow in a faceted glow, the effort, the inconvenience of rising, made an occasion of the view, and so became all the more worthwhile.

The End

On one of the busiest streets in Paris, a freestanding public toilet is visible within a glass wall next to a bus stop. At first glance, a toilet in so public a place comes as a complete surprise. Is the private act of urination or defecation to be performed in full view of the passengers waiting at the bus stop? The fact is that as a person enters the toilet, the walls of double glass fill with a fine mist, rendering the actions inside invisible and private. On release of the door, the toilet inside becomes visible once more.

Often, architecture's most persistent urban refrain demands a complete physical reversal of convention. It doesn't call for a rebellion, but a way of restating convention itself. In my own work I have often used a similar reversal of expectation to arrive at a rational basis for architecture. To make privacy public and shift public actions into the innermost sanctum, to place the valuable within the vulnerable: bank lockers and vaults made of glass, not buried in sub-basements, but exposed to a public street; private actions like a spa-massage, steam and bath, placed similarly in an open landscape; a roofless vacation home, an apartment without walls, a closed plan office, basement walls retaining earth inside glass, a swimming pool inside a research centre, a library in a suburban subway station, a road that runs inside a building, a bridge that is also an office building.

The urge to magnify an architectural intention is formed of unexpected, and implausible placements. The public toilet at a busy bus stop in Paris is an extreme case, where private actions can be performed in glass-walled interiors, suddenly privatized. The building performs, as does its use, in a seemingly irrational position, whose mist-enveloping enclosure makes unlikely associations between private necessity and public event. The line in *The Godfather* only endorses such kinship. "When you gotta go, you gotta go."

The rational impulse in architecture springs from the view that building is a problem-solving activity: the functions and efficiency demanded by people in need of homes, shelters and offices, and the statistical requirements of housing. India's national surveys underscore critical needs and place undue demands on a profession that is not used to big challenges. The bureaucratic mind uses architecture, first and foremost, as a safety net for allaying statistics.

■ India Gate painted, simulation, 2012

The numbers of bridges built, people housed, etc., are the literal strengths of and reasons for architecture. The current state of expectation in architecture becomes a rallying point against such conformity. The gesticulation of design in the city is only a measure of its nascent physical difference with others of its kind. In the urge to escape the death knell of atrophy, architecture offers a form of resistance to cultural norms, and becomes an art form outside the recognizable context of imitation.

The reduction of architecture to private object destroys its inherent strength as a force offering social context. The deadweight of design in most emerging economies confuses architecture with design, and nullifies its impact on the landscape or urban setting. In fact the equation of architecture with design robs the profession of its true calling, and reduces its relevance to simplistic decoration. When new models of cars are announced, they are merely harping about looks and performance. Automotive design offers no measure of improving the quality of lives. Architecture does. By ridiculing architecture as an object of personal desire, it is removed from the utopian discourse that believes that there is value in its existence beyond that of its immediate function.

When architecture becomes a service divorced from social criticism, its value is suspect. The contempt for this larger intent comes as much from the nature of derivative design practice as from the insistence on authorship; the power of celebrity that links shape to face, and face to fame. The resulting building assumes the label of "iconic" only in the narrow frame of celebration. Indian urbanism celebrates the iconic in an unusually long list that includes India Gate, the DDA flat in Delhi, the Taj Mahal, the Taj Mahal Hotel, Dharavi in Mumbai, Corbusier's Secretariat in Chandigarh and the Union Carbide plant in Bhopal. The iconic currency of these structures shatters their value in cultural terms only because they offer no constructive observation of life in their cities and neighbourhoods, nor do they offer any means to renew the connection between life and art.

The unwillingness to be ridiculed, over being celebrated, makes architects and artists resistant to exploration and the adoption of new strategies of autonomous thinking. I was trying to get away

■ Pedestrian Crossing, simulation, 2012

from the rational quantification of the planner. My own work was too minor to make a public impact. It could not test the available statistics of a city, its demography and its problems. Nor could I use the data like a scientist to construct a new model for architecture. The idea was not to negate this reality but to find more valuable indicators in the realm of my own experience, to not search from the perspective of an existing frame work of judgement, but to construct a psychological rationale out of private perceptions.

The integration of a disparate reality, the mixing of unmixable and contradictory images, surely are worth the freelancer's efforts to build a more liberated and richly imagined life. The privacy of private practice has its own rewards. With it comes the tendency, first to irrational thought, then to irrational actions. Yet the subversion of architectural convention was not a form of lunacy for me. It was more of an intentional, momentary derangement that attempted to presage a new discovery of design—the search for a contradictory assembly that enhanced architectural experience, and turned the insanity into a surprising reality. In part, the altered state proposed a perspective that was reactionary and inclusive, taking in ideas of irreverence, play, exaggeration, satire and irony. And it endorsed a multiple sensibility that brought in arts like graphics, sculpture and scenography, all of which help architecture communicate.

Since psychological ideas are best conveyed through language—like in drama and film—architecture's intuition cannot but grasp this new dimension and absorb it in some form of spatial experience. For me, the early work of Sculpture in the Environment (SITE) architects in New York was a confirmation of the brief that architecture must display a psychological dimension. Though they built little, project after project questioned people's relationship with the building, the building's relationship with landscape, ideas of entrance and enclosure, role of facades, methods of parking and links between cars and buildings. Most important was the question of permanence.

At BEST products showrooms across America, building facades peeled away, parking lots rose upwards and enveloped whole buildings, brick walls collapsed on entrance canopies, tree plantations ripped apart structures, sometimes appearing behind dismembered walls. Though sensational to the conventional eye, in every one of these acts was the admission that there are innumerable new ways of seeing and testing the environment. The unmaking and destruction of buildings was the clearest message about how they were really made. Architecture's self-importance was not essential. SITE systematically ripped apart the inconsequential and gratuitous so that a complete cross-section of

■ Cadillac Apartments, watercolour, 2011

viewers, from artists and intellectuals to garbage collectors, could participate in the message.

The irrational urge of the architect is then not intentionally non-serious, a source of facile amusement or irrationality for its own sake. It hovers between two evocations, first, to make a critical assessment of convention itself and ask the old question, "Why does the bank vault live below ground? Is it possible to situate it in a way that ensures security in a different way?" Second, the fresh placement initiates a parallel thought process that is more experimental and imaginative. You think differently because the image that confronts you has transferred your attention on to a surreal and potentially paranoid direction.

How the hell do you secure the currency notes visible to passers-by on the street? Can architecture ever have such an outlandish rendition? The necessity of architecture to address real, day-to-day issues makes every such attempt a carefully planned subversive experiment. Will it work? In designing a spa, an outdoor shower was placed, like the French toilet, in the middle of a public barbeque deck, surrounded for privacy by one-way glass, completely shrouded from the public gaze. However, the fear that the enclosure may not actually protect them from prying eyes kept most bathers away from the shower. The erosion of architecture's most basic performance of the right to privacy raised suspicion, and subjected the design idea to criticism. Without the potential risk of exposure, privacy in the shower had become an ordinary task, a routine. The building's visible reassurance of its function to the resident was essential, and it was the only obvious value of architecture in this instance.

When architects consider function as merely one of the many ingredients that contribute to performance, the open basket of variables surrenders more easily to a concert of unlikely associations. Banks no longer need security, newly wedded couples do not need privacy, an office doesn't require an open plan and commerce dispenses with the need for public viewing. Architecture realigns its conventional message and calls for irrational tangential links; intuitive, rather than evolved from precedence and formula. In the spa, many stood outside on the wooden deck testing the invisibility of the shower stall; looking uncomfortable and out of sync with the experimental idea. Despite the thrill, it was a risk not worth taking.

People observed the shower with incredulity and a smirk like it was an anthropological specimen in a museum. The shower stall was akin to the glassy restaurant enclosures that project on busy

■ Gateway of India airlifted, simulation, 2012

city sidewalks and forcibly bring together two opposing functional conditions: the anonymity of people in rapid public movement juxtaposed against a secret moment in seclusion; a person sipping coffee with indolent ease despite the agitated crossfire of pedestrians in steady flight, barely a foot away from the table. The signal to risk mixing these inherently paradoxical activities makes architectural reasoning and analysis an unlikely partner in such unusual circumstances. Less a risk, more of a deliberate and delicate balance of activities that gains meaning from the overlap.

The idea of straddling the edge of contradictory places enhances the inherent actions, adding a frisson of pleasant disturbance and discomfort on both sides of the glass partition. Design's movement to the extreme position is the first step towards dispensing with conventional logic. One of sculptor Anish Kapoor's more spatially arresting architectural projects is a subway entrance. By turning an ordinary escalator that moves underground into one where its descent into the earth is exaggerated by the earth itself, the building becomes sculpture and architecture all at once. Its shape rises around the escalator, forming a thick, rounded lipping, and immediately induces a sense of the ground's catastrophic gorging. As he goes down, or comes up, the escalator rider is a surprised and shocked participant in the experience. By adding a sculpted form to the humdrum movement of a set of rising steps, architecture changed the site's topographical character, making the earth seem deeper, the sky higher and humanity insignificant.

Gripped by the urge to come up with such unusual answers, the architect subverts convention to seek more substantial solutions. Consequently, the irrational impulse is all the more powerful in a discipline that actively relies on defining physical control in the environment. Whereas the first idea that needs to be sought is the loss of control itself. In the conceptual exercise of design, the early stage of any conception relies on that loss to seek as wide and limitless an arc of possibilities—there, in the unconscious, contradictory experiences find full play. Without it, architecture as problem solver itself becomes a problem.

Gandhiji's lesser known architectural maxim states that "the ideal Indian house will be built by materials gathered from within five kilometres of the building site". It was a statement that encapsulated a particular idea about building, material resources, labour and skills. At the time he said this, the words had a less prophetic feel because they echoed his larger message of "self reliance and swadeshi". They were traditionalist, as they saw the core of rural life as just and

■ Grass Maze, watercolour, 2011

good and worthy of perpetuation. They echoed too, the environmental plea that the best form of conservation was not to build at all.

If indeed any building was to be done, the reliance on local knowledge and material was the closest approximation of that standard. The pastoral image of Thoreau's life in New England has direct parallels with Gandhi's rural Gujarat. But in the intervening years the shift of population has defeated the idea of home as god's little acre, greened and set apart from each other. Conservation of ecology has always been part of an Indian architect's work ethic. But today, Gandhi's references to the larger context of city building would perhaps not hold true. In the agrarian rural surroundings, the ethics of his land use would ring true. But the enlarged scale of the city requires both a moral view on private land ownership and a radical shift of the Gandhian call for an untested technology.

The right to land needs to be critically divorced from the right to a home. Nowhere is the need more desperate than in the Indian city of the future. Twentieth-century ideals of conservation fall apart when applied to the numbers game of urbanization and migratory shifts. Everywhere you look there are signs of fatigue. Overstretched by agriculture, the spread of relentless suburbia, the blight of industry and the bigger blight of farm houses with swimming pools, architecture's private optimism takes a severe public beating. Travel to any place beyond the few remaining stretches of ethereally melancholic, beautiful and soon-to-be invaded countryside, the approach to any Indian city is like a pus-filled wound, a shattering eruption of surface despair that deepens as you venture further in. Cancerous and debased, it is a frontal attack, like an ancient battleground; the war over, and everything abandoned in the smoldering, smoking wind.

Nowhere is this more apparent than around India's biggest cities; the vast stretches of amassed and often unrelated buildings with an imprecise network of seemingly disjointed neighbourhoods. Do enlarging road networks and concrete trails of metro lines form the only links between the disparate sections of the city, so isolated they remain unknown to residents of the same city? The psychological dilemma of the spreading city is an unfortunate fuel for both private aspirations and public apathy; people are privately demanding and indifferent in public. They want more electricity, more water, more entertainment, more shopping options, more and bigger cars, better schools, better medical care and more servants. They keep pets and protect their turf by hiring guards. As restaurants sprout on the streets, their social life grows; then they apply for club memberships. All life is built on material expectations and the promise of quick delivery.

■ Pedestrian Tube, watercolour, 2011

In contrast, public life is steeped in abject squalor. The inability to share urban resources equitably makes for lowering standards of city life: air pollution, uncollected garbage and litter, encroachments, stolen electricity, water wars, road rage, crime and sexual assault. The divisions grow shamelessly large, but always go unnoticed. The approach to the shopping mall is across a sea of stinking garbage; there are several choices of Mediterranean restaurants, but not enough public health clinics. One home is guarded with electrified fences, the other located in the mouth of an open drain.

I was born and bred into the same ecology, but without the contrast of such unkind juxtapositions. I grew up with the old idea of life on the land, a single-floor house with an ornamented garden and a cultivated vegetable patch whose yield kept the family fed, summer and winter. The house was measured in acreage; a low, oblong building set in a tended garden. Behind the car porch was a green, painted jaffrey fluffed white with jasmine; you could hear the quiet hiss of the summer grass on a hot day; at night, mosquito nets were hung above beds tucked in with white sheets, scented with *motia* petals. To dissolve the day's heat, the grass was sprayed with a fine mist. It was the same everywhere, on every lawn and house down the street, the whole neighbourhood. A pleasant sameness, a sort of colourless homogeneity. City architecture was more a show of public contentment then private aspiration. For all intents and purposes, it was a rural life arranged in neat rectangles and called city.

In a different situation, such a life would be seen as a gross misuse of resources, and would call for serious architectural re-organization. In fact, for too long now, the Indian misunderstanding of architectural ideals has been the unfortunate outcome of a clash of cultures; the great historical background of the East pitted against the seductive cultural power of the West—an invasion, superior in the arsenal of imagery and technology. An East that flounders without a language of architecture, and consequently leans heavily on the West as the only possible model, however calcified and useless it may be. Partly of course, the fault lies with making only a half-hearted engagement with the ideas of the West. A will perhaps, to be Indian first, then Western, then regional, then...

Hard-pressed as we were at the time of Independence to seek the new symbols of progress, the heartstrings also tugged away at the idea that the expression of Indian identity was equally valid. The industrial model, however, applied as it was during Nehru's time, made sense in untested, open continents—with regard to the colonization

■ Circle Maze, watercolour, 2011
■ Whisky Apartment, watercolour, 2011

of America, and to an extent even to the new colonialism in Africa. But in the densely populated, traditional culture of India it produced an unfortunate anomaly, a confusion that only exaggerated the divide between rational professional action and a culture of identity and tradition. Moreover an under-achieving culture could only absorb Western technology and imagery like a sponge, but produce nothing new on its own.

For this reason perhaps the dimly comical underbelly of modernism is best seen in India, where buildings mimic visible modernity without following through on the essential measures of the work. There never was any evolved Indian alternative to Western modernism. Was an architectural opportunity missed? Was Indian independence really just another defeat since it produced no lasting cultural alternative to the Empire? In the current scramble for funds and building resources, the urge to industrialize and produce more, the fear of environmental catastrophe, the urgency of "green" amid the material demands of growing populations, the demographics of migrant cities, the requiem of endless growth, all call for yet another model. Sadly, the great economic and social divide in India and the utter lack of will ensures that the model will again emerge from the West, or perhaps from China, which is now the West's ideological equal. To my mind, there are only two ways of enabling an understanding of contemporary Indian architecture today. One, as an episode, a private encounter, a mere incident in a city of many incidents—like a *paan* shop, a road accident, a rape. Architecture as just another jay walker comfortably crossing the road at his own pace, oblivious to the consequences of his actions, his presence. Just a fleeting disturbance in the life of the road. In the larger culture of the city such architecture is entirely insignificant. Merely a private moment, petrified.

Usually such architecture exists with a distinct, well-defined boundary within which there is a building, an object of gratification surrounded by garden and landscape. Other than affecting its occupant, its owner, its architect, it has no social dimension. It raises no questions about urbanity, or visual import, says nothing about the values inherent in its materials, structure and construction, communicates nothing about the methods of occupying space, or about its place in the community. In the cultural milieu of its surroundings, enclosed by boundary walls, it is entirely irrelevant. An end in itself. It does, however, ask one pertinent question: if it is not for public consumption, is it even architecture? If it qualifies as architecture, is it worthy of discussion outside the subjective strain of beauty, design and aesthetics?

The other is an architecture culled from the despairing mess, the gut-wrenching, palpitating putrification of the daily wounds and fissures of discontent that make up urban Indian reality. The soiled streetscape, the loosely strung wires hanging across markets, the peeling monsoon-stained walls of government housing, the streets without sidewalks, the overflowing garbage dumps, the plastic bags blowing in the wind, the defecating mass of immigrant life in ancient monuments, the French restaurants in Lal Dora land, the glass mall lobbies baking in the noonday sun, the broken roads and sewer pipe houses—the tiresome, demanding, life sapping, life enriching, continually unfolding contaminating experience that makes architecture a deeply heartfelt social and cultural call.

There, where the relentless physical crush of life swallows you up completely, where observation and visibility have no academic meaning, there, where you make all the theoretical and demographic assumptions about the city and shops and hoardings and street people and the informal sector and ineffective master plans, but to no avail. There, among the spirited mess, where the architect stands, entirely defenseless, a desperate failure, viewing everything in his mind as squalid, second-rate and Third World. Any bit of construction enacted there, is that a worthwhile measure of architecture?

Architecture falls so unevenly between art and science, sociology and engineering, culture and anthropology, even between democracy and authoritarianism, that the question will never answer itself. But the current crisis of architecture also conceals something else: a disturbing paradox. In the widened arc of influences, building has become a world-wide expression of an expanding reality. A reality that includes film, magazines, travel and movement across borders, transport of produce, technology, automobiles, expansion of professional boundaries, exchange of fast food and coffee shops, transport of wood from Malaysia, kiwi fruit from New Zealand, new trade policies, open borders...

In a world where commodities and the market place determine the laws of acquisition, the private life of places is merely a direct representation of economic forces. People possess, make, build, add and replace in a continuum of living the spectacle. Yet, instead of bringing the world closer, this euphoria of globalization, with all its common design ideals and shared technology, has a tendency to isolate acutely.

In architecture, the isolation takes two forms. The first stems from the concept of entropy, where the proverbial disorder and unpredictability of life get packaged into newer, smaller states of order. Fear of randomness and a loss of physical control confines architecture to more manageable private realms. Building becomes a series of closed systems. The house is surrounded by high boundaries; it relies on itself for utilities like water and electric power; it employs guards and electronic surveillance for its security. Within, the rooms, each equipped with gadgets like an entertainment system and a fridge become a self-contained site of private privilege. Isolated from the neighbourhood, the house is further separated from the city by a self-proclaimed gated community.

The quest for protection from migrants makes the city itself take defensive and closed positions. This raises the all too evident question: do any of the solutions today, say, to the energy crisis, the search for identity in building, the loss of a sense of place, etc., and the resultant messages of "going green," recycling waste, attempting to reduce consumption, or enacting laws on preservation, make any difference within such closed and finite systems? When the loss of control in the wider world is so acute, you are ironically left with a feeling of complete, almost authoritarian control within the smaller one. When the supposedly classless landscape becomes the most class-conscious and insecure one, does the answer lie in enlarging the scope of architecture by drawing on people, situations and urban circumstances? To make places contaminated by people and their experiences? To build what hasn't been, to see what has long since been rendered blind, is now a quest that survives outside the current, limited boundaries of the profession.

The second is a more physical measure of architecture itself. Since architecture had embarked into a new future buttressed by commercial hopes and impulses, the structure need say nothing about bringing its occupant in tune with the surroundings. Instead building was merely a technological device, an instrument of expediency. It was as simple as that. The better architecture was the one with greater inputs of wiring, more kilowatts, more generators, better alarm systems, greater fire-fighting equipment. A state of architecture could be achieved by programming the building to make provisions for all desires, and at the same time, react against all possibilities of threat. Consequently the experience of day-to-day living has slowly disappeared from architecture.

Since all the choices have been made for you, you no longer open windows, bang doors, look for the light switch, change a bulb, feel enclosed by walls, draw curtains, shut blinds, repaint ceilings, wash floors, get lost in corridors, get stung by a hive under the eaves, smell the thick air of a summer cooler, feel the heat of a coal fire in the fireplace, watch the monsoon rain seep in through the glass, rub your nose in the frosted fog of a winter mirror, lie on a water-cooled stone terrace on summer nights. No. Architecture requires no exertion, no effort. You are no longer the cause of the transformation you enact to space. Merely a cautious recipient like a monkey in the closed environment of a zoo.

This is one of the primary failures of recent architecture, one among many, the incapacity to engage the users in its forms. To respond to the topography, the climate, the seasonal variation, or the thematic ideas of space and requirement is often used as an abstract justification for its design. Adjustments to excessive rain or sun, the movement of people indoors, the placement of furnishings and equipment are an obvious set of essential measures in a building's performance, merely part of architecture's expectations, and can hardly be viewed as an insight into design. This is just as domesticity is expected of houses, as clerestory light is desirable in churches, as darkness is relief in Hindu temples. Something else is a desperate need. Unknown, secret, random and imprecise moments, that even hint at a lack of control, are now unfortunately absent in architecture, and in the city.

The weary and unremarkable quests in which architecture is adrift today offer little optimism, and the profession is mired in unrest. Can the value of architecture survive the disdain and indifference felt by the larger population living within it? Is it a culturally binding force, a form of social cohesion that contributes to the community? Why then has it failed to create universally symbolic forms, forms that generate a common interest among ordinary people? Why indeed has architecture aligned itself to formalist design, when it belongs so clearly in the realm of informed day-to-day art, to forms derived from ordinary urban situations? In today's denuded landscape, does architecture offer life-supporting, indeed life-changing possibilities? Or has the new architecture destroyed all sense of hope?

Within the rising tide of pessimistic pronouncements, the reason for this exercise is neither to make a record of failure nor to make a passing remembrance of times and opportunities lost. Nor is to attempt to reclaim and recover a wilderness long since passed. Architecture has, and always will, represent transition. Within its parochial idealism, it was never possible to change the world, the city, or the profession itself. But it was possible to change the practitioner. In the process of growing old and approaching one's own physical end, there arose a need to free oneself from professional burden and assessment, free oneself in the work. My own professional life unfortunately has oscillated between hope and nostalgia. And however hard I have tried, the nocturnal smells of the past proliferate and permeate any call to architectural assembly.

An early life spent in rest houses in the remote mountains, and a childhood lived in colonial bungalows, the resistance to a changed modernism was the manifest disconnection with the professed values of the present. It was not that too much water had flowed under the bridge, but the bridge on which I stood now was itself barely passable. Besides, for too long I had been hardened by practice, and the incessant need to build in a conforming world. I hoped to look elsewhere now, beyond my little box of repeated failures, to ask if there were possibilities outside it. Outside the wish list of performance, outside the medium of judgment, beyond the refrains of the creative, brilliant, innovative and original.

Architecture had for too long been a basis for personal reaction, the desecrating judgment that immediately placed and defensively positioned each building in society, its place in history, its position in the social order of the day. The dilemma of instant recognition was also tied closely to abject failure, and it relegated the vast majority of the architecture that had been created by market forces to the dung heap. The monosyllabic world of advertising had sadly engulfed architecture and made it as precious as a piece of gold jewelry. A branded piece that shone in the dark, with 23 jewels, and designer door knobs. Success in such a framework was marked by equally palpable amnesia. The trophy cabinet was a sign of too easy a victory. And now, interest in updating the office portfolio had begun to flag. The practice of architecture, more and more, was not only falling away as a useless appendage. It was also building up a fierce rage, a sentiment soaked in the acid and brine of middle-class helplessness. I was waiting then for the rage to erupt, unsure when it would, and what form it may take.

For long, I had approached architecture as a problem to be solved, much like a surgeon treating a cancer patient. It took some doing to understand that such an approach was not only flawed but also filled with the quotients of perennial defeat. The shadowed life of architecture held no interest beyond the mere act of design. A passionless, defeated state of building, just another way of making a living, ensuring that the rent was paid and there was enough money for the kids' school fees. I had begun to suspect that places too easily designed and built without pain were in the end not worth doing. I had become suspicious of fluency, that earlier case of facility that flew from the hand to paper, and eventually to the building site.

Over time, design was becoming increasingly difficult; each decision to build was wracked with uncertainty as if a reversal was taking place now. Outside the reference of rhetoric and theory, the mere act of building was a form of decline, not in physical terms, but an atrophy of the spirit. A form of self-indulgence from which the only escape was to build that which had not been asked; to build for the imagination, or not build at all. It was a strange sort of liberation that was far more enticing than the standardized routine of design. And it left you conditioned to a wholly new and pleasantly perplexing enterprise. Pretentious as it may seem, I no longer felt any of the professional constants of playing architect, but rather as if I had been chosen, or had chosen for myself, to resolve a peculiar human condition. And that I had been placed at the centre of this inquiry.

It is then that I began to see that the spirit of architecture had very little to do with the actions of building, that some of the most serious efforts at architecture were at times totally devoid of building. The idea was not to falsify the present, but to truthfully imagine a more prolific future. Problem solving was forever the casual mask of a profession that skillfully avoided the two essentials of any art: risk and pleasure. In that regard it was easy to see that the only possibilities of architecture lay in its remotest reaches. If any useful work was to be attempted it was at the far ends of the economic spectrum. It was to be done for people too poor to afford architecture or those too rich to cultivate an interest in it.

In the standard practice, architecture had been an additive science, an enabling structure that lent coherence by the inclusion of various devices. I was no longer just looking for a form of professional satisfaction, but for something larger—a form of happiness even, where architecture was intrinsically tied to my own movement through life—a progression to some immeasurable, undefined and elusive truth. In an effort to give credibility to a wholly personal endeavour, I started to think of the practice of architecture in evolutionary terms, and to see in the passing years, a pattern of growth.

If the present battle between the self and architecture only resolves into plunder and violence, then it raises the need to eradicate the boundary between the two. When the self is fully aware, free of itself—a state defined philosophically as *moksha*—it loses its personal identity, and then, in every way, becomes community, ecology, history, tradition, landscape; a boundless territory beyond description. I have often wondered, if in one's own practice, there lay a possibility of such an obliteration, such relief. Was it then possible to deviate from the physical effort of building altogether, or rather, to stretch the physical order of architecture into other states—the sensory, experiential, emotional, even spiritual?

The architectural journey then became, like the yogic, a transformation from the self to a sort of material freedom. Such an exercise was of course fraught with the misgivings of oversimplification, but it had to be done, if only to explain to myself that the daily routine of architecture had the rigour of a mentally strenuous discipline like yoga. And like the yogi, the path to architecture was a progress to some unknown inner state for me. Its sequence could not be easily charted, but it did follow a cyclical trajectory, a circumnavigation into deeper and deeper embryonic states that would lead to an inner core. If not a form of joy, it would be at least a kind of healing, a balm.

So came the idea of circles, a spiral of intersections. In the outermost circle, at the fringe of the spiral, architecture was a physical thing, a gross manifestation of personal desire, a rank invasion of the self against the world, a disgorging of wish fulfillment into the open field for all to see. A visible, observable thing. Outwardly, architecture performs the task for which it is made—a bridge allowing for the easy crossing of a river, a roof sheltering one from a storm. At its most whimsical, it may lose contact with its intention but for all purposes, it remains a physical imposition on the site and sight.

By and large, this is the most pervasive outer cycle of architecture, and whole lifetimes are spent encircling it, often without any wish or hope to part with it. The Zaha Hadid phenomenon leaves you with the mistaken belief that the final proof of architecture was the physical form of the building itself. At the start, the practitioner remains mired in selfishness and despite many ambulations around the circle is left without awareness of the particular goodwill and fellowship that building entails. There is no semblance of any moral or ethical code, a strategy of practice that thrives in blindness. This is architecture as a form of nourishment of the baser appetites. You are part of an escaping mob, a momentary thrill seeker moving away from himself before he spots his reflection in the mirror.

Progress to the next state causes an ethical correction where the personal is perhaps elliptically present, but in subdued form. Its place is taken by a more complete sensory experience—the tactile, visual, olfactory, historical and personal, submerge their individual identities into a seeming continuity that enlarges perception and gives due credence to the belief that the building is more than the sum of its parts. Architecture is historically correct, aesthetically right, and acceptable in the community of buildings. Beyond just the visible, the experience is evocative and illusory. It remains, and remains for long. This is for me most palpable in Mughal monuments, especially in the controlled sequence through tombs, past gates along waterways, and the constant play of miniaturization and monumentalism, edged by fine details and devices, correct in proportion and perspective, true to the treatise.

It is the slow unfolding of a deeply-felt and orchestrated story. At this stage of its life, architecture is an enlargement of the visible into the personal, the public and the formal. In one sense it is akin to the way a pen not only fulfills the function for which it is made, but also promotes the idea of writing with its presence. It resembles a thoughtfully designed school for the visually impaired where the students are entirely unaware of their disability. A place where they move around with ease, relying naturally and unselfconsciously on touch, smell and hearing to make their orientation in space easier.

Architecture compensates and provides in a way in which people are barely aware of the arrangement of things. In such situations, the mind reacts to buildings without contemplation but through association. Houses are expected to be domestic, factories practical; a shiny brass door knob is an invitation to touch, a cobblestone texture evokes the sound of horse hoofs. The material nature of architecture is sensory and tactile, and linked to past associations. In this, the second circle of architecture; memory, sound and smell become personal possessions, sifting surfaces and textures, and connecting them to earlier places. Of course many of the links and associations are related less to professional knowledge than to the mind's capacity to constantly re-order and re-interpret the surroundings. Consequently architecture becomes not just the personal possession of its maker, but that of all those who experience it.

The third circle's evolution is a result of the complete abandonment of architecture's physical dimension, and so a sheering away of the discordance associated with visibility. You have moved beyond the worship of components that can be seen, touched and felt to a completely different motivation. This is a repeal of architecture's first law of materiality. The visible was in fact the first lie of architecture. In such an architecture you are drawn away from its details, deeper and deeper into an architecture beyond sensation, into a place where the building loses its individuality and its attributes of location, all its surface decoration, weight of gravity, definition of structure, and drops below the surface of judgement.

The strength of such architecture lies in its capacity to rekindle something of the spirit with which it is built, the way it is conceived. A bounty achieved through some difficult distillation. By dissociating the structure from the flesh and bones and skin, it frees itself from the burden of examination. And for a brief moment, when it invades the mind with the force of its solitude, you feel gratified. You feel you are its architect.

No longer limited by the compulsions and inhibitions of structure, you transcend. In this, the circle of architectural enlightenment, is the consciously inward journey, a detached observation of the implements of the trade till they are stilled over and over again, and lost to (self) awareness. It remains still, an entirely architectural experience, for its humbling, and at times humiliating action frees you from the greed of your self-inflicted professional ideals and desires.

It is here that I recall most vividly the experience of a crematorium in Scandinavia. Each time I think of it, I see the place condensed in winter light, where the sky is lit from a source so low on the horizon that it becomes a shallow, depthless dome. A processional path took me slowly uphill, into an open endlessness, rising up slowly across a grassy mound, a great earthen breast. Something kept pushing me along the graded walk to no particular end. I was moving from a moment of life to one of death; the geography at the bottom of the hill where I had begun the journey was the outpost of a visible reality—a gate, a cross—but along the rise I had become intrinsically bound to the sky and the eternal space it inhabited.

An ancient rootedness said something about the age of the place. At the top, the actual crematorium was just a minor feature in the fundamental frame of the surroundings binding itself to the eternal lines of earth and sky, assuring its place so firmly in the scheme of things that it had eradicated its individual self wholly, and become part of the background, dissociating itself from its material form. The immeasurable aspect of its architecture was in the fusion of all things unrelated to building—materials, site, silhouette, the details, sky and grassy, rounded earth—all the elements that made the reading possible in the first place. As if in order to arrive at its own imminent truth, the structure had absorbed all its extraneous physical details to reveal its core. It had discarded all the individual voices that described it—the materials and styles and protective layers of aesthetic armour—till it became apathetic to its fate as a conscious piece of architecture.

In the fourth circle, reality disappears altogether and architecture descends into a meditative state. As in the yogic frame of mind, a withdrawal of the senses, and an absence of focus and concentration, but a state of complete awareness. The practice of architecture dissolves all physical encumbrances and becomes devotional. You no longer feel the authorship of buildings, you are only an instrument who merely happened to be, so to say, in the moment. You are in a way without sensation, but you have complete equilibrium.

I spent a few hours inside Tiruvalla temple straining hard to make its darkness visible, drawing the experience away from physical dimensions altogether. The building merely wished to lower me slowly into its gray areas of darkness, a dark that described the complete blackness inside. Unable to see, smell, or hear, the structure was a source of all denial, and in the absence of sight—the very essence of boundlessness. Yet, on the outside the temple displayed a territorial integrity so formal, so geometric and finite it was hard to imagine so great a contrast within. The memory of the outer profile stuck with me—the rectangular geometry of the outer courtyard, the perfect circle of the temple wall, the precise cone of the roof. But as I stood inside, my bare feet on the ground the only connection between skin and cold stone, the physical sensation had slowly begun to dissipate.

I lost all sense of the temperature, the stone damp of the air. Eyes open or shut, made no difference at all. I felt like a particle in a great void. The inside of the temple was speaking, as if through me. And this left me wondering how someone could create a structure so precise, so carefully executed in height, scale and dimension; something so visually perfect outside, and then deny its very existence on the inside. Darkness acted as a shroud, covering the inessentials, and so touching a chord so personal that it denied all formal structures of existence. Formlessness was a form of celebration—a proclamation—an escape from appearances into transcendence. A meditation brought on by the dark, by the belief in the transition inherent in all physical things. This was the final inner circle of architecture...

Endnote

For the most part, now that the book is done, I realize that the position I have stated in these chapters is merely a concern for design. I began to write the book for an altogether different reason: to examine the way architecture had shaped my life. It was not meant to be a narration of a professional career, but rather an account of how the engagement with building had shaped me. No easy task! Throughout its lengthening conception, I was riddled by the excess knowledge of practice; practice gained in the way of a more personal exploration.

For this, I blame myself less than the profession itself. By its very nature, architecture is a practice of contradictions. Unlike many other professions, it opens you up to a host of influences and ideas that include sociology, design, engineering, landscape, anthropology, urbanism and civic practices; its asks you to develop the skills to draw, construct, narrate, engage and express in a variety of mediums. Yet, the reality of its many expressions forced me into a form of linear thinking that is a useful tool in resolving problems. Architecture then became a conquest of reality for me, rather than that of the imagination. Just like my own, the longer practices we know of are invariably careers in design, not art.

Yet, every time I built, I also saw a place for architecture in eternity. The impulse originated perhaps from the archaic view that a building's hold on the earth was longer than one's own; and indeed in that elongating time frame, it wizened and metamorphosed into something precious. Such a condition was doubtless formed out of erosion, and the endless weight that time imposed on buildings. The ruin was not a celebration of a ruinous state, but the natural process of ageing, newness slowly converting to residue. This was the lay of the land, its materials, landscapes, climate; and human occupation ultimately condensed into the structure; a gnawing physical atrophy that elevated it to architecture.

In placing buildings on the river-edge, or on the shelf of a steep cliff, constructing a new structure with the very stone excavated from a building's plinth, or allowing a forest cover to submerge a building's outline, were all an acceptance of the conditions that inevitably hastened the archaic processing of building. I wanted the building to look old before its time, each blemish extending the place beyond the present as if its sights and surfaces were always in the past or the future. The collective of buildings cited in this book is thus not a record of a personal or professional legacy. I use it merely to examine my life in architecture. I was not interested in the design of specific or generic space, nor in describing the various catchments of landscapes and settings that have brushed against my career. No. For me, architecture hovers between the destructive, illusory imagination of design, and the more vivid making of an assured reality.

To physically will a building onto a site is an act of design, but to set it free onto a course of transformation is an act of architecture. To set it free into a realm beyond the present, where the place is not just made, but lives and dies.

Project Profile

Architects: Gautam Bhatia/Navin Gupta with Chitra Viswanath for Lake House
Structural: A.K. Gupta/S.K.Arora
Mechanical: Vinod Sharma
Electrical: R.M. Singh
Interiors: Rajiv Saini for Devigarh
Furniture: Sameer Jain for Kalmatia Sangam
Panorama of Devigarh, Courtesy: Samar Jodha

Acknowledgements

Arup Giri
Ankita Karmakar
Rajat Arora
Navin Gupta
Shibu M.P.
Shankar Bhopa
Hamdan Mohammad
Sumaiya Muslim
Meghna Roy